189124I

CHARITY
IN SCOTL.

CHARITY LAW
IN SCOTLAND

edited by

Dr Christine R. Barker
(Principal Editor)

Patrick J. Ford

Susan R. Moody

Robert C. Elliot

W. GREEN/SWEET & MAXWELL
EDINBURGH
1996

First Published 1996

© 1996
W. Green & Son Ltd

ISBN 0 414 01141 4
A catalogue record for this book is available
from the British Library

Typeset by Trinity Typesetting, Edinburgh
Printed and bound in Great Britain by Butler & Tanner Ltd,
Frome and London

FOREWORD

Until fairly recently charities did not come much to the notice of the public or of lawyers. They did good by stealth and lawyers in Scotland wrestled with their special legal problems only comparatively rarely. There was, of course, a famous storm in the early 1950s about the application of English rules in connexion with taxation but, once that matter was resolved, lawyers' interest in the subject subsided.

All that changed when Part I of the Law Reform (Miscellaneous Provisions) (Scotland) Act 1990 came into force in July 1992. The Act itself was passed because Parliament recognised that charities were playing a larger part in our national life and were administering correspondingly larger funds than ever before. Since that time well-publicised cases of abuse and the introduction of the National Lottery have served only to increase the public's awareness both of the importance of the work done by charities and of the opportunities which they may offer to the unscrupulous. The legislation introduced what was seen as a suitable measure of regulation and created a wholly new and important role for the Lord Advocate. This in turn led to the creation of the specialist group of officials in the Scottish Charities Office which forms part of the Crown Office.

As Lord Advocate I was privileged to watch and participate in the development of this new area of the law and to observe how the volume of enquiries addressed to the Charities Office increased steadily as people became aware of its existence and of the ways in which it might help them. In my experience the Office was well able both to give advice and guidance and, where appropriate in more serious cases, to obtain remedies from the Court. But, having seen this new area of law spring into life, I am particularly conscious of the need for a book which will guide charity officials and their lawyers and accountants through the new legislation. This book not only sets out the new law, but it also places the legislation in the context of the pre-existing Scots law, while at the same time highlighting the important issues which arise for the many bodies which operate not only in Scotland but in England and Wales also. The problems are by no means easy to resolve and — however unpalatable this may be — in certain cases advisers may find it hard to give any very positive steer until the point has been considered by the Court. In the meantime, however, the authors identify the difficulties and discuss them in a practical way which should help charities to take the most prudent course, having regard to their own particular resources and requirements.

The authors are to be congratulated on producing a book which answers a real need in an important area. I wish it all success in this edition and in the editions which will follow as the law develops.

January 8, 1996   Rodger of Earlsferry

ACKNOWLEDGEMENTS

The impetus for this book came from research we have been conducting since 1993 on the implications of Part I of the Law Reform (Miscellaneous Provisions) (Scotland) Act 1990, which came into effect in July 1992. This work began as a pilot project funded by Dundee University and the Carnegie Trust and subsequently developed into a full-scale research project with the aid of funding from the Nuffield Foundation. The members of the Charity Law Research Unit are very grateful to all of these bodies for the funding they supplied.

In the course of our research and in the writing of this book we have received encouragement and assistance from many quarters, and we would like to thank in particular the following: all those who kindly agreed to participate in interviews; our invaluable research assistant, Dr Elizabeth Hunter; the staff of the Scottish Council for Voluntary Organisations (SCVO), in particular Lucy Pratt and Martin Sime; Jean Warburton and Debra Morris of the Charity Law Unit at Liverpool University; Lord Rodger of Earlsferry for kindly agreeing to write the foreword to this book; our colleagues in the law department for their support and encouragement, and the secretarial staff for assistance in producing the final manuscript.

In 1995 members of our Charity Law Research Unit gave seminars on charity law organised by Central Law Training and the Legal Services Agency (both in Glasgow), and also gave talks at meetings of the Society of Trust and Estate Practitioners in Dundee and Edinburgh. The feedback from these has been very useful in determining the issues which need to be addressed.

We have also benefited from conferences organised by the Scottish and National Councils for Voluntary Organisations, the Directory of Social Change, the Charities Aid Foundation, and the Charity Law Association.

Dr Christine R. Barker
Senior Research Fellow
Charity Law Research Unit
Department of Law
University of Dundee

CONTENTS

TABLE OF CASES

TABLE OF STATUTES

xi

TABLE OF STATUTORY INSTRUMENTS

INTRODUCTION

Part I of the Law Reform (Miscellaneous Provisions) (Scotland) Act 1990 **1.1.1** represents a watershed in the law governing charities in Scotland. The Act introduced a system of regulation for bodies which are recognised in Scotland as charitable for tax purposes, describing such bodies as "Scottish charities" (section 1 (7)). This book follows the example of the Act by adopting eligibility for tax relief as the defining characteristic of a "charity" in Scotland and accepting, therefore, the criteria of recognition of what is "charitable" developed by English law.

Before July 1992, when Part I of the 1990 Act came into force, charity **1.1.2** law in Scotland was not an area which required specific legal expertise. Indeed, it could hardly have been regarded as a specialism in its own right, since indigenous Scots law did not recognise its existence. Members of the legal profession who specialised in the law of trusts were associated most closely with it but there was little to distinguish their work in relation to private trusts from trusts for charitable purposes.[1] Trusts for charitable purposes were themselves subsumed under the general head of trusts for public benefit. It was only in the field of tax law that Scottish charities were given a special status, enabling them to claim tax and rates exemptions.

The 1990 Act for the first time acknowledged the need for separate **1.1.3** regulation of charities and introduced a régime which aimed to strengthen internal management and instigate measures designed to produce external accountability. In the three years since it came into force it has had a significant impact on charities in Scotland: changing accounting and reporting practices, altering management structures, facilitating investigations by the Lord Advocate and providing authority for intervention by the Court of Session in several cases. Its provisions appear, however, not to be known and understood by all professional advisers to charities or by charity managers and decision-makers. This is not surprising given difficulties in identifying and making contact with charities and their professional advisers and the absence of any previous legal foundation on which to develop charity law.

Some of the material for the book has been assembled in the course of **1.1.4** research carried out since 1993 by members of Dundee University's

---

[1] The most noteworthy exception is the *cy-près* doctrine.

1

Charity Law Research Unit. This has involved monitoring the effects of the provisions introduced by the 1990 Act, mainly for a project funded by the Nuffield Foundation.[2] The purpose and scope of the 1990 Act provisions, different forms of regulation over charities — both internal and external — and the effectiveness of these controls were key issues addressed in the study.[3]

1.1.5   We also considered the degree of awareness among charity administrators and advisers about the requirements of the legislation, its impact on the structure and operation of charities and specific issues such as fundraising and campaigning. (Where relevant the research findings have been incorporated into the text of this book.) Perhaps the most important finding was the degree of ignorance which still persisted about the legislative changes introduced in July 1992 by the 1990 Act and the Charities Accounts (Scotland) Regulations 1992, which came into effect on September 30, 1992. It emerged from in-depth interviews that the majority of interviewees knew very little about this legislation and some knew nothing at all, even though all were in senior posts in the charities concerned. Understandably, perhaps, most charities said they relied on their professional advisers to keep them abreast of what was required of them, but it was clear that not all advisers had been doing so.

SCOPE AND PURPOSE

1.2.1   This book is designed to fill that knowledge gap by offering a comprehensive review of the current legal position of charities in Scotland (as at November 30, 1995). It explores the question of what constitutes "charity law" in Scotland, it describes the different legal forms in which charities can be constituted, it analyses the provisions of the Law Reform (Miscellaneous Provisions) (Scotland) Act 1990,[4] explaining the background to the legislative changes and their implications, and provides information on other legal issues. The contributors are all specialists in their chosen fields and include academics, solicitors with practical experience of charity law and a charity accountant.

---

[2] Our research was first funded by Dundee University's Research Initiatives Fund and the Carnegie Trust, and then for a further year by the Nuffield Foundation.

[3] A report on the study is awaiting publication. See also Barker, C.R., Elliot, R.C. and Moody, S.R., "The Impact of the New Regulatory Framework on Scottish Charities", 1994 S.L.T. (News) 331, "The Impact of Regulation on Charitable Trusts and other Recognised Charities in Scotland" (1995) *Law Teacher*, Vol. 29, No.1, 97 and "Charity Law: The New Minefield" (1995) 40 J.L.S.S. 460.

[4] Subsequently referred to as "the 1990 Act".

It is addressed to legal advisers, accountants, and business advisers
who offer professional advice to charities, and to office bearers and
administrators of Scottish charities. It is the first book to provide
coverage of charity law as a subject in its own right in Scotland. It
aims to assist professional advisers in offering appropriate and
accurate advice to their clients in this rapidly-developing area and to
help those running charities to meet their legal obligations.

1.2.2

What is Charity Law?

A lawyer trained in the English common law tradition would have
little difficulty in identifying what in England is meant by "charity law".
Charitable trusts have been an important aspect of English law for
centuries.[5] Nevertheless, even in that jurisdiction the scope of the law
relating to charities is very much wider than simply trust law. The legal
form in which a charity is constituted, usually as a trust, unincorporated
association or company,[6] has important implications for the powers
and duties which may be exercised by its members. In addition, such
diverse areas as tax law, the law relating to street collections and the
negotiation of service contracts are key areas for charities.

1.3.1

Scots law now gives specific recognition to charities, described as
"recognised bodies" in the 1990 Act.[7] The provisions of that Act and
the accompanying regulations must therefore provide the main focus
of a book on charity law in Scotland. But again, as in England and Wales,
professional advisers to Scottish charities and charities themselves need
to be aware of the legal form adopted by a charity and the powers and
duties determined by that form. They also need guidance on taxation
and rating issues and on fundraising, which are not included in the
1990 Act. The particular situation of charities which are "cross-border",
and therefore may be subject to two regulatory régimes, deserves
consideration. Finally, the "contract culture" has a profound impact on
the charitable sector so that negotiation of contracts between charities
and local or central government for the provision of services must be
included in any book which seeks to be comprehensive in its coverage
of legal issues important to Scottish charities.

1.3.2

This book, therefore, looks at the following:

1.3.3

Chapter 1
Terminology and definitions in "charity law", charities and political
purposes, background to charity law and practice, the current situation
under the 1990 Act.

---

[5] See Chap. 8 and paras. 1.4.2–1.4.4, 1.4.11–1.4.12.
[6] See also friendly societies, industrial and provident societies discussed
in Chap. 2, paras. 2.5.1 *et seq.*
[7] s. 1(7).

Chapter 2
The different legal forms of charities: unincorporated charities (except for charitable trusts), charities incorporated as companies under the Companies Acts 1985–1989, industrial and provident societies, friendly societies.

Chapter 3
Charitable trusts: the administration of public trusts under the general law of Scotland, statutory amendments of the law of public trusts contained in the 1990 Act, the regulatory provisions of the 1990 Act as they affect trusts, and criteria to be taken into account in choosing the trust as the legal form in which to constitute a recognised body.

Chapter 4
Management and accountability: regulation of charities before 1992, general requirements under the 1990 Act, duties imposed on recognised and non-recognised bodies, misconduct and mismanagement, persons concerned in management or control, disqualification, designated religious bodies.

Chapter 5
The powers of the Lord Advocate, the Court of Session and the Scottish charities nominee under the 1990 Act.

Chapter 6
Statutory financial accounting requirements for unincorporated and incorporated charities in Scotland, comparative regulations affecting charities in England and Wales, the statement of recommended practice and other additional accounting requirements.

Chapter 7
Application of the English definition of what is charitable for tax purposes in Scotland and the reliefs available, in particular those available from the Inland Revenue and Customs and Excise.

Chapter 8
English charity law and the four "heads" of charity, cross-border issues in the context of the differing regulatory frameworks for charities in Scotland and those in England and Wales.

Chapter 9
Public charitable collections, lotteries, disaster appeals, commercial fundraisers and sponsorship.

Chapter 10
Charities as service providers, the contract culture, key issues in contracting with local authorities and others.

Chapter 11
Charities and regulation, future directions, opportunities and challenges.

TERMINOLOGY AND DEFINITIONS

It is difficult in the area of charity law in Scotland to find precise **1.4.1** terminology and clear definitions, first because there was no need for such terms before the 1990 Act, and secondly because the use of English concepts tended to confuse rather than clarify the common law meaning of key terms in Scotland.

The English Definition of "Charitable"

The meaning, or content, of the word "charitable" has never been **1.4.2** definitively established in Scots common law. It was never the subject of exhaustive judicial definition in the Scottish courts as it was in the Court of Chancery in England, where it has an elaborately developed technical meaning. It is this meaning which is applicable in Scotland in the interpretation of taxation and rating statutes, and it is this meaning also which defines what is a "charity" for the purposes of this book. The English definition is dealt with more fully in Chapter 8 but may be summarised here as incorporating four main heads of charity: the relief of poverty, the advancement of education, the advancement of religion, and purposes beneficial to the community not falling under the first three heads. There is an overriding requirement of public benefit applicable to each of the four heads.[8] The common law definition has been extended by the Recreational Charities Act 1958 to cover the provision of facilities for recreational or other leisure time occupation, if the facilities are provided in the interests of social welfare.[9]

The English definition of "charitable" has its origin in the Preamble **1.4.3** to the Charitable Uses Act 1601, sometimes referred to as the Statute of Elizabeth, which struck at the use of charitable endowments for private purposes. The preamble contains an almost random list of charitable uses, including the relief of "the aged, impotent and poor", the maintenance of "sick and maimed soldiers and mariners, schools of learning, free schools and scholars of universities", the repair of "bridges, ports, havens, causeways, churches, sea banks and highways", and the "marriages of poor maids".

The Court of Chancery used the preamble as the basis for deciding **1.4.4** what purposes should be treated as charitable in the application of the English rule against perpetuities, under which only trusts for charitable purposes may continue in perpetuity, and of the Mortmain Act in 1736, an English statute directed against the deathbed disinheritance of heirs by bequest to charity. By the time the House of

---

[8] *Inland Revenue Special Commissioners* [1891] A.C. 531, *per* Lord Macnaghten at 583.

[9] s.1(1).

Lords came to decide (in *Inland Revenue Special Commissioners v. Pemsel*[10]) how the word "charitable" should be understood in a United Kingdom taxation statute, the law of charities in England had developed its own elaborate jurisprudence, from which Lord Macnaghten was able to draw the four heads of charity mentioned above.[11]

"Charitable" in Scots Law

1.4.5 Attempts have been made to compare the Scots and English law meanings of "charitable", but have been confronted by the basic difficulty that it is not a comparison of like with like. Before tax relief became the dominant issue there was never the same reason in Scots law to define the limits of the term as there had been in England, where charitable status had long carried other significant consequences.

1.4.6 When (in *Baird's Trustees*[12]) the Court of Session was faced with the task of interpreting "charitable" for the purpose of applying tax relief under a United Kingdom taxation statute it was held that the word had no technical meaning in Scots law. The court fell back on what Lord President Inglis called the "popular and ordinary signification" of the word, which he considered to be limited to the relief of poverty. The decision in *Baird* was disapproved by the House of Lords in *Pemsel*,[13] which established (by a majority decision) that the word "charitable" in a taxation statute must be understood in its technical meaning in English law. *Pemsel* was an English appeal, but the House was fully aware of the effect its decision would have in Scotland. The result is that in applying a taxing provision in Scotland the Scottish courts must use the English definition of "charitable".[14]

1.4.7 Lord Watson, the only Scottish judge in *Pemsel*, also disagreed that the word had no technical meaning in Scots law. He reviewed past decisions in Scottish cases and, while accepting that they contained no definition of the word, concluded that:

> "In the first place, they establish positively that charity is not limited to relief of the physical wants of the poor, but includes their intellectual and moral culture; and, in the second place, they suggest very strongly that purposes which concern others than the poor may nevertheless be charitable purposes in the sense of Scotch law."[15]

---

[10] *supra*, n. 8.
[11] *ibid.* at 583.
[12] *Baird's Trustees v. Lord Advocate* (1888) 15 R. 682.
[13] *supra*, n. 8.
[14] *Inland Revenue v. City of Glasgow Police Athletic Association*, 1953 S.C. (H.L.) 13 at 21; 1953 S.L.T. 105 at 106.
[15] at 561.

This remains perhaps as complete a judicial definition as any of the word "charitable" in Scots common law.

Perhaps embarrassed by the thought of imposing the English definition on Scottish courts, even for tax purposes, Lord Watson was at pains to minimise the difference between the two systems. He reviewed both the old Scottish cases and the statutes of the Scottish Parliament, rejected the attempt by the Court of Session in *Baird* to define a "popular and ordinary meaning" of "charitable", and concluded:

1.4.8

> "I have been unable to find that the word "charitable", taken by itself, has any well-defined popular meaning in Scotland or elsewhere. It is a relative term, and takes its colour from the specific objects to which it is applied. Whilst it is applicable to acts and objects of a purely eleemosynary character, it may with equal propriety be used to designate acts and purposes which do not exclusively concern the poor, but are dictated by a spirit of charity or benevolence. In the latter sense the meaning of the term is practically, although not absolutely, co-extensive with that which has been attributed to it by the Courts of Chancery. Assuming, as the Court of Session has decided [in *Baird's Trustees v. Lord Advocate*], that the term has no technical meaning in Scotch law, ought "charitable", as it occurs in [a taxation statute], to receive that wide yet legitimate popular interpretation which practically harmonises with its import in English law, or must its narrowest conventional use be accepted as matter of fixed legal construction? I have not found it necessary for the purposes of this case to determine these questions, because I am satisfied that, in legislative language, at least, the expression "charitable" has hitherto borne a comprehensive meaning according to Scotch as well as according to English law."

The fact remains, however, that the significance of the word "charitable" is fundamentally different in the two systems, and the unification of meaning achieved in *Pemsel* is strictly limited to the interpretation of taxation and rating statutes. For that limited purpose the meaning of "charitable" appearing in a Scottish deed can be taken to be, if not identical with the English meaning, then at least included within it,[16] so that a Scottish trust for "charitable" purposes in its undefined meaning in Scots law will be eligible for tax relief as being also "charitable" in the English sense. In other respects, however, the force of the term in the common law of Scotland remains exactly as it was before the decision in *Pemsel*, in particular in the construction of deeds and the constitution of public trusts in Scotland.[17]

1.4.9

---

[16] *Jackson's Trustees v. Lord Advocate*, 1926 S.C. 579.
[17] See Chap. 3, para. 3.2.19.

Recognised Bodies

1.4.10   The 1990 Act introduced a new concept, that of a "recognised body",
and related this concept to that of a "Scottish charity". In terms of
section 1(7) of the Act, a recognised body is one which is recognised
by the Inland Revenue in Scotland[18] as eligible for tax relief on the
grounds that its purposes are exclusively charitable in the technical
meaning of the word in English law. A recognised body is one which
is established under the law of Scotland or which is managed or
controlled wholly or mainly in or from Scotland. This means that
companies registered in England or trusts created under English trust
law can also be recognised bodies for the purposes of the Act if
administered in Scotland. A recognised body is entitled to describe
itself as "a Scottish charity" (section 1(7)), and the inclusion of bodies
managed or controlled in or from Scotland means that a charity
registered in England and Wales may also be a recognised body under
the terms of the 1990 Act.

Definitions

1.4.11   Charity law in Scotland may be defined as the law governing the
formation and operation in Scotland of bodies capable of recognition
by the Inland Revenue as charitable for tax purposes. The following
key terms are accordingly used throughout this book:

"Charitable"
Used throughout the book in its technical English meaning as applied
for tax purposes unless otherwise stated.[19]

"Charitable body", "charitable organisation", "charitable company",
"charitable association", "charitable trust"
All used to mean bodies which are charitable for tax purposes
according to the English definition, unless otherwise stated.

"A charity"
Used to mean any body with charitable purposes in the English sense
as applied for tax purposes.

"Recognised body"
As in its definition in section 1(7) of the 1990 Act, namely, "any body to
which the Commissioners have given intimation, which has not
subsequently been withdrawn, that relief will be due under section 505
of the Income and Corporation Taxes Act 1988 in respect of income of
the body which is applicable and applied to charitable purposes only,
being a body (*a*) which is established under the law of Scotland; or (*b*)
which is managed or controlled wholly or mainly in or from Scotland".

---

[18] *i.e.* by the Financial Intermediaries and Claims Office (FICO) in
Edinburgh.
[19] See above and Chap. 8, paras. 8.2.1–8.2.7.

"Scottish charity"
Used as synonymous with "recognised body".

"Non-recognised body"
Section 2 of the 1990 Act defines a non-recognised body as any body which is not (*a*) a recognised body or (*b*) a body which is (i) registered as a charity in England and Wales or (ii) a charity which is not required to register in England and Wales.

Terms from English Charity Law

Certain terms from English charity law are sometimes used for convenience by voluntary sector professionals in Scotland although, strictly speaking, foreign to Scots law.[20] It may be helpful to conclude this section by isolating some of the most common of these in order to emphasise that they do not form part of Scots law.

1.4.12

"Charity"
In terms of section 96(1) of the Charities Act 1993 in England and Wales a "charity" means any institution, corporate or not, which is established for charitable purposes and is subject to the control of the High Court in the exercise of the court's jurisdiction with respect to charities. The term "institution" includes a trust and the term "charitable" is to be understood in its technical meaning in English law. In Scotland a recognised body is entitled to describe itself as "a Scottish charity", but the term "charity" on its own has no equivalent statutorily-defined meaning. The English statutory definition should be distinguished from the working definition of a "charity" given on the previous page and used throughout this book.

"Registered charity" and *"non-registered charity"*
A "registered charity" is a charity registered by the Charity Commissioners under section 3 of the 1993 Act. Subsection (5) provides that certain types of charity are not required to register, and such a charity is a "non-registered charity". Both terms are used in the 1990 Act in exempting English charities from the provisions which prohibit non-recognised bodies from holding themselves out as charities. Otherwise, the concept of "registration", as opposed to "recognition", has no meaning in charity law in Scotland.

"Charitable trust"
The term "charitable trust" has a technical meaning in English law which it does not have in Scots law. Charitable trusts in England form a distinct class of trusts governed by rules originally developed by

---

[20] The English law of charities is foreign to Scotland except in so far as it affects fiscal matters. See *Glasgow Police Athletic Association* at n. 14, *supra*.

the Court of Chancery and now administered by the Charity Commissioners under the overall jurisdiction of the High Court.[21]

"Charity trustees"

The term "charity trustees" has a technical meaning in English law but not in Scots law. Section 97(1) of the Charities Act 1993, which does not apply to Scotland,[22] defines charity trustees as "the persons having the general control and management of the administration of a charity". This extended definition includes directors of companies and office bearers of unincorporated associations formed for charitable purposes, as well as trustees in the strict sense. The term is not used in the Scottish legislation, and the nearest equivalent in the 1990 Act is the expression "persons concerned in management or control", which seems to cast a wider net than the English definition, in particular by using the word "or" instead of "and", but it certainly includes trustees in the strict sense.[23] There is an approximation to the English usage in the Charities Accounts (Scotland) Regulations 1992,[24] in which the term "trustees" (but not "charity trustees") is extended to include, in relation to any recognised body, "the persons in management or control of that body".[25] Similarly, in the Charities (Scheme for the Transfer of Assets) (Scotland) Regulations 1992[26] "trustees" is used to mean, in relation to any transferor or transferee body, "the persons concerned in the management or control of that body".[27]

1.4.13 It is also necessary to look to English law when considering certain activities, particularly political campaigning, which may be associated in the public mind with charities but which may in fact not be permissible for recognised bodies wishing to retain their "charitable" status. The linkage of charities with political purposes has been one of the most contentious developments in recent years and the next section considers this issue.

POLITICAL PURPOSES[28]

1.5.1 Charities are increasingly associated in the public mind with "pressure

---

[21] In particular, they are the only form of trust which in English law may continue in perpetuity.

[22] Certain other sections of the 1993 Act do apply to Scotland and are discussed in Chap. 8, paras. 8.3.1 *et seq.*

[23] See ss.6–8 of the 1990 Act and paras. 4.8.1-4.8.7. The expression seems wide enough to include solicitors and other agents concerned in the management of a recognised body.

[24] S.I. 1992 No. 2165.

[25] reg. 2.

[26] S.I. 1992 No. 2082.

[27] reg. 2.

[28] For a comprehensive study of constraints on political action see Randon, A. and 6, P., "Constraining Campaigning: the legal treatment of non-profit policy advocacy across 24 countries" (1994) 5(1) *Voluntas* 27.

groups" which seek to encourage changes in law or executive decision-making by government. Difficulties have been experienced in England and Wales by certain bodies seeking to register as charities which are actively involved in campaigning for a particular political stance and/or for changes in the law. Before 1992 these difficulties did not arise in Scotland except for those bodies which sought exemption from taxation under section 505 of the Income and Corporation Taxes Act 1988. However, in applying the general law to investment powers of trustees, it was held in the Court of Session in a recent case that a local authority which administered a public trust could not use its position as a trustee to further political aims extraneous to the purposes of the trust.[29]

Section 1(1) and (2) of the 1990 Act now enable the Inland Revenue to disclose to the Lord Advocate information on Scottish charities which appear to the Revenue to be carrying on activities which are not charitable, no doubt as a prelude to investigation and possible action by the Court of Session under the Act. It seems clear that the limitations concerning political purposes laid down by English cases would be relevant and that Scottish charities would be well advised to follow the guidance laid down by the Charity Commissioners on this issue.

1.5.2

Promotion of Political Views

Charities under English law are not permitted to have as their overriding purpose the furthering of the interests of a particular political party. Thus, a charitable trust whose purpose was to campaign for the Conservative Party was deprived of its charitable status.[30] Where the main purpose of the charity is to educate the public about a particular political doctrine this may well be valid under the object of advancement of education.[31] It is clear from decided cases that the courts will give education a wide meaning but will draw the line at propaganda.[32] However, cases earlier this century appear to have adopted a strict approach to bodies designed to further international relations or promote good relations between different racial and cultural groups.[33] Since 1983 the Charity Commissioners have permitted bodies which seek to eliminate racial discrimination to be registered as charities.[34]

1.5.3

---

[29] *Martin v. Edinburgh District Council,* 1988 S.L.T. 329. For trustees' duties in relation to investments see Chap. 3, paras. 3.3.20–3.3.21.

[30] *Bonar Law Memorial Trust v. IRC* (1933) 17 T.C. 503; (1933) 49 T.L.R. 220.

[31] See *Re the Trusts of Arthur MacDougall Fund* [1957] 1 W.L.R. 81.

[32] *Re Bushnell* [1975] 1 W.L.R. 1596.

[33] See, for instance, *Buxton v. Public Trustee* (1962) 41 T.C. 235.

[34] [1983] Ch. Comm. Rep., para. 15 *et seq. Decision of the Charity Commissioners on Charitable Status: Recreational Charities Act 1958 — Community Associations and Other Recreational Charities Established by Reference to Race, Nationality, Ethnic or National Origins or Religion* (1995) *Decisions of Charity Commissioners,* Vol. 4,

Promotion of Changes in the Law and Government Policy

1.5.4   Charities which have as their main purpose, or one of their principal purposes, promotion of or opposition to changes in legislation or government policy are not charitable. This restriction applies not only to changes in the United Kingdom but to the laws and government of a foreign country. Such purposes have included a ban on vivisection,[35] the promotion of prohibition laws in the United Kingdom[36] and the release of prisoners of conscience by reversal of government policy, both here and abroad.[37] The main justifications for this restriction are that the court does not usually have sufficient information to judge whether the changes which are proposed will be for the public benefit and that, in any case, taking such a decision would be a usurpation of the functions of Parliament or the executive.

Guidance from the Charity Commissioners

1.5.5   The Charity Commissioners have provided helpful guidance to charities in England and Wales to assist them in distinguishing between "political purposes" and "political activity to secure charitable purposes". If the constituting document of a body includes as its stated purpose or one of its stated purposes the attainment of a political purpose as defined above then it cannot be a charity. However, a charity may "do things of a political nature as a means of achieving the purposes of that charity".[38]

1.5.6   Such activities must be ancillary to the main purpose of the charity, must not become the sole focus of that charity's activities and there must be a reasonable expectation that these activities will further the purposes of the charity. Charities are therefore permitted to enter into debate with government about changes in the law, to make their concerns known and to seek to educate the public, provided two conditions are met. The first concerns the focus for their activities, which must relate to and be *intra vires* the purposes of their charity. Thus a charity whose purposes included the provision of material and emotional support to war widows could campaign for improvements in war widows' pensions, but could probably not be actively involved in efforts to ban the use of certain chemical weapons

---

September 1995, 17; *Decision of the Charity Commissioners on Charitable Status: Animal Abuse, Injustice and Defence Society* (1993) *Decisions of the Charity Commissioners*, Vol. 2, April 1994, 1.

[35] *Animal Defence and Anti-Vivisection Society v. I.R.C (No. 2)* (1950) 66 T.L.R. 1112.

[36] *IRC. v. Temperance Council of The Christian Churches of England and Wales* (1926) 10 T.C. 748.

[37] *McGovern v. Att.-Gen.* [1982] Ch. 321.

[38] Charity Commissioners for England and Wales, *Political Activities and Campaigning by Charities* (1995), HMSO, at para. 7.

by British and foreign governments. The second requirement refers to the form which such activities should take, necessitating the expression of views which are "based on a well-founded and reasoned case and are expressed in a responsible way".[39]

Charities may use emotive material to further their campaign but the information must be accurate and as full as possible, given the often limited nature of media coverage. Charities must not seek to organise public opinion to support or oppose one political party or another, but they may organise campaigns which involve sending material direct to the public and to Members of Parliament or encouraging supporters to lobby others, provided their arguments are well-founded and reasoned. They may also actively support or oppose legislation or policy changes and may spend charitable funds on this work.

1.5.7

BACKGROUND TO CHARITY LAW AND PRACTICE

Prior to the 1990 Act

For centuries charities have enjoyed a privileged legal status in England and Wales and in Scotland. As early as the twelfth century, philanthropists were giving money for relief of the poor using the legal mechanism of the trust to ensure that their wishes were fulfilled.[40] While the State was not always keen to encourage the development of charitable giving,[41] for the most part it was regarded as desirable to support philanthropy. However, charities were also seen by classical economists like de Tocqueville as a bulwark against State encroachment in democratic societies, standing "in lieu of those powerful private individuals whom the equality of conditions has swept away".[42] The flexibility of the trust, the judicial policy of benignant construction of charitable trusts, the opportunity to alter trust purposes by applying the *cy-près* doctrine and, from 1799 onwards, the exemption from taxation afforded to charities helped facilitate their development.[43] By Victorian times charities were the major providers of social services, the pioneers of new developments in social welfare

1.6.1

---

[39] *ibid.* at para. 12.

[40] See, *inter alia*, Jones, G., *History of the Law of Charity* (1969), Cambridge University Press; Chesterman, M., *Charities, Trusts and Social Welfare* (1979), Weidenfeld and Nicolson; Keeton, G. and Sheridan, L.A., *The Modern Law of Charities* (1963), Northern Ireland Law Quarterly.

[41] See, for example, the Mortmain Act 1736 which was designed to protect private property rights against dispositions to charity, reflecting the interests of the great landowners. This Act applied to England and Wales only.

[42] de Tocqueville, A., *Democracy in America* (1968), Collins.

[43] See Income Tax Act 1799.

and vigorous campaigners on a wide range of social and cultural issues.[44]

1.6.2   The development in the twentieth century of State benefits and welfare services was not welcomed by many of the established charities.[45] Not only did such apparently comprehensive provisions undermine their philosophy of individual reliance but their influence and prestige were also threatened. The Webbs, in their major contribution to the welfare debate, offered voluntary organisations a choice of role.[46] Either they could operate a system which would parallel or duplicate State provision, the "parallel bar" notion, or they could offer services which went beyond the State system, described as the "extension ladder" approach.

1.6.3   The advent of the Welfare State did not, perhaps surprisingly, lead to the demise of the charitable sector. The architect of the benefits system, Lord Beveridge, was keen to emphasise the continuing role for charities even within the new *dirigiste* order.[47] A report on the future of voluntary organisations (as charities were increasingly being called) stated that "the voluntary system complements, supplements, extends and influences the informal and statutory systems".[48] New types of charities flourished, particularly self-help groups, pressure groups and voluntary organisations moved into new areas of work, such as advice-giving and counselling, environment and conservation.[49]

1.6.4   In the 1990s, with attempts by government over the last 15 years to roll back the boundaries of State intervention, the voluntary sector has assumed renewed importance. Conservative philosophy, particularly that of the "new right", sees private philanthropy and individual responsibility as partners in creating a more robust, entrepreneurial society.[50] The scale of voluntary endeavour has never been greater, both in terms of its contribution to the gross domestic product (GDP), approximately five per cent in 1995, the central role

---

[44] See, for instance, the Charity Organisation Society which sought to find systematic means of relieving poverty without recourse to State intervention. The society, which flourished between 1869 and 1914, was heavily influenced by the ideas of the Scottish divine Dr Thomas Chalmers. Mowat, C., *The Charity Organisation Society* (1961), Collins.

[45] See the campaign waged by the COS and others.

[46] See Webb, B. and S., *The Prevention of Destitution* (1912), Methuen.

[47] See Beveridge, W., *Voluntary Action: A Report on Methods of Social Advance* (1948), HMSO.

[48] *The Future of Voluntary Organisations: Report of the Wolfenden Committee* (1977), Croom Helm.

[49] Kramer, R., *Voluntary Organisations in the Welfare State* (1981), London School of Economics.

[50] For a useful article see King, D.S., "Voluntary and state provision of welfare as part of the public-private continuum: modelling the shifting involvements in Britain" in Ware, A. (ed.), *Charities and Government* (1989), Manchester University Press, 29.

of charities in articulating and implementing policy and the power and control exercised predominantly by voluntary management boards.[51] There are some 170,000 registered charities in England and Wales generating £16-17 billion each year and 23,000 recognised bodies in Scotland with an estimated income of over £2 billion,[52] and British charities are reported to hold £30 billion in investments.[53]

Voluntary organisations are fulfilling all the roles envisaged for them by the Wolfenden Committee and are also being encouraged to take on direct service-provision, competing with the profitmaking private sector. The importance of the voluntary sector to the European community is explicitly recognised in the Maastricht Treaty. The mechanisms by which the voluntary sector is funded have changed significantly, with moves away from individual philanthropy to corporate giving through schemes such as Gift Aid and Give as You Earn (GAYE)[54] and government subsidy.[55] Funding by the State has increasingly been subsumed into the contract culture, with the 1990s being described as the "decade of the contract".[56] In this climate charities have, quite literally, become big business and the scope and influence of the third sector is unlikely to diminish in the foreseeable future. At the same time, charities apparently maintain "a special place in the minds of the general public ... and there is a high degree of public expectation that they should be properly controlled and efficiently managed".[57]

1.6.5

Yet there are major questions about the legal status of charities, the appropriateness of their favoured position, particularly in relation to taxation (see Chapter 7) and the ways in which they should be regulated by law to secure efficiency and accountability. Such concerns have led at least one commentator to recommend the abolition of charitable status in its present form, which he regards as an outdated medieval concept.[58] These questions are especially germane to Scotland, where charities have been virtually unregulated since their inception in medieval times.

1.6.6

---

[51] An estimated 50,000 people are employed in voluntary management in Scotland (figures from the Scottish Council for Voluntary Organisations - (SCVO).

[52] The figures for registered charities in England and Wales and for recognised bodies in Scotland are not directly comparable as the Scottish recognised bodies include many which in similar circumstances would be exempt from registration in England and Wales.

[53] *The Sunday Times*, May 21, 1995.

[54] See paras.7.4.23–7.4.24, 7.4.34.

[55] See Leat, D., Tester, S., Unell, J., *A Price Worth Paying?* (1986), PS1 No. 651, London Policy Studies Institute.

[56] Warburton, J. and Morris, D., "Charities and the Contract Culture", (1991) 55 *The Conveyancer* 419.

[57] Woodfield, P. et al, *Efficiency Scrutiny of the Supervision of Charities; Committee of Public Accounts* (1987), at para. 1.

[58] Knight, B., *Voluntary Action: Report for the Home Office* (1993), HMSO.

Unlike the situation in England and Wales where numerous statutes have dealt with charities and charitable trusts since the thirteenth century, there were few legislative provisions (although some old Scots statutes did deal with "pious uses") applicable to Scotland until 1990, with the exception of United Kingdom taxing statutes. Legal obligations did arise, of course, depending on the particular method of organising the charity, whether as a trust, a company limited by guarantee or an unincorporated association, but such accountability was not directly related to charitable status.

1.6.7   Some disquiet had been expressed about this by, among others, the then Scottish Council for Social Services (now known as the Scottish Council for Voluntary Organisations) which sought some form of registration for Scottish voluntary organisations.[59] A discussion paper and a report produced by the Scottish Home and Health Department at last provided a means for exploring different methods of regulating Scottish charities.[60] This discussion should be located within its particular social, economic and political context. Scottish charities were receiving substantial sums of government money.[61] A recent efficiency scrutiny of government funding of the voluntary sector in the U.K. and a report by the National Audit Commission had been very critical of the unco-ordinated way in which government money was awarded, without in some cases proper feedback mechanisms, performance indicators and evaluated outcomes.[62] There had been a few well publicised incidents of major fraud within voluntary organisations.[63] Government was actively encouraging corporate and individual giving through covenants, GAYE schemes and appeals to philanthropy. Corporate givers in particular, it was felt, would want to be kept informed of the activities of charities which they funded and would give more if there were regular checks on the efficiency and effectiveness of charities, especially in financial matters. The larger voluntary organisations were themselves aware of the dangers of inefficient rivals fouling the nest for them and giving charities a bad name. In addition, government had, and continues to have, an uneasy

---

[59] *Supervision of Charities in Scotland: A Consultative Memorandum* (1988), Scottish Home and Health Department, at para. 4.2, Option 2.

[60] *ibid.* and *Charities in Scotland: A Framework for Supervision* (1989), Scottish Home and Health Department.

[61] In 1993–94 the Scottish Office gave £24.2 million to Scottish charities in the form of direct grants, £48.06 million through Urban Programme projects in Scotland, £5.1 million from the Mental Illness Specific Grant and £273.3 million through Housing Associations. (Statistics from *Funding the Voluntary Sector 1993-94*, SCVO.)

[62] Woodfield, P. et al, *Efficiency Scrutiny of the Supervision of Charities; Committee of Public Accounts* (1987) and *Monitoring and Control of Charities in England and Wales* (1988), HMSO.

[63] For a practical article on how to prevent fraud see Huntington, I., "Charity Fraud - disarming the enemy within" (1993) *NGO Finance* 3(3) 22.

relationship with certain charities, particularly those which are campaigning or which do not fit into the traditional mould.[64]

Research literature in the 1970s and 1980s shows that long-established charities tended to have "a cosy relationship" with government and that in such a climate overt regulation was superfluous.[65] Since the huge growth in pressure groups and self-help agencies, that cosy relationship may increasingly be a thing of the past. Attempts by the courts and the Charity Commissioners to demarcate satisfactorily the line between charitable and political endeavours have also pointed in the direction of greater accountability.[66] Finally, much emphasis has been placed by the present administration on accountability to the public, and it was felt that charities should be accountable to members of the public who give money to them as well as to funding bodies such as local and national government which give grants to charities. The provisions of the 1990 Act relating to the supervision of Scottish charities were therefore "enacted against a background of a greater public awareness of the risks which may arise due to their mismanagement".[67]

1.6.8

THE CURRENT SITUATION

New legislation governing charities in the United Kingdom was brought into force in 1992. In Scotland this took the form of Part I of the Law Reform (Miscellaneous Provisions) (Scotland) Act 1990, which came into effect on July 27, 1992, closely followed by the Charities Accounts (Scotland) Regulations 1992 which came into effect on September 30, 1992. Parallel, but by no means identical, legislation was introduced in England and Wales by the Charities Acts 1992 and 1993.[68]

1.7.1

Purpose and Scope of the Legislation[69]

One of the main aims of the 1990 Act was to make all charities in Scotland publicly accountable by ensuring that members of the public could readily obtain reliable information about any charity's activities. Prior to the implementation of the Act it was not possible for members of the public or official bodies to obtain information from the Inland

1.7.2

---

[64] For one solution to this perceived problem see Knight, B. (1993) *op. cit.*, n. 58.

[65] Kramer, R. *op.cit.*, n. 49.

[66] In particular *McGovern v. Att-Gen.* [1982] 1 Ch. 321 and guidelines issued by the Charity Commissioners. See paras. 1.5.1-1.5.7 above.

[67] *Governors of Dollar Academy v. Lord Advocate*, 1995 S.L.T. 596 *per* the Lord President at 600.

[68] The 1993 Act consolidated previous Acts.

[69] See Chaps. 4 and 5.

Revenue about whether organisations had charitable status for tax purposes, because the Inland Revenue had a statutory duty to treat all information with absolute confidentiality. The lack of a Charity Commission or register of charities in Scotland meant that there was no public access to information about charities. Now, however, the Inland Revenue has compiled an Index of Scottish Charities and is able to disclose to any member of the public whether or not a body is recognised by it as a Scottish charity and will also provide the name and address of its contact for the charity and the date of the last communication with the charity. In addition, the 1990 Act makes provision for members of the public to obtain from a recognised body a copy of its latest annual accounts and its "explanatory document" (*i.e.* trust deed, constitution or other statement of the charity's objects), upon payment of a "reasonable charge" for photocopying and postage.[70]

1.7.3　The supervisory function of the Inland Revenue before 1992 was limited to preventing and detecting tax abuse. It had no responsibility in relation to non-tax abuses and prior to the 1990 Act there was no body which could act in the public interest to investigate cases of suspected wrongdoing in areas unrelated to tax abuse, except for the plenary jurisdiction which the Court of Session could exercise in the case of public trusts. "The lack of anybody who may act in the public interest in the field of charitable supervision has been one of the most persistent complaints which persuaded the government that this legislation was required."[71]

1.7.4　The 1990 Act gives the Lord Advocate powers to investigate charities and bodies holding themselves out as charities and to apply to the Court of Session to prevent or remedy misconduct or mismanagement. The Lord Advocate has the power to suspend those concerned in management or control during any investigation and may apply to the Court of Session to interdict a charity and anyone concerned in its management or control, to freeze bank accounts and to transfer assets to another charity.[72] These powers also extend to non-recognised bodies which represent themselves as charities.[73]

1.7.5　The 1990 Act makes it an offence for an undischarged bankrupt or anyone who has an unspent conviction for an offence involving dishonesty to be concerned in the management or control of a charity.[74] The Lord Advocate may consider applications for waiver of the disqualification. Trustees are also given new powers to reorganise and amalgamate public trusts, under the overall supervision of the Lord Advocate, in order to make better use of small and obsolescent trusts[75]

---

[70] ss.1(4) and 5(7).
[71] Lord Fraser of Carmyllie, *Hansard,* H.L. Vol.517, col. 742.
[72] 1990 Act, ss.1(6), 5(13), 6(2), 7(4) and (6)-(9).
[73] s.2(3).
[74] s.8.
[75] s.9.

and "dormant" charities can be investigated and their funds transferred.[76]

Regulatory Bodies

Inland Revenue

Under the 1990 Act the Inland Revenue continues to be the body granting or refusing charitable status in Scotland and, when tax relief is sought, checking from charities' accounts that income has been applied for charitable purposes. The Inland Revenue also gives whatever assistance it can to charities in the form of guidelines contained in a series of booklets and a telephone helpline. (The latter was set up in 1992 when the Index was established.) Charities seeking assistance with book-keeping procedures, perhaps when a new treasurer takes over, can request a visit by an Inland Revenue auditor. In recent years the auditors have also adopted the practice of visiting on a rota basis charities reclaiming tax in order to check that records are being kept in such a way as to substantiate claims for repayment of tax in respect of deeds of covenant and Gift Aid.[77] The booklets produced by the Inland Revenue give advice, *inter alia*, on setting up a charity in Scotland, how to obtain tax relief, and on fundraising and trading. The 1990 Act, rather surprisingly, does not impose an obligation on charities to file accounts annually, but the Inland Revenue expects to receive them periodically and may insist on doing so prior to making any repayment of tax.

1.7.6

Registrar of Companies

Incorporated charities continue to file accounts with Companies House which, while endeavouring to ensure that accounts are filed timeously and in accordance with the appropriate accounting provisions laid down by the Companies Acts, has no regulatory function specific to charities.

1.7.7

Scottish Charities Office/Lord Advocate

The Scottish Charities Office (SCO), newly established as a division of the Crown Office in 1992 in order to implement the provisions of the 1990 Act relating to the supervision of charities in Scotland, has the remit generally of carrying out the functions of the Lord Advocate under the 1990 Act. The SCO has a multi-disciplinary legal, accountancy and investigative staff. Under the 1990 Act the Lord Advocate has powers to take action where non-recognised bodies represent themselves as charities, in cases of misconduct and mismanagement by those concerned in management or control of

1.7.8

---

[76] s.12.

[77] The Inland Revenue does not regard it as being within its remit to advise on the form which accounts should take and whether they satisfy the requirements of the Charities Accounts (Scotland) Regulations 1992.

recognised bodies and also may investigate those involved in the management and control of charities who do not respond to a request from members of the public for copies of annual accounts or explanatory documents.[78]

Court of Session

1.7.9   The SCO has brought court proceedings in a number of cases, leading to the suspension of persons concerned in management or control. Court proceedings in one of the SCO's first major investigations reached their conclusion in 1995 with the removal from office of the managing director of the Leukaemia and Cancer Children's Fund following orders made in the Court of Session. Interdicts were granted against the disposal of specific property belonging to the charity by the remaining members of the management committee. Orders were also obtained from the Court of Session suspending the trustees of the Care for People Appeal following investigations revealing evidence of misconduct or mismanagement in the administration of the charity. Action was taken to "freeze" bank accounts, and judicial factors were appointed to take over the administration of the charities and to assist SCO officials in the tracing and recovery of assets and funds.[79] Commenting after the final order preventing the managing director of the Leukaemia and Cancer Children's Fund from taking any part in its management, Mr Brian Logan, Director of the SCO, said:

> "The terms of the final orders will reassure the public that charities are closely supervised and that the Crown Office will act decisively in any cases of maladministration. This was a primary concern of the legislation."[80]

The Public

1.7.10   Members of the public play an important role in the regulatory process. The entitlement under the 1990 Act to receive copies of a charity's explanatory document and latest set of accounts means that for the first time members of the public have a right to check the purposes and financial viability of a charity to which they may wish to make a donation or which has aroused their suspicions in some respect.

---

[78] See Chap. 5, paras 5.1.2 and 5.2.1 *et seq.*

[79] In 1995 the SCO reported that its staff had given counsel and assistance to 25 charities where its inquiries discovered maladministration of a lesser degree, in comparison with 35 such cases in the period from the establishment of the SCO in July 1992 to March 31, 1994. There were a further 23 cases where the evidence revealed sufficient grounds for full investigation and the possibility of court proceedings, as compared with 17 cases in the previous reporting period: *Crown Office and Procurator Fiscal Service Annual Report 1994/95*, pp.11-12.

[80] Reported in *The Scotsman*, June 14, 1995.

Conclusions

The major developments in the role of charities over the years, the   **1.7.11**
numbers of people involved in working for them, both in a voluntary
and a paid capacity, and the large sums of money given to charities
by funding bodies and members of the public have made legislative
changes inevitable and in many respects desirable. In Scotland in
particular, where prior to 1992 there was no accountability directly
related to charitable status, new regulatory measures were long
overdue. The chapters which follow examine the provisions
introduced by the 1990 Act in the context of other legislation which
Scottish charities need to consider.

CHAPTER 2

INCORPORATED CHARITIES AND OTHER BODIES

MAIN TYPES OF BODY

2.1.1 While neither of the two statutes[1] which are the principal sources of regulation of charitable bodies in Scotland require the use of any specific legal form by a charitable body, there are in practice four forms of status which are commonly used: an association; a trust (both of which are often referred to as unincorporated bodies); a registered company; or an industrial and provident society (often referred to as incorporated bodies). It is possible for any of these legal forms to be used in such a fashion that an organisation may be a recognised body under the 1990 Act[2] and as a consequence describe itself as "a Scottish charity".[3]

2.1.2 While it is also possible for a charity to be a friendly society, a body constituted by Royal Charter or constituted by Act of Parliament,[4] the most commonly encountered forms are the trust, the association, and the registered company.

UNINCORPORATED CHARITIES

Unincorporated Associations

2.2.1 In describing the nature of organisations involved in charitable activities reference is often made to bodies within the voluntary sector.

---

[1] Law Reform (Miscellaneous Provisions) (Scotland) Act 1990 and Income and Corporation Taxes Act 1988.

[2] s. 1(7) of the Law Reform (Miscellaneous Provisions) (Scotland) Act 1990 specifies that a recognised body shall be any body which has been afforded relief under s. 505 of the Income and Corporation Taxes Act 1988, and has been established under the law of Scotland or is managed or controlled wholly or mainly in or from Scotland.

[3] s. 1(7).

[4] An example of such a body is the National Trust for Scotland.

22

The most common form of organisation within the voluntary sector is the unincorporated association.[5]

There is no Act of Parliament defining or organising the nature and structure of unincorporated associations and perhaps the simplest definition of this type of body is to be found in the *Stair Memorial Encyclopaedia of The Laws of Scotland* where it is described as "a group of persons bound together by agreement for a particular purpose".[6] This type of structure is often adopted by individuals who have decided to pursue collectively a purpose or activity which is charitable in nature although it is by no means restricted to charitable bodies. One of the most frequent examples of an unincorporated association is a members' club where individuals gather to pursue a common interest in a broad range of concerns such as sporting, leisure or cultural activities.[7] Associations with charitable purposes are no different in legal form from those involved in sporting, leisure or cultural activities, with the obvious exception that their activities will be directed towards charitable ends such as the relief of poverty or distress. This difference does, however, have an important effect on the way property is held for the association.[8]

2.2.2

Constitution

At the core of an unincorporated association is a group of individuals who have agreed to gather together to pursue a particular purpose. The relationship between the individual members of the organisation is contractual and in stark contrast to the incorporated charity the association has no existence or personality separate from its individual members. Given that the relationship between those involved in an association is contractual[9] it is perfectly possible that there may be no single document, or no document at all, which clearly sets out the purposes of the association or the rights and duties of the individual members.

2.2.3

While there may be no document setting out the purposes and constitution of the association, or there may simply be an informal record or minute of the first meeting of those involved, clearly it is preferable that some form of written constitution is adopted by an association.

2.2.4

---

[5] The trust, which is the other form of organisation most commonly found within the voluntary sector, and which is also the other type of unincorporated body most frequently used by charitable organisations, is considered in Chap. 3.

[6] *Stair Memorial Encyclopaedia of The Laws of Scotland*, Vol. 2, p. 291.

[7] Such bodies are often simply referred to as clubs, which are perhaps the most commonly encountered forms of unincorporated associations.

[8] See below and Chap. 3, paras. 3.3.32–3.3.33.

[9] The relationship depends simply upon the agreement of all the parties involved.

2.2.5   Normally the constitution will deal with the appointment of office
bearers such as a chairperson, secretary and treasurer with specific
duties and roles and the election of additional members to form a
management committee.[10] Often the constitution or rules of an
association will regulate how members may be introduced and
expelled, what payments require to be made by members and what
interests they have in the assets of the association, what powers,
responsibilities and duties are delegated to office bearers and to the
management committee and in addition deal with a whole range of
other issues, such as the conduct of meetings.[11]

2.2.6   Members of an association may from time to time wish to alter its
purposes or the arrangements for the conduct of the affairs of the
association. Unless there are any express rules governing the changing
of the purposes or rules of the association it is presumed that changes
can only be made with the consent of all the members of the
association.[12] In addition where new members join an association they
are taken to have accepted in advance any alterations which have
been made to the constitution of an association and to be bound by
those alterations.

Management Committees and Office Bearers

2.2.7   Frequently, the constitution of an association will provide for office
bearers and a management committee to be appointed by the members
of the association. The powers and duties of the individual office
bearers and the committee will be set out in the constitution and,
particularly where a large organisation is involved, it will provide for
the use of sub-committees whose responsibilities and duties will also
be outlined.

2.2.8   Irrespective of the size of the association or the complexity of its
constitution or rules, the authority of the office bearers and the
management committee (under whatever name it operates) derives
from the contractual agreement that exists between the members of
the association. The office bearers and the committee simply act as

---

[10] The three matters which are usually dealt with first, often being perceived
as the most important issues to be addressed, are the name, the objects of the
association and the nature of and rights attached to membership. In addition
it is useful to have rules dealing with issues such as subscription, expulsion,
committees, officers, meetings, arrangements for property and change of rules.

[11] The courts will normally choose not to intervene in the affairs of an
association or club, preferring to leave it to regulate its own activities in
accordance with its rules/constitution. *Gardner v. McLintock* (1904) 11 S.L.T.
654.

[12] *Re Tobacco Trade Benevolent Association, Sinclair v. Finlay & Co. Ltd.* [1958]
3 All E.R. 353. But see Chap. 3, para. 3.2.9 for the position where an association
amounts to a quasi-public trust.

agents of the members and exercise the powers and duties delegated to them as agents for the members. As agents of the members of the association, the office bearers and committee members[13] will (subject to the terms of the rules or constitution of the association) be authorised to enter into contracts and arrangements on behalf of the association. The duties of the office bearers and committee members should be clearly stated in the rules or constitution of the association but, irrespective of the exact content of the constitution or rules, it will always be a matter of fact whether or not an office bearer, committee member or, for that matter, any other ordinary member of the association is a person concerned in the management or control of a recognised body and as such bound by the duties imposed on such persons by the 1990 Act.

Branches and Affiliation

Increasingly, it is possible that an unincorporated association may have contacts or links with other organisations which go beyond mere working arrangements. The true legal nature of such links will depend upon the facts and circumstances and, in particular, the rules of each body involved. A number of common linkages are encountered, such as branches and affiliations, but unfortunately the words used to describe such relationships have no technical definition and there may be overlap in the actual status of an association. **2.2.9**

The use of branch status is likely to prove attractive where a large association seeks to establish a new presence in a hitherto unrepresented area or region. In this situation it is simply a convenient grouping of members within a large organisation. No one can be a member of the branch without also being a member of the association and the rules of the branch (if there are in fact branch rules which differ from the rules of the association) should closely reflect the rules of the association and indeed the branch rules should be controlled by the rules of the association. **2.2.10**

The separate concept of affiliation arises where a number of quite separate and distinct associations exist and they have agreed that the rules and structures of a larger organisation will, in fact, control the smaller constituent or affiliated bodies. The attraction of the affiliation structure for smaller local associations is that it may open access to skills and resources within the larger, often national, body and provide a level of professional and administrative support which might otherwise have been beyond the means of the smaller organisation. One potential risk may lurk in this structure for the unwary administrator or officer of the national body. This is quite simply that **2.2.11**

---

[13] It will frequently be the case that the office bearers will be members of the management committee.

the extent of reliance placed by, for example, one local organisation upon the expertise of an official of the national body could put the official at risk of being considered a person involved in the management or control of the local association. Once again, the provisions of the 1990 Act could extend to individuals other than those considered as being involved in management or control were it not for the statutory provisions.

Property and Liability

2.2.12   Normally the property and assets of an association which has been formed for the benefit of its members only will belong to those members jointly in equal shares.

2.2.13   Conversely, where the association exists for the benefit of others the property will be deemed to be held in trust for the purposes of the association. The result is that where the object of the association is to benefit a section of the public its assets are treated as held in a quasi-public trust.[14]

2.2.14   One of the key distinguishing features between an association and any form of incorporated body adopted by a charitable organisation is that the association is not a separate or distinct legal personality from those individuals who have gathered together to form the organisation. However, any sheriff court case involving the association may run in its name.[15] In respect of the property of an association this absence of separate legal personality means that heritable property cannot be taken in the name of the association and must be vested in trustees on behalf of the association. Again, where the purposes of the association are public, the trustees are treated as the trustees of a public trust.[16]

2.2.15   In the absence of any rules in the constitution of the association to the contrary the basic liability of a member (once admitted as a member) is to pay his or her subscription (if any) for the duration of the membership.[17] As far as liability under contract is concerned members will not be liable for contracts undertaken on behalf of the association unless the member has in fact authorised the contract in question.[18] On the basis of the normal rules of agency the committee has implied authority to employ staff and enter into contracts for the purchase of goods and materials necessary for the association's activities.

---

[14] *Anderson's Trustees v. Scott*, 1914 S.C. 942, and see Chap. 3, para. 3.2.9.
[15] rule 5.7 of the Ordinary Cause Rules 1993. There is no equivalent rule in the Court of Session.
[16] *supra*, n. 14.
[17] *Re New University Club (Duty on Estate)* [1887] 18 Q.B.D. 720 at 727.
[18] *Thomson and Gillespie v. Victoria Eighty Club* (1905) 13 S.L.T 399.

The essential question in any dealings on behalf of an association by **2.2.16** the committee members will always be the extent to which they are authorised to act. If the committee members or any office bearers are acting within the extent of the authority granted to them by the rules or constitution of the association, or are otherwise authorised by the members of the association, then they will be in a position to bind the association and its members. Conversely, if committee members or office bearers (or for that matter any ordinary members) purport to bind the association outwith the extent of any express or implied authority, they will be personally liable as agents who have exceeded their authority. The prospect of personal liability for the obligations of an association is one reason why larger charitable bodies may seek to incorporate and obtain the benefit of limited liability status, thereby removing the potential risk of personal liability from members, office bearers and committee members.

While it may be perfectly possible to monitor the activities of office **2.2.17** bearers and the management committee when an association is still relatively small in size, this can become increasingly difficult as the association grows. This can cause difficulties, particularly as regards the potential liability of members. As the management committee will almost certainly be authorised to enter into contracts on behalf of the association the individual members may find themselves personally liable for contracts. Normally this should not worry members unduly as the first call on assets to cover any such liability will be the association's own. But as associations grow in size and members perhaps find themselves at a greater remove from the management committee and from its decision-making, they may well find themselves potentially liable for obligations arising from the committee's activities of which they have no knowledge.

Trusts

Charitable trusts are dealt with in Chapter 3.   **2.2.18**

INCORPORATED CHARITIES

There are three principal types of incorporated charities: **2.3.1**

(A) those incorporated under the Companies Acts 1985 to 1989;
(B) those incorporated under the Industrial and Provident Societies Act 1965;
(C) those incorporated by Royal Charter.

This chapter concentrates on the first two types of body, which are those most commonly encountered. For the sake of completeness, the friendly society should also be noted, although it is no longer possible to register an entirely new organisation using the original friendly society structure.[19]

(A) CHARITIES INCORPORATED AS COMPANIES UNDER THE COMPANIES ACTS 1985 TO 1989

(i) General Features

2.4.1   Companies can be incorporated with either unlimited or limited liability.[20] The prospect of a charity incorporating as a company with unlimited liability seems extremely remote, as it is difficult to see why a charity would wish to adopt this form of status, which leaves the members of the company entirely liable on a personal basis for all the obligations and liabilities of the company. It is mentioned simply for the sake of completeness.

2.4.2   Much more common is the limited liability company which can take one of two forms: a company limited by guarantee or a company limited by shares. Both forms are used by charities in differing circumstances. The main difference between the two forms is that a company limited by shares has shareholders (often also called members) who purchase shares in the company, while a company limited by guarantee has members who do not purchase shares but simply guarantee to pay the company's debts. In a guarantee company, therefore, the members do not make any initial payment of money to the company to become a member but guarantee that they will contribute a fixed sum into the company, should it be wound up. The maximum extent of the members' liability under this guarantee is limited to an agreed amount when they become members and the sum involved is usually £1 per member. With a company limited by shares, however, the members initially pay money to the company when they subscribe for shares and their liability is limited to the value of the shares purchased. Once members have paid for their shares in full they have no further liability.

2.4.3   Subject to this fundamental difference between the two forms of limited liability company, the provisions of the Companies Acts 1985 to 1989 apply in like fashion to both. While it is perfectly possible for a company limited by shares to be used as a legal structure by a charity, it is an option which is seldom pursued.

2.4.4   This arises primarily because the whole structure of such a company is directed towards making profits for distribution to shareholders.

---

[19] The Friendly Societies Act 1992 was designed to enable existing friendly societies to convert to more modern forms, so as to be able to compete with companies registered under the Companies Acts 1985 to 1989.

[20] Companies Act 1985, ss.1(1)(2)(*a*)–(*c*).

Such a structure is inappropriate for a charity, where the principal activity may not be (by definition) the attainment of profit. Charities do, however, use companies limited by shares for non-charitable purposes incidental to their principal activities such as the conduct of trading activities where the making of profits is a key objective.[21] Where companies limited by shares arise within the charity sector they tend to be used in this type of ancillary role rather than as the primary legal structure for the charity itself. Accordingly, the company structure which is usually used for a charity is a company limited by guarantee.[22]

In this case the members are the equivalent of the shareholders and they also exercise the powers of the company in general meeting, including the power of appointment of the directors who actually run the charity.

2.4.5

(ii) Limited Liability

The benefit of limited liability status is likely to be one of the main reasons for those involved in a charity choosing to incorporate rather than opt for any form of unincorporated structure. This is particularly likely to be the case for charities where substantial financial commitments are involved, *e.g.* salaries for employees and lease or rental payments for premises and/or equipment.

2.4.6

As a legal personality quite separate from its members and officers,[23] the limited liability company itself will be responsible for meeting its commitments rather than the members or officers. This may be contrasted with, for example, the position of the management committee of an unincorporated association. Members of such a committee have unlimited liability and as a consequence, should an unincorporated association fail to meet its debts, the committee members may be required to settle those debts personally.

2.4.7

It can be seen, therefore, that limited liability status is likely to be attractive to many charitable bodies. Organisations with large numbers of staff may seek to protect their members and officers against personal liability for redundancy payments in the event of a withdrawal of funding. Those involved in ancillary trading activities may seek to protect against the vagaries of an income shortfall through poor trading. In short, as the levels of income and the extent of the

2.4.8

---

[21] See Chap. 7, paras. 7.4.15 *et seq.*

[22] If a company limited by guarantee is utilised it should be noted that such a company need not incorporate the word "limited" at the end of its name if its objects are charitable and the company complies with the provisions contained in s.30(3) of the Companies Act 1985.

[23] *Salomon v. A. Salomon & Co. Ltd.* [1897] A.C. 22.

commitments of charitable bodies increase in size, the desire to protect
those involved in the promotion and operation of charities from
potential personal liability through the use of a limited company is
likely to remain high.

(iii) Constitution

2.4.9   Both forms of limited liability company are established as a result of
registration with the Registrar of Companies.[24] As part of the
incorporation procedure, there must be lodged with the Registrar of
Companies two documents, known separately as the memorandum
of association and the articles of association, which in large part may
be considered as equivalent to the trust deed of a trust and the
constitution and rules of an unincorporated association.

2.4.10   The memorandum of association is the company's link with the
outside world and specifies (often in considerable detail) what the
company may do and what are its objects. The articles of association
are essentially the internal regulations of the company and regulate
such matters as the convening and conduct of meetings and
appointment and removal of directors.

2.4.11   While the Companies Act 1985 provides specimen memoranda and
articles of association[25] both for companies limited by guarantee
and those having a share capital and the Charity Commissioners
for England and Wales have published a booklet incorporating an
approved form of memorandum and articles of association for use
by a company limited by guarantee,[26] there is no obligation upon a
company to adopt either form. Provided the versions used are
drafted in such a manner as to satisfy the requirements of the
Companies Act 1985 and the Inland Revenue, there is virtually
complete freedom to draft the memorandum and articles of
association in such a fashion as to satisfy the particular
requirements of the charity in question. For example, where a group
of individuals choose to form a charity but also require to work
for it and receive a salary because they have no other means, they
would be unable to be trustees of a charity because of the general

---

[24] While the Companies Acts 1985 and 1989 apply both in Scotland and in
England and Wales, registered companies may be separately domiciled in
either Scotland or England and Wales. This is established at the point of
incorporation and may not be altered subsequently.

[25] Tables A and C of the Companies Regulations 1985 (S.I. 1985 No. 805).

[26] The model memorandum and articles of association are incorporated in
Charity Commission booklet GD1. This is drafted to take account of English
charities legislation and would require re-drafting for Scotland. Nonetheless,
the style is a useful guide for drafting purposes. The Scottish Council for
Voluntary Organisations also incorporates useful style memorandum and
articles of association in its *Guide to Constitutions and Charitable Status in
Scotland* (1995) SCVO.

prohibition on a trustee profiting personally from the trust. They could, however, in addition to being employees also be members of the company and, in that capacity, they would still be able to exercise control over key issues such as the appointment of the company's directors.

(iv) The Officers of the Company and their Duties

Directors and Secretary

Every limited company must have at least one director and a secretary,[26] both of whom are generally referred to as being the officers of the company.

2.4.12

While it is difficult to generalise, as roles differ from one company to another, directors are likely to be responsible for the day to day conduct of the affairs of the company, often also being full-time employees of the company, while the secretary is likely to be responsible for the administrative activities of the company and often, in addition, its financial affairs.

2.4.13

Shadow and Other Directors

Confusion can arise as to the exact legal status of an individual involved in the activities of a company when job titles such as "local" or "branch" director are used. In such a case there will be no doubt as to the individual's status if the individual has consented to act as a director of the company and a formal appointment as a director has been made and notified to the Registrar of Companies. Conversely, the individual may simply be an employee of the company who has been given a job title which includes the word director. In virtually all situations any doubt over the status of someone described as being a director can be overcome by testing whether the individual consented to act as a director and has been appointed as such.

2.4.14

However, in the absence of such an appointment it is still possible that the individual may be held to be a "shadow director" of the company[27] and as such responsible for the company's affairs in exactly the same way as formally appointed directors of the company. Given that many charitable organisations now operate through local units or branches where considerable authority may have been devolved to one or more individuals operating locally, the concept of being a shadow director could be important for organisations with local or branch administrators, and they should regularly assess the

2.4.15

---

[26] Where the company has only one director, that person may not also be secretary of the company — Companies Act 1985, s.283(2).

[27] A shadow director "means a person in accordance with whose directions or instructions the directors of a company are accustomed to act" — Companies Act 1985, s.741(2).

extent to which the appointed officers of the company act in accordance with the administrators' directions and instructions. A perfectly innocent and well intentioned local charity administrator could well be considered to be a shadow director of a charitable company by virtue of his or her actions and the actions of appointed directors of the company, while remaining entirely unaware that this is the case.

Qualifications of Directors

2.4.16 Interestingly, there are no minimum qualifications required for anyone who wishes to be a director of a registered company, although an individual may in certain circumstances be prevented from becoming a director of a company; for example, if he or she has already been disqualified from acting as a director in another company.[28]

Duties of Directors

2.4.17 Directors do not have unfettered powers to make decisions and take action on behalf of the company and are subject to control by the company in general meeting. New directors may be appointed or existing directors removed.[29] Nevertheless, it tends to be the case that the directors are responsible for the day to day running of a charitable company. As a result of this exercise of authority (particularly where those involved are not only directors but are also employed by the company) it will almost certainly be the case that such directors will be construed as being "persons concerned in the management or control of a recognised body" under the Law Reform (Miscellaneous Provisions) (Scotland) Act 1990 and will be subject to the duties imposed on such persons under the Act, such as the duty to keep accounting records. In addition to their duties under the 1990 Act, which arise as a result of their position of management or control within a charity, directors are bound, in their capacity as directors, to observe a number of additional duties arising both from statute and common law.

Common Law Duties

2.4.18 The principal common law duties are known as fiduciary duties and duties of skill and care. In observing their fiduciary duties directors must act bona fide in the best interests of the company and in so doing must not make any secret profit or gain at the company's expense, fetter their discretion to act in the best interests of the company, or place themselves in a position where their interests may conflict with those of the company.

2.4.19 This would tend to suggest that in the case of a charitable company observance of the duty to act in the best interests of the company would lead the directors to be predominantly concerned with

---

[28] Company Directors Disqualification Act 1986, s.6.
[29] An example of the power to remove directors is to be found in s.303 of the Companies Act 1985.

furthering the charitable objects of the company. It should be clearly noted, however, that there is no authority to the effect that a director's obligations in respect of a charitable company are any different from those which apply in the case of a trading company.

Directors' duties of skill and care in relation to a company are generally less onerous than those which might be expected of a trustee in relation to a trust. **2.4.20**

This is an area where the common law has failed to keep up to date with modern developments and the position at common law is contained in *Re City Equitable Fire Insurance Co. Ltd.* [1925] Ch. 407, which establishes that a director need not exhibit in the performance of his/her duties a greater degree of skill than may reasonably be expected of a person of his/her knowledge and experience. It is a subjective test with no minimum reasonable amount of skill being required and, accordingly, under such a test the less knowledge and experience a director has the less skill is expected of him/her. So a director responsible for the financial affairs of an incorporated charity is likely to have a higher level of responsibility in fulfilling his/her duties of skill and care in financial matters if qualified as a chartered accountant than would have been the case if (s)he had originally qualified in another discipline not involving financial expertise. This being the case, it is likely that a director will not be held liable for breaching the duty of skill and care and acting negligently unless (s)he has been grossly negligent. It is, however, extremely important to note that in assessing whether a director has breached his/her duties of skill and care to the company no assessment is being made as to whether or not the director has breached duties which may be owed to other bodies. In particular it may be the case that a director's actions, while less than satisfactory, do not constitute a breach of the duties of skill and care but in the director's other capacity as a person concerned in the management or control of a recognised body such actions may be more than adequate to form the basis of an application by the Lord Advocate to the court for his/her suspension under section 6 of the 1990 Act. **2.4.21**

Statutory Duties

In addition to their common law duties, directors require to observe a number of statutory duties, many of which arise under the Companies Act 1985.[30] These duties largely apply in situations where the interests of the directors diverge from the interests of the company. Certain transactions are prohibited (*e.g.* a company may not make a loan to a director) while others require the consent of the members of the company (*e.g.* when a director acquires something of value from the company). Even when a proposed transaction falls within the latter category and requires approval under the Companies Act it should be borne in mind that the memorandum of association of a charitable **2.4.22**

---

[30] Part X of the Companies Act 1985 contains most of the statutory duties.

company will invariably forbid any benefits to members irrespective of whether otherwise permitted by the Companies Act 1985. So a director of a charitable company who is also a member is likely to be affected by this type of restriction in the memorandum of association.

Insolvency

2.4.23   Two other statutory duties are particularly noteworthy and both are connected with the insolvency of a company. The first duty arises under section 214 of the Insolvency Act 1986 and refers to what is known as "wrongful trading". If a company gets into financial difficulties the directors may be tempted to continue the company's activities while they try to obtain additional funding. If, however, the directors realise that the company is insolvent and that there is no reasonable prospect of avoiding liquidation or receivership they should take action to minimise the potential loss to creditors. Failure to do so may require the directors to make personal contributions to any shortfall in the monies available to be distributed to creditors.

2.4.24   With personal liability as a potential consequence of wrongful trading, directors should adopt a cautious approach in dealing with financial difficulties. While it remains uncommon to encounter charitable companies in real financial difficulties, particularly by comparison to the numbers of commercial/trading companies experiencing problems, the significance of section 214 should not be underestimated.

2.4.25   Many charities now conduct their trading and ancillary activities, such as charity shops, through the medium of a wholly owned or associated trading company. The provisions relating to wrongful trading will apply to the wholly owned subsidiary or associated company in exactly the same way as they apply to the charitable company. Furthermore, if any director (or employee) of the charitable company gives directions or instructions to the directors of the subsidiary, who are accustomed to acting on such instructions, the individual giving the instructions may be held to be a shadow director. As a shadow director, (s)he may be held to have traded wrongfully along with the other appointed directors of the company with the consequent risk of having to contribute personally to any shortfall arising from the insolvency.

2.4.26   The other statutory duty associated with insolvency arises under section 213 of the Insolvency Act 1986, which refers to fraudulent trading. This is a much more clear-cut situation than that relating to wrongful trading and the section strikes at the directors of any company which on winding up appears to have carried on its business with the intention of defrauding its creditors or for any other fraudulent purpose. Once again, directors breaching this section are liable to contribute personally to the company's assets.

Deregulation

2.4.27   In summary, all directors of registered companies require to observe a combination of statutory and common law duties which are largely applicable to all registered companies. It seems unlikely that there will be any substantial increase in the extent of the general duties under company law which require to be observed by directors whilst current trends to deregulate limited companies continue.

The significant exception to this is, of course, the increase in regulation of charitable bodies where directors of charities which have opted for incorporation will almost certainly be persons concerned in the management or control of a recognised body and, as such, will be obliged, in addition to their duties as directors, to observe the regulatory régime applicable to recognised bodies. **2.4.28**

Directors as Persons "Concerned in Management or Control"

While it is understandable that those involved in the administration of charitable organisations will be particularly concerned to ensure compliance with the provisions introduced by the 1990 Act, it is important that directors of charitable companies should remain aware of their other common law and statutory duties. The need for vigilance by directors in complying with their common law and statutory duties when they are also persons concerned in the management or control of a recognised body can be seen in the interaction of section 8 of the 1990 Act and the provisions of the Company Directors Disqualification Act 1986. The 1986 Act provides the means for disqualification of a director of a company on a number of different grounds. While a number of the grounds relate to circumstances where a company has become insolvent, section 3 of the 1986 Act permits the court to disqualify from acting as a director any person who has persistently breached his or her statutory duty to file documents required by the registrar of companies. The additional consequence of this is the disqualification of that person from acting as a person concerned in the management or control of a recognised body. This interaction between the observance of directors' duties generally and the specific obligations arising under the 1990 Act can also be seen in the provisions of section 7 of the 1990 Act. **2.4.29**

One of the powers reserved to the court on the application of the Lord Advocate is the suspension of any person concerned in the management or control of a recognised body.[31] Interestingly, however, there is no provision linking this suspension to any such suspended person's position as a director of a company where the registered body is in fact a company. This would appear to give rise to a potential situation whereby a person involved in management or control may **2.4.30**

---

[31] 1990 Act, s.7(4)(*b*). s. 7 deals generally with the management of charities in circumstances where there is or has been misconduct or mismanagement in the administration of a recognised body or it is necessary or desirable to act for the purpose of protecting its property or securing proper application of such property for its purposes.

have been suspended from such a position but can continue to be a director of the company in question albeit unable to exercise any powers of control or management. To prevent this situation from prevailing, one possible course of action would be to ensure that a charitable company's articles of association contain a regulation to the effect that any director who is suspended pursuant to the provisions of section 7 of the 1990 Act should forthwith cease to be a director of the company.

Corporate Governance

2.4.31 Before leaving the area of directors, their role and their duties, one final issue is worthy of brief consideration. That is the question of corporate governance. Quite simply, corporate governance is the system by which companies are directed and controlled. This has already been touched on in the form of shareholder-control over the appointment and removal of directors. Similarly, auditors of a company have a role to play in satisfying themselves that an appropriate governance structure is in place and, finally, the directors themselves have overall responsibility for the governance of their company. In the aftermath of high profile company collapses such as Polly Peck, concerns over the effectiveness of the controls exercised by shareholders, directors and auditors over companies in the United Kingdom led to the setting up of a committee known as the Cadbury Committee.[32]

2.4.32 The committee reported in 1992 and one of the key recommendations was that companies listed on the Stock Exchange should comply with a Code of Best Practice prepared by the committee. This dealt with a whole series of issues such as the accountability of directors to shareholders, the appointment and roles of non-executive directors and the use of remuneration committees to decide on directors' remuneration. Obviously, the application of the Code of Best Practice is limited to a small group of companies although the report of the Cadbury Committee sought to encourage companies to adopt it on a voluntary basis. Given the nature of the activities of many charitable organisations where donated funds are administered and the desire for transparency in activity and accountability, there must be a significant possibility that discussions over corporate governance will spread from the corporate sector to the voluntary sector in the near future. While drafted with the needs and interests of trading companies largely in mind, the Cadbury Committee's Code of Best Practice may be a useful starting point for any organisation looking to improve its own procedures on governance.

---

[32] The committee was set up in 1991 by the Financial Reporting Council, the London Stock Exchange and the accountancy profession. The Committee's remit was relatively narrow and was focused on reviewing the financial aspects of corporate governance.

Regulatory Régime

While the potential benefits of limited liability represent one of the principal reasons for a charitable organisation to choose to incorporate, the extent of the regulatory régime to which a company is subject is often cited as a reason not to incorporate.

2.4.33

The régime may be considered conveniently under four main headings:

2.4.34

(a) cost
(b) publicity
(c) annual requirements
(d) inflexible procedures.

(a) Cost

There are undoubtedly costs involved in incorporating a company but there is no reason why these should be excessive by comparison to those involved in, for example, the constitution of a trust. The fee charged by the Registrar of Companies on incorporation is £20 and, in addition, there will be the cost of either having a solicitor prepare appropriate forms of the memorandum and articles of association or purchasing an "off-the-shelf" company from a company formation agent. While it is possible that the costs involved in instructing a solicitor may be higher than those involved in simply purchasing an off-the-shelf company, it should be borne in mind that this cost should result in a suitable and appropriately defined constitution in the form of the memorandum and articles of association. Where professional advice is taken on the terms of a trust deed or the rules of a voluntary association, it is perfectly possible to assume that the cost of that advice would be largely similar to that involved in registering the company. In addition, it should be borne in mind that low cost assistance with the formation process may be available from other charitable bodies.

2.4.35

The second area of concern over costs has been in relation to the statutory requirement for an annual audit. Historically, this has been a major concern, especially for smaller organisations. While the provisions in the Companies Act 1985 which differentiate between companies of differing size have an impact upon the extent to which they are required to disclose financial information and as a consequence may have an impact on the extent to which their financial records require to be audited,[33] they do not deal with the fundamental issue of whether or not an audit is required.

2.4.36

In 1994, as part of the present government's programme of deregulation for private limited companies, new provisions were introduced which were designed to streamline the audit procedure for small and medium-sized companies. The statutory audit obligation

2.4.37

---

[33] See Chap. 6, paras. 6.4.9–6.4.11.

was removed for certain companies and amended for other companies with a slightly higher turnover.[34] While these alterations to the existing audit régime appear to favour smaller companies with restricted budgets, it remains to be seen how effective they will be for charitable companies where external funders may still insist upon an annual audit irrespective of the fact that the company may be exempt from the statutory audit requirement or may only require an accountant's report under the audit exemption regulations.

(b) Publicity

2.4.38   The provision of information to the public lies at the core of many of the provisions in the Companies Acts and the Registrar of Companies provides what is effectively no more than a sophisticated filing system designed to make information available to the public about registered companies. This procedure starts with formation of the company when, along with the memorandum and articles of association and the statutory filing fee, details are required of the first director(s) and secretary of the company. All of this information is freely available for inspection by the public. On an ongoing basis, details of changes in directors, shareholders and the company secretary are required, together with the annual filing of copies of a company's accounts and details of any borrowing arrangements the company might arrange where such arrangements involve giving security to the lender.

2.4.39   All of this information is readily available to any member of the public who seeks to access it. It should perhaps be queried why this situation is sometimes regarded in a negative sense, since charitable companies, particularly those receiving public funding, should be answerable to members of the public.

(c) Annual Requirements

2.4.40   Companies are required to hold at least one general meeting of members in each calendar year (referred to as an annual general meeting) before which accounts are laid.[35] In addition to filing a copy of its annual accounts, a company must also file a document, known as an annual return, which discloses details of any significant changes which have taken place in the relevant year in relation to such matters as the shareholders and directors of the company.[36]

(d) Inflexible Procedures

2.4.41   It is often suggested that limited companies are administratively cumbersome. If a meeting of members is required to consider, for example, a change in either the memorandum or articles of association, detailed procedures require to be observed which may be both costly and time-consuming.

---

[34] *ibid.*
[35] Companies Act 1985, s.366(1).
[36] *ibid.* s. 363.

However, it is now possible for private limited companies to "elect" to dispense with observance of a number of provisions in the Companies Act 1985 which deal with internal administration or procedure.[37]

2.4.42

Section 379A(1) of the 1985 Act permits a company, *inter alia*: (i) to dispense with laying accounts before a general meeting; (ii) to dispense with an annual general meeting; and (iii) to dispense with the annual appointment of auditors.[38]

2.4.43

It is undoubtedly the case that the regulatory régime applicable to limited companies is extensive and potentially complex, requiring discipline in record keeping on the part of a company. In recent years, however, attempts have been made to simplify the administrative régime which applies to companies and it must be questioned whether this need for discipline should be considered by companies as unnecessarily onerous, particularly for charitable companies in receipt of public funding.

2.4.44

(B) INDUSTRIAL AND PROVIDENT SOCIETIES

The industrial and provident society is a form of constitution which is used less frequently than it might be. It is perhaps best considered as representing a cross between a registered company and an unincorporated association. Its constitution takes the form of rules of association in much the same way as an unincorporated association, but it is an incorporated body and enjoys the benefit of limited liability. To qualify for registration as an industrial and provident society, a body must either be a bona fide co-operative society for the mutual benefit of members or a society for the benefit of the community, which is clearly the category most relevant to charitable organisations. Although the industrial and provident society is now used less commonly than the registered company, one area where it remains significant is in respect of housing associations.

2.5.1

It is now the case that any body which seeks registration with Scottish Homes as a housing association must be an industrial and provident society, having its registered office in Scotland.[39] While this does not mean that any such body will automatically seek to obtain charitable status, those that do will be subject to a regulatory régime different

2.5.2

---

[37] *ibid.*, s.379A(1).

[38] It is also possible for a private limited company to elect to reduce the majority needed to consent to short notice of meetings and also to specify the duration of directors' authority to issue shares.

[39] Housing Associations Act 1985, ss.2A(1), 3(10).

from that which applies to other incorporated bodies, such as the registered company.

2.5.3   Industrial and provident societies are regulated by and registered with the Registrar of Friendly Societies under a régime which is similar to that for registered companies, but which is overall less onerous.

2.5.4   Undoubtedly, the industrial and provident society has attractions in that it provides the benefit of limited liability without all the requirements associated with limited liability under the Companies Acts. That said, however, the incorporation procedure can be expensive and time-consuming and few professional advisers will be familiar with the industrial and provident societies' régime. It is, therefore, probable that the more readily-understood process of incorporation as a registered company will be recommended to charitable organisations, particularly as administrative obligations continue to be reduced in comparison with those which apply for other incorporated bodies.

(C) FRIENDLY SOCIETIES

2.6.1   Friendly societies are often confused with industrial and provident societies because historically both forms of organisation have been administered by the Registrar of Friendly Societies. Although this is no longer the case,[40] confusion continues.

2.6.2   Originally the friendly society was an unincorporated association formed for the mutual relief and maintenance of its members (primarily in sickness and old age). From this original form of association, the form of the friendly society extended to include a total of six permitted types of society which were registrable under the Friendly Societies Acts 1974. While many of the functions of friendly societies which dealt with provision of benefits for members in the event of sickness, retirement and the like have now been taken over by the state and commercial insurance companies, a number of large insurance organisations still retain their mutual status and are registered as friendly societies.

2.6.3   Upon registration, a friendly society remained unincorporated but, in like fashion to industrial and provident societies, became subject to a regulatory régime similar to that applicable to registered companies. Members did not enjoy limited liability.

---

[40] s. 1(1) of the Friendly Societies Act 1992 created the Friendly Societies Commission which is charged with regulating friendly societies.

While many charitable organisations still exist in the form of friendly   **2.6.4**
societies, it has not been possible to create a new friendly society of
the original type since February 1993, by virtue of the Friendly Societies
Act 1992. The primary purpose of this Act was to enable existing
friendly societies of the original kind (mainly mutual insurance
societies), particularly those dealing in financial services, to re-register
as incorporated friendly societies with limited liability. New societies
could also be formed in this format.[41]

It is clearly the intention that pre-1992 forms of friendly society should   **2.6.5**
gradually cease to exist. The 1974 Act will continue in force to regulate
those pre-1992 societies which still exist, but no new societies in the
old style will be registrable under the 1974 Act.

CONCLUSION

It is undoubtedly still the case that instances will arise where the choice   **2.7.1**
of legal form for a charitable organisation will be a simple exercise as
one particular form is ideally suited to the charitable purpose
involved.[42] Increasingly, however, those involved in the formation
and promotion of a charitable organisation will require to reflect in
greater depth than has hitherto been the case on which legal form is
most appropriate for their proposed organisation. The use of an
incorporated body as a suitable form for a small charitable organisation
may in the past have been discounted out of hand as being too
complex, too expensive or too inflexible for small or medium-sized
charities. In any event, it was assumed that it would be possible to
incorporate at a later stage if necessary without undue expense or
inconvenience. It is no longer the case that such assumptions are
automatically valid.

The pace of deregulation in company law is increasing and the burden   **2.7.2**
of administration on small charities which opt to adopt an
incorporated form may be nowhere near as extensive as might
previously have been assumed. Similarly, the prospect of incorporation
at a later stage may in itself give rise to cost and complexity where an
established body with numerous employees, properties and
obligations has to arrange for all of these to be transferred to a new
legal entity in the form of a company. This narrowing of the differences
between incorporated and unincorporated bodies is one reason why

---

[41] Sched. 2 to the Friendly Societies Act 1992 specifies the activities which
may be carried on by newly-formed societies. These are essentially restricted
to financial services.

[42] Where, for example, the charity will be involved exclusively in the award
of grants with no other activities being carried on, the use of a trust will readily
recommend itself.

the incorporated form may begin to be used more regularly, particularly as promoters start to look at all possible forms prior to formation rather than simply assuming that a natural evolution from one form to another will take place as the charity grows larger and its structures require to be changed. In addition, providers of funding, particularly public sector bodies, are likely to play an important role in seeking to influence the nature of the structure of the body they intend to fund.

2.7.3   It does not at present seem likely that the choice of legal form for a charitable organisation will be driven in large part by differences in the application or effect of the provisions of the 1990 Act to differing legal forms. The trust, the unincorporated association and the incorporated charity are all affected by the 1990 Act. While the interaction of the obligations arising under the 1990 Act and the separate régimes applying to, for example, trusts and limited companies may well give rise to quite distinct régimes for trustees as opposed to company directors, it is difficult at the moment to identify such radical differences between the overall effect of both régimes as to justify a preference for one legal form as opposed to another. The only conclusion to be drawn at this stage is that those involved in the the formation of charitable bodies will now require to be much more aware of all the options which are available rather than simply maintaining familiarity with one type of structure and shying away from consideration of others.

Chapter 3

CHARITABLE TRUSTS

Introduction

This book is concerned principally with bodies which are "charitable" **3.1.1**
in the technical English sense applied for the purposes of tax relief and
which are therefore capable of becoming recognised bodies in terms of
Part I of the Law Reform (Miscellaneous Provisions) (Scotland) Act 1990.
A Scottish trust is one of several legal forms in which a recognised
body may be constituted, but the formation of a trust which is charitable
for tax purposes must be looked at in its context within the general law.
The indigenous concept of the public trust and the peculiar function of
the word "charitable" in Scottish deeds together form the common law
background onto which the English concept of charity has been
superimposed for tax and regulatory purposes. The importation of the
English definition has, inevitably, given rise to confusion in the use of
the word "charitable", and the expression "charitable trust" when found
in Scotland must be treated with caution.

This chapter seeks to clarify in a preliminary section the meanings of **3.1.2**
the terms "public trust" and "charitable trust" and associated
expressions. A second section looks at the administration of public
trusts under the general law, and a third at the statutory amendments
of the law of public trusts contained in the 1990 Act. A fourth section
deals with the regulatory provisions of the 1990 Act as they affect
trusts in particular, as opposed to other forms of recognised body,
and a final section considers the criteria to be taken into account in
choosing the trust as the appropriate "vehicle" when forming a body
which is to be charitable for tax purposes and regulated by the Act.

Clarification of Terms

The terms considered below come from three sources: first, the common **3.2.1**
law of Scotland; second, the law of England as it has been imported into
Scots law for the purposes of taxation; and third, Part I of the 1990 Act.
The obvious starting point is the Scots common law term "trust".[1]

---

[1] It should be acknowledged at the outset that this and the following section
rely heavily on the standard works on trusts, in particular Wilson, W.A. and

"Trust"

3.2.2   Trusts in general take a wide variety of forms, and it is difficult to find a definition which fits them all. Lord Normand's often-quoted description of a Scottish trust, given in an English case in the House of Lords and offered as one applicable to trusts in both jurisdictions, perhaps serves to emphasise the difficulty of providing a formula which is both legally accurate and gives a real flavour of the operation of an ordinary trust in practice:

> "a fund is held as their property in law by persons who are directed to hold it, subject to purposes which operate as a qualification of their rights and constitute a burden on the property preferable to all claims by or through them".[2]

3.2.3   In a typical case what happens is that a benefactor (the truster) makes over property (the trust fund) to persons who become its legal owners (the trustees) under obligation to administer the trust fund in accordance with directions (the trust purposes) recorded at the outset by the truster in writing (the trust deed), and by virtue of powers (the trustee powers) granted expressly or impliedly by the truster, for the benefit of certain persons (the beneficiaries) chosen by the truster. These components may appear in various forms and combinations. For instance, there may be more than one truster, a truster may also be a trustee, and the beneficiaries need not be personally named but designated by reference to a wide class.

"Public Trust"

Public and Private Trusts

3.2.4   In the common law of Scotland, every trust belongs in principle to one of two classes.[3] It is either a private trust or a public trust. A private trust is formed for the benefit of an ascertainable individual or a number of ascertainable individuals, more often than not members of the truster's family. A public trust is formed for the benefit of the public, or at least of a section of the public. For instance, a trust for the protection of the environment generally would be a trust for the benefit of the public at large, but a trust for the control of pollution in the City of Glasgow would be a trust for the benefit of a section of the public.

3.2.5   The question can arise whether the class of beneficiaries defined represents a large class of ascertainable individuals, making the trust

---

Duncan, A.G.M., *Trusts, Trustees and Executors* (2nd ed., 1995), W. Green; *Stair Memorial Encyclopaedia of the Laws of Scotland*, Vol. 24; and Norrie, K., and Scobbie, E., *Trusts* (1991), W. Green.

[2] *Camille and Henry Dreyfus Foundation v. Inland Revenue Commissioners* [1956] A.C. 39 at 48, 1955 S.L.T. 335 H.L. at 337.

[3] But see *Glentanar v. Scottish Industrial Musical Association*, 1925 S.C. 892, which suggests that a private trust may display some of the characteristics of a public trust.

a private trust, or a small section of the public, making it a public trust. The key to the distinction between private and public trusts has been said to lie in the truster's intention,[4] and the best approach is probably simply to ask, in a case of doubt, whether the truster intended to benefit a number of individuals connected with him personally, for example as relations, friends, or employees, or whether his intention was to do good to a class of people in the world at large, such as "the poor".[5] It has also been suggested that a trust is presumed to be a private trust until it has been shown to be a public trust.[6]

Public and "Charitable" Trusts

Confusion has been caused in the past by the fact that many of the old Scottish cases treat the terms "charitable trust" and "public trust" as synonymous. The view of Lord McLaren that in the common law of Scotland trusts for charitable purposes are only one possible manifestation among others of the wider class of public trusts is, however, now firmly established as correct.[7] Lord McLaren's statement was adopted judicially in *Anderson's Trustees v. Scott*[8] and has been legislatively endorsed by the use of the term "public trust" in sections 9, 10 and 11 of the 1990 Act. Accordingly, trusts for purposes which may not be charitable in the Scots law sense, such as for the promotion of sport, or the social welfare of persons who are not necessarily in need, will still be public trusts if they are intended to benefit a section of the public. Because of the indistinct meaning of "charitable" in Scots law, however, it is impossible to say exactly what purposes are included in the term "public" but not in the term "charitable".

3.2.6

If the correct term of art, therefore, is "public trust" it seems to follow that characteristics attributed by the courts to "charitable trusts" when they should properly have used the term "public trusts" should now be attributed to all public trusts. Recent judicial confirmation of this view is to be found in the Outer House case of *Russell's Executor v. Balden*,[9] in which Lord Jauncey treats the rule of benignant construction as applicable to a deed constituting a public trust, although the rule was earlier said to have been developed out of the favourable bias of the courts towards charity.[10]

3.2.7

In summary, the correct term in the common law of Scotland for trusts constituted for public as opposed to private benefit is "public trust", and not, as in English law, "charitable trust". It might even be

3.2.8

---

[4] *Stair Memorial Encyclopaedia*, Vol. 24, para. 86.
[5] *Salvesen's Trustees v. Wye*, 1954 S.C. 440.
[6] *Glentanar v. Scottish Industrial Music Association, supra* (n. 3).
[7] McLaren, J., *Wills and Succession*, W. Green, at para. 1691.
[8] 1914 S.C. 942.
[9] 1989 S.L.T. 177.
[10] *Blair v. Duncan* (1901) 4 F. (H.L.) 1 *per* Lord Robertson at 6.

suggested that the Scottish term is more logical, and certainly less confusing, than the English one, because the expression "charitable" in English law includes a wide variety of purposes which are of general public benefit but which have little to do with charity in the ordinary sense of the word.[11]

Unincorporated Association as "Quasi-Public Trust"

3.2.9   An unincorporated association has no legal personality distinct from that of its members and its heritable assets must be held by trustees on behalf of the association as a whole. Such trustees will hold the property in trust for the purposes of the association as disclosed in its constitution or other contract of association. Where those purposes are public, in the sense that the object of the association is to benefit a section of the public, the heritable property is to be treated as held in a public trust.[12] Moveable property may be held less formally, but subscriptions or donations paid over by members for application to the public purposes of the association will be treated as held in quasi trust.[13] The application of the general law of trusts to such quasi trusts presents some difficulties, which are considered more fully in the next section.

"Charitable" in Scots Law

3.2.10   It might be said that in the common law of Scotland the meaning of the word "charitable" is less important than the fact that it is used at all. Its use in a testamentary or other trust deed has two consequences: first, the direction to the trustees to apply the trust fund for charitable purposes is regarded as a sufficiently clear designation of the class of beneficiaries to constitute a valid trust; and second, the trust constituted will be classified as a public trust. The exact meaning or content of the word, on the other hand, has never been definitively established in Scots common law.

Effect of "Charitable" in a Scottish Deed

3.2.11   It is a well established general rule that a testator or other truster may designate intended beneficiaries by reference to a specified class, subject to the proviso that trustees or others are appointed with power to select particular beneficiaries from within the class.[14] A second proviso is that the truster specifies the class in terms sufficiently definite to enable the trustees to proceed to a selection which can be

---

[11] See Chaps. 1 and 8.

[12] *Anderson's Trustees v. Scott, supra* (n. 8).

[13] *Ewing v. McGavin* (1831) 9 S. 62; *Connell v. Ferguson* (1857) 19 D. 482.

[14] *Dundas v. Dundas* (1837) 15 S. 427; *Crichton v. Grierson* (1828) 3 W. & S. 329.

said truly to reflect the truster's own intentions.[15] If the definition of the class is too vague, the truster will be taken to have delegated the power of disposal of his estate, and this the law does not permit him to do. A living truster might correct the deficiency with a supplementary deed, but where the deficiency exists in a will, the testator's heirs may successfully challenge the purported transfer to trustees. In considering such a challenge, the court must interpret the language of the will on its merits, treating the deed as "its own lexicon",[16] but rules of construction have accumulated in a long line of cases which are dealt with fully in the specialist textbooks on trusts.[17] One of these rules is that specification of a class of beneficiaries or objects by reference to the word "charitable", used alone or in conjunction with similar words such as "benevolent", is sufficient specification. By contrast, the word "benevolent" on its own, and words such as "social", "public", "useful", and "deserving" are not regarded as giving sufficiently clear guidance to trustees. On the other hand, "educational" has been held, like "charitable", to have a sufficiently definite meaning in itself.

This rule of construction has been treated as evidence of the special favour accorded by the courts to charitable purposes in particular, and it has also been said that the rule of benignant construction in itself amounts to nothing more than the court's acceptance that the word "charitable" has a definite meaning.[18] This is a narrow interpretation of the rule, however, and an alternative view is that the courts should take a generally benignant approach to the construction of deeds which disclose an intention of public benefit, whether or not the word "charitable" is in issue. Thus in *Russell's Executor v. Balden*,[19] Lord Jauncey adopted a benignant approach in giving effect to a bequest for the provision of sporting facilities for the people of North Berwick as a section of the public. The underlying principle, assumed

3.2.12

---

[15] *Denny's Trustees v. Dumbarton Magistrates*, 1945 S.C. 147.

[16] *Wink's Executors v. Tallent*, 1947 S.C. 470, *per* Lord President Cooper at 478.

[17] See n. 1 *supra*.

[18] *Angus' Exrx. v. Batchan's Trustees*, 1949 S.C. 335 *per* Lord President Cooper at 367.

[19] 1989 S.L.T. 177. Lord Jauncey treats the benignant approach as due to public trusts generally, and if this does amount to an extension of the earlier rule, it might be justified on at least three grounds: (1) that it is no more desirable to frustrate a desire for general public benefit than an intention to promote the narrower range of public benefit represented by the word "charitable" in Scots law; (2) that a similar rule of benignant construction exists for English charitable trusts, which form in English law a wide general class broadly equivalent to the class of public trusts in Scotland, and it seems equitable that the benefit of the Scots rule should also be enjoyed by the wider class and not confined to a part of the class only (see *Guild v. Inland Revenue Commissioners* [1992] 2 A.C. 310); and (3) that this is the logical result of the decision in *Anderson's Trustees v. Scott*, which equated the term "charitable trust" as used in earlier decisions with "public trust", at least for the purposes of *cy-près*.

but not discussed by Lord Jauncey in his opinion, is that an intention to benefit the public in any way is as worthy of favourable consideration as an intention to benefit objects which are specifically "charitable". There is no suggestion, however, that the wider application of the benignant approach can cure the fundamental deficiency of vague words such as "public" and "benevolent" as guides to the intention of the truster, and to that extent the word "charitable" continues to perform a special function.

3.2.13   Once the validity of a trust has been established, there is nothing to distinguish the treatment of trusts for "charitable" purposes in its Scots law sense from any other type of public trust, and while it has been said that "the prominence of charitable trusts in legal decisions results from nothing more than their being the most numerous class of public trusts",[20] it may be safest not to regard them as forming a separate class or sub-class at all, any more than trusts for religious purposes or sporting purposes form distinct classes within the definitive class of public trusts. What is certain, however, is that a trust which is charitable in the Scottish sense is also a public trust.

Meaning of "Charitable" in Scots Common Law

3.2.14   The meaning of the word "charitable" in Scots common law is less certain than its effect. Precisely because it was established early on that the meaning of "charitable" was sufficiently self-evident in itself to direct trustees in the selection of beneficiaries[21] the word has never been the subject of exhaustive judicial definition in the Scottish courts, as it has in England.[22] It may be convenient to repeat here the conclusion to Lord Watson's review of the early cases which has been quoted in Chapter 1:

> "In the first place, they establish positively that charity is not limited to relief of the physical wants of the poor, but includes their intellectual and moral culture; and, in the second place, they suggest very strongly that purposes which concern others than the poor may nevertheless be charitable purposes in the sense of Scotch law."[23]

3.2.15   Given the limited, if important, function of the word "charitable" in the interpretation of Scottish deeds, Scots law has no requirement for a more exact definition than this, and the temptation to confine the meaning of the word to the relief of poverty or, worse still, to assimilate the technical English definition into the common law of Scotland (as opposed to its tax law), should be firmly resisted.[24]

---

[20] Wilson and Duncan, p. 196; *Blair v. Duncan* (1901) 4 F. (H.L.) 1, *per* Lord Robertson at 6.

[21] *Dundas v. Dundas* (1837) 15 S. 427.

[22] *Income Tax Special Commissioners v. Pemsel* [1891] A.C. 531, *per* Lord Watson at 560.

[23] *ibid*. at 561.

[24] *Wink's Executors v. Tallent, supra* (n. 16).

In summary, therefore, the significance of the word "charitable" in the common law of Scotland is twofold: first, that its use to define a class of beneficiaries provides sufficiently clear direction to trustees to create a valid trust; and secondly, that a trust for charitable purposes is a public trust. On the other hand, Scots common law provides no clear definition of the word "charitable", but does not restrict its meaning to the relief of physical poverty.

3.2.16

"Charitable" in English Law

Definition

The word "charitable" in English law has an elaborately-developed technical meaning, which is dealt with more fully in Chapters 1 and 8. It is this meaning which is applicable in Scotland in the interpretation of taxation and rating statutes. The English definition has its origin in the Charitable Uses Acts 1601, known as the "Statute of Elizabeth", and incorporates four main heads of charity: the relief of poverty, the advancement of education, the advancement of religion, and purposes beneficial to the community not falling under the first three heads. There is an overriding requirement of public benefit applicable to each of the four heads. The English meaning has been defined and redefined as the courts have sought at times to restrict and at others to extend the range of activities capable of enjoying the benefits (in English law not exclusively tax benefits) associated with charitable status.

3.2.17

Comparison with Meaning in Scots Law

Attempts to compare the meaning of the term "charitable" in the English and Scottish systems have ranged from the robust, such as Lord Chelmsford's remark in *Magistrates of Dundee v. Morris* that he could not "discover any great dissimilarity between the law of Scotland and the law of England with respect to charities",[25] to the conciliatory, exemplified by Lord Watson's studious reconciliation of the two meanings in *Pemsel*. Lord Watson concluded that, in legislative language at least, the term bore a "comprehensive" meaning in both systems.[26] In *Jackson's Trustees v. Lord Advocate,* Lord President Clyde treated it as established that the English meaning was wider than the Scots meaning, so that a trust which was charitable under Scots law would automatically qualify for tax relief as also charitable in the English sense.[27]

3.2.18

Application of English Definition in Scotland

Lord Watson's objective in *Pemsel* was to justify the application of the English technical meaning of "charity" and "charitable" for tax purposes in Scotland, and the case established that those words

3.2.19

---

[25] Quoted by Lord Macnaghten in *Pemsel, supra,* at 582.
[26] *Pemsel, supra,* at 558.
[27] 1926 S.C. 579.

appearing in a taxation statute should be construed in the English sense throughout the United Kingdom.[28] In other respects, however, the force of the term in the common law of Scotland remains exactly as it was before the decision in *Pemsel*, in particular in the construction of deeds and the constitution of public trusts in Scotland.

Continuing independence of Scots common law

3.2.20 The continuing differences between the two systems were summarised by Lord President Cooper in *Wink's Executors v. Tallent*[29]:

> "In England, the whole subject is overshadowed by the statute of Elizabeth and the artificial structure which has been erected upon it; but that statute is unknown to Scots law. The Scottish rules affecting charitable and public trusts are the product of our common law without any significant interference from the legislature."

3.2.21 In construing the word "charitable" and associated terms in a Scottish deed, the principles developed in Scotland before *Pemsel* remain valid, even where the result would be different if the English rules were applied. Thus in *Wink's Executors* the Court of Session upheld the rule in *Hay's Trustees v. Baillie*[30] that the expression "charitable or benevolent" is a sufficiently clear declaration of purposes to create a valid Scottish trust, refusing to follow a decision of the House of Lords to the opposite effect in an English case in which the same combination of words had been used in an English will.[31] The difference between the two systems was, and remains, that the word "charitable" carries in Scots common law a broad, general meaning to which a further exegetical word such as "benevolent" can safely be added without harm to the established effect of the term "charitable" itself. In England, on the other hand, a general word such as "benevolent" cannot logically be exegetical of a highly technical expression such as "charitable", so that the addition of the vague alternative invalidates the certainty of the whole.[32]

3.2.22 The general law of public trusts in Scotland also remains unaffected by the introduction of the English definition of "charitable" for tax purposes. In *Russell's Executor*,[33] Lord Jauncey, when considering the applicability of the *cy-près* jurisdiction to a trust in Scotland, cited Lord President Cooper in *Wink's Executors* in refusing to identify the term "public" in Scots law with "charitable" in English law, and rejected as

---

[28] *supra, per* Lord Macnaghten at 587.

[29] *supra*, at 476.

[30] 1908 S.C. 1224.

[31] *Chichester Diocesan Fund and Board of Finance (Incorp.) v. Simpson* [1944] A.C. 341.

[32] There is not sufficient space here to analyse the exegetical and alternative uses of "and" and "or". See the specialist works cited at n. 1 above.

[33] *supra*, n. 9.

irrelevant English authority on the meaning of the word "charitable" in the context of *cy-près*.

In conclusion, therefore, no comparison of the meanings of the word "charitable" as it is used in Scots common law and in English law can be anything but approximate because of the quite different functions performed by the term in each of the two systems. The importation of the English definition of the word for the purposes of taxation in Scotland has left its function in the common law of Scotland entirely unaffected.

3.2.23

Trust as "Recognised Body"

A trust may be a "recognised body" under the 1990 Act. In terms of section 1 (7) of the Act, a recognised body is one which is recognised by the Inland Revenue in Scotland[34] as eligible for income tax relief on the grounds that its purposes are exclusively charitable in the technical meaning of the word in English law. "Body" is not exhaustively defined in the Act but is stated to include the sole trustee of any trust and certainly includes a trust established under the law of Scotland.[35]

3.2.24

"Recognised Body Trusts" and "Public Trusts" Compared

The 1990 Act contains certain provisions directed at recognised bodies, including trusts, and others directed at public trusts as such. The vast majority of trusts which are recognised bodies are likely also to be public trusts. On the other hand, not all public trusts will be eligible for recognition by the Inland Revenue as recognised bodies.

3.2.25

It seems clear that in principle all recognised body trusts will also be public trusts. This is because the English definition of charity contains an overriding requirement of public benefit.[36] To be charitable in the English sense, a trust's purposes must both fall within one or more of the four heads of charity identified by Lord Macnaghten in *Pemsel* and be of benefit to the public or to a section of the public. A trust constituted in Scotland which satisfies both parts of the English test and becomes a recognised body will be by definition a public trust.[37]

3.2.26

---

[34] *i.e.* by FICO in Edinburgh.

[35] See ss. 1 (7), (9) (*a*) and 15 (1). It appears that a trust established under the law of England may also be a recognised body if "managed or controlled wholly or mainly in or from Scotland", but only a body established in the United Kingdom may be recognised for the purposes of tax relief: *Camille and Henry Dreyfus Foundation v. Inland Revenue Commissioners* [1956] A.C. 39 at 48; 1955 S.L.T. 335 at 337.

[36] See Chap. 8.

[37] There are, however, two possible exceptions to the principle that all recognised body trusts are public trusts. The first arises from an anomaly in

3.2.27 Not all public trusts, however, are necessarily recognised bodies. In practice, it is likely that the trustees of many small public trusts which would be eligible for recognition by the Inland Revenue on the English test choose not to apply because the value of tax relief would be marginal. There will also be public trusts which do not qualify for recognition because they fail to satisfy the first part of the English test. The most obvious example is a trust for the promotion of sporting facilities for the public. Such a trust is a public trust by the Scottish test, but it is well-established that the promotion of sport in itself, unless its underlying object is the advancement of education or social welfare, does not fall within any of the four heads of charity under English law and is not therefore eligible for tax relief.[38]

Trust as "Non-Recognised Body"

3.2.28 A trust may be a "non-recognised body" under the 1990 Act. Section 2 of the Act provides that a non-recognised body is any body which is not (a) a recognised body or (b) registered as a charity in England and Wales or a charity which is not required to register. The Lord Advocate and the Court of Session are given powers under the Act in relation to non-recognised bodies which will be looked at later in the chapter as they apply particularly to trusts.

---

the case of trusts for the relief of poverty. Trusts for the relief of poverty suffered by persons connected with the truster by blood relationship or employment have been held in England to be charitable (*Re Scarisbrick* [1951] Ch. 622, *Dingle v. Turner* [1972] A.C. 601), but similar trusts are probably private in Scotland, on the authority of *Salvesen's Trustees v. Wye, supra* (n. 5). The English authorities make it clear, however, that the exception to the normal requirement of public benefit is anomalous and will not be extended beyond trusts for the relief of poverty. The second arises from the terms of the Recreational Charities Act 1958, which seems to leave open the possibility that a truster in Scotland could constitute a private trust for the provision of recreational or leisure time facilities for the benefit of young or aged persons connected with the truster personally which would nevertheless qualify for recognition by the Inland Revenue as charitable. See also *Glentannar v. Scottish Industrial Musical Association*, 1925 S.C. 226, in which a trust promoting a music competition for schools was held to be a private trust, but might have qualified as charitable in the English sense had tax relief been an issue. It appears, therefore, that in certain circumstances a private trust in Scotland might be capable of becoming a recognised-body, but for practical purposes it seems safe to assume that the vast majority of recognised body trusts in Scotland are also public trusts.

[38] *Re Nottage* [1895] 2 Ch. 649; *Inland Revenue v. Glasgow Police Athletic Association*, 1953 S.C. (H.L.) 13. The cases of *Russell's Executor v. Balden, supra*, n. 9 and *Inland Revenue v. Guild, supra*, provide an interesting illustration of the application of the Scots common-law test and the taxation test to the same trust.

"Charitable Trusts" in Scotland

It will be seen from what has gone before that the term "charitable   3.2.29
trust" when used in Scotland is capable of several meanings. First, it
can be used simply as "a convenient general name".[39] In this case, the
adjective "charitable" is used without any technical intention and
"takes its colour from the specific objects to which it is applied".[40]
Secondly, it can be used as a synonym for the technical Scots law term
"public trust". This use is found in many of the older cases but is no
longer regarded as correct. Thirdly, it can be used to designate a trust
constituted for purposes which are "charitable" in the indefinite
meaning of the word in Scots common law. It is suggested that this is
a misleading usage, because trusts which are charitable in this sense
are administered on exactly the same principles as other public trusts
and cannot truly be said to form a separate class in Scots law. Fourthly,
the term can be used to mean a trust which is recognised by the Inland
Revenue in Scotland as eligible for tax relief because its purposes are
exclusively charitable in the technical sense developed by English law.
Such a trust would be a recognised body under the 1990 Act and
entitled to describe itself as "a Scottish charity".[41] Lastly, the term
"charitable trust" might correctly be used even in Scotland to mean a
trust registered as a charity in England and Wales (or charitable in the
English sense but not required to register), but active in Scotland.

The scope for confusion is obvious and it is tempting to say that in   3.2.30
Scotland the term "charitable trust" should be avoided altogether. It
seems unlikely, however, that its use as "a convenient general name"
will ever be abandoned completely, but because of the practical
importance of tax relief the term is probably most often used by
"charity" administrators and their advisers to mean a trust which has
been officially accepted (in Scotland by recognition and in England
and Wales by registration) as eligible for relief.

ADMINISTRATION OF PUBLIC TRUSTS

The purpose of this section is to give a brief account of the law   3.3.1
governing the administration of public trusts in Scotland, as a prelude
to the final section, which deals with the choice of the public trust as
a vehicle for achieving objects which are charitable for tax purposes.

Subject to the differences set out below, and to the special treatment   3.3.2
under the 1990 Act of public trusts and trusts which are recognised

---

[39] McLaren, at para. 1691.
[40] *per* Lord Watson in *Pemsel, supra,* at 558.
[41] 1990 Act, s. 1(7).

bodies, public and private trusts in Scotland are governed by the same general rules. These rules are fully discussed in the specialist works on trusts.[42] Just as on registration a company enters the jurisdiction of the Registrar of Companies, on constitution a trust comes within the plenary jurisdiction which the Court of Session exercises over all trusts,[43] but the régime for trusts is quite different from the régime for companies. It is largely a development of the common law, supplemented by the Trusts (Scotland) Acts 1921 and 1961 and by the Trustee Investments Act 1961, which governs the management of trust investments in so far as alternative provision is not made in the trust deed.

Public Trusts and Private Trusts: Administrative Differences

3.3.3   It may be helpful to summarise the administrative differences between public and private trusts at the outset.

Benignant Construction

3.3.4   The courts will take a benignant approach to the construction of a deed disclosing an intention of public benefit by favouring an interpretation which will give the deed effect.[44] Deeds intended to constitute private trusts, on the other hand, are construed strictly.

Appointment of Trustees

3.3.5   A truster who sets up a private trust retains a residual right at common law to appoint new trustees in the event that the trustees die out without having assumed successors. No equivalent common law right exists for the truster of a public trust, unless specifically reserved in the trust deed. Only the court can appoint new trustees where the trustees of a public trust have died out.[45]

Trustees' Liablity on Distribution

3.3.6   The trustees of a public trust have a duty to take all reasonable care to distribute the trust fund in accordance with the trust purposes. However, they will not be personally liable where they have proceeded on a reasonable misunderstanding and in good faith.[46] The trustees of a private trust, on the other hand, will be personally liable for any error of distribution, even if committed in good faith.[47]

---

[42] See n. 1.

[43] *Pemsel, supra, per* Lord Watson at 560.

[44] *Russell's Executor v. Balden,* 1989 S.L.T. 177. The rule is not so much a rule of administration as of construction, but is included here for completeness. See para. 3.2.12.

[45] *Glentanar v. Scottish Industrial Musical Association,* 1925 S.C. 226.

[46] *Andrews v. Ewart's Trustees* (1886) 13 R. (H.L.) 69; *Free Church of Scotland v. MacKnight's Trustees,* 1914 2 S.L.T. 329.

[47] *Lamond's Trustees v. Croom* (1871) M. 662.

Role of Lord Advocate

A beneficiary, or potential beneficiary, of a public trust may raise an **3.3.7** action against the trustees to enforce fulfilment of the trust purposes, but because there may be difficulty in identifying those who have title to sue, and because the public as a whole has an interest in seeing that the truster's intention of public benefit is given effect, the Lord Advocate may raise an action against the trustees on behalf of the public.[48] The Lord Advocate has no such role in the enforcement of private trusts.

Role of Court of Session—*Cy-près*

Although the Court of Session has plenary jurisdiction over all trusts, **3.3.8** it has more extensive powers of supervision over public trusts than private trusts.[49] The exact scope of this additional supervisory function is uncertain, but includes power to approve schemes for the variation of public trusts under the common law doctrine of *cy-près*.[50] The *cy-près* jurisdiction has no application to private trusts.

Variation under 1990 Act

Public trusts may also be varied in certain circumstances under **3.3.9** sections 9, 10 and 11 of the 1990 Act.[51] The statutory provision for the variation of private trusts, on the other hand, is contained in the Trusts (Scotland) Act 1961.

Elements of a Public Trust

The principal elements of a trust have been identified in the previous **3.3.10** section (para. 3.2.3), and manifest themselves in a variety of ways in public trusts. Some of the peculiarities of unincorporated associations as quasi-public trusts are dealt with separately below (paras. 3.3.31–3.3.39).

Truster

A public trust may be set up by a single philanthropic individual, by **3.3.11** lifetime transfer of assets to trustees or by will. Alternatively, a number

---

[48] *Mitchell v. Burness* (1878) 5 R. 954, *per* Lord Deas at 959. The Lord Advocate's role in the enforcement of public trusts at common law is independent of his statutory powers under the 1990 Act.

[49] *Dundas* (1869) 7 M. 670, *per* Lord Deas at 672. He refers to "charitable" trusts, a reference which since *Anderson's Trustees* might be taken to include all public trusts. These powers arise at common law and are independent of the court's statutory powers under the 1990 Act in relation to trusts which are recognised bodies.

[50] *Anderson's Trustees v. Scott*, 1914 S.C. 942; *Wink's Executors v. Tallent*, 1947 S.C. 470. And see para. 3.4.4.

[51] See para. 3.4.4.

of like-minded individuals may set up a trust to promote a common cause. The promoters normally contribute funds themselves and invite contributions from others. The usual form is a declaration of trust by the promoters, who are both trusters and the first trustees. Additional donors are also trusters because they make a disposition to the trustees of part of their personal estate, however small, for application according to the trust purposes. Where the common cause is the promotion of a benefit to a section of the public, the donations will not be returnable.[52]

Trustees

3.3.12   The norm is that the truster appoints named trustees in the trust deed, who have power by virtue of the Trusts (Scotland)1921 Act, if not granted in the deed itself, to assume others.[53] A truster may sometimes reserve the right to appoint new trustees, or may provide that trustees should be certain persons *ex officio*, such as the holders of designated public offices. Unless the trust deed provides otherwise, a majority of trustees constitutes a quorum, and in the event of disagreement among the trustees, the view of the majority prevails.

Trust Fund

3.3.13   Almost any asset may form part of a trust fund, but a trust cannot be constituted without the transfer of some item of property, however small, to the trustees.[54] It is common to constitute a trust by transfer of a nominal sum, such as £10, which forms the initial trust fund and is supplemented by subsequent transfers. Trustees take title to heritable property in their own names as trustees. In the special case of Stock Exchange investments it is increasingly the practice for trustees to hold through the medium of a nominee company. Different views are held, but the pragmatic approach is that this does not amount to the delegation of a non-delegable trustee function, provided the trustees make the substantive investment decisions themselves. It is otherwise increasingly difficult for even a small body of trustees to sign transfer documents within the short time limits now imposed for Stock Exchange transactions.[55]

Trust Purposes

3.3.14   The trust purposes are those declared by the truster or trusters. By definition, the purposes of a public trust will bestow a benefit on a

---

[52] *Ewing v. McGavin* (1831) 9 S. 62; *Anderson's Trustees v. Scott*, 1914 S.C. 942.
[53] Trusts (Scotland) Act 1921, s. 3.
[54] *Clark Taylor & Co. Ltd. v. Quality Site Development (Edinburgh) Ltd.*, 1981 S.L.T. 308. In *Glentanar v. Scottish Industrial Musical Association*, 1925 S.C. 226, the trust fund consisted of an ornamental shield which was to be the prize in an annual music competition.
[55] See para. 3.3.21. The same considerations apply to the use by trustees of the new system of electronic share registration and transfer, CREST, to be introduced in July 1996 as an optional alternative to the existing paper-based system.

section of the public. In Scots law a trust with public purposes is nonetheless public although it contains other purposes which are not.[56]

Trustee Powers

The constituting deed will normally invest the trustees with a full range of powers and discretions to be exercised in fulfilment of the purposes. The 1921 Act contains a list of powers which are deemed to be available to all trustees in so far as not at variance with the terms or purposes of the trust.[57] It is usual for the truster to grant powers of investment which are far more comprehensive than those supplied by the Trustee Investments Act 1961, which are generally regarded as unsuited to modern investment conditions.[58] There are also statutory restrictions on the period during which income may be accumulated with capital in a trust,[59] which it is not open to the truster to override. Their normal effect for a public trust will be to prohibit the accumulation of income after a period of 21 years from the constitution of the trust.

3.3.15

Beneficiaries

The beneficiaries of a public trust will not be named individuals but a section of the public designated in sufficiently clear terms to enable the the trustees to give effect to the truster's own wishes. The use of the word "charitable" to designate a class of objects or institutions is a sufficiently clear direction to trustees to enable them to proceed. Most other general and vague words, including "public", are not sufficient when used on their own.[60] It would be quite possible to define the beneficiaries by reference to purposes which are "charitable" under section 505 of the Income and Corporation Taxes Act 1988, thus ensuring that the trust would be both valid as a public trust in Scotland and assured of being recognised as charitable for tax purposes in terms of the English definition.

3.3.16

There is much to be said for expressing charitable purposes in very general terms, leaving much to the discretion of the trustees but recording the specific intentions of the truster in a separate, non-binding letter of wishes. This will enable trustees to meet changing circumstances without recourse to a formal variation of the terms of the trust.

3.3.17

---

[56] *Ossington's Trustees*, 1966 S.L.T. 19. The reference is to a "charitable trust", used synonymously with "public trust". On the other hand, a trust which has a mixture of charitable and non-charitable purposes in the English sense is not charitable for tax purposes.

[57] Trusts (Scotland) Act 1921, s. 4.

[58] See para. 3.3.20. The Charities (Trustee Investments Act 1961) Order 1995 (S.I. 1995 No. 1092) goes some way to easing restrictions where the trust in question has been recognised as a charity by the Inland Revenue. Reform of the Trustee Investments Act 1961 is now under active consideration.

[59] Trusts (Scotland) Act 1961, s. 5, as amended by the Law Reform (Miscellaneous Provisions) (Scotland) Act 1966.

[60] See para. 3.2.11, and the specialist works on trusts referred to in n. 1.

Liability of Trustees

Duties of Trustees

3.3.18   The fundamental duty of a trustee is to fulfil the purposes of the trust. It follows that the trustee must know what the purposes are, and should be familiar with the terms of the trust deed, obtaining advice if necessary to understand its terms. The standard of care expected in the administration of any trust is "the same degree of diligence that a man of ordinary prudence would exercise in the management of his own affairs".[61] (The standard of care expected in the distribution of the funds of a public trust is, however, less strict than in the case of a private trust.[62]) The duty of care involves taking appropriate professional advice, for example from stockbrokers.[63] A trustee may not, however, delegate a decision to an adviser. According to the maxim *delegatus non potest delegare* a trustee, who is in the first place a delegate of the truster, may not delegate trustee duties to someone else.

3.3.19   A second maxim is that a trustee may not be *auctor in rem suam*, in other words may not allow personal interest to conflict with the interests of the trust. Where a trustee acting as an individual does transact with the trust, and is enriched, the effect of the rule is that the enrichment constructively forms part of the trust fund. This is so even when the transaction has been carried out as if at arms' length. The truster may, however, provide that the rule should not apply in all circumstances, and the most obvious example is the standard provision that a trustee who is also a professional adviser should be entitled to reasonable remuneration. Where there is no such provision, however, a trustee is only entitled to reimbursement of expenses incurred in the fulfilment of trustee duties. Trustees must act within their powers and in pursuance of the trust purposes. If they act *ultra vires*, and loss results, they may be called to account in the Court of Session, in the case of public trusts by a person with an interest or potential interest in the trust or at the instance of the Lord Advocate.

Investment of Trust Funds

3.3.20   The trustees have a duty to invest the trust funds. If the trust deed does not contain wider powers (as is normal) they must do so in terms of the Trustee Investments Act 1961. The Act provides, in essence, for the division of the trust fund into two parts, one to be invested in "narrower-range" investments, such as government stocks, the other in "wider-range" investments such as equities. Once divided, the two funds are to be managed separately, and it has been clear over the period since the passing of the Act that narrower-range funds have performed very poorly by comparison with those in wider-range

---

[61] *Rae v. Meek* (1889) 16 R. (H.L.) 31 *per* Lord Hershell at 33.

[62] *Andrews v. Ewart's Trustees*, (1886) 13 R. (H.L.) 69; *Free Church of Scotland v. MacKnight's Trustees*, 1914 2 S.L.T. 329. See para. 3.3.6.

[63] *Martin v. Edinburgh District Council*, 1988 S.L.T. 329.

investments. The Charities (Trustee Investments Act 1961) Order 1995[64] goes some way to easing restrictions where the trust in question has been recognised as charitable by the Inland Revenue, by allowing a further division of funds so that 75 per cent of the trust fund may now be placed in wider-range investments. Further division is not compulsory, for instance where the wider-range fund has already outperformed the narrower-range fund to the extent that it represents more than 75 per cent of the funds invested.

In the case of investment, as in other matters, trustees must take advice but make their own decisions. Strictly speaking, therefore, the trustees of a Scottish trust should not enter into an arrangement under which stockbrokers or other fund managers make substantive investment decisions at their discretion. Trustees are not entitled to make investment decisions on the basis of extraneous political or moral grounds, such as the withdrawal of investment from a particular country as a protest against its governmental policies, without considering what is in the best interests of the beneficiaries and taking advice on what is in their best interests. The issues are dealt with fully in *Martin v. City of Edinburgh District Council*,[65] in which Lord Murray in the Outer House comments on general propositions derived from the English case of *Cowan v. Scargill*.[66] *Martin* dealt with disinvestment from South Africa in disapproval of apartheid, but the principle seems applicable more widely, and might disallow, for instance, a policy decision by trustees not to invest in a tobacco company. The underlying principle is that investment decisions should be made on investment grounds, with proper advice and in furtherance of the trust purposes. A decision not to make an investment patently at odds with the primary purposes of the trust, such as an investment in a distilling company by a trust promoting abstinence from all alcohol, might therefore be justified by the terms of the trust itself.
3.3.21

It should be noted that there is no equivalent in Scotland to the concept of a common investment fund under section 24 of the Charities Act 1993, which permits small charities to pool assets in a common investment scheme approved by the Charity Commissioners.
3.3.22

Liability in Contract and Delict

The liability of the trustees to beneficiaries for mismanagement of the trust has already been touched on, and the trustees' liabilities to third parties in contract and delict are a logical extension. If the trustees enter into a contract in pursuance of the trust purposes and within their powers while exercising the overall standard of care demanded
3.3.23

---

[64] S.I. 1995 No. 1092, introduced under s. 70 of the Charities Act 1993, which applies to both English charities and recognised bodies under the 1990 Act. Wholesale reform of the Trustee Investments Act 1961 is now under active consideration.

[65] 1988 S.L.T. 329.

[66] [1984] 3 W.L.R. 501; [1985] Ch. 270.

of them, any liabilities under the contract will be met by the trust fund. If they act *ultra vires* or without due care they will be liable personally to the beneficiaries. They may also be personally liable to the third party if the liability exceeds the value of the trust fund.

3.3.24   In questions of delict, the same considerations apply. The trustees might, for instance, own heritable property, in which case they should see to it that there is adequate public liability insurance against claims by third parties. If they fail to do so, they will have failed in their duty as prudent trustees, and will bear the liability to the third party personally.

Relief from Liability at Discretion of the Court

3.3.25   Under section 32 (1) of the Trusts (Scotland) Act 1921 the court may relieve a trustee wholly or partly from personal liability for a breach of trust where the trustee has acted honestly and reasonably, and ought fairly to be excused for the breach.

Trustee Indemnity Insurance

3.3.26   The cost of insurance against damage to trust assets or delictual liabilties which may arise as the result of the trust's ownership of property is a legitimate trust expense as a necessary protection of the trust fund. The cost of insurance to cover the personal liability of trustees may also be legitimate.

3.3.27   The question was considered by Lord President Hope, sitting in the Outer House, in a petition under the Education (Scotland) Act 1980 by school governors who sought approval of an amendment to the trust scheme under which they acted, in the following terms:

> "The governing body may purchase and maintain for any governor insurance against (i) any liability which by virtue of any rule of law may attach to him in respect of any negligence, default, breach of duty or breach of trust of which he may be guilty in his capacity as a governor; (ii) all costs, charges and expenses which may be incurred by him in contesting any such liability or alleged liability but always excluding liability arising from any act or omission which the governor knew to be a breach of trust or breach of duty or which was committed by the governor in reckless disregard of whether it was a breach of trust or breach of duty or not."[67]

3.3.28   The cost of insurance was to be met from the income of the trust. The Lord President approved the amendment, remarking that its wording derived from two sources, the Companies Acts and a decision of the

---

[67] *Governors of Dollar Academy Trust v. Lord Advocate*, 1995 S.L.T. 596 at 598. Part VI of the Education (Scotland) Act 1980, as amended by the Education (Scotland) Act 1981, provides a statutory system for the reorganisation of endowments and trusts for educational purposes. Only s. 1 of the 1990 Act applies to educational endowments.

Charity Commissioners on trustees' indemnity insurance.[68] Factors taken into account in the decision were: (1) that the principle that the governing body should represent a wide cross-section of interests should not be put at risk by the unwillingness of elected governors to serve because of a lack of insurance cover for personal liability; (2) that the nature and scale of the activities for which the governors were responsible showed a real risk of liability; (3) that the statutory relief available under section 32(1) of the Trusts (Scotland) Act 1921 did not provide a satisfactory alternative to contractual insurance; and (4) that the Charity Commissioners had approved similar insurance for charitable companies in England and Wales and that the governors' position was indistiguishable from that of a charitable company.

Care should be taken in applying these principles to public trusts at common law but it seems possible to offer the following propositions: **3.3.29**

1.   Trustees are free to take out their own insurance to cover personal liability for their actings as trustees.
2.   The cost of insurance cover for personal liability may only be met from trust funds where there is authority in the trust deed or approved scheme.
3.   Where such authority exists the trustees must consider before availing themselves of it whether the activities for which they are responsible are really of a kind which might give rise to liability.
4.   If insurance cover is justified by the nature of the trustees' activities then the expenditure of trust funds to meet the premiums is unlikely to be considered expenditure of a non-charitable nature in questions with the Inland Revenue, because not so considered by the Charity Commissioners.
5.   The extent of cover, where cover is justified, should not normally exceed that permitted under the amendment approved by the Lord President.

The Charity Commissioners have recently made a further decision on the subject of trustee indemnity insurance. They have decided that, in cases where the purchase of indemnity insurance is appropriate, it would be acceptable for charity funds to be used to pay for insurance which includes cover indemnifying trustees against the costs of a successful defence to a criminal prosecution against them in their capacity as charity trustees. It remains to be seen whether a Scottish court would approve a power to insure in similar terms.[69] **3.3.30**

Unincorporated Associations as Quasi-Trusts

It has been mentioned in the previous section that property held for the purposes of an unincorporated association whose object is to **3.3.31**

---

[68] *Decision of the Charity Commissioners on Trustees' Indemnity Insurance* (1993), *Decisions of the Charity Commissioners*, Vol. 2, April 1994, 24.

[69] *Decisions of the Charity Commissioners*, Vol. 4, September 1995, 28. It seems unlikely that the Inland Revenue would object to a power in a new trust deed to insure in terms of the Commissioners' latest decision, but trustees of an existing trust without such a power would have to apply to the court.

benefit a section of the public is held in trust or at least quasi-trust. The underlying principle is that those who hold assets for the purposes of the association, whether as formally-appointed trustees or incidentally as office bearers, do so not for the members but for the public purposes of the association which are declared and recorded in the constitution. The application of the general law of public trusts to such associations is not wholly clear, but the following principles may be derived from the cases.

Property Held by Trustees

3.3.32   Trustees who hold heritable property on behalf of an association do so as trustees for the purposes of the association as disclosed in the constitution or other document or documents forming the contract of association. In practice the trustees, who may themselves be office bearers, will act in effect as nominees under direction from the office bearers as a body. The office bearers themselves are bound to act within the terms of the contract of association, but difficulties have arisen where the terms of the contract have been in dispute.

3.3.33   In many cases it is not simply a question of ascertaining the terms of association from a single, unambiguous constitution but instead from a series of perhaps conflicting minutes and resolutions. In such cases the underlying principle remains that the trustees hold the assets of the association for its original purposes, and any dispute as to the destination of heritable property is to be resolved by establishing what the purposes are. The principle is illustrated by the nineteenth-century cases in which the doctrines of dissenting protestant churches were examined in detail by the courts in an effort to establish which of the disputing factions within the given church could be said to have remained faithful to its original principles.[70] Property held in trust for a church congregation is held in a public trust because the purpose of a church is to assure public worship for those members of the public who share the beliefs of the congregation in question.[71]

Application of *Cy-près* Jurisdiction

3.3.34   It appears that if the constitution of the association does not itself contain provision for winding up or for the alternative application of funds in the event of failure of the original purposes, then the members must apply for approval of a scheme under the *cy-près* jurisdiction.[72] Those acting by appointment or *de facto* as trustees of a quasi-public trust are no more in a position at common law to alter the purposes of the association without court approval than the trustees of an ordinary

---

[70] *Craigdallie v. Davidson* (1813) 5 Pat. 719; *Free Church of Scotland General Assembly v. Lord Overtoun* (1904) 7 F. (H.L.) 1; (1904) 12 S.L.T. 297.

[71] *Anderson's Trustees v. Scott, supra,* n. 8. The congregation of a church other than the Church of Scotland is in law nothing more nor less than an unincorporated association: see *McMillan v. Free Church* (1861) 236, 1314.

[72] *ibid.*

public trust, unless, in either case, the founding document provides for alteration. The members of the association are in the same position as the truster of an *inter vivos* public trust, who having once declared the purposes of the trust is not entitled to intervene to change them unless under a reserved power to do so. The public has an interest in the original purposes of the association which is safeguarded by the court. It follows that even the unanimous agreement of members to alter the purposes is not competent without court approval. The trust may, in fact, outlive the association itself, as in the case of property held in trust for a religious congregation which has been disbanded, so that the original purposes can no longer be fulfilled. This was the position in *Anderson's Trustees.*

Where the original constitution incorporates a formula for amendment, for instance by qualified majority of the members in general meeting, the difficulty does not arise because the formula is integral to the terms of the quasi trust.[73] The same is true where the original constitution provides for an alternative application of the association's funds, for instance by transfer to a body with similar aims, in the event of winding up. Such provisions are, of course, normal and desirable, and care should also be taken to ensure in the case of an association which is to be a recognised body that any alternative application of funds is restricted to charitable purposes in the English sense required for tax relief.   **3.3.35**

Trustees' Powers

If an association with public objects is a quasi-public trust, it follows that the powers of those who hold property on behalf of the association are governed by the general law of trusts. It appears, therefore, that trustees who hold property in trust for an association with public purposes will have the powers granted to them in the constitution, and that the powers can be extended by the membership in accordance with any formula for amendment contained in the original constitution. Where the constitution contains no formula for amendment, the membership will not be at liberty to alter the trustees' powers because, on the analogy of the argument developed in *Anderson's Trustees* in applying the *cy-près* doctrine, the terms of the trust are fixed and cannot be altered without the authority of the court. This is admittedly an odd result, and probably ignored in practice by a great many small associations formed for a public purpose which see the need to alter their trustees' powers as the activities of the association develop. Not all will have had the foresight to include an amending formula in their original constitution.   **3.3.36**

The question arises whether the trustees enjoy the powers set out in section 4 of the 1921 Act in addition to those in the constitution. It seems clear that where trustees are nominated or appointed as such   **3.3.37**

---

[73] *Trustees of Leven Penny Savings Bank,* 1948 S.C. 147.

they will be trustees under the Act and will benefit from the statutory powers.

Powers of Investment

3.3.38   The same considerations apply to the special case of the investment powers of trustees who are nominated or appointed to hold the moveable property of an association. If the constitution is silent on powers of investment, and contains no formula for amendment, then it appears that the Trustee Investments Act 1961 (and the Charities (Trustee Investments Act 1961) Order 1995 if the association is a recognised body) will apply.

Accumulation of Income

3.3.39   The question also arises whether the restrictions on the accumulation of income contained in the Trusts (Scotland) Act 1961 apply to funds held in quasi trust for an association with public purposes. There is authority in an English decision which considered similar provisions applying to English trusts to the effect that the restrictions do not apply.[74]

Variation

3.3.40   Once a public trust has been constituted, it will continue in existence until the trust purposes have been fulfilled. There is no reason why a public trust should not continue indefinitely. There is, however, provision for the variation of public trusts both at common law under the *cy-près* jurisdiction of the Inner House and under the 1990 Act. There is no provision for the dissolution of a trust as such, and the trustees of a public trust who feel that the trust no longer serves its original purpose must avail themselves of either the *cy-près* or the statutory jurisdiction described below.

Public Trusts and the 1990 Act

Impact of the 1990 Act on Trusts

3.4.1   It will be seen from the origins of the terms discussed in the preliminary section that the law of trusts for public benefit in Scotland has undergone three main stages of development. The first was the common law stage, which developed the idea of the public trust and the special function of the word "charitable" in a Scottish will or trust deed. The second stage began with the introduction by *Pemsel* of the

---

[74] *Re A.E.G. Unit Trust (Managers) Ltd.'s Deeds* [1957] Ch. 415.

English definition of "charitable" into Scots law for the purpose of interpreting a taxation statute. This second layer of development was superimposed on the existing common law and left it intact. The third stage began more recently, with the coming into force, in July 1992, of Part I of the Law Reform (Miscellaneous Provisions) (Scotland) Act 1990.

Part I of the 1990 Act divides broadly into two main sets of provisions. **3.4.2**
The first (sections 1 to 8 and 12 to 15) introduces a system of regulation for bodies which have been recognised in Scotland as charitable for tax purposes, whether constituted as trusts or otherwise. The second set of provisions (sections 9 to 11) deals with the reorganisation of public trusts as a class, whether recognised bodies or not. The overall effect of Part I is to add a further, statutory layer to the law of public trusts, but, again, to leave the underlying common law intact. The provisions for the reorganisation of public trusts are dealt with at this point in the chapter because they amend the general law of public trusts described in the preceding section.

Reorganisation of Public Trusts (Sections 9–11)

Sections 9, 10 and 11 of the 1990 Act are concerned not so much with **3.4.3**
regulation as with assisting the trustees of outmoded and ineffective public trusts to bring their funds back into full use for public benefit. The sections apply to public trusts as a class, irrespective of their status for tax purposes. The term "public trust" is not defined in the Act and must therefore be understood in its common law meaning. The sections apply only to trusts and not to organisations for public benefit constituted in other legal forms, except in so far as the assets of an unincorporated association may be regarded as held in quasi-public trust. The sections supplement the existing power of the Court of Session under the *nobile officium* to approve schemes for the application of the funds of public trusts *cy-près*.

Cy-près at Common Law

The *cy-près* jurisdiction applies to all public trusts.[75] It is an exercise of **3.4.4**
the *nobile officium*, or equitable jurisdiction, of the Court of Session. In exercise of the *cy-près* jurisdiction the court may intervene to give effect to the underlying wishes of the truster of a public trust in cases where the trustees are unable to do so in accordance with the actual directions of the truster.[76] The court may sanction a scheme by which the truster's underlying intentions are given effect by means which approximate as closely as possible to the specific directions given by the truster. The jurisdiction is exerciseable by the Inner House of the Court of Session.

---

[75] *Anderson's Trustees v. Scott, supra,* n. 8; *Wink's Exrs. v. Tallent, supra,* n. 16; *Russell's Executor v. Balden, supra,* n. 9.
[76] *Clephane v. Magistrates of Edinburgh* (1869) 7 M. (H.L.) 7, *per* Lord Westbury at 15.

3.4.5   The *cy-près* jurisdiction is exerciseable both in preventing the failure *ab initio* of a testator's wish to constitute a trust for public benefit where there is some deficiency in the instructions contained in the will,[77] and in allowing variation of the terms of an established public trust which have been rendered unworkable by changing circumstances. Sections 9, 10 and 11 are concerned only with the second of these situations. Under the common law doctrine of *cy-près*, the court may sanction a scheme for altering the purposes of an existing public trust either where it is impossible to carry out the original purposes or where it is strongly expedient that the purposes should be changed.[78] Lord President Hope has described the recent exercise of the jurisdiction as follows:

> "It is a matter for the Inner House of the Court of Session to define the limits of its cy près jurisdiction in the exercise of the nobile officium. Recent decisions of the court have demonstrated that, while at one time a strict approach was taken to this matter, the court is now willing to exercise its power in cases of strong expediency falling short of impossibility of performance. The flexibility of approach which is inherent in the nobile officium enables the Inner House to take full account of the circumstances of each case and to act in accordance with principle as each case requires."[79]

3.4.6   The Lord President made his remarks in an opinion delivered in the Outer House refusing a petition presented under section 9 of the Act. The trustees of two public trusts had applied for approval of a scheme for their amalgamation and for the future administration of their combined assets. At the Lord President's suggestion, the trustees subsequently petitioned the Inner House and were successful, so the facts provide an illustration of the circumstances in which the court is prepared to exercise its *cy-près* jurisdiction today.

3.4.7   Both trusts were linked with the mining industry and both were shortly to benefit from a substantial bequest. The trustees of one trust had found that as a result of changing social and economic conditions surrounding the industry there was less need than formerly for the use of the trust funds in the way envisaged by the existing purposes, and the trustees of the other sought approval of the scheme as a means of extending the range of possible beneficiaries and of streamlining the administration of the trust, which was managed as a series of separate funds. In neither case was it averred that the trustees would be unable to apply the increased funds in terms of the existing purposes. The Lord President found that in these circumstances the

---

[77] *e.g. Russell's Executor v. Balden, supra*, n. 9.

[78] *e.g. Provost and Magistrates of Forfar*, 1975 S.L.T. (Notes) 36 in which approval was granted for the amalgamation of a number of small trusts to enable efficient administration.

[79] *Mining Institute of Scotland Benevolent Fund Trustees, Petrs.*, 1995 S.L.T. 785 at 786.

statutory jurisdiction did not apply but pointed out that the trustees were in a position to say that in view of the social and economic changes identified and in the interests of the better management of the trust funds, the scheme for amalgamation should be approved as a matter of expediency. It was presumably on the basis of such expediency that *cy-près* approval was granted in the Inner House.

It is against the background of the *cy-près* jurisdiction that sections 9, 10 and 11 were enacted as a means by which public trusts could be reorganised without recourse to a petition to the Inner House. In many cases the cost of such a petition would be wholly disproportionate to the value of the trust fund. In others, the preconditions of impossibility or strong expediency might not exist, but the trust might be difficult to administer effectively in practice. The sections supplement the existing *cy-près* jurisdiction but do not replace it.[80] **3.4.8**

Section 9 — Reorganisation Approved by the Court

Conditions of Statutory Jurisdiction

Section 9 lays down a total of eight sets of circumstances in which the court may approve a scheme for reorganisation proposed by the trustees of a public trust. The court in this case is the Outer House of the Court of Session or, from such day as the Lord Advocate may appoint, in relation to a public trust having an annual income not exceeding such amount as the Secretary of State may prescribe, an appropriate sheriff court.[81] The statutory jurisdiction exists where: **3.4.9**

1. The purposes of the trust, whether in whole or in part, have been fulfilled as far as it is possible for them to be fulfilled.
2. The purposes of the trust, whether in whole or in part, can no longer be given effect to, whether in accordance with the directions or spirit of the trust deed or other document constituting the trust or otherwise.
3. The purposes of the trust provide a use for only part of the property available under the trust.
4. The purposes of the trust were expressed by reference to an area which has, since the trust was constituted, ceased to have effect for the purpose described expressly or by implication in the trust deed or other document constituting the trust.
5. The purposes of the trust were expressed by reference to a class of persons or area which has ceased to be suitable or appropriate, having regard to the spirit of the trust deed or other document constituting the trust, or as regards which it has ceased to be practicable to administer the property available under the trust.

---

[80] s. 9(7).
[81] s. 9(5). No orders have yet been made.

6.   The purposes of the trust, whether in whole or in part, have, since the trust was constituted, been adequately provided for by other means.
7.   The purposes of the trust, whether in whole or in part, have, since the trust was constituted, ceased to be such as would enable the trust to become a recognised body.
8.   The purposes of the trust, whether in whole or in part, have, since the trust was constituted, ceased in any other way to provide a suitable and effective method of using the property available under the trust, having regard to the spirit of the trust deed or other document constituting the trust.

Conditions of Approval

3.4.10   In approving a scheme the court must be satisfied (1) that one or more of the eight sets of circumstances exists and (2) that the trust purposes proposed in the scheme will enable the resources of the trust to be applied to better effect consistently with the spirit of the trust deed,[82] having regard to changes in social and economic conditions since the time when the trust was constituted.

Form of Scheme

3.4.11   A scheme may take one of three forms:

1.   For the variation or reorganisation of the trust purposes.
2.   For the transfer of the assets of the trust to another public trust, whether involving a change to the trust purposes of such other trust or not.
3.   For the amalgamation of the trust with one or more public trusts.

Lord Advocate

3.4.12   An application for approval of a scheme must be intimated to the Lord Advocate, who may enter appearance as a party in any proceedings.[83] It might be said that the Lord Advocate's statutory role in such proceedings has a parallel in his role at common law in the enforcement of public trusts on behalf of the public as a whole.

Effect of Provisions

3.4.13   The provisions of section 9 have their origin in provisions introduced in the Charities Act 1960 for the application of charitable gifts *cy-près*

---

[82] English authority has defined the phrase "spirit of the gift" appearing in parallel English legislation as meaning "the basic intention underlying the gift". See *Re Lepton's Will Trusts* [1972] Ch. 276. See also *Governors of Dollar Academy Trust v. Lord Advocate, supra* (n. 67), on "the spirit of the intention of the founders" of an educational endowment under the Education (Scotland) Act 1980.

[83] s.9(6).

under English law, and now contained in a further developed form in section 13 of the Charities Act 1993. The impact of the provisions is twofold. First, they provide for approval of trust reorganisations by a single judge, whether in the Outer House of the Court of Session or, in appropriate circumstances, by a sheriff. Secondly, they provide for approval of a scheme in certain circumstances in which the the Inner House would not normally grant approval under its *cy-près* jurisdiction, even if in theory the *nobile officium* permits a highly flexible exercise of the jurisdiction.

There is some overlap between the conditions in which approval may be granted under the section and under the *cy-près* jurisdiction, but the statutory jurisdiction of the Outer House and the sheriff court on the one hand and the common law jurisdiction of the Inner House on the other should be seen as different, if similar. Only if one or more of the eight sets of circumstances laid down in section 9 applies will the statutory jurisdiction be available, and a petition under the section should be framed with particular reference to the terms of the section. If the statutory jurisdiction is not available, however, it is possible that the particular circumstances of the trust may nevertheless justify a petition to the Inner House under its *cy-près* jurisdiction.[84]

3.4.14

Section 10 — Reorganisation by Resolution of Trustees; Small Trusts

Section 10 provides for the reorganisation of small public trusts by determination of the trustees. By subsection (1), a trust to which the section applies is one whose annual income does not exceed £5,000, although the Secretary of State has power by order to substitute a different figure.[85]

3.4.15

Conditions of Trustee Determination

Before a determination is made, a majority of the trustees must be of the opinion that one or more of the eight sets of circumstances described in section 10(1) exists in relation to the trust. The eight situations are the same as those listed above as to which the court must be satisfied in terms of section 9 before approving a scheme. In terms of subsection (2), a determination by the trustees[86] is to be made to enable the resources of the trust to be applied to better effect consistently with the spirit of the trust deed or other document constituting the trust,[87] and may take one of three forms:

3.4.16

---

[84] *Mining Institute of Scotland Benevolent Fund Trustees, Petrs., supra* (n. 79), *per* Lord President Hope at 787.

[85] s.10(15).

[86] A majority is not specified, as in subs. (1).

[87] s. 10(2).

1. That a modification of the trust purposes should be made.
2. That the whole assets of the trust should be transferred to another public trust.
3. That the trust should be amalgamated with one or more public trusts.

Modification of Purposes

3.4.17 Where the trustees determine that a modification of the trust's purposes should be made, they may pass a resolution under subsection (3) that the trust deed be modified by replacing the trust purposes with new trust purposes specified in the resolution, but subject to the following four conditions:

(1) They must ensure that, so far as practicable, the new purposes are not so dissimilar in character to the original purposes that the modification would constitute an unreasonable departure from the spirit of the trust deed.

(2) They must have regard, where the trust purposes relate to a particular locality, to the circumstances of that locality.

(3) They must have regard to the extent to which it may be desirable to achieve economy by amalgamating two or more trusts.

(4) They must ensure, as regards a trust which is a recognised body, that the proposed new purposes are such as to enable the trust to remain a recognised body.

3.4.18 The modification will not take effect before expiry of a period of two months from publication of an advertisement giving notice of the proposed changes. In response to the advertisement any person with an interest in the purposes of the trust may make an objection in writing to the trustees. The terms of the resolution and of any objections received must be notified to the Lord Advocate, who may under section 10(14) direct the trustees not to proceed with the modification. The form of the advertisement and the procedures and timetables governing notification to the Lord Advocate and the handling of objections are laid out in detail in the Public Trusts (Reorganisation) (Scotland) Regulations 1993.[88] The purpose of the regulations is to enable the Lord Advocate to ensure that all the steps envisaged as a prelude to the taking effect of the modification have been properly taken.[89]

3.4.19 If the Lord Advocate makes no direction under section 10(14), the resolution will become effective after the expiry of two months from the date of the advertisement. Where the trust is a recognised body, the

---

[88] S.I. 1993 No. 2036. See Legal Materials section.
[89] The Scottish Charities Office carries out the functions of the Lord Advocate under the section, and has in practice adopted a general advisory role to trustees wishing to proceed under the section.

trustees must within seven days send to the Inland Revenue a copy of the resolution and a statement of the date on which it took effect.[90]

Transfer to another Public Trust

Where the trustees determine that the whole assets of the trust should be transferred to another public trust or trusts, the transfer will amount to a winding up of the trust. The trustees may pass a resolution under section 10(8) that the trust be wound up and its assets transferred, subject to the following four conditions: **3.4.20**

(1) That the purposes of the transferee trust are not so dissimilar in character to those of the trust to be wound up as to constitute an unreasonable departure from the spirit of its trust deed.
(2) That the trustees have regard, where the purposes relate to a particular locality, to the circumstances of the locality.
(3) That the trustees ensure, as regards a trust which is a recognised body, that the transferee trust is either a recognised body or capable of being recognised as such.
(4) That the trustees ascertain that the trustees of the transferee trust will consent to the proposed transfer of assets.

The assets may be distributed among a number of other trusts, so long as the conditions are met in relation to each tranferee trust. **3.4.21**

The transfer must not be effected until the expiry of a two month notice period similar to that required for a proposed modification of trust purposes, and similar procedures as to notifications and objections are prescribed in the 1993 Regulations. In this case, however, provision is made for a joint advertisement by two or more trusts which are to be wound up simultaneously. There is also a requirement in the regulations, which does not appear in the Act, for a statement as to how any liabilities of the transferor trust are to be dealt with. The transfer may be effected after the two month period has elapsed unless the Lord Advocate has directed under subsection (14) that it should not. Where the trust being wound up is a recognised body, the Inland Revenue must be informed of the date on which the resolution took effect. **3.4.22**

Amalgamation

Where the trustees of two or more public trusts determine that the trusts should be amalgamated, the determination amounts to a decision to constitute a new trust. The trustees of each of the amalgamating trusts may pass a resolution under section 10(10) that the trust is to be amalgamated, subject to the following four conditions: **3.4.23**

---

[90] reg. 6 of the Public Trusts (Reorganisation) (Scotland) Regulations 1993. The trustees will already have been in touch with the Inland Revenue as part of the requirement to ensure in advance that the modifications will be compatible with recognised body status.

(1) The purposes of the new trust will not be so dissimilar to those of the trust to which the resolution relates as to constitute an unreasonable departure from the spirit of its trust deed.

(2) The trustees have regard, where the purposes relate to a particular locality, to the circumstances of the locality.

(3) The trustees ensure, as regards a trust which is a recognised body, that the transferee trust is either a recognised body or capable of being recognised as such.

(4) The trustees ascertain that the trustees of any other trust to be involved in the proposed amalgamation will agree to participate.

3.4.24   What seems to be envisaged is that the trustees of one or more trusts with broadly similar purposes will co-operate in settling the purposes of a new trust, no doubt to be declared in a separate deed of trust. The purposes of the new trust will be designed to fall within the spirit of the trust deeds of each of the amalgamating trusts. The trustees of each of the amalgamating trusts will then pass a resolution that the trust should be amalgamated with the other participating trusts by reference to the new deed of trust.

3.4.25   The two month notice period applies as in the case of modifications and transfers, with the same opportunity for objections by members of the public. Procedures are laid down in the 1993 Regulations, and there is specific provision for a joint advertisement by the amalgamating trusts. The amalgamation may be effected at the expiry of the two month period unless the Lord Advocate has directed that it should not, and the effective date of an amalgamation involving a recognised body should then be notified to the Inland Revenue.

Effect of Provisions

3.4.26   The provisions of section 10 are based on provisions introduced in England and Wales in the Charities Act 1985 and now contained in section 74 of the Charities Act 1993. The Charity Commissioners perform the overseeing role given to the Lord Advocate by the Scottish legislation. The overall effect of section 10 is to introduce into the law of Scotland for the first time a means by which the trustees of a public trust with assets of only modest value may themselves, without recourse to the court, alter the purposes of the trust where no authority to do so exists in the trust deed. The interest of the public is safeguarded by the objections procedure and the right of veto vested in the Lord Advocate.[91]

Section 11 — Reorganisation by the Trustees; Expenditure of Capital

3.4.27   Section 11 applies only to public trusts whose annual income does not exceed £1,000[92] and whose trust deed prohibits the expenditure

---

[91] s. 10 (16) provides that s.10 shall apply to any trust under which property is held in trust by a local authority under s. 223 of the Local Government (Scotland) Act 1973.

[92] By s. 11(5), the Secretary of State may substitute a different figure.

of trust capital. In many cases the trustees of such trusts will find it impossible to give meaningful effect to the trust purposes by application of the income only. The section provides an alternative to the recourse which is theoretically available of an application to the *nobile officium* of the Court of Session, either for approval of a *cy-près* scheme or for the grant of a power to expend capital.

The section applies where the trustees have: 3.4.28

1. Resolved unanimously (not by majority) that, having regard to the purposes of the trust, the income of the trust is too small to enable its purposes to be achieved.
2. Satisfied themselves *either* that there is no reasonable prospect of effecting a transfer of the trust's assets under section 10 of the Act *or* that the expenditure of capital is more likely to achieve the purposes of the trust.

Where both conditions are satisfied, the trustees may proceed with the expenditure of capital in pursuance of their resolution, but subject to the following: 3.4.29

(1) They must advertise their intention to expend capital (in the form prescribed in the Public Trusts (Reorganisation) (Scotland) Regulations 1993).
(2) They must notify the Lord Advocate.

Role of Lord Advocate

Under section 11(4), the Lord Advocate may apply to the court for an order prohibiting expenditure of capital if it appears to him that there are insufficient grounds for such expenditure, and the court may grant the order if it is satisfied that there are insufficient grounds. If no such order is granted, the expenditure may take place at the expiry of the two months' notice. Neither the section nor the regulations provide for objections by members of the public and the onus rests with the Lord Advocate to take any protective action which may be necessary. No doubt in practice the Lord Advocate would consider objections submitted to him by persons having an interest in the trust. The Lord Advocate might also be expected to consider action in a case where the capital was in fact substantial but the income had been kept artificially low in order to bring the trust within the ambit of the section. There appears to be no requirement that a trust which is a recognised body should notify the Inland Revenue of its intention to expend capital. 3.4.30

Regulation 7 and the form of advertisement set out in Schedule 6 to the 1993 Regulations envisage expenditure of the entire capital of the trust, but it seems from the language of the section itself that the trustees, having once acquired authority to expend capital in terms of the section, may do so in whole or in part at their discretion. They may in fact decide to expend the whole capital in a single payment by making it over to a body with similar purposes, and that would seem an attractive alternative to proceeding under the more onerous provisions of section 10. 3.4.31

Effect of Provisions

3.4.32   The origin of section 11 lies in the Charities Act 1985, although the provisions for England and Wales are now contained in section 75 of the Charities Act 1993, and include a procedure for representations to the Charity Commissioners by persons having an interest in the charity seeking to expend capital. The general effect of section 11 is similar to that of section 10, in that it introduces into Scots law a means by which trustees of a public trust may acquire a power to expend capital where none exists in the trust deed without the expensive, and therefore impractical, recourse of petitioning the *nobile officium* for a formal variation of the terms of the trust.

3.4.33   It should be emphasised that the provisions of sections 9, 10 and 11 apply only to public trusts and not to recognised bodies generally. The Lord Advocate's role in safeguarding the interest of the public in any reorganisation proposed under the sections should also be distinguished from his power to apply to the court for approval of a scheme for the transfer of assets under section 7.

TRUSTS AS RECOGNISED BODIES UNDER THE 1990 ACT

Regulatory Provisions of the 1990 Act (Sections 1–8 and 12–15)

3.5.1   The main business of Part I of the 1990 Act is to introduce a system of regulation for bodies which have been officially recognised as charitable for tax purposes or which improperly hold themselves out as charitable. The system regulates such bodies generally, but certain provisions are directed specifically at trusts. The purpose of this section is to look at the regulatory provisions of Part I as they apply particularly to trusts. The remaining provisions of Part I, which amend the law of public trusts in Scotland, have been dealt with above.

Application of the Act to Trusts — Sections 1 and 2

Recognised Bodies, Non-recognised Bodies and English Charities

3.5.2   It has been mentioned in the preliminary section of the chapter that a Scottish trust may be either a recognised body under the Act or a non-recognised body. A non-recognised body is not entitled to hold itself out as a charity, and may be interdicted from doing so at the instance of the Lord Advocate. It follows that the trustees of a "charitable trust" in the Scots common law sense are not entitled to describe the trust as "a charity" unless the trust is also a recognised body (or possibly, if the trust has been constituted in Scotland but operates principally in England and Wales, a registered or non-registered charity).

The Act also contains provision for the regulation of English registered   **3.5.3**
and non-registered charities active in Scotland. In theory, the
underlying legal form of such a charity might be a trust established
under the law of Scotland, in which case the relevant provisions would
be applicable to a Scottish trust.

Accounting — Sections 4 and 5

Accounting for recognised bodies generally is dealt with in Chapter   **3.5.4**
6, and it is sufficient to mention here that compliance with the Charities
Accounts (Scotland) Regulations 1992 can be taken to satisfy any
concurrent common law obligation to prepare accounts which may
be incumbent on the trustees of a recognised body trust.

Suspension by Lord Advocate — Section 6

Under section 6, the Lord Advocate has power to suspend any person   **3.5.5**
concerned in the management or control of a body from the exercise
of his or her functions (but not for a period longer than 28 days) in
circumstances which are set out in section 6(2).[93] It seems clear that a
trustee is by the nature of the office a person concerned in the
management or control of a trust, and the effect of the power appears
to be that a person suspended remains a trustee but cannot exercise
the functions of a trustee during the period of suspension. It follows
that if the period of suspension ends without further steps having
been taken by the Lord Advocate under section 7, the person will be
restored to the full exercise of the functions of a trustee. It also appears
that if the suspension leaves a quorum of trustees in place, the quorum
may continue to manage and control the trust, subject to the
supplementary power of the Lord Advocate under section 6(2) to
"make provision as respects the period of the suspension for matters
arising out of it".

Suspension, Appointment and Removal by Court of Session — Section 7

Under section 7, the Court of Session is granted a range of powers   **3.5.6**
for the control of recognised bodies, non-recognised bodies, and
certain English charities, any of which might be a Scottish trust in
form. The powers which directly affect the status of trustees are as
follows, listed by reference to the relevant paragraphs of section 7 (4):

(*b*)   to suspend any person concerned in the management or control
of the body;

---

[93] See Chap. 5 for a full analysis of the circumstances in which the Lord
Advocate may exercise the power.

(c) to appoint *ad interim* a judicial factor to manage the affairs of the body;

(f) to appoint a trustee, "and section 22 of the Trusts (Scotland) Act 1921 shall apply to such a trustee as if he had been appointed under that section";

(h) to remove any person concerned in the management or control of the body;

(j) to appoint a judicial factor to manage the affairs of the body.

The effect of each of the powers (b), (c), (f), (h) and (j) on the office of trustee may be analysed as follows:

(b) Power of Suspension

3.5.7 The power of the court to suspend a trustee, as a person concerned in the management or control of a trust, appears to have the same effect as the power of the Lord Advocate discussed above, except that the suspension is not limited to a period of 28 days. It seems that the period of suspension may be indefinite, although the court has power to recall it at any time under section 7(9)(b). If an indefinite suspension is to be distinguished from a removal (under paragraph (h) of subsection (4)), then the trustee must remain a trustee while under suspension, even if unable to exercise the functions of a trustee.

(c) Power to Appoint a Judicial Factor *Ad Interim*

3.5.8 Walker in *Judicial Factors* suggests that there is little room for the appointment of a judicial factor to a public trust, except as an interim measure. An interim appointment is one which is made without intimation and service and is to take immediate effect.[94]

(f) Power to Appoint a Trustee

3.5.9 This power, unlike the others discussed, appears to be directed specifically at trusts, and in particular at Scottish trusts. The term "trustee" is not given an extended meaning in the 1990 Act as the term "charity trustee" is in the Charities Act 1993 and must be taken to refer only to a trustee in the usual sense of the term. The reference to section 22 of the Trusts (Scotland) Act 1921 seems to restrict the effect of the section to trusts to which the 1921 Act would apply. It would be meaningless to provide that section 22 should apply to a trustee appointed to a trust governed by English law (and in particular by the Trustee Act 1925). The provision is therefore much narrower than its equivalent in the 1993 Act, which allows the Charity Commissioners in certain circumstances to appoint a person as a charity trustee, that is as a person having the general control and management of the administration of a charity whatever its legal form.[95]

---

[94] Walker, N.M.L., *Judicial Factors* (1974), W. Green, pp. 41 and 61.
[95] Charities Act 1993, ss. 18 and 97. See also s. 80, under which the provisions of s. 18 (except subs. (2)(ii)) apply to a recognised body which is managed or controlled wholly or mainly in or from England or Wales; and see Chap. 8.

Possible uses of the power might be to supply trustees where the previous trustees had all died (on the ground that it was necessary to secure a proper application of the trust property to its purposes) or to replace trustees removed from office under power (*h*) in a case of misconduct or mismanagement.

3.5.10

(h) Power to Remove

The court has power to remove "any person concerned in the management or control" of a body to which the section applies. Like the Lord Advocate's and the court's own powers to suspend such a person, the power of removal is expressed in general terms and there is no suggestion that it is specific to trusts. Likewise, it appears to be exerciseable in respect of bodies, including trusts, established under the law of England.

3.5.11

It is not provided that a trustee (in the strict sense) who is removed from management and control under the section is removed as a trustee in terms of section 23 of the Trusts (Scotland) Act 1921, and it may be prudent for the remaining trustees to obtain a minute of resignation from the person removed in the usual form for the purposes of future conveyancing. Unlike the equivalent provisions in the Charities Act 1993, the section is silent on the question of the vesting of the property of a recognised body in the wake of a removal.[96]

3.5.12

(j) Power to Appoint a Judicial Factor

See comments on paragraph (c) above. Walker suggests that the appropriate course in the case of a public trust is the appointment of new trustees, not a judicial factor.

3.5.13

Scheme for the Transfer of Assets — Section 7(5)

Under section 7(5) the court may in certain circumstances intervene in the management of (1) a recognised body, (2) a registered or non-registered charity which is managed or controlled wholly or mainly in or from Scotland, and (3) a non-recognised body, by approving a scheme presented to it by the Lord Advocate for the transfer of any assets of the body to another body which is either (i) a recognised body or (ii) a registered or non-registered charity which is managed or controlled wholly or mainly in or from Scotland. The circumstances in which the court may intervene are set out in the subsection,[97] but the underlying object is to provide a mechanism by which assets which are being unsatisfactorily managed by one body in Scotland may be transferred to another selected by the Lord Advocate. Procedures to be followed by the Lord Advocate in preparing a scheme are laid down

3.5.14

---

[96] Charities Act 1993, ss. 16 and 18.
[97] See Chap. 5, para. 5.3.26.

in the Charities (Scheme for the Transfer of Assets) (Scotland) Regulations 1992.[98]

3.5.15 The effect of the transfer will be to leave the transferor body without assets, and where the body is a trust the result will be to bring the trust to an end. In the case of a Scottish trust there seems to be little difficulty in regarding the provision as an amendment of the substantive law of trusts in that it provides a new means by which the court may vary the purposes of a trust or at least accelerate the fulfilment of its purposes by transfer to another body with similar aims. There is a case for saying that the court has always had such power under the *nobile officium*. The court now on the face of it has a similar power in respect of trusts established under the law of England.

3.5.16 The court's power to approve a scheme for transfer proposed by the Lord Advocate under section 7(5) should be distinguished from the court's power to approve a scheme for the reorganisation of a public trust under section 9.

Section 8 — Disqualification

3.5.17 Section 8(4) provides that the acts of any person disqualified under the section from being concerned with the management or control of a recognised body shall not be invalid only by reason of the person's disqualification. The sanction for acting while disqualified is a criminal one, directed against the individual so acting and not against the body with whose management or control the individual is concerned. It appears therefore that a disqualified trustee could continue to act as such and would not cease to be a trustee by virtue of disqualification. A disqualified person could likewise be validly assumed as a trustee. In practice, however, the trustees of a recognised body trust would be wise both to insist on the resignation of a trustee who became disqualified while in office and to take reasonable steps to ensure that no disqualified person was assumed.

Transfer from Dormant Accounts — Section 12

3.5.18 Section 12 provides machinery by which funds lying in a dormant bank or building society account to the credit of a named recognised body may be transferred to another recognised body.[99] The object is to bring back into charitable use funds which have lain unadministered for a period of 10 or more years. The section applies only to recognised bodies and not to the other bodies to which sections 6 and 7 apply.[1]

---

[98] See Chap. 5 and Legal Materials section.

[99] See Chap. 5, para. 5.4.1.

[1] *i.e.* registered and non-registered charities managed or controlled wholly or mainly in or from Scotland and non-recognised bodies holding themselves out as charities.

The power to transfer funds is vested in the Scottish charities nominee, an official appointed by the Secretary of State.[2] The functions of the nominee are described more fully in Chapter 5, but there is provision in certain circumstances for the Lord Advocate to intervene either by appointing new trustees under section 13(2) or by applying to the Court of Session for the appointment of an interim judicial factor under section 7(4)(c).[3]

Section 12 applies to trusts as to other forms of recognised body, and it is not difficult to imagine circumstances in which, with the passage of time, trustees will have died or forgotten the existence of small sums of money held in a bank account, especially where the trust has no other assets and has ceased to be active. In such circumstances a transfer by the nominee will have a parallel effect in winding up the trust as the approval by the Court of Session of a scheme for transfer under section 7(5). Where the nominee's inquiries reveal other assets, however, that is no doubt a circumstance which would be drawn to the Lord Advocate's attention so that the appointment of new trustees or a judicial factor could be considered.

3.5.19

Section 13 — Appointment of Trustees by Lord Advocate

Section 13(1) provides that where a recognised body is a trust the trustees shall have power to appoint such number of additional trustees as will secure that the number of trustees shall not be less than three, notwithstanding anything to the contrary in the trust deed. The power might be necessary where the trust deed restricts the number of trustees to one or two, or provides for appointment of trustees by reference to a formula which can no longer be applied,[4] so that the existing trustees cannot assume successors.

3.5.20

There is no requirement in the general law that a trust, public or private, should have three or any other set number of trustees, although three is often considered a good number in practice because it is safer than a sole trustee, likely to produce decisive management by majority if not always unanimously, and more convenient administratively than a larger number. The effect of the section is not to set in terms a statutory minimum of three trustees for recognised body trusts as a class, but by subsection (2) the Lord Advocate may in particular cases where the number of trustees is less than three exercise the power of appointment provided by subsection (1) on the trustees' behalf. The Lord Advocate may make an appointment where it appears to him that the trustees will not, or are unable to, exercise the power for themselves and it appears to him that it is expedient to do so.

3.5.21

---

[2] s. 12(1).
[3] s. 12(6).
[4] *e.g. ex officio* of a body which no longer exists.

3.5.22   Possible circumstances for the Lord Advocate's intervention might be the wilful refusal of a sole trustee (falling short of misconduct or mismanagement) to assume additional trustees, or the incapacity of a sole trustee or one of two trustees.[5] It does not appear that the Lord Advocate may appoint new trustees under section 13 where all the previous trustees have died, because subsection (1) seems to give the principal power of appointment to the existing trustees and the Lord Advocate's role under subsection (2) is limited to exercising the power as their substitute. This is perhaps an over-literal reading of the section and it does sit oddly with section 12(6)(*a*), which appears to envisage the intervention of the Lord Advocate where a dormant account is held for trustees who cannot be traced.

3.5.23   The effect of an appointment under section 13 is presumably, as the exercise of a power by the existing trustees or on their behalf, equivalent to an assumption of a trustee under section 3(*b*) of the Trusts (Scotland) Act 1921.

THE TRUST AS CHARITY VEHICLE

3.6.1   This section of the chapter reviews the criteria to be taken into account in choosing a trust, in preference to other possible forms, as the vehicle for achieving charitable objects. The criteria will be summarised under the same heads as used in the consideration of companies in the preceding chapter. It may be helpful first, however, to mention some common examples of the use of trusts as "charities" in the taxation sense.

Examples of Charitable Trusts

Grant-making Trusts

3.6.2   Probably the most familiar example of a charitable trust is the grant-making trust set up by a single philanthropic individual. The truster may grant the trustees a very wide discretion in the selection of charitable objects, and may well appoint himself as a trustee. A grant-making trust of this kind is a public trust even if run in practice by a small body of family trustees who meet in private. A grant-making trust may also be formed by a group of like-minded individuals anxious to promote a particular cause in much the same way as the members of an unincorporated association.

---

[5] Where there were two trustees who were both *incapax*, the appointment of a third, *capax*, trustee would not help because a quorum of *capax* trustees could not be mounted.

Service-providing Trusts

A service-providing charity may be constituted in the form of a trust, **3.6.3**
and its trustees may participate in service provision either directly or
through the employment of specialist staff. Increasingly, however,
trustees are advised to put themselves at one remove from the risks
inherent in service provision by offering services and employing staff
through the medium of a limited company.

Trusts Ancillary to other Organisations

A trust may be ancillary to a body constituted with similar purposes **3.6.4**
under another legal form. For instance, a trust may be constituted as
a separate recognised body to hold and manage investments and other
property on behalf of a members' organisation formed as an
association or a company. The members' organisation may itself be a
recognised body, but if not, the trustees would be obliged to restrict
financial support of the organisation to such of its activities as qualify
for tax relief. As the activities of organisations in the voluntary sector
become more complex, use is now frequently made of trusts as part
only of a composite structure designed to maximise fiscal reliefs and
afford some degree of protection from personal liability to those with
primary responsibility for decision-making.

Choice of Trust as Charity Form

Regulatory Régime

The legal forms described in the previous chapter all require the **3.6.5**
participation of members. They represent different means of
organising a greater or smaller number of individuals uniting in a
common purpose. The organisation may or may not require
substantial assets to achieve its purpose, but the juridical heart of the
organisation is the relationship of the members to each other. A trust
is different in kind. It is a means of consecrating property rather than
people to a chosen purpose. If the purpose is charitable within the tax
definition the trust will almost certainly be a public trust. The
regulatory régime for public trusts under the general law and under
the 1990 Act has been described above, and against that background
the criteria to be looked at in considering the trust as charity vehicle
might be summarised as follows.

(a) Cost

The cost of a professionally-drafted trust deed is not likely to exceed **3.6.6**
the cost of purchasing an off-the-shelf company. Many solicitors base
their drafts on standard styles, and costs will increase to the extent
that the deed is tailored to special requirements. Trust deeds are
generally much simpler, and therefore cheaper to draft, than the
constitutions of associations. Model deeds for all types of organisation
are, however, available from bodies such as the Scottish Council for
Voluntary Organisations. Not surprisingly, it is the view of many

solicitors that the use of such models by non-professionals may still require professional guidance. There is no registration fee as such for trusts, although the deed is often voluntarily registered, at the cost of a few pounds, in the Books of Council and Session for the purposes of preservation.

3.6.7   Annual costs will be those associated with preparing annual accounts to meet the requirements of the 1990 Act. Changes of trustee and minuting of trustee meetings will involve continuing costs where professional agents are involved. Major changes, such as a variation of trust purposes, will require expert legal advice. It might be said generally that the trust environment, if not the exclusive preserve of lawyers, is territory in which their specialist knowledge is difficult to do without. Many professional firms and banks provide a range of services to trusts which includes day to day administration as well as legal, accountancy and banking advice as such. The level of costs will depend on the particular agents used and any special feeing policy they may adopt towards charitable organisations.

(b) Publicity

3.6.8   There is no equivalent for a trust of the public file held for every registered company by the Registrar of Companies. A trust deed recorded in the Books of Council and Session is theoretically available for public inspection, and a person with a potential interest in a trust has a limited right to information, but in practice the management of even a public trust is a private affair, apart from the duties of disclosure under the 1990 Act which apply to all recognised bodies.

(c) Annual Requirements

3.6.9   The trust régime brings with it no equivalent of the statutory annual general meeting for companies or of the annual submission of accounts to the Registrar of Companies. In Scotland, however, annual accounts are the norm for all but the smallest trusts, if only because they assist in the preparation of annual tax returns. It might also be said that a trustee anxious to fulfil the general duty of care owed by trustees to their beneficiaries would want to study and approve annual accounts as a matter of course. For trusts which are recognised bodies, however, the common law duty to account to beneficiaries is in practice superseded by the requirements of the 1990 Act.

(d) Procedures

3.6.10   Likewise, there are no statutory procedures laid down for the conduct of trustees' meetings, but it is prudent, if only as evidence of the conscientious discharge of their duties, for trustees to minute their principal decisions in writing. The trust deed itself may lay down certain procedures to be followed at meetings and in decision-taking generally. In practice, much trustee business may be conducted by post. Inevitably, the larger the number of trustees the more cumbersome and expensive the administration of the trust will become.

Conclusion

A trust which is a recognised body under the 1990 Act will almost certainly be a public trust. Its administration will therefore be governed not only by the regulatory provisions of the 1990 Act but also by the general law of trusts in Scotland as it applies particularly to public trusts. If the trust's terms are not themselves sufficiently flexible to allow the trustees to adapt their administration to changing circumstances, it may be varied either by recourse to the Inner House of the Court of Session under the common law doctrine of *cy-près* or by petition to the Outer House under the statutory provisions contained in the 1990 Act.[6] **3.6.11**

A trust is different in kind from the other legal forms which may be adopted in the constitution of a recognised body, and in some limited respects is differently regulated under the 1990 Act. It is not a suitable form for a charitable body which is intended to become a members' organisation, nor for one likely to engage in providing services or to employ substantial numbers of staff. On the other hand, it is well-adapted to the management of assets held for charitable purposes either as an independent grant-making trust or as a trust ancillary to a service-providing charity constituted in another form. The trust is perhaps at its best as a "charity vehicle" where the tasks to be performed are the management of substantial assets and the distribution of cash grants and where the administration of the trust will be undertaken by a small body of experienced trustees with ready access to professional advice. **3.6.12**

---

[6] Jurisdiction under s.9 has not yet been extended to the sheriff court.

CHAPTER 4

MANAGEMENT AND ACCOUNTABILITY OF SCOTTISH CHARITIES

INTRODUCTION

Regulation of Charities Before 1992

4.1.1　Before the 1990 Act the legal responsibilities which charitable bodies[1] in Scotland owed to their members and to external agencies depended on the particular legal form in which they were constituted. As earlier chapters have demonstrated,[2] charitable bodies may take a variety of legal forms including public trusts, limited companies, friendly societies, industrial and provident societies or unincorporated associations. Each of these legal forms brings with it certain legal obligations. These obligations will generally govern not only dealings between members *inter se* but also duties, such as the provision of information, which enable outside agencies to exercise some control over the conduct of the body. In this chapter "management" issues are defined as matters pertaining to the internal arrangements of charitable bodies whereas "accountability" refers to those obligations which require charitable bodies to inform and account for their actions to others outside the organisation.

4.1.2　Thus, directors of companies which have charitable purposes are subject to the accounting requirements prescribed by the Companies Acts, particularly Part VII of the 1985 Act, which enable members of the company to be kept informed of the company's financial position. For the purposes of accountability and for the protection of third parties, company directors may be disqualified from holding office under the Company Directors Disqualification Act 1986. In relation to public and private trusts governed by the law of Scotland, trustees are subject to a common law duty of accountability to their beneficiaries who, in the case of a public trust, may be represented by the Lord Advocate. Public trusts whose purposes have failed are also subject to the plenary jurisdiction of the Court of Session, which in the exercise of the *nobile officium* may approve a *cy-près* scheme to enable the truster's underlying intention of public benefit to be implemented. For unincorporated associations, which is the legal

---

[1]See Chap. 1, paras. 1.4.5–1.4.9 for definition.
[2]See Chaps. 2 and 3.

form most commonly used by Scottish charitable bodies, management within the organisation is governed by contract and dealings with third parties are regulated according to the normal rules of contractual and delictual liability.[3] Friendly societies and industrial and provident societies have their own statutory rules regulating internal management and external accountability.[4] In addition, the constituting documents of these bodies, whether establishing a trust, a company, an unincorporated association, a friendly society or an industrial and provident society, may contain other management and accountability requirements which are not derived from statute or common law.

This patchwork of different legal forms has enabled the charitable sector to develop flexibly and in response to social and economic change with few of the legal constraints which have for many years been a feature of the regulation of charities in England and Wales.[5] Indeed, under Scots law as it operated before the implementation of the Law Reform (Miscellaneous Provisions) (Scotland) Act 1990 no distinction was drawn, other than for tax and rating purposes, between charitable and other bodies having the same legal form, and the word "charitable" at common law had a very general meaning, unlike the artificial definition which is applied in English law.[6] Before Part I of the 1990 Act came into force recognition of a body as charitable for tax purposes brought with it no general public accountability beyond compliance with the legislation itself. Since July 27, 1992, however, those bodies which have been recognised by the law as charitable for tax purposes do have to meet certain obligations specific to them as "recognised bodies", regardless of legal form. At the same time, each recognised body has to adhere to the requirements of management and accountability which are imposed generally on bodies having the same legal form and also any particular obligations stated in its constituting document. **4.1.3**

Since the general legal framework for the management and accountability of charities in Scotland is contained in the 1990 Act, this chapter concentrates on the provisions of the Act and on the duties prescribed in that Act and the regulations issued under its authority. Chapter 5 considers the powers which are given to the Lord Advocate and the Court of Session under the Act over recognised and non-recognised bodies, and in relation to English charities. **4.1.4**

---

[3]See Chap. 2, paras. 2.2.1 *et seq.*

[4]See the Industrial and Provident Societies Acts 1965, 1968, 1975 and 1978 and the Friendly Societies Acts 1974 and 1992. See also Chap. 2, paras. 2.5.1–2.6.5.

[5]English law on charities is now contained in the Charities Acts 1992 and 1993.

[6]See Chaps. 1 and 8 for fuller consideration of English law.

GENERAL REQUIREMENTS UNDER PART I OF THE LAW REFORM
(MISCELLANEOUS PROVISIONS) (SCOTLAND) ACT 1990

4.2.1   Part I of the Law Reform (Miscellaneous Provisions) (Scotland) Act
1990 imposes important new forms of accountability on charities
operating in Scotland. Recognition by the Inland Revenue of a given
body as charitable now gives Scottish bodies not only the right to tax
exemptions and preferential treatment in rating but also renders such
bodies accountable to the public, the Lord Advocate and the Court of
Session in the fulfilment of their charitable purposes. These obligations
are similar to those which have been imposed on charities in England
and Wales since 1960 and which are now consolidated in the Charities
Act 1993. However, the extensive powers given to the Charity
Commissioners in England and Wales do not extend to Scotland and
there is no comparable regulatory body in this jurisdiction. It should
be noted that the Act imposes duties not only on bodies recognised as
charitable but provides authority for the Lord Advocate to investigate
bodies which are not recognised by the Inland Revenue but which
nevertheless represent themselves as "charities". The legislation
therefore has an important role to play in protecting the public from
"bogus" charities and in maintaining the good reputation of *bona fide*
charities.

4.2.2   The need for greater public accountability was recognised in the
Scottish Home and Health Department's paper on charities in
Scotland,[7] which preceded and helped to shape the provisions of the
1990 Act. The importance of securing the public's continuing
confidence in charities could, according to the paper, "best be achieved
by ensuring that all charities are open about the conduct of their
affairs".[8]

4.2.3   The paper proposed three ways in which charities might be more open
to public scrutiny:

(1)   the establishment of an index of "recognised" charities;
(2)   the provision of information by charities to the public on request;
(3)   minimum requirements for the keeping of charity accounts.

These proposals were all included in the legislation, which was
generally welcomed within the voluntary sector. Nevertheless,
concern was expressed that the provisions lacked rigour and might
fail to provide an effective means of subjecting charities to public
scrutiny.[9] For instance, the Inland Revenue's Index contains
information only on those bodies which are known to the Revenue
because they have sought tax exemption or claimed tax rebates. This

---

[7]Scottish Home and Health Department, *Charities in Scotland: A Framework
for Supervision* (1989), Scottish Office.
[8]*ibid.* para. 2.3.
[9]*ibid.* para.2.7.

does not include bodies which have not had contact with the Revenue since 1970. In addition, it is estimated that the information which the Inland Revenue has on such bodies may be out of date and that 25 per cent of the entries may well be inaccurate.[10]

Recognised Bodies

The Act introduced the new concept, in section 1(7), of a "recognised body". A recognised body is one which the Inland Revenue accepts as having objects which are exclusively charitable for tax purposes,[11] applying the definition under English law set down initially in the Statute of Charitable Uses 1601 and developed in subsequent case law. Thus the charity must have one or more of the following purposes: **4.3.1**

(1)   the relief of poverty;
(2)   the advancement of education;
(3)   the advancement of religion;
(4)   other purposes beneficial to the community.

It has been suggested that this definition does not accord either with what the layperson would define as charitable or with the Scots law meaning of the word. Lord Macnaghten, in the leading case of *Income Tax Special Commissioners v. Pemsel* [1891] A.C. 531, noted the difficulty which the public might have in understanding the meaning in English law of the word "charity":   **4.3.2**

> "Of all words in the English language bearing a popular as well as a legal signification I am not sure that there is one which more unmistakeably has a technical meaning in the strictest sense of the term, that is a meaning clear and distinct, peculiar to the law as understood and administered in this country, [*i.e.* in England]"[12]

The meaning of charitable in Scots common law, as has been noted in earlier chapters, is much less definite and technical than in English law. The 1990 Act has reinforced the significance of the imported English definition in Scotland but at the same time does nothing to assist either legal system in dealing with the difficulties arising from such an artificial definition.   **4.3.3**

If a body is to be recognised as charitable for tax purposes in Scotland, therefore, it must provide the Inland Revenue with evidence that it has been established for "charitable purposes" according to the English definition. A copy of the constitution, memorandum and articles of association or trust deed must be submitted and the approval of the   **4.3.4**

---

[10]See *Faith and Hope in Charity* (1994) SCVO.
  [11]According to s. 1(8) a certificate from the Revenue is sufficient evidence that a body is a recognised body.
  [12]*Pemsel* at 581–582.

Inland Revenue secured before any body can describe itself as a charity, for example on its headed notepaper, in fundraising appeals or for publicity campaigns. Interdict may be granted to prevent a body which has not been recognised by the Inland Revenue from representing itself as a charity, upon application by the Lord Advocate to the Court of Session.[13]

Non-Recognised Bodies

4.4.1   Under section 2 a body is not entitled to represent itself as a charity unless it is either a "recognised body" in terms of section 1(7) of the 1990 Act or a body registered as a charity in England and Wales under section 3 of the Charities Act 1993 or a charity established in England and Wales which is not required to register by virtue of section 3(5) of the 1993 Act. Before the 1990 Act came into force in 1992 there was no bar on bodies which were not recognised as charitable for tax purposes calling themselves charities. Criminal charges might have been brought where a body representing itself as a charity was in fact acting fraudulently and misapplying funds given for charitable purposes.[14] But until the provisions of the 1990 Act came into force Scots law did not afford any special status to charitable bodies other than for tax purposes and did not impose particular obligations on such bodies *per se*. The legislation therefore represents a decisive step in creating a category of "recognised bodies" which alone have the right to call themselves charities. In addition, certain of the extensive regulatory powers to investigate and control the activities of recognised bodies which are given to the Lord Advocate and the Court of Session under sections 6 and 7 extend to non-recognised bodies.[15]

DUTIES IMPOSED ON RECOGNISED BODIES

The Duty to Provide Information to the Public

4.5.1   Under section 1(1) the Inland Revenue is released from its conventional obligation of confidentiality in relation to information supplied to it. The Lord Advocate is entitled under section 1(1)(*a*) to receive information about any recognised body where it appears to the Commissioners that the body has not been devoting its funds or confining its activities to charitable purposes, or in relation to a "dormant" charity.[16] In addition, any person may now request the

---

[13] s.7(4)(*a*). To date no such interdicts have been granted.

[14] In relation to public trusts the Court of Session might also have had authority to intervene in such cases.

[15] See Chap. 5, paras. 5.3.14 and 5.3.25.

[16] s. 12. See Chap. 5, paras. 5.4.1 *et seq.* for an analysis of this provision.

Inland Revenue to supply him or her with the name and last known address of any recognised body and the last year in which communication was made by the Revenue with that body.

Recognised bodies must themselves provide a copy of their "explanatory document" to any person who requests it, within one month of such a request.[17] This provision not only enables a member of the public to find out about the nature and purpose of a recognised body but also provides a means by which the public may alert the Lord Advocate in the case of recognised bodies which appear to be applying their funds to non-charitable purposes or carrying out activities which are not charitable.

4.5.2

The Act defines an explanatory document as either the trust deed of a body or other document constituting the body or such other document as the Lord Advocate may approve.[18] It appears not to be necessary, therefore, to supply the full text of the constitution, memorandum and articles or trust deed in all cases. Where the Lord Advocate considers that an abridged version of this document describes the nature of the body and its charitable purposes that version may be approved by the Lord Advocate as an explanatory document within the meaning of the Act. Bodies which have complicated and lengthy constituting documents, such as certain religious bodies, may be permitted by the Lord Advocate to submit a much simpler explanatory document to meet the requirements of the Act.

4.5.3

The recognised body may levy a reasonable charge in respect of copying and postage.[19] It is doubtful whether the practice adopted by some professional advisers of charging a fee including the cost of their time in dealing with such requests is permitted under a strict interpretation of the Act. The Scottish Charities Office has recommended that charities should charge no more than £10 for the supply of this information and usually the fee is considerably less.[20]

4.5.4

Where this information is not provided within one month of a request, the person seeking the information may make a complaint to the Lord Advocate. Application can then be made by the Lord Advocate to the Court of Session, except in the case of designated religious bodies,[21] seeking interdict to prevent the body from engaging in "any activity specified in the application" made by the Lord Advocate,[22] for instance holding a fundraising event or providing a service to the public. The Lord Advocate may also direct that the failure to provide a copy of the explanatory document be noted by the Inland Revenue so that

4.5.5

---

[17]s.1(4) and (5).
[18]s.1(9).
[19]s.1(4).
[20]In the Nuffield research most charities did not charge any fee.
[21]See s.3(3).
[22]s.1(6).

any person who subsequently asks the Revenue for details on a recognised body will receive notification of such failure.[23] In the Nuffield study, involving 150 bodies in the fields of social welfare and the environment drawn from the Inland Revenue's Index, 100 recognised bodies failed to provide such information within a month of receipt of the request.[24]

The Duty to Keep Accounting Records and to Prepare Accounts[25]

4.5.6   All recognised bodies are now under an obligation to keep accounting records which are sufficient to show and explain the body's financial transactions. The aim of this provision is to ensure that the body can at any time "disclose with reasonable accuracy" its financial position at that time.[26] The accounts of a recognised body must show income and expenditure on a day to day basis and must record the assets and liabilities of the body. Accounting records must be kept for six years. In addition, annual accounts must be prepared, including a balance sheet, an income and expenditure account and a report on the charitable activities of the body.[27] A modified form of accounts is prescribed for smaller recognised bodies. More detailed requirements are laid down in the Charities Accounts (Scotland) Regulations 1992.

4.5.7   As with the obligation to provide an explanatory document, recognised bodies, for a reasonable charge, must make their most recent set of annual accounts available to a member of the public who requests them and also to the Lord Advocate free on request. Where accounts are not provided within a month to members of the public, the Lord Advocate may apply to the Court of Session for interdict to prevent the body from engaging in any activity specified in the application. Where no accounts have been prepared within 10 months of the end of the financial year the Lord Advocate may require their preparation and may appoint a suitably qualified person to carry out that task.

4.5.8   Designated religious bodies are exempt from certain of these duties[28] as are recognised bodies which are companies within the meaning of section 735 of the Companies Act 1985 or unregistered companies to which the accounts and audit requirements of that Act apply.[29]

---

[23]s.1(3) and (5).

[24]This included 22 whose addresses had changed, seven which had been wound up and four which were no longer charities. For further information about this study, see Chap. 1, paras. 1.1.4–1.1.5 and Chap. 11, paras. 11.3.4 *et seq*.

[25]For more detailed consideration of the accounting requirements, see Chap. 6.

[26]s.4(1)(*a*).

[27]s.5.

[28]See s.3(2)(*c*) and section 4.10 below.

[29]s.5(14). See also Chaps. 2 and 6.

The Implied Duty to Administer Honestly and Competently

Sections 6 and 7 of the Act, which grant the Lord Advocate and the   **4.5.9**
Court of Session powers to intervene in the management of a
recognised body in certain circumstances, imply positive duties on
the part of persons concerned in the management or control of the
recognised body.[30] First, there is an implied duty to administer the
charity honestly and competently; and second, such persons are under
an obligation to ensure the sound management and proper application
of its assets. These duties are the corollary to the powers given to the
Lord Advocate and the Court of Session to investigate allegations of
"misconduct or mismanagement" in relation to the administration of
a recognised body, or to intervene where it is necessary or desirable
for the purpose of protecting that recognised body's property or
securing its proper application.

Misconduct or Mismanagement

One of the triggers for the Lord Advocate's and the Court of Session's   **4.6.1**
intervention in the affairs of a recognised body is the appearance of
"any misconduct or mismanagement in its administration".[31] The same
expression is used in English provisions introduced under section 20
of the Charities Act 1960 and consolidated in section 18 of the Charities
Act 1993. According to section 18(3) of that Act, misconduct or
mismanagement includes the payment of excessive remuneration to
persons acting on behalf of the charity. Some further guidance is given
about the meaning of "misconduct" in sections 2 to 5 of the Company
Directors Disqualification Act 1986 which give examples of situations
in which a director may be disqualified for misconduct. They include
conviction for an indictable offence in connection with the formation
and management of a company, persistent breaches of statutory duties
to provide information to the Registrar of Companies, and fraudulent
trading or fraud. The term "misconduct" is a familiar one in the field
of professional negligence and usually connotes intentional conduct.
However, mismanagement is a far more nebulous concept. The term
"maladministration" was used in the debate on the Law Reform
(Miscellaneous Provisions) (Scotland) Bill and the term "malpractice"
also appears in *Hansard*.

The Charity Commissioners' annual reports provide some useful   **4.6.2**
material on the ways in which they interpret misconduct or
mismanagement. Their most recent report, for example, cites
inadequate management or financial controls, misunderstanding and
difficulties with associated trading organisations, fundraising abuse,

---

[30]See paras. 4.8.1–4.8.7 below for further consideration of "persons
concerned in management or control".
    [31]s.7(1)(*a*).

deliberate malpractice, improper political activities and tax abuse as grounds for investigation by them.[32] In England and Wales the term has been deemed by the Commissioners to cover excessive remuneration or other administrative outlays in relation to property which is likely to be applied for the purposes of a charity, including the fees of professional fundraisers. So far, no specific official guidance is available to recognised bodies in Scotland. It appears from newspaper reports of cases brought under the 1990 Act that the same general approach has been taken by the Court of Session, but there have been no officially reported cases to date.

4.6.3   A report on the work of the Scottish Charities Office in recent major inquiries into misconduct and management notes, as matters which resulted in investigation and intervention by the Court of Session, the following: payment of a salary to a trustee without express authority in the constitution; abuse of the position of trustee to secure financial advantages for members of the family of a trustee; and the maladministration of funds requiring the appointment of a judicial factor to trace and recover funds which had gone missing.[33] Although these proceedings were brought under the 1990 Act, it is possible that they could also have justified actions for breach of trust at common law, at the instance of an interested beneficiary or the Lord Advocate, where the body in question was a public trust.[34] In addition, the Lord Advocate might have been able to prosecute for fraud under the criminal law. However, the 1990 Act does give the Lord Advocate very specific powers to investigate in such cases which involve negligence as well as those where fraud is suspected and also provides the Court of Session with a wide range of powers to deal with all such cases. The Scottish Charities Office records that since 1992, when it began its operations, funds belonging to charities have been frozen and judicial factors appointed in two cases. In three cases trustees have been removed from office and are now disqualified from involvement in the management or control of charitable organisations anywhere in Great Britain.[35] Under section 8(1)(c) of the 1990 Act the effect of removal of a person from being concerned in management or control of a body under section 7 is to disqualify such a person from fulfilling that role for any recognised body.

DUTY IMPOSED ON NON-RECOGNISED BODIES

Prohibition against Representation as a Charity

4.7.1   The regulation of bodies which have not been recognised as charitable

---

[32]*Report of the Charity Commissioners for England and Wales for the Year 1994* (1995), HMSO, pp. 11–12.
[33]See *Annual Report of Crown Office and the Procurator Fiscal Service 1994/5.*
[34]See Chap. 3, para 3.3.7.
[35]See s.8 and paras. 4.9.1 and 4.9.2 below on disqualification.

for tax purposes is as much a feature of the Act as the regulation of recognised bodies. Non-recognised bodies have only one duty under the Act, which is not to hold themselves out as charities.[36] The Lord Advocate and the Court of Session can exercise a wide range of powers against a non-recognised body, ranging from interdict[37] to suspension and removal of persons concerned in management or control, and including the appointment of a judicial factor[38] and the transfer of its assets to another body.[39]

Persons Concerned in Management or Control

The duties outlined above are laid on "the persons concerned in the management or control" of the body in question. This expression is used throughout the Act but is not defined. In a debate as to its meaning in the House of Lords, prompted by Lord Morton's attempt to amend the Bill,[40] it was indicated by the Government that the addition of "or control", which Lord Morton sought to delete, extended the ambit of people who might come within the accountability requirements of the legislation. Lord Grimond thought it was essential that those who chose to give their time to charitable works should know what responsibilities they were undertaking. In reply, Lord Fraser took a broad "common sense" approach to the definition of "or control". He states that "management" is intended to cover managers as distinct from "control" which includes a wider group of people. He appears to be equating management with paid employees and control with decision-making committees, saying that the exclusion of the words "or control" would enable unscrupulous members of decision-making committees to avoid any liability under the Act by dismissing persons in management, leaving no one to whom the Act could be applied. Lord Fraser was unable to give a checklist of those offices which would be included under the umbrella of management or control, simply advising those involved in charities to decide whether their office imposed upon them "a degree of control or alternatively management".[41]

4.8.1

In England and Wales equivalent responsibility rests with "charity trustees", who are defined as "persons having the general control and management of the administration of a charity".[42] (The term "charity trustees" is therefore used in a much wider sense in the English

4.8.2

---

[36]s.2(1).
[37]s.2(3).
[38]s.7(4).
[39]s.7(5).
[40]Amendment of Bill No. 30. *Hansard*, H.L. Vol. 517, col. 284.
[41]*ibid.* col. 290.
[42]See Charities Act 1993, s.97(1) incorporating the same definition used in the now repealed Charities Act 1960.

definition than the meaning attached to the term in Scots law and is applied to all charities whether they are companies, unincorporated associations or trusts.) Research carried out for the National Council for Voluntary Organisations (NCVO) in 1991 revealed that only one in three of those people involved in the general control and management of an English charity actually knew that they were charity trustees in terms of the statutory definition.[43] Confusion arose particularly in the case of unincorporated associations, where management committee members tended to assume that only the office bearers were charity trustees, whereas no such distinction would be presumed in law. In fact, as the Charity Commission explains, in terms of the English definition members of management or executive committees of charitable associations, directors of charitable companies as well as trustees of charitable trusts are all charity trustees.[44]

4.8.3   The expression "persons concerned in management or control" appearing in the 1990 Act seems to cast a much wider net than the English definition for two reasons. First, the Scottish term covers persons concerned only in "management" and persons concerned only in "control" and, of course, those concerned in both. Under the English definition, however, it is necessary for a person to be involved in both management and control. Secondly, the Scottish term strikes at persons "concerned in" management or control whereas the English definition includes only persons "having" the general control and management of the administration. Thus a person involved in fairly mundane duties, such as a correspondence secretary employed by a charity, would hardly be considered to be a person "having the general management" of its administration, but might well be regarded as being "concerned" in the management of that body. However, the distinction between English and Scots law may in practice be of little significance since the Charity Commissioners may exercise their regulatory powers not only against charity trustees but also against officers, agents or employees of a charity under a separate section of the 1993 Act.[45] The main concern in both jurisdictions is to control the activities of persons involved in the work of a charity who may be in a position to prejudice the fulfilment of that charity's purposes by their mismanagement or misconduct, and to render them accountable for such actions.

4.8.4   In Scotland the definition of persons concerned in management or control has yet to be judicially considered. The Scottish Charities Office

---

[43] *On Trust:Increasing the Effectiveness of Charity Trustees and Management Committees* (1992), Report of a Working Party on trustee training set up by NCVO and the Charity Commission, London: National Council for Voluntary Organisations, p. 1.

[44] Charity Commissioners for England and Wales, *Charities: The New Law: A Trustees' Guide to the Charities Acts 1992 & 1993* (1994).

[45] Charities Act 1993, s.18.

may be adopting a restrictive approach to the term, although it is impossible to draw firm conclusions from the information currently available. According to its first report, of the 17 applications made for waiver of disqualification, 11 were found after examination not to involve persons concerned in the management or control of the body involved.[46] It has been suggested that the expression "will certainly include the trustees, and in appropriate circumstances will also include employees and professional advisers of the trust".[47] For example, a financial adviser who deals with the implementation of a grant-making trust's investment policy, a solicitor who "runs" a trust in between trustees' meetings, or a medical expert who recommends which research projects should be funded by a cancer charity, might all be considered persons concerned in the management or control of a given body.

The position of honorary patrons and presidents may require clarification. Their status in terms of the Act will depend on the degree to which they are in practice involved in the running of the body. Similarly, those who sit on advisory groups to which certain responsibilities have been devolved by the main decision-making organ of the body, for instance a fundraising subcommittee, may not be persons concerned in the management or control of the body if their role is purely advisory and they have no executive power to take decisions themselves. However, in all cases it will be necessary to consider what role a person performs in fact rather than notionally.   4.8.5

Finally, the position of representatives of other organisations needs to be examined carefully. Such representatives may, for instance, attend meetings as mere observers on behalf of another organisation. On the other hand they may play an active part in the management or control of the body, for example as members of a co-ordinating body formed by a group of charities, such as a fundraising consortium. The absence of voting powers would seem to indicate that such representatives were not "concerned in management or control".   4.8.6

However, it seems clear that a paid employee who does not have a vote may nevertheless be regarded as a person "in management". While not all paid employees of a body will be persons concerned in its management or control in terms of the Act, it should not be forgotten that the body may nevertheless be vicariously liable under the general law for delictual or even criminal actions by employees in the course of their employment, regardless of any culpability on the part of those who manage or control the organisation.[48]   4.8.7

---

[46] *Annual Report of the Crown Office and Procurator Fiscal Service 1993/94*, p.23.
[47] Norrie, K. and Scobbie, E., *Trusts* (1991), p. 32.
[48] The usual requirements for establishing vicarious liability must be present, so that the wrongdoer must be an employee and be acting within the scope of his or her employment.

DISQUALIFICATION

4.9.1   Apart from the accountability requirements imposed on persons concerned in management or control, section 8 of the Act also stipulates that a person who has been convicted of a crime of dishonesty, is an undischarged bankrupt,[49] has been removed from office in another or the same recognised body as the result of proceedings under the Act, or is subject to a disqualification order under the Company Directors Disqualification Act 1986, is disqualified from being concerned in the management or control of a recognised body. The Rehabilitation of Offenders Act 1974 applies so that "spent" convictions will not count for the purposes of section 8. A person who breaches this section may be liable to imprisonment and/or a fine and may be tried summarily or on indictment. There is a limitation period of three years from the date of the offence within which court proceedings must be commenced. Any prosecution under this section must be brought within six months of the date when the procurator fiscal is satisfied that there is sufficient evidence to proceed. Disqualification does not invalidate dealings between the disqualified person as a person in management or control and third parties.

4.9.2   The Lord Advocate has the power to grant a waiver of disqualification. However, the Scottish Charities Office notes that pending the application for a waiver those persons affected by the provisions must not continue in office.[50] No guidance has been given as to the procedure and criteria which are applied in considering a request for waiver although evidence from some charities suggests that the process requires the recognised body to provide much additional information to the Scottish Charities Office and that it takes a considerable time. The Charity Commissioners provide some guidance about the circumstances in which a waiver will be granted under the equivalent English provisions. The burden of demonstrating why a waiver is justified rests with the disqualified person. In permitting the disqualification to be waived the Charity Commissioners may insist on conditions which limit the involvement of that "charity trustee" in the administration of the body, particularly in financial matters.[51] It appears that the responsibility to disclose information about disqualifying factors rests with the individual concerned in management or control and not with the charity. Indeed in most cases

---

[49]According to s.8(6), "undischarged bankrupt" means a person whose estate has been sequestrated, who has been declared bankrupt or who has made an arrangement with creditors to reimburse them but has not yet discharged such debts.

[50]*The Supervision of Charities in Scotland: A Brief Guide*, Scottish Charities Office.

[51]*Decision of the Charity Commissioners on the Effect of Disqualification from Acting as Charity Trustee and Criteria for Grant of Waiver* (1993) *Decisions of the Charity Commissioners*, Vol. 2, April 1994, 11.

it will not be possible for charities themselves to obtain information about previous convictions. However, it is suggested that where a charity knew or ought to have known that a person concerned in management or control of that charity is disqualified under section 8 from holding such office the failure to take immediate steps to remove that person from office might constitute "mismanagement" under the Act.

DESIGNATED RELIGIOUS BODIES

Introduction

Charitable giving was in origin a means by which in the middle ages   **4.10.1**
people of wealth could atone for their sins through the donation of moveable and heritable property to the church. The term "mortification" which still applies to certain charitable trusts today demonstrates how closely charitable giving was associated with the saving of souls. In addition, religious bodies have traditionally provided the means by which charitable giving is translated into the provision of services, for example through an almshouse or hospital. The development in England and Wales of the definition of "charitable purposes" to include the advancement of religion illustrates the important role of religious bodies in this area. The advancement of religion is a distinct head of charity in English law following the Preamble to the Charitable Uses Act 1601 and is included in the United Kingdom definition of charitable objects for tax purposes.[52] A body seeking charitable status in Scotland for tax purposes which identifies the advancement of religion as its sole charitable purpose must show that the religion involves some belief in and worship of a deity or deities.[53] In addition, under English law the activities of the religious body must include some element of public instruction or promotion of such beliefs. Therefore an enclosed order of contemplative nuns was not permitted to register as a charity in England and Wales.[54]

Definition

Given the historic importance of religious bodies, it is not surprising   **4.10.2**
that legislation on charities in all United Kingdom jurisdictions acknowledges their unique position in relation to charitable giving

---

[52]See *Income Tax Special Commissioners v. Pemsel* [1891] A.C. 531 (H.L.) and Income and Corporation Taxes Act 1988, s.505.

[53] The religion need not be monotheistic.

[54]*Cocks v. Manners* (1871) L.R. 12 Eq. 574; but see also *Decision of the Charity Commissioners on Charitable Status: The Society of the Precious Blood* (1989) *Decisions of the Charity Commissioners*, Vol. 3, Jan. 1995, 11.

and the provision of charitable services. The 1990 Act accords exemption from virtually all of the enforcement provisions relating to accountability to "designated religious bodies". Similar exemptions apply to certain religious bodies in England and Wales under the Charities Act 1993.

4.10.3 Section 3(1) and (2) define those bodies which may be designated by the Secretary of State as designated religious bodies. The following requirements must be met:

(1) the body must be a recognised body;
(2) the body must have as its principal purpose the promotion of a religious objective;
(3) the body must have as its principal activity the regular holding of public acts of worship;
(4) the body (or in the case of amalgamations or splinter groups the bodies which form the amalgamation or from which the splinter group secedes) must have been in existence for at least 10 years[55];
(5) membership of the body must be not less than 3,000 persons over the age of 16 resident in Scotland[56];
(6) the internal organisation of the body must be such that one or more authorities exercise "supervisory and disciplinary" functions in relation to the component elements of the body, particularly for the purposes of financial accounting.

4.10.4 It is not enough, therefore, that the body which seeks designation under section 3 has purposes which are conducive to the advancement of religion, the third "head of charity" specified by Lord Macnaghten in *Pemsel*.[57] While a designated religious body need not have as its sole purpose the promotion of a religion and as its only activity the regular holding of acts of public worship, these two requirements must form the principal focus of the body. Thus an organisation in which acts of public worship take place each week and where Bible classes are held regularly would not meet the test laid down in section 3 if its principal object was in fact the promotion of leisure activities for young people. On the other hand, a church which provides a range of services to the needy in fulfilment of a stated object in its constituting document will not be prevented from becoming a designated religious body, unless the provision of such services is its principal purpose.

4.10.5 The requirements of durability and size are clearly designed to discourage transient groups attracting hundreds rather than thousands of adherents from obtaining designated status. Perhaps

---

[55]Under subs. (4) the Secretary of State can determine, in cases involving amalgamations of, or splinter groups from, designated religious bodies, whether the requirement of membership numbers given in subs. (2) does not need to be satisfied in relation to the new grouping.

[56]The Secretary of State has to be satisfied that the body has sufficient members to meet this figure.

[57]For the significance of this case for English and Scottish charities see Chap. 1, paras. 1.4.6–1.4.9 and Chap. 8, paras. 8.2.2–8.2.7.

the most significant obstacle for many organisations seeking designation is the need to establish that the activities carried out at all levels within the organisation are subject to appropriate supervision. The function of supervising and applying disciplinary measures to "the component elements" of the body is to be exercised internally by one or more authorities within the organisation itself. A religious body which seeks designation must lay down mandatory standards about the keeping of accounting records and the auditing of accounts for each constituent element of that body. Thus the Church of Scotland is a designated religious body but Baptist congregations are not.[58] These exemptions are granted both to the body as a whole and to its constituent parts. The Secretary of State has designated the following recognised bodies:

(1) The Church of Scotland;
(2) The Free Church of Scotland;
(3) The Free Presbyterian Church of Scotland;
(4) The Roman Catholic Archdiocese of St Andrews and Edinburgh;
(5) The Roman Catholic Archdiocese of Glasgow;
(6) The Roman Catholic Diocese of Argyll and the Isles;
(7) The Roman Catholic Diocese of Dunkeld;
(8) The Roman Catholic Diocese of Galloway;
(9) The Roman Catholic Diocese of Paisley; and
(10) The Scottish Episcopal Church.

Exemptions granted to Designated Religious Bodies under the 1990 Act

The Duty to Keep Accounting Records

The duty to keep accounting records laid down in section 4 does not apply directly to designated religious bodies. However, under section 3 the accounting standards laid down by the body itself must approximate to the standards set down for other recognised bodies.[59]   **4.10.6**

Enforcement of Duty to Provide Annual Accounts

Although designated religious bodies are required to furnish their annual accounts to the Lord Advocate or any person on request (under subsections (6) and (7) of section 5) there is no action which the Lord Advocate can take against that body for failure to comply, except to require that such failure be noted in the Inland Revenue's Index of Recognised Bodies. The Lord Advocate cannot therefore compel persons concerned in the management or control of a designated religious body to provide accounts or appoint a person to carry out that task or seek interdict to curtail the activities of the body.   **4.10.7**

---

[58]The Charities (Designated Religious Bodies) (Scotland) Order 1993 (S.I. 1993 No. 2774).
[59]See Chap. 6.

Enforcement of Duty to Provide Explanatory Document

4.10.8 A similar exemption applies in relation to the provision of the designated religious body's explanatory document. While the requirement to provide such a document, under section 1(4), applies to all recognised bodies, the Lord Advocate cannot seek interdict to prevent a designated religious body which has failed to comply with that duty from continuing with its activities. Failure to comply with section 1(4) can, however, be noted on the Inland Revenue Index at the Lord Advocate's request.

Lord Advocate's Power of Suspension

4.10.9 The Lord Advocate cannot exercise the power of suspension (under subsection (2) of section 6) in the case of any person concerned in the management or control of a designated religious body. The other powers granted to the Lord Advocate under section 6 are not affected.

The Sheriff's Power to order the Provision of Information

4.10.10 The power to order the production of information which is given to the sheriff under subsection (6) of section 6 does not apply in the case of designated religious bodies. An officer nominated by the Lord Advocate can carry out investigations into a designated religious body and require that body or any person having relevant information to provide it. However, in the case of a designated religious body a sheriff cannot order a person to attend to answer questions or provide information, to give copies or extracts of relevant records or to transmit the records themselves to a nominated officer. The offence of failure to comply with the requirements of subsection (6) is not applicable in the case of designated religious bodies.

The Powers of the Court of Session

4.10.11 The extensive powers given to the Court of Session under section 7 of the Act do not apply to designated religious bodies. In cases involving designated religious bodies which are subject to investigation by the Lord Advocate it is assumed that such steps as require to be taken to prevent further misconduct or mismanagement or to protect the property of the body in question will be taken by the supervisory authority within the designated religious body itself.

Disqualification of Persons Concerned in Management or Control

4.10.12 The disqualification provision under section 8 of the Act does not apply to designated religious bodies so that people with unspent convictions for dishonesty, undischarged bankrupts, disqualified company directors and those who have been disqualified from being concerned in the management or control of another recognised body (which is not a designated religious body) are not, apparently, disqualified from being concerned in the management or control of a designated religious body and are not guilty of a criminal offence for so acting.

Powers of the Secretary of State

The Secretary of State alone has the power to designate recognised **4.10.13**
bodies as designated religious bodies. In cases where a designated
religious body was found after investigation to have been
mismanaged, it would be open to the Secretary of State to withdraw
designated status from that body, thus rendering it open to the full
range of regulatory powers available to the Lord Advocate and the
courts under the Act.

CONCLUSION

The 1990 Act has provided a new régime of accountability in Scotland   **4.11.1**
for bodies which lay claim — properly or improperly — to the status
of "charitable", that word being understood in its technical meaning
for tax purposes. The new régime is superimposed on the existing
systems of accountability associated with the different legal forms in
which such bodies may be constituted and leaves those systems intact
and fully operative. The question which cannot yet be answered, given
the short time during which the new régime has been in force, is
whether the new Act has struck the right balance between, on the one
hand, controlling the activities of the unscrupulous and the
incompetent and, on the other, allowing sufficient freedom of action
to the altruistic and the inspired to develop a flourishing and effective
voluntary sector. The balance lies between insufficient regulation and
too much, between an environment which may be abused and one
which stifles. It is likely to be some time before a pattern emerges in
the way the regulatory powers are used by the Lord Advocate and
the courts and before the true impact of the Act can be properly
assessed.

CHAPTER 5

REGULATORY POWERS UNDER THE 1990 ACT

INTRODUCTION

5.1.1   The duties, express or implied, imposed by the Law Reform (Miscellaneous Provisions) (Scotland) Act 1990 on persons concerned in the management or control of recognised bodies, of certain English charities, and of non-recognised bodies have been considered in the preceding chapter. The task of enforcing those duties rests principally with the Lord Advocate and with the Court of Session acting at the instance of the Lord Advocate, and this chapter examines their powers under sections 6 and 7 of the Act. The Lord Advocate's other powers are summarised below for convenience but are dealt with more fully elsewhere in the book,[1] and their interaction with those of the Charity Commissioners is considered more fully in Chapter 8. This chapter also considers the powers of the Scottish charities nominee in dealing with dormant charity accounts. It should be emphasised that although the Inland Revenue performs the crucial function of establishing whether or not a body is to be a recognised body, its policing role under the 1990 Act is otherwise confined to the provision of information to the Lord Advocate and the public. It is worth noting that the functions shared out by the Act among the Inland Revenue, the Lord Advocate, the Court of Session and the Scottish charities nominee are all performed in England and Wales by the Charity Commissioners.

Powers of the Lord Advocate — Summary

5.1.2   The role of the Lord Advocate is pivotal under the 1990 Act, and it may be helpful to summarise here the regulatory powers exercisable by the Lord Advocate under the Act other than those contained in sections 6 and 7. The Lord Advocate's powers in relation to public trusts under sections 9, 10 and 11 are omitted here because they are not, strictly speaking, part of the regulatory scheme associated with charitable status for tax purposes.[2] The regulatory powers are as follows:

---

[1] For the Lord Advocate's powers under ss.1 and 2, see Chap. 4; under s.5, Chap. 6; under s.13, Chap. 3, para. 3.5.20.

[2] See Chap. 3, paras. 3.4.9 *et seq.* for the Lord Advocate's role in relation to public trusts.

Section 1(5):   Power to direct that failure to provide an explanatory document be noted by the Inland Revenue as public information.

Section 1(6):   Power to apply to the court for an interdict in the event of a failure to provide an explanatory document.

Section 1(9):   Power to approve an alternative to the trust deed or other constituting document of a body as its explanatory document.

Section 2(3):   Power to apply for an interdict where a non-recognised body represents itself as a charity.

Section 5(6):   Power to require that a recognised body furnish a statement of accounts.

Section 5(8):   Power to require that a failure to prepare accounts be noted by the Inland Revenue as public information.

Section 5(9):   Power to direct that accounts be prepared.

Section 5(10):   Power to appoint a person to prepare accounts in place of the body.

Section 5(12):   Power to direct that failure to provide a member of the public with a copy statement of accounts or with an accounting reference date be noted by the Inland Revenue as public information.

Section 5(13):   Power to apply to the court for interdict where there has been a failure to prepare accounts or provide copy accounts or the accounting reference date to a member of the public.

Section 8(2):   Power to grant waivers of disqualification of persons concerned in the management or control of recognised bodies.

Section 13(2):   Power to appoint trustees to a trust which is a recognised body.

Section 14(3):   Power to present a petition for the winding up of a charitable company.

Section 15(8):   Power to object to a change in an accounting reference date.

Designated Religious Bodies

The privileged status of designated religious bodies is dealt with in the previous chapter. Section 3 of the Act provides that certain of the powers of the Lord Advocate (and of the court) are not exerciseable in the case of designated religious bodies.   **5.1.3**

POWERS OF THE LORD ADVOCATE UNDER SECTION 6

The Scottish Charities Office

By section 6 of the Law Reform (Miscellaneous Provisions) (Scotland) Act 1990 the Lord Advocate has power to investigate   **5.2.1** both bodies which have been officially recognised as charitable for tax purposes and bodies which unjustifiably claim the mantle of official recognition. The Lord Advocate also has power under the section to suspend persons concerned in the management or control of such bodies for a maximum period of 28 days. In practice, investigations under the section are the responsibility of the Scottish Charities Office, a division of the Crown Office, which recently reported that during the period from the establishment of the Charities Office in July 1992 to March 31, 1995 its inquiries revealed sufficient grounds for full investigation and the possibility of court proceedings in some 40 cases and "maladministration of a lesser degree" in a further 60 cases which were resolved by counsel and assistance.[3]

Power to Investigate

Jurisdiction

5.2.2   Under section 6(1) the Lord Advocate may investigate the following types of body:

(1)   a recognised body;
(2)   an English registered or non-registered charity operating as such in Scotland; and
(3)   a non-recognised body which appears to him to hold itself out as a charity and which (a) is established under the law of Scotland or (b) is managed or controlled wholly or mainly in or from Scotland or (c) has moveable or immoveable property in Scotland.[4]

The investigatory jurisdiction extends to English charities "operating as such" in Scotland, whether or not managed or controlled in or from Scotland. "Operating as such" presumably covers fundraising in the name of the charity and administration of a Scottish branch or branches as well as the provision of services.[5]

5.2.3   Similarly, jurisdiction over non-recognised bodies is not confined to those whose management or control is centred in Scotland. It seems that a non-recognised body which is managed or controlled wholly or mainly in or from England and carries out its operations there may competently be investigated by the Lord Advocate if it is a body constituted under Scots law.

---

[3]*Annual Report of the Crown Office and Procurator Fiscal Service 1994/95*, pp. 11–12.
[4]The expressions "recognised body" and "non-recognised body" are defined in ss.1(7) and 2(2) of the Act respectively. A "registered charity" means a body which is registered in England and Wales under s.3 of the Charities Act 1993, and a "non-registered charity" is one which by s.3(5) of the 1993 Act is not required to register.
[5]See also Chap. 8.

The Lord Advocate may make inquiries with regard to "any class" of the bodies mentioned in section 6(1). Presumably these provisions are designed to facilitate a systematic investigation into all bodies sharing a particular characteristic, for instance those claiming to fund hospital treatment for children.

5.2.4

Conditions of Exercise

In the case of recognised bodies and English charities there is no precondition that the Lord Advocate should suspect impropriety before undertaking an investigation. The Lord Advocate's power in terms of section 6(1) is simply to "make inquiries, either generally or for particular purposes". It seems therefore that, resources permitting, the Scottish Charities Office could institute random or "spot" inquiries. In the case of non-recognised bodies, on the other hand, it is a precondition of an inquiry under the section that the body appears to the Lord Advocate to represent itself or hold itself out as a charity.

5.2.5

Nominated Officers

Under section 6(3) the Lord Advocate may appoint "nominated officers" to make inquiries on his behalf. No criteria for the appointment of nominated officers are laid down in the Act. It appears that they may be members of the Scottish Charities Office but *ad hoc* appointments might also be made of solicitors, accountants or others with special expertise. A nominated officer may exercise the following powers under section 6:

5.2.6

(1) By notice in writing, to require any person the nominated officer has reason to believe has relevant information to answer questions or furnish information.[6]
(2) To require a person in possession or control of records relating to a body under investigation to furnish a copy or extract of such records, or the original record unless it forms part of the records of a court, public body or local authority.[7] A "record" means a record held in any medium.[8]
(3) Without payment, to inspect and take copies of or extracts from records the originals of which cannot be transmitted to the nominated officer for inspection, and to keep such copies or extracts.[9]

Reasonable expenses incurred in complying with a requirement of a nominated officer will be reimbursed.[10]

Criminal Offences under Section 6

If a person fails or refuses to comply with a requirement made by the

5.2.7

---

[6] s.6(4).
[7] s.6(5).
[8] s.6(13).
[9] s.6(11).
[10] s.6(10).

nominated officer the person may be ordered to do so by the sheriff on a summary application by the nominated officer.[11] Failure to comply with the sheriff's order is a criminal offence for which a fine may be imposed on summary conviction.[12] A person is not excused from obeying an order of the sheriff to answer questions on the ground that the answers might be self-incriminating, but a statement made in response to such an order is not admissible in evidence in subsequent criminal proceedings against the person, except under the False Oaths (Scotland) Act 1933.[13] It is also a criminal offence wilfully to alter, suppress, conceal or destroy any record which is the subject of a requirement by a nominated officer, in this case punishable on summary conviction by a fine or up to six months' imprisonment, or both.[14]

Power to Suspend

Jurisdiction

5.2.8   The Lord Advocate may suspend for a maximum of 28 days any person concerned in the management or control[15] of the following types of body:

(1)   a recognised body;
(2)   an English registered or non-registered charity operating as such in Scotland; and
(3)   a non-recognised body which appears to the Lord Advocate to hold itself out as a charity.

In each case, however, the Lord Advocate has power to suspend only if the body is managed or controlled wholly or mainly in or from Scotland.[16] The jurisdiction is therefore narrower than for the power of investigation, since it is restricted to bodies whose management or control is centred in Scotland. Thus, for instance, the Lord Advocate may make inquiries into an English charity managed and controlled outside Scotland provided some part of its operation takes place in Scotland, but if further action is to be taken the Lord Advocate must refer the matter to the Charity Commissioners. Similarly, the Lord Advocate may not act alone to suspend those responsible for a non-recognised body managed and controlled outside Scotland even if it is, for instance, constituted as a Scottish trust, or owns property in Scotland, though he may apply to the Court of Session to take action in such circumstances.

---

[11]s.6(8).
[12]s.6(8).
[13]s.6(7).
[14]s.6(9).
[15]The expression "person concerned in the management or control" of a body is discussed in the previous chapter.
[16]s.6(2).

Conditions of Exercise

The Lord Advocate may suspend in the case of a recognised body or **5.2.9**
English charity only where it appears to him:

(a) that there is or has been misconduct or mismanagement in the
    administration of the body, or
(b) that it is necessary or desirable to act for the purpose of protecting
    the property of the body, or securing a proper application of its
    property for its purposes.

The Lord Advocate may suspend a person concerned in the
management or control of a non-recognised body only if it appears
to him that the body is representing itself or holding itself out as a
charity.

In the case of recognised bodies and English charities the **5.2.10**
preconditions for exercise of the power of suspension are therefore
stricter than for the power of investigation. Inquiries may be made
into a recognised body or English charity whether or not there is a
suggestion of impropriety, but suspension may follow only where
there is an appearance of misconduct or mismanagement or some
other reason for acting to safeguard the body's assets.[17] In the case
of a non-recognised body the Lord Advocate may both investigate
and suspend where it appears to him that the body improperly
represents itself as a charity, regardless of whether there has been
other misconduct or impropriety. Curiously, however, it seems that
the Lord Advocate may neither investigate nor suspend under
section 6 in the case of a non-recognised body which does not hold
itself out as a charity, even if there are grounds to suspect
misconduct or mismanagement or there is some other reason to
act. It seems quite possible that a body might raise funds for
apparently public purposes without actually claiming to be a
charity, in which case it would escape the net of the Lord Advocate's
powers under the Act and other remedies would have to be found
to control misconduct or mismanagement. In such a case the Lord
Advocate would presumably proceed under the general criminal
law or, conceivably, under the law of public trusts.[18] Perhaps,
however, the Lord Advocate would take a broad view of what is
meant by a body "holding itself out" as a charity. It may be that
the act of soliciting funds from the public amounts in itself to an
implied claim to charitable status.

Purpose and Effect of Powers under Section 6

Section 6 gives the Lord Advocate a wide investigative jurisdiction, **5.2.11**
but limits his power of suspension to cases where those responsible

---

[17]The expressions "misconduct" and "mismanagement" are discussed in
the previous chapter.
[18]See Chap. 3, para. 3.3.7.

for undesirable activity have their base in Scotland. Under section 6(2) the Lord Advocate may make provision for matters arising out of a suspension, presumably to safeguard, where possible and appropriate, the continuing work of the body concerned. The section allows for a process of initial inquiry followed by emergency action in appropriate cases by the Lord Advocate acting alone. It appears that on the expiry of 28 days from the date of suspension the person suspended will then be restored to the full exercise of his or her functions unless the Lord Advocate has taken further action by applying to the Court of Session under section 7.[19]

POWERS OF THE COURT OF SESSION

Jurisdiction

5.3.1 The Court of Session has always had plenary jurisdiction at common law to intervene in the management of public trusts so as to ensure the proper application of their funds for public benefit.[20] The 1990 Act has, however, extended the court's jurisdiction to cover all bodies, whether constituted as trusts or otherwise, which are:

(1) recognised bodies;
(2) English registered and non-registered charities which are managed or controlled wholly or mainly in or from Scotland; and
(3) non-recognised bodies which (a) represent themselves as charities and (b) are established under the law of Scotland or are managed or controlled wholly or mainly in or from Scotland or have moveable or immoveable property situated in Scotland.[21]

5.3.2 These bodies are the same as those in respect of which the Lord Advocate may exercise his power of suspension under section 6 except that in the case of a non-recognised body the court's jurisdiction may derive from the fact that the body is established under Scots law, or from its ownership of property in Scotland, as well as from the concentration of its management or control in Scotland. The court also has a limited jurisdiction for specific purposes over English registered or non-registered charities which are managed or controlled wholly or mainly outside Scotland but on behalf of which a bank or other person in Scotland holds moveable property. The jurisdiction of the court under section 7 is therefore wider than the Lord Advocate's jurisdiction to suspend under section 6.

---

[19]The Lord Advocate might also refer the case of an English charity to the Charity Commissioners.

[20]*Income Tax Special Commissioners v. Pemsel* [1891] A.C. 531, *per* Lord Watson at 560; *Anderson's Trustees v. Scott*, 1914 S.C. 942.

[21]s.7(1) and (2).

Although the court's common law jurisdiction over public trusts is notionally very wide, and enables the court to consider among other things the enforcement of trust purposes at the instance of the Lord Advocate, its most frequent exercise has been the approval of *cy-près* schemes proposed by trustees.[22] In such cases the intervention of the court is invoked in order to assist the trustees in the conscientious exercise of their duties. The purpose of section 7 of the 1990 Act, on the other hand, is to enable the court to intervene on the application of the Lord Advocate where there is reason to fear that those responsible for a body which is ostensibly devoted to charitable purposes are not in reality acting in the body's or the public's best interests.

5.3.3

Interim Powers

The powers of the court may be roughly divided into powers intended to be used on an interim or emergency basis and powers intended to bring about a permanent change in the management of the body concerned. All powers are to be exercised on the application of the Lord Advocate. The interim powers are as follows.

5.3.4

Section 7(4)(a): Interim Interdict

The court may interdict a body *ad interim* from representing itself or holding itself out as a charity, or from such other action as the court may (on the application of the Lord Advocate) think fit. Such "other action" might, for instance, be the disposal of property held for the purposes of the body.

5.3.5

Section 7(4)(b): Power to Suspend

The court may suspend any person concerned in the management or control of a body. The suspension may be recalled under section 7(8)(*c*), and the effect of recall is presumably to restore the person to the full exercise of his or her powers. Presumably, suspended persons themselves may move the court for a recall.

5.3.6

Section 7(4)(c): Interim Judicial Factor

The court may appoint a judicial factor *ad interim* to manage the affairs of a body. An interim appointment is made without intimation and service and to take immediate effect. It seems that a factor appointed under the paragraph may have a role in both tracing and safeguarding assets.[23]

5.3.7

Section 7(4)(d): "Freezing Order"

The court may order a bank or any other third party holding money or securities on behalf of a body or of a person concerned in its "control

5.3.8

---

[22]See Chap. 3, para. 3.4.4.
[23]*Crown Office and Procurator Fiscal Service Annual Report 1994/95*, pp. 11–12.

and management" not to part with the money or securities without the court's approval. An order made under subsection (*d*) may be varied or recalled under section 7(9)(*a*). The intention is that funds held by third parties may be "frozen" to protect them on an interim basis. Such funds are frequently held in the names of trustees or of officials acting in a fiduciary capacity, and the phrase "person concerned in control and management", as opposed to the term "management or control" used in the rest of the Act, no doubt refers to such persons.

Section 7(4)(e): Restriction on Transactions and Payments

5.3.9   The court may override the trust deed or other constituting document of a body to restrict the transactions which may be entered into in its administration and the nature or amount of payments which may be made without the court's approval. Again, the underlying purpose is the interim safeguarding of assets, and an order under the paragraph may be recalled (or varied) under section 7(4)(*a*). It seems that in the absence of a recall, a restriction made under the power would remain in force indefinitely, but the court might be reluctant to allow what is in effect a temporary variation of the constituting deed to become permanent.

Section 7(4)(f): Power to Appoint a Trustee

5.3.10   The power to appoint a trustee is exercisable by the court both in "emergency" conditions where it is necessary to act on a provisional basis, and in circumstances where the court is satisfied that a permanent change is required (see below). The appointment of a trustee by the court in either situation is, however, a full and permanent appointment as a trustee, as if made by the court under section 22 of the Trusts (Scotland) Act 1921. The reference to the 1921 Act appears to restrict the effect of the power to trustees in the strict sense of the word. The term "trustee" does not have an extended meaning under the 1990 Act, as the term "charity trustee" has under the English legislation,[24] and cannot be taken to refer to persons concerned in management and control generally. The 1921 Act regulates the administration of Scottish trusts, and has no application to other legal forms[25] or trusts established under the law of England. It seems, therefore, that the court does not have power under the paragraph (or otherwise under the Act) to appoint directors to a company or officers to serve on the management committee of an unincorporated association. This is in contrast to the position in England and Wales, where the equivalent power of the Charity Commissioners is expressed by reference to the inclusive term "charity trustee".[26]

---

[24]See Chap. 1 and Charities Act 1993, s.97.
[25]But see Chap. 3 on unincorporated associations as quasi-public trusts.
[26]Charities Act 1993, s.18(1) and (5).

Section 7(6): Freezing Order — English Charities

The court has power to order a bank or other person in Scotland   **5.3.11**
holding moveable property on behalf of an English charity, registered
or non-registered, which is managed or controlled wholly or mainly
outside Scotland, not to part with the property without the court's
approval. The court may act on the application of the Lord Advocate,
who acts on information received from the Charity Commissioners.
The process would no doubt begin with an investigation of an English
charity by the Commissioners, who would seek interim protection of
the charity's moveable assets in Scotland by recourse, through the
Lord Advocate, to the jurisdiction of the Court of Session. After further
inquiry, permanent action might be taken under subsections (7) and
(8) of section 7 (see below).

Conditions of Exercise of Interim Powers

Recognised Bodies and English Charities

The conditions in which the court may exercise its interim powers   **5.3.12**
under section 7(4) are as follows. In the case of (1) a recognised body
and (2) an English registered or non-registered charity managed or
controlled wholly or mainly in or from Scotland, the court may exercise
any of the powers specified in paragraphs (*a*) to (*f*) of subsection (4)
(listed above) where it appears to the court that:

(a)   there is or has been misconduct or mismanagement in the body's
      administration, or
(b)   it is necessary or desirable to act for the purpose of protecting
      the property of the body or securing its proper application for
      the purposes of the body.

The expression "misconduct or mismanagement" has been discussed   **5.3.13**
in the previous chapter, but it is worth noting here that the equivalent
provisions in the Charities Act 1993 define the same term as extending
to "the employment for the remuneration or reward of persons acting
in the affairs of the charity, or for other administrative purposes, of
sums which are excessive in relation to the property which is or is
likely to be applied or applicable for the purposes of the charity" and
that notwithstanding what is provided in the constituting document
of the charity.[27] The court may take provisional action, however, under
paragraph (b), even where there is no suggestion of impropriety on
the part of the persons concerned in management or control. It appears
that the court might, for instance, appoint a new trustee under
paragraph (*f*) where the previous trustees had all died, in order to
secure the proper application of the trust's property.

---

[27]*ibid.* s.18(3).

Non-Recognised Bodies

5.3.14   In the case of a non-recognised body the court may exercise the interim powers where it is satisfied that the body represents or holds itself out as a charity.[28] The fact that it merely appears to the court to do so is not sufficient. It seems that the court has no power to act against a non-recognised body unless it represents itself or holds itself out as a charity. The court is in the same position in this respect as the Lord Advocate in exercising his powers under section 6. This may be a serious deficiency in the 1990 Act, although there is insufficient statistical information available to justify a firm view. It seems possible, however, that there are large numbers of bodies active in Scotland which are not technically eligible for recognition by the Inland Revenue as charitable because their purposes are not exclusively charitable. Such bodies will be non-recognised bodies in terms of the 1990 Act but in all other respects, such as their management, objectives and activities, will closely resemble bodies which have in fact been recognised and are subject to the powers of the court and the other regulatory provisions of the 1990 Act. It appears that such bodies remain outside the ambit of the court's powers under the 1990 Act even where there is misconduct or mismanagement of their affairs, so long as they do not hold themselves out as charities. Again, however, it seems open to the court to take a broad view of what activities amount to an implied claim to charitable status.

Powers with Permanent Effect

5.3.15   The court also has powers under section 7 enabling a definitive intervention in the affairs of a body which has been investigated by the Lord Advocate. The powers are as follows.

Section 7(4)(f): Power to Appoint a Trustee

5.3.16   The power to appoint a trustee is exercisable in both the "emergency" conditions described above and where the court is satisfied that a longer-term remedy is required. It seems that the appointment of a trustee may therefore form part of a "package" either of provisional remedies sought by the Lord Advocate in terms of the court's interim powers or of permanent measures designed to assure the long-term future of a trust.

Section 7(4)(g): Interdict

5.3.17   The court's power to interdict a body from representing itself as a charity or from such other action as the court (on the application of

---

[28]The court must also satisfy itself as to the basis of jurisdiction, *i.e.* that the non-recognised body is established under the law of Scotland or is wholly or mainly managed or controlled in Scotland or has moveable or immoveable property in Scotland.

the Lord Advocate) may think fit is the permanent equivalent of the court's interim power under paragraph (*a*) of subsection (4). It might be used, for instance, to prevent a body holding fundraising events. The court may, however, on a change of circumstances, grant authority to carry out an action which would otherwise be in breach of a perpetual interest.[29]

Section 7(4)(h): Power to Remove

Likewise, the court's power to remove a person concerned in the management or control of a body goes beyond its power to suspend under paragraph (4)(*b*). There is no provision for recall of a removal and it is clear that removal is intended to have permanent effect. The effect of a removal under this paragraph on the status of, for instance, a director under the Companies Acts, a trustee, or an officer of an unincorporated association, is less clear. While persons removed under the section will certainly be unable to exercise their functions as directors, trustees or other office bearers on pain of criminal prosecution as persons disqualified under section 8 of the Act, it may be that a further administrative step will be required to complete their removal in terms of company law[30] or trust law,[31] or of the constitution of the particular association involved. The person removed by the court may, for instance, be required to submit a letter of resignation to comply with the terms of the constitution of an association unless there is provision for automatic termination of office on removal by the court or other disqualification under the 1990 Act.   **5.3.18**

Section 7(4)(j): Judicial Factor

The court may appoint a judicial factor to manage the affairs of a body or to wind them up. An appointment under the paragraph might form part of the long-term solution to the difficulties of the body exposed at the interim stage, but the functions of the factor would be in principle the same as under an interim appointment.   **5.3.19**

Section 7(5): Transfer of Assets

The court may approve a scheme, presented to it by the Lord Advocate, for the transfer of a body's assets to another body specified by the Lord Advocate in the scheme. The Lord Advocate is to prepare the scheme in accordance with regulations made by the Secretary of State, and the court's power and the obligations of the Lord Advocate under the regulations are considered further below.   **5.3.20**

---

[29]*Stair Memorial Encyclopaedia of the Laws of Scotland,* Vol. 13, paras. 17 *et seq.*
[30]See Chap. 2.
[31]See Chap. 3, para. 3.5.12.

Section 7(7) and (8): Power to Transfer Moveable Property — English Charities

5.3.21   In the special case of an English registered or non-registered charity which is managed or controlled wholly or mainly outside Scotland but on behalf of which a bank or other person in Scotland holds moveable property the court may confirm a freezing order made by it under section 7(6) requiring the bank or person not to part with the property without the court's approval. The court may make the order subject to such conditions as it thinks fit. No doubt the court's wide discretion is intended to allow flexibility in the disposal of property belonging to bodies otherwise regulated by the Charity Commissioners and to enable the court to match its own orders with those of the Commissioners.

5.3.22   There is power in section 7(9)(*a*) for the variation or recall of freezing orders made under subsections (6) and (7), and no doubt recall will be appropriate where the difficulties of the English charity in question have been resolved by the Commissioners. The court also has power, however, where in its opinion the moveable property which is subject to a freezing order would not be applied for the purposes of the charity, to transfer the property to a body specified by the Lord Advocate. The transferee body must be a recognised body or an English registered or non-registered charity, the purposes of which "closely resemble" those of the charity from which the assets are transferred. Before a transfer may be made, the transferee body must have intimated that it will receive the property.

Conditions of Exercise of Powers with Permanent Effect

Recognised Bodies and English Charities

5.3.23   In the case of (1) a recognised body and (2) an English registered or non-registered charity managed or controlled wholly or mainly in or from Scotland, the court may exercise any of the powers specified in paragraphs (*f*) to (*j*) of section 7(4) where it is satisfied that both:

   (a)   there is or has been misconduct or mismanagement in the body's administration; and
   (b)   it is necessary or desirable to act for the purpose of protecting the property of the body or securing its proper application for the purposes of the body.

5.3.24   The conditions are therefore stricter than for the exercise of the interim powers in that (1) the court must satisfy itself as to the information put before it by the Lord Advocate and may not act on appearances alone, and (2) both impropriety in the administration of the body and some prejudice to its property or its proper application must be present before the court may intervene. Before granting approval of a scheme for the transfer of assets under section 7(5) the court must satisfy itself on two additional points:

   (a)   that it is not practicable nor in the best interests of the body to retain its existing administrative structure and, if appropriate, trustee body; and

(b) that (in the court's opinion) the body's purpose would be achieved better by transferring its assets to another similar body.

The transfer of assets under section 7(5) is considered more fully below.

Non-Recognised Bodies

In the case of a non-recognised body the court may exercise the powers in section 7(4)(*f*) to (*j*) and the power to approve a scheme for transfer under section 7(5) where it is satisfied that the non-recognised body represents itself or holds itself out as a charity. Neither administrative impropriety nor the need to protect the body's property or to secure its proper application are preconditions of the court's intervention, nor would they justify the court's intervention against a recognised body which did not hold itself out as a charity. This is the same apparent deficiency in the Act as has been noted above in relation to the Lord Advocate's powers under section 6 and the court's interim powers.   **5.3.25**

Schemes for Transfer of Assets

Preparation of Scheme by Lord Advocate

Section 7(5) empowers the court, in the circumstances described above, to approve a scheme for the transfer of assets from: **5.3.26**

(1) a registered body;
(2) an English registered or non-registered charity wholly or mainly managed or controlled in or from Scotland; and
(3) a non-recognised body which represents itself or holds itself out as a charity.

The transferee body is to be specified by the Lord Advocate and may be either (1) a recognised body or (2) an English registered or non-registered charity wholly or mainly managed or controlled in or from Scotland. The intention is, therefore, to ensure that the assets transferred will continue to be either managed or controlled (if not both) in or from Scotland.

The scheme is to be prepared by the Lord Advocate in accordance with regulations which have now been made by the Secretary of State as the Charities (Scheme for the Transfer of Assets) (Scotland) Regulations 1992,[32] which came into force in September 1992. Under these regulations the Lord Advocate must have regard to the spirit of the constituting document or the intentions of the body from which assets are to be transferred and must obtain a written statement from the "trustees" of the transferee body that they are willing to accept   **5.3.27**

---

[32]S.I. 1992 No. 2082.

the transfer and meet any liabilities of the transferor body. The term "trustees" is defined in the regulations (but not the 1990 Act) to mean "persons concerned in the management or control" of the body in question.

Procedure under the Regulations

5.3.28   Before presenting a scheme to the court the Lord Advocate must notify the trustees of the transferor body of his intention to do so by posting to such of them as are known to him at their last known address in the United Kingdom (1) a draft of the scheme and (2) a notice of his intention to present the scheme for approval by the court. He must give the trustees an opportunity to make representations in writing about the proposed scheme within four weeks, and must consider such representations.

5.3.29   The public must also be advised of the proposed scheme by publication of a notice in at least one newspaper selected by the Lord Advocate. Any person may make representations about the proposed scheme in writing to the Lord Advocate within four weeks from the date of publication, which the Lord Advocate must consider.

5.3.30   The scheme must include (so far as is known to the Lord Advocate) the names and addresses of the transferor and transferee bodies and of their trustees. A list and valuation of all assets and liabilities of the transferor body, the proposed date of transfer and a statement of what provision is being made to meet any liabilities of the transferor body must also be included in the scheme. The scheme must contain a statement (1) of the reasons for the presentation of the scheme, (2) of the Lord Advocate's compliance with the procedures set out in the regulations, (3) of any representations made by the trustees of the transferor body or by any member of the public and (4) of the Lord Advocate's observations on them. A copy of the written statement by the transferee body indicating acceptance of the assets must also be appended to the scheme.

Effect of a Scheme

5.3.31   The effect of a transfer of assets under section 7(5) will be to leave the transferee body without assets and, in effect, in the case of a trust or association to wind it up.[33] The regulations are designed to ensure that a radical step of this kind is not taken without adequate opportunity for representations and without due provision for the transferor body's liabilities.

---

[33] The court's power to approve a scheme presented by the Lord Advocate under s.7(5) should be distinguished from its powers in relation to public trusts under s.9.

Expenses — Publicity — Lord Ordinary

Section 7(10) permits the court to exercise discretion in awarding expenses which would otherwise have been awarded against the body involved in proceedings against the persons concerned in its management or control. The court thus has the power to prevent the assets of the body from being diverted from charitable purposes to costs incurred by the body through the fault of those responsible for its administration. Section 7(11) enables the Lord Advocate to direct that the exercise of any of the court's powers under section 7(4) and (5) be noted by the Inland Revenue as a matter to be included in information about a recognised body provided in response to a request from a member of the public.[34] Section 7(12) provides that "the court" means the Court of Session, and in practice the powers of the court are exercised by the Lord Ordinary in the Outer House.

5.3.32

First Use of Powers under Section 7

The Annual Report for 1994/95 of the Crown Office and Procurator Fiscal Service records that during the course of the year the Scottish Charities Office obtained orders from the Court of Session removing three trustees from office following investigations conducted into maladministration of funds. The grounds for intervention in one case included payment of a salary to "the principal trustee" in the absence of authority to do so in the constitution of the body and abuse of the body's funds to secure financial advantage for members of the trustee's family. It may be that the word "trustee" is used in the Report in an extended sense to mean a person concerned in management or control, whether or not a trustee in the strict sense. In two cases action was also taken to "freeze" funds held in bank accounts, and judicial factors were appointed not only to carry on the administration of the bodies concerned, but also to assist in the discovery of evidence of misconduct and to trace and recover missing assets.

5.3.33

Such other information as is publicly available suggests that the cases have not raised any questions of law on the extent of the court's powers under section 7. Orders granted by the court have included interdict under paragraphs (*a*) and (*g*) of paragraph 4, suspension under paragraph (*b*) of persons concerned in a body's management and control, and an order made under paragraph (*e*) restricting the body concerned and the members of its committee from entering into certain specified transactions affecting the body's heritable property.[35]

5.3.34

---

[34]1990 Act, s.1(3).
[35]Petitions by the Lord Advocate in the cases of *Leukaemia and Cancer Fund* and *Care for People*, both 1994/95, unreported.

Scottish Charities Nominee

Dormant Accounts

5.4.1   It was suggested during the consultation process which led to the passing of the 1990 Act that there might be significant numbers of charitable bodies in Scotland which had ceased to be active but for which funds were still held by banks and other financial institutions. The banks and other institutions were not permitted to disclose the existence of dormant accounts and there was no mechanism by which balances lying unadministered and apparently abandoned could be brought back into charitable use. Section 12 of the 1990 Act provides such a mechanism, and allows funds lying in a dormant account to the credit of one recognised body to be transferred to another recognised body. The power to transfer funds is vested in the Scottish charities nominee, an official appointed by the Secretary of State.[36]

Jurisdiction

5.4.2   Section 12(1) provides that the Secretary of State may appoint a person to be the Scottish charities nominee. The jurisdiction of the nominee is confined to the dormant accounts of recognised bodies and does not extend to accounts held for English charities or non-recognised bodies. The nominee acts on information received from banks and other "relevant institutions", but the nominee appears to have no power to compel the provision of information.[37] An account is dormant if (1) there has been no transaction during the 10 years preceding the date of review by the institution and (2) the institution is unable to identify any person concerned in the management or control of the body in whose name or on whose behalf the account is held.[38]

Relevant Institutions

5.4.3   A relevant institution is a bank, building society or other approved deposit-taking institution prescribed by the Secretary of State in regulations made under the section.[39] Relevant institutions are released from normal obligations of confidentiality where every account held for a body which appears to be a recognised body is dormant.[40] Where a number of accounts are held for a body of which at least one is

---

[36]The equivalent provisions for England and Wales are contained in the Charities Act 1993, s.28 under which the Charity Commissioners have power to give directions to financial institutions for the transfer of funds in dormant accounts.
[37]s.12(2).
[38]s.12(1) and (13).
[39]s.12(13); Banking Act 1987, Pt. I and Sched. 2.
[40]s.12(11).

active the section will not apply because the identity of persons concerned in the management or control of the account-holding body would presumably be known to the institution. The waiver of the obligation of confidentiality enables an institution to inform the nominee of (1) the balance on any dormant account, (2) the date of the last transaction other than an accrual of interest, and (3) the terms of the trust deed or other constituting document of the body or any other information as to the purposes of the body so far as known to the institution.[41]

Power to Transfer

Conditions of Exercise

On being informed by a relevant institution (1) that every account it holds for a named body is dormant, and (2) of the amount of the balances standing to credit of each account, the nominee may act if satisfied that the named body concerned is a recognised body. The nominee has power to transfer the aggregate of the credit balances to such other recognised body as the nominee may determine, having regard to the purposes of the "transferor" body and those of the proposed transferee. If the purposes of the transferor body cannot be ascertained, the nominee may choose the transferee body at discretion. The transferee body is entitled in either case to apply the funds transferred for its own purposes as it thinks fit.[42] The remaining conditions of exercise vary according to the amount to be transferred.

5.4.4

£5,000 Threshold

Where the aggregate amount standing to the credit of the transferor body does not exceed £5,000 the nominee may proceed with a transfer unless it appears to the nominee either (1) that there is a person concerned in the management or control of the transferor body or (2) that there are circumstances relating to the body which would make it inappropriate to do so. In either of these events, the nominee must inform the Lord Advocate. Where the aggregate of credit balances exceeds £5,000, the nominee must in all cases inform the Lord Advocate.[43] The threshold figure of £5,000 may be varied by the Secretary of State by regulation.[44]

5.4.5

Role of the Lord Advocate

On receiving information from the nominee the Lord Advocate may (1) appoint new trustees to a recognised body which is a trust, under

5.4.6

---

[41]s.12(12).
[42]s.12(3) and (4).
[43]s.12(3).
[44]s.12(10).

section 13(2) of the Act,[45] (2) apply to the Court of Session for the appointment of an interim judicial factor under section 7(4)(c), or (3) refer the matter back to the nominee. The Lord Advocate may receive additional information from the Inland Revenue before making a decision.[46] If the matter is referred back to the nominee, the nominee may then proceed with a transfer without further reference to the Lord Advocate.

Accountability

5.4.7   The nominee has power to operate accounts and effect transactions without liability other than for a criminal offence.[47] The nominee's powers in relation to a body's accounts come to an end, however, if (1) the Lord Advocate decides to appoint trustees or apply for the appointment of an interim judicial factor, (2) the accounts cease to be dormant, or (3) the identity of any person concerned in the management or control of the body becomes known. The Secretary of State has issued regulations under section 12(10) which lay down in detail the procedures to be followed by the nominee and which provide for public notice of any proposed transfer and an opportunity for representations.[48] The nominee must keep accounts, which are to incorporate details of his outlays and expenses, and submit an annual report to the Secretary of State to be laid before each House of Parliament.[49]

Implementation

5.4.8   A solicitor recently retired from full-time practice has been appointed as the first Scottish charities nominee, taking up his duties at the beginning of September 1995. A press report suggests that the nominee will take as his point of reference the Index of Recognised Bodies maintained by the Inland Revenue and will invite banks and building societies to check their account holders against it. The secretary of the Committee of Scottish Clearing Bankers has drawn attention to the fact that words such as "charity" are not always included in an account holder's designation, so that dormant accounts for recognised bodies may be difficult to trace. The total held in dormant charity accounts throughout Scotland has been variously estimated at hundreds of thousands, and tens of thousands of pounds.[50]

---

[45]See Chap. 3.
[46]ss.1(1) and (2), 12(6).
[47]s.12(8).
[48]Charities (Dormant Accounts) (Scotland) Regulations 1995 (S.I. 1995 No. 2056).
[49]s.12(10).
[50]*The Scotsman*, September 2, 1995.

CONCLUSION

There is still insufficient evidence on which to base useful comment **5.5.1**
about the effectiveness of the powers conferred on the Lord Advocate
and the Court of Session by sections 6 and 7 in securing the honest
and efficient management of charitable resources in Scotland. It is
also too soon to attempt any assessment of the operation in practice
of the powers of the Scottish charities nominee under section 12. The
effect of the 1990 Act is to distribute regulatory functions which in
England and Wales are performed by a single authority in the form of
the Charity Commission (sharing jurisdiction in certain circumstances
with the High Court) among the Inland Revenue, the Lord Advocate,
the Court of Session, and the Scottish charities nominee. The role of
the Lord Advocate, and in practice of the Scottish Charities Office, is
central, and future reports of the Crown Office may give a clearer
picture of how and to what extent the regulatory powers are being
exercised.

CHAPTER 6

FINANCIAL ACCOUNTING REQUIREMENTS

6.1.1 One of the main aims of the Law Reform (Miscellaneous Provisions) (Scotland) Act 1990 ("the 1990 Act") was to make all Scottish charities publicly accountable by ensuring that members of the public could readily obtain reliable information about their activities. One of the most important means of obtaining this information is through a charity's accounts. This chapter examines the current statutory requirements in relation to financial accounting for all Scottish charities, the impact of the revised Statement of Recommended Practice (SORP) for charities and other accounting standards. It also examines other issues such as the accounting requirements for branches of charities, and the position with regard to consolidated accounts.

6.1.2 First, it is helpful to appreciate the legal framework (as at November 30, 1995) within which Scottish charities are required to account for their operation and subject themselves to external review.

UNITED KINGDOM			
CHARITY ACCOUNTING AND AUDIT REGULATIONS			
INCORPORATED	**UNINCORPORATED**		
U.K. Wide(*)	England & Wales	Scotland	N. Ireland
Companies Act 1985 (incl. N. Ireland eqvnt. 1986)	Charities Acts 1992 & 1993	1990 Act(*)	Charities Act (N.I.) 1964
Companies Act 1985 (Audit Exemption) Regs. 1994	Charities (A/cs & Reports) Regs. 1995	Charities A/cs. (Scotland) Regs. 1992	Charities (N. Ireland) Order 1987
influenced by	based on	influenced by	influenced by
Statement of Recommended Practice — Accounting by Charities (SORP)			

(*) The 1990 Act affects all charities in Scotland, including incorporated charities, in respect of:

(1) recognition as a charity,
(2) monitoring of people "concerned in the management or control of Scottish charities",[1]
(3) obligation to supply accounts and legal documents on request.

STATUTORY ACCOUNTING REQUIREMENTS FOR ALL SCOTTISH CHARITIES

Sections 4 and 5 of the 1990 Act detail the accounting requirements for recognised bodies. **6.2.1**

Section 4 deals with the basic obligations relating to the keeping of financial records and imposes a duty on the persons concerned in the management or control of the recognised body to keep accounting records which are sufficient to show and explain the body's transactions and which: **6.2.2**

(1) disclose with reasonable accuracy at any time the financial position of the body;
(2) contain entries showing sums of money received and expended by the body from day to day and the matters in respect of which the receipt or expenditure takes place;
(3) contain a record of the assets and liabilities of the body.

Accounting records must be preserved for six years from the date on which they are made.

Section 5 elaborates on the basic obligations contained in section 4 by listing a number of specific obligations covering issues as diverse as the format of the annual statement of accounts and the obligation to make financial records available for inspection. **6.2.3**

An annual statement of accounts must be prepared which must comprise either **6.2.4**

> (a) a balance sheet, an income and expenditure account and a report on the activities of the body, having regard to its charitable purposes; or

> (b) a statement of balances, a receipts and payments account and a report on the activities of the body.

The category of recognised bodies to which the latter applies is defined in the Charities Accounts (Scotland) Regulations 1992.

The Lord Advocate may request a free copy of the statement of accounts and it must also be made available to any other person requesting it, upon payment of a reasonable charge. Failure to supply a statement of accounts within one month to a person who has **6.2.5**

---

[1]See Chap. 4, paras. 4.8.1–4.8.7.

requested it may result in a complaint to the Lord Advocate, and failure to prepare a statement of accounts within 10 months of the year end may entail the intervention of the Lord Advocate.

6.2.6   The Lord Advocate may require those in management or control to prepare a statement of accounts by a date determined by him. He has power to have accounts prepared, at the expense of those in management or control, by a qualified person who reports to the Lord Advocate and sends a copy to those "concerned in the management or control" of the recognised body.

6.2.7   In the case of a company under the Companies Act 1985 the normal accounting régime under the 1985 Act remains in force, and the only additional requirements in relation to accounts under the 1990 Act are to provide accounts to the Lord Advocate and to the public on request. References to "income and expenditure account" and "report" are to be construed as references to the company's "profit and loss account" and "directors' report". The remaining provisions of the 1990 Act, dealing with non-accounting requirements, apply to incorporated charities as well as unincorporated.

Designated Bodies

6.2.8   Certain designated recognised bodies are exempted from section 4 and parts of section 5 of the 1990 Act by statutory instrument, namely, the Charities (Exemption from Accounting Requirements) (Scotland) Regulations 1993[2] and the Charities (Designated Religious Bodies) (Scotland) Order 1993[3]. Such recognised bodies are:

(1) Scottish charitable statutory corporations (which are still subject to section 5(6)-(7), section 5(12) and section 5(14));
(2) local authority trusts (exempted from section 4 and subsections (2), (3), (4), (5) and (13) of section 5);
(3) registered housing associations (which have the same exemptions as local authority trusts and are subject to their own accounting and SORP requirements); and
(4) designated religious bodies[4] (which are, however, still subject to section 5(6)-(8) and section 5(12)).

UNINCORPORATED CHARITIES IN SCOTLAND

6.3.1   Unincorporated charities in Scotland, other than the above designated bodies, are governed by the accounting requirements contained in

---

[2]S.I. 1993 No. 1624.
[3]S.I. 1993 No. 2774.
[4]See also Chap. 4, paras. 4.10.1 *et seq.*

sections 4 and 5 of the 1990 Act. Subsequent to section 5(5) of the 1990 Act, the Charities Accounts (Scotland) Regulations 1992[5] were laid before Parliament and came into force on September 30, 1992. These regulations set out the detail of the accounting requirements which apply to unincorporated charities. They introduced many important new provisions and merit detailed examination.

Definitions

Regulation 2 defines major terms such as founding deed, gross income/expenditure/receipts, permanent endowment fund and records. Interestingly, trustees are defined in these regulations as "the persons in management or control" of the recognised body.[6]   **6.3.2**

Accounting Regulations

Regulation 3 gives the financial limit for the preparation of the alternative statement of accounts referred to in section 5(3) of the 1990 Act. Receipts and payments accounts and a statement of balances are sufficient where the body's gross receipts do not exceed £25,000 and there is no requirement in the founding deed that the statement of accounts shall be audited.   **6.3.3**

Regulation 4 refers to the form and content of the statement of accounts, of which further particulars are given in schedules to the regulations. The statement of accounts must show: **6.3.4**

(i) the duration of the financial year to which they relate and the immediately preceding financial year; and
(ii) for every item the corresponding amount for the preceding financial year.

The report to which subsections 5(2) and (3) of the 1990 Act refer must be approved by the "trustees" (*i.e.* those in management or control) and signed by one of their number as authorised. Every copy of the report which is circulated must state the name of the person who signed the report.   **6.3.5**

The accounts themselves must also be "approved by the trustees and signed by one of their number on their behalf and as authorised by them". The signature should be on the balance sheet or statement of balances as appropriate, and all copies issued must state the name of the signatory and the date of approval (regulation 6).   **6.3.6**

---

[5]S.I. 1992 No. 2165.
[6]See Chap. 4, para. 4.8.2.

External Review Regulations

6.3.7   Regulation 7 relates to audit requirements. Where gross income or expenditure in the current or either of the preceding two years exceeds £100,000, or where there is a requirement for an audit in the founding deed, or where the "trustees" elect to have an audit, then an audit by a person eligible for appointment as a company auditor under the provisions of the Companies Act 1989[7] is required. The remainder of regulation 7 sets out conditions for the appointment and resignation of the auditor together with the major requirements for the auditor's report.

6.3.8   If the income criteria in regulation 7 above are not relevant, then the charity need only submit accounts to an "independent examiner". An independent examiner is described as "an independent person who is reasonably believed by the trustees to have the requisite ability and practical experience to carry out a competent examination of the accounts" (regulation 8). "Independent" is not defined. There follow conditions for the appointment and resignation of the independent examiner, together with major requirements for the independent examiner's report.

6.3.9   The accounting regulations impose a duty on the auditor or independent examiner to consider whether the accounts have been properly prepared from the charity's records and whether the information given in the charity's report is consistent with the accounts. The report by the auditor or independent examiner must record any shortcomings, including a failure to obtain all the information and explanation required to carry out a satisfactory audit or examination.

6.3.10 The major difference between an auditor's opinion and an independent examiner's report is that the auditor states whether in his/her opinion the accounts give a true and fair view of the state of affairs at the end of the financial year and of the surplus or deficit for the year, whereas the independent examiner need only say whether or not the accounts are in agreement with the records and comply with the terms of the regulations and the body's founding deed.

6.3.11 The regulations for England and Wales go further than this and require auditors to write to the Charity Commissioners regarding any matters which they have reasonable cause to believe are of material

---

[7]s. 24(2) of the 1989 Act states that a "company auditor" means a person appointed as auditor under Chap. V of Pt. XI of the Companies Act 1985, and s. 25 adds that a person is eligible for appointment as a company auditor only if (*a*) a member of a recognised supervisory body, and (*b*) eligible for the appointment under the rules of that body. Schedules to the 1989 Act give the criteria for recognition and eligibility. An individual or a firm may be appointed a company auditor.

significance to the functions of the Commissioners under section 8 of the Charities Act 1993 (the general power to institute inquiries) or under section 18 (the power to act for the protection of charities).[8] This raises the question of the precise regulatory role of the auditor or independent examiner. The provisions of the English regulations imply that (s)he will need to consider whether trustees are fulfilling their duties and responsibilities and whether there have been any breaches of trust which may jeopardise the charity's funds. There is at present no equivalent statutory "whistle-blowing" role in Scotland.

Retention of Records

Regulation 9 states that the accounting records must be stored at the main office of the recognised body or such other place as determined by the "trustees", but they may not be stored outside Great Britain. The 1990 Act gives a time limit of six years from the date of the transaction (not the year end as in England and Wales).

6.3.12

Schedules to the Regulations

Schedule 1, Parts 1 and 2 detail the information to be shown in the balance sheet (or statement of balances as appropriate) and the income and expenditure account (or receipts and payments account as appropriate). The key provision is that the accounts must be set out in sufficient detail to "reasonably enable the user to gain a proper appreciation of the transactions and the surplus or deficit for that year". There follows a long list of categories of income and expenditure to be shown separately.

6.3.13

An income and expenditure account comprises "receipts and receivables" and "payments and payables" for the accounting period under review whereas a receipts and payments account merely reflects actual cash movements in the period under review. Netting off, whereby related expenditure is deducted from income, is discouraged.[9] An important aspect of the statement should be the inclusion of any appropriations (transfers) between funds and they should be shown separately below the "surplus/deficit for the year".

6.3.14

Schedule 1, Part 3 gives the information which should appear in the trustees' report. This includes details of the legal and administrative arrangements, the names and designations of trustees at any time during the year, the principal address of the body, an explanation of its objectives and organisational structure, a review of the financial position, a review of the year's activities and details of any connected bodies.

6.3.15

---

[8]S.I. 1995 No. 2724 at para. 6.5.

[9]For example, expenditure on fundraising should not be netted off against the funds raised. Both income and expenditure should be shown gross.

6.3.16   Schedule 2, Parts 1 and 2 detail the additional information required
by way of notes to the accounts including: accounting policies; **nature
and purpose of each fund**; movements on permanent endowment
funds; **reconciliation of opening and closing balances of funds;
details of non-personal grants paid (greater of £1000 or 2% of gross
income)**; material commitments; guarantees and other contingent
liabilities; **remuneration and reimbursements to trustees**; average
number of employees and total emoluments paid and **such other
information as may assist the user to understand the statement of
accounts.** Only those items which are highlighted above need to be
included as notes to the receipts and payments account.

6.3.17   As is apparent, the regulations contain considerable detail about the
information to be included in the annual accounts of unincorporated
Scottish charities and the obligations of those in management or
control. It is particularly important to realise that the preparation of
the accounts and the report is the responsibility of those in
management or control. It is they who must approve and sign both
documents, and responsibility cannot be transferred to an auditor or
independent examiner, although their advice regarding best practice
can be sought separately from their review role.

INCORPORATED CHARITIES

Accounting requirements

6.4.1   As noted earlier, charitable companies have a quite separate régime
regulating their accounting and audit obligations, and these are found
in Part VII of the Companies Act 1985 (sections 221-262). In many
areas the requirements are very similar to those which apply to
unincorporated charities. The directors of a charitable company will
almost invariably, in the terminology of the 1990 Act, be persons
concerned in its management or control.[10]

6.4.2   Section 221(1) sets out the basic requirement that a company must
maintain its own accounting records. In particular it specifies that:

> "every company shall keep accounting records which are
> sufficient to show and explain the company's transactions
> and are such as to: (*a*) disclose with reasonable accuracy at
> any time the financial position of the company at that time;
> and (*b*) enable the directors to ensure that any balance sheet
> and profit and loss account prepared under this Part complies
> with the requirements of the Act."

---

[10]See Chap. 2, para. 2.4.17.

The section goes on to describe what the accounting records should contain, including entries from day to day of all sums of money received and expended, a record of the company's assets and liabilities, and a statement of stock held at the year end. **6.4.3**

Section 222 covers the storage and retention of records, which should be kept at the company's registered office or such other place as determined by the directors, and should be open to inspection by the company's officers at all times. Subsection (5) refers to the obligation of private companies (which most incorporated charities will be) to retain accounting records for three years from the date on which they are made. However, it is important to realise that section 4(3) of the 1990 Act requires all recognised bodies to preserve their accounting records for six years. **6.4.4**

Sections 223 to 225 deal with the "financial year" and "accounting reference date" (this is often referred to as the company's year end). Where a company has not notified the Registrar of Companies of its accounting reference date within the prescribed period of nine months from the date of its incorporation, its accounting reference date is March 31 for companies incorporated before April 1, 1990, and for those incorporated after April 1,1990 it is the last day of the month in which the anniversary of its incorporation falls. However, a company may, by duly notifying the Registrar of Companies, change its accounting reference date. **6.4.5**

Section 226 requires the directors:

(1) to prepare for each financial year a balance sheet as at the last day of the year, and a profit and loss account.
(2) to ensure that these documents give a true and fair view of the state of affairs of the company for the year and at the year end.

Nowhere in the legislation is the term "true and fair" defined. One wag has stated that the only "true" figure on the accounts is cash which can be counted; all the remaining figures are "fair" based on directors' valuations and judgments. This is a good yardstick with which to work. Section 226(3) states that the accounts shall comply with Schedule 4 (to the Act) as to form and content and section 256 refers to accounting standards applicable to a company's annual accounts where relevant to the company's circumstances. (See paragraph 6.6.1 below.) **6.4.6**

The 1985 Act incorporates the requirements of the EEC Fourth Directive in that balance sheets and profit and loss accounts must now adhere to one of a limited number of formats which are detailed in Schedule 4 to the Act. Unfortunately the formats for the profit and loss account are not helpful for charities. However, formats from the specified list should be tailored for the use of charities by using section 3(3) of Schedule 4, which states: **6.4.7**

> "In preparing the company's balance sheet or profit and loss account the directors of the company shall adapt the

arrangement and headings and sub-headings as required in respect of items to which an Arabic number is assigned in the format adopted, in any case where the special nature of the company's business requires such adaptation."

In relation to all recognised bodies, best practice is to adapt the profit and loss account (which is really applicable to commercial companies) to an income and expenditure account with headings similar to those for an unincorporated charity or in line with the Statement of Recommended Practice "Accounting by Charities". This will yield a more meaningful financial statement for the user of the accounts.

6.4.8 If an incorporated charity is part of a group of companies, section 227 lays a duty on the parent company of the group to prepare individual accounts for the parent company together with consolidated accounts for the group (*i.e.* parent company and subsidiary undertakings). A subsidiary undertaking in relation to a charity means any entity in which the charity as parent or its directors or trustees hold or control the majority of the voting rights, or have the right to appoint or remove a majority of its board of directors or trustees. Sections 258 and 259 of the Companies Act provide a fuller definition of parent and subsidiary undertakings.

6.4.9 Sections 246 to 247 permit exemption from certain disclosure requirements in the accounts and reports for small and medium-sized companies. The exemptions are detailed in Schedule 8 to the Companies Act.

6.4.10 Sections 248 to 249 allow small and medium-sized groups exemption from preparing group accounts, unless any of the members of the group are public companies or banks or insurance companies or an authorised person under the Financial Services Act 1986. Most small or medium-sized charity groups will not be caught, but the last point may involve charities giving debt advice. All charities are encouraged to prepare group accounts.

6.4.11 The financial criteria quoted in the 1985 Act for identifying whether companies are small or medium-sized groups were amended upwards in November 1992 by statutory instrument.[11] Details of the current financial criteria are given in Appendix 6:1.

6.4.12 If consolidated accounts are required these should be prepared in line with current Companies Act and accounting standards guidance. The SORP recommends that the accounts of trading subsidiaries of a charity should be consolidated.

External Review

6.4.13 The 1985 Act requires accounts to be reported upon by external

---

[11]The Companies Act 1985 (Accounts of Small and Medium Sized Enterprises and Publication of Accounts in ECUs) Regulations 1992 (S.I. 1992 No. 2452).

auditors (section 235) following audit, and the accounts together with the auditor's report and a directors' report (section 234) must then be sent to the members of the company (section 238), considered in general meeting, usually the annual general meeting (section 241), and, if adopted, shall be delivered to the registrar of companies (section 242). Private companies have 10 months from the end of their financial year to deliver accounts (section 244).

In August 1994, under sections 245(3)–(5) and 257 of the Companies **6.4.14** Act 1985, the Audit Exemption Regulations[12] were introduced as part of the Government's desire to assist small business by reducing red tape. The regulations afford certain exemptions to incorporated charities with a gross annual income under £250,000, namely, no audit or independent examination is required if the income is under £90,000, an independent accountant's report will suffice if the income is between £90,000 and £250,000 and only thereafter is a full audit needed as was previously the case. (Companies other than charities require a full audit only if their income is over £350,000.) Groups of companies, whether charitable or not, are not exempted, and all parent companies and subsidiary undertakings require an audit regardless of size.

A summary of Scottish accounting and external review requirements **6.4.15** appears in Appendix 6:1.

COMPARATIVE REGULATIONS AFFECTING CHARITIES IN ENGLAND AND WALES

The accounting regulations for England and Wales, due to be **6.5.1** implemented in 1996, require:

(1) an independent examination for unincorporated charities whose income exceeds £10,000 but does not exceed £250,000, and
(2) a professional audit for those with gross income or total expenditure over £250,000 in the relevant year or in either of the immediately preceding two years.

There is a recommendation that where gross income is more than £100,000 (or assets are in excess of £1,000,000) a qualified accountant should carry out the independent examination. Charities whose income does not exceed £100,000 can also elect to prepare receipts and payments accounts.

Following the recommendations of the Deregulation Task Force[13] **6.5.2** which were incorporated in the English regulations, small charities

---

[12]The Companies Act 1985 (Audit Exemption) Regulations 1994 (S.I. 1994 No. 1935).
[13]Charities and Voluntary Organisations Task Force, *Proposals for Reform* (1994), Deregulation Task Forces.

in England and Wales have seen some easing of the accountancy burden previously outlined in the Charities Act 1993. The Deregulation and Contracting Out Act 1994 introduced the first of these by freeing charities whose income does not exceed £10,000 from the obligation to have an independent examination or audit.[14]

6.5.3 All U.K. charities should be aware that funders such as government departments, local authorities and health boards often require an audit whatever the size of the charity, and contracts frequently stipulate this. This audit may differ in presentation and format from that set out in the statutory requirements and may also be required to be presented more frequently.

6.5.4 Scotland's unincorporated charities are currently subject to more stringent accounting and external review requirements than their counterparts in England and Wales, but former Scottish Office minister Lord Fraser of Carmyllie did indicate that it is anticipated that the Scottish accounting regulations will be revised once the English regulations are brought into effect.[15] An argument which has been put forward for retaining stricter accounting and external review requirements for Scottish charities is that in England and Wales the Charity Commissioners, with whom accounts must be filed annually, carry out their own routine checks, whereas Scotland does not have a body which fulfils this function.

ADDITIONAL ACCOUNTING REQUIREMENTS

6.6.1 Cognisance must be taken in preparing the statutory accounts, whether for an incorporated or unincorporated charity, of the various Statements of Standard Accounting Practice (SSAPs)[16] and Financial Reporting Standards (FRSs)[17] which are in force. Charities should check with their auditor or independent examiner as to which of these may apply to the charity's circumstances and its accounts.

6.6.2 The underlying SSAP affecting all U.K. accounting, including charity accounting, is SSAP2 which deals with accounting concepts, standards and policies. The fundamental accounting concepts are:

---

[14]s. 28 of the Deregulation and Contracting Out Act 1994 amends s.43 of the Charities Act 1993 which required an audit or independent examination for charities with an income of £100,000 or less. Charities whose governing instrument requires them to have an audit must, however, still do so.

[15]*Hansard*, H.L. Vol. 560, cols. 1053–1054.

[16]SSAPs 1–25, not all current.

[17]FRSs 1–8.

(1) **going concern**[18] basis;
(2) **matching** income with expenditure — **accruals**[19] basis;
(3) **prudence** in acknowledging losses, but not assuming gains until they are reasonably assured;
(4) **consistency** in presentation year on year.

Policies appropriate to the charity but consistent with SSAP2 and also with the "true and fair" concept should be adopted. There is an obligation to prepare "true and fair" accounts, so those in management or control are required to follow SSAPs and FRSs as relevant. Departure therefrom without adequate justification may lead a court to hold that the accounts are not "true are fair"! There is an obligation to disclose in the notes to the accounts the accounting policies which have been adopted.

STATEMENT OF RECOMMENDED PRACTICE (SORP)

Aside from the statutory requirements and the SSAPs and FRSs already outlined, there is in existence *Accounting by Charities: Statement of Recommended Practice* (SORP), first issued in 1988 by the Accounting Standards Committee of the Committee of Chartered Accountancy Bodies (CCAB). A major revision of the SORP has taken place. Reissued in 1995, it is now the basis of the English and Welsh regulations for accounting by charities (issued under Part VI of the Charities Act 1993). With its 240 sections and four detailed appendices, SORP contains best practice and will be required reading for all lawyers, accountants and auditors advising charities as well as those in management or control of charities. **6.7.1**

At paragraph 6, the SORP emphasises the intention that it will apply to all charities in the U.K. and the Republic of Ireland regardless of size, constitution or complexity. However, where a separate SORP exists for a particular class of charity, those in management or control of such a charity should adhere to the specific SORP instead. **6.7.2**

Paragraph 7 suggests that each recommendation be considered in the context of what is "material" to the particular charity. **6.7.3**

Integration of the SORP with Legislation

The SORP impinges on all the legislation governing charity accounting, and paragraph 8 notes that the recommendations should **6.7.4**

---

[18]This means that the charity will continue in operational existence for the foreseeable future. In particular the accounts assume no intention to liquidate or to curtail significantly the scale of operation of the charity.

[19]That is, recognised when earned or receivable or when expenditure is incurred, not as money is received or paid.

be adapted to meet any statutory requirements such as are contained in:

(1)   the Companies Acts 1985 and 1989;
(2)   the Industrial and Provident Societies Acts 1965 to 1978[20];
(3)   the Registered Housing Associations Regulations (Accounting Requirements) Order 1992;
(4)   the Charities Accounts (Scotland) Regulations 1992; and
(5)   any requirements imposed by the charity's own governing instrument, *e.g.* a trust deed or constitution.

6.7.5   The particular references to the SORP and Scottish charities can be found in Appendix 6:2, but both the general and specific guidance contained in the SORP applies to Scotland and should be followed, unless there is a specific Scottish requirement.

Format for Smaller Charities

6.7.6   A small charity is allowed by the SORP to elect to prepare a receipts and payments account and statement of assets and liabilities (in England and Wales) or a statement of balances (in Scotland) unless dictated otherwise by its own governing instrument (paragraph 5). The SORP goes on to state that for accounting purposes a small charity is eligible as such if:

(1)   it is not a limited company, and
(2)   the prescribed threshold of gross income or gross receipts in any one year is not exceeded (paragraph 13).

In England and Wales this is the amount of its gross income (not receipts), and the threshold is currently £100,000; in Scotland it is the amount of its gross receipts (not income), and the threshold is currently £25,000 (paragraphs 234-235).

6.7.7   It should be recognised that because only receipts and payments are disclosed, the accounts do not give a true and fair view of the charity's affairs. Therefore the only fundamental accounting concept in terms of SSAP2 which is assumed is consistency. Paragraphs 13–20 refer to this and other issues relating to small charities. Paragraphs 18 and 19 point out that much of the remainder of the SORP still applies in some degree to small charities as well as to larger ones; for example, the charity's unrestricted funds should still be distinguished from any permanent endowment and other restricted funds.

Statement of Financial Activities (SOFA)

6.7.8   The most revolutionary development in the SORP is a Statement of

---

[20]See Chap. 2, paras. 2.5.1–2.5.4.

Financial Activities (SOFA) which is the new primary accounting statement for unincorporated charities in England and Wales.[21]

Paragraph 69, which introduces the SOFA, states that the traditional income and expenditure account, which distinguishes between revenue and capital, does not always fully explain the charity's activities. The primary purpose of charitable endeavours must be the provision of benefits to its beneficiaries rather than the corporate pursuit of gain for the benefit of the shareholders. The introduction of the SOFA should overcome these limitations by showing all incoming resources during the year and how they are expended for the benefit of the beneficiaries.

6.7.9

Furthermore, charities also receive significant amounts of restricted funds which affect the type and level of service they can provide. The SOFA is a single accounting statement analysing all capital and income resources and expenditures by type of fund and contains a reconciliation of all movements in the charity's funds.

6.7.10

A *pro forma* of the SOFA with explanatory notes appears in Appendix 6:3.

6.7.11

Other Important Aspects of SORP

Accounting for Separate Funds

Where more than one fund is under the control of the charity then a summary of the main funds is required in the accounts, with details in notes. The summary should differentiate between:

6.7.12

Permanent endowment funds
where there is no power to convert capital into income so the capital must be held indefinitely but funds can be homogenous in nature, *e.g.* investments can be bought and sold within the heading of investments;

Restricted funds
where donor or appeal restrictions imposed within the objects of charity mean that restricted income funds are only expendable in furtherance of a particular aspect of the charity's work, or where the assets of restricted capital funds are to be invested or retained for actual use rather than expended;

Unrestricted funds
expendable at the discretion of those in management or control and of which part may be "designated funds" for particular purposes in the near future.

---

[21]See Charity Commissioners for England and Wales, *Accounting by Charities: Statement of Recommended Practice* (1995), Charity Commission, paras. 69-165.

Assets and liabilities representing each fund must be clearly analysed and any funds in deficit always separately disclosed. Persons in management or control should carefully review the performance of each fund to ensure that no fund is in deficit, particularly an unrestricted fund, as a cross-subsidy from a permanent endowment or restricted fund could be construed as transacting *ultra vires*.

Balance Sheet

6.7.13   Funds should be grouped and there should be segregation of permanent endowment funds, restricted funds and unrestricted funds (designated and otherwise). Details of the funds should appear in the notes if required.

6.7.14   Revaluations and diminutions in fixed assets will appear as adjustments in the SOFA, but in the case of an unincorporated Scottish charity it will currently appear as part of the funds directly on the balance sheet, possibly segregated as a revaluation reserve. This is one area which may be amended by the Scottish Office to harmonise with the SORP. Where there is a conflict between the SORP and the 1992 accounting regulations it is the latter which must be complied with.

6.7.15   Cash flow and summary income and expenditure statements are to be presented in the form required by legislation, regulation and the relevant accounting standard.[22]

CHARITIES WITH BRANCHES

6.8.1   Charities use branches primarily to raise funds, to increase public awareness and to carry out their charitable objectives. It can be argued that any money raised using the charity's name must belong to the charity and that the branch is acting in a trustee capacity, for instance, in relation to membership subscriptions.

6.8.2   The accounts of branches (known as "quasi-subsidiary undertakings" in accounting jargon) should be included (aggregated) in the accounts of the main charity if the branch falls within the definition given below. Separate legal entities which may be known as branches but which do not fall within the definition should prepare their own annual report and accounts. They may still be considered as "connected charities" in relation to the main charity.

6.8.3   The SORP defines branches (which may also be known as supporters' groups, friends' groups, members' groups) as:

> "entities or administrative bodies set up, for example, to

---

[22]A summary of the primary documents for Scottish charities appears in App. 6:4.

conduct a particular aspect of the business of the main charity, or to conduct the business of the main charity in a particular geographical area. They may or may not be legal entities which are separate from the main charity".[23]

As far as Scottish bodies linked to charities registered in England and Wales are concerned, it is important to establish whether they are autonomous Scottish charities, to which the Scottish accounting and external review requirements will apply, or branches of an English charity, in which case they will need to comply with the legislation, including accounting and external review requirements, which prevails in England and Wales.

Ideally, there should be a statement in the appropriate document(s) constituting the charity which clarifies whether a branch is: **6.8.4**

(a) an administrative arm of the parent charity; or
(b) a separate legal entity which is administered by or "on behalf of"[24] the parent charity and whose funds are held for specific purposes which correspond to the general purposes of the parent charity, but are confined to the area in which the entity operates. Such funds would be restricted funds.

A separate legal entity may be known as a "branch", but if it is not within the definition at (b) above, then it is not a branch for accounting purposes.

If the branch is not a separate legal entity, all funds held by a branch will be the legal property of the parent charity whether or not it has a separate bank account. **6.8.5**

Charities, therefore, must establish the legal status of the entities through which they operate. The attitude of branch members or of head office is not the deciding factor. **6.8.6**

With the more prescriptive SORP as "best practice", there are more detailed requirements regarding branch operations. Questions which may assist in establishing the status of a "branch" appear in Appendix 6:5. **6.8.7**

Connected Charities

Connected charities are dealt with in paragraphs 50–53 of the SORP and are those with common, parallel or related objects; and either common control, or unity of administration. If there are connected charities then the annual report should include names and addresses **6.8.8**

---

[23]Charity Commissioners for England and Wales, *op. cit.* (1995), App.1.1.

[24]The words "on behalf of" should be taken to mean that under the constitution of the separate entity a substantial degree of influence is exerted by the parent charity over the administration of its affairs.

and material transactions between the connected bodies.[25] If the connection between the charities is such that one is under the control of another to the extent of being subordinate to it, the subordinate charity will be a "branch" of the primary charity (see above).

Consolidated Accounts

6.8.9   A charity may have a number of subsidiary undertakings whose activities are not of a charitable nature. Typically, such subsidiary undertakings conduct a trade and pass any profits up to the parent charity.[26] Consolidated accounts should be prepared in all cases as set out in FRS2, subject to paragraphs 62-66 of the SORP which describe the different presentation methods in the SOFA; these being consolidation on a line by line basis, a single line for net profit or loss, or by segregating and summarising the results of the subsidiary undertaking. The choice of method will be dependent on the circumstances described in the SORP aligned to the charity's circumstances. On the balance sheet, however, the assets and liabilities of all subsidiaries should be consolidated on a line by line basis in the normal way.

CONCLUSION

6.9.1   The provisions governing charity financial accounting and external review are complex and each charity will have to pick its own way through the maze with the assistance of professional advisers.

6.9.2   It is important to appreciate that:

(1)   for all recognised bodies in Scotland the 1990 Act is mandatory;
(2)   for all unincorporated recognised bodies in Scotland the accounting and external review régime laid down in the 1992 Regulations is mandatory;
(3)   for all incorporated recognised bodies in Scotland the Companies Act 1985 is mandatory and its accounting and auditing requirements prevail;
(4)   for all U.K. charities, including all recognised bodies in Scotland, the SORP is acknowledged best practice. Auditors of recognised bodies are bound to adhere to best practice.

---

[25]The term "affiliate", which is often used in the charity sector to describe a loose relationship between two charitable bodies, is defined by the *Oxford English Dictionary* as meaning "to adopt or attach or connect as member or branch to or with", which raises the question of whether an affiliated body is a branch (a quasi-subsidiary undertaking) or a connected body (and therefore autonomous).

[26]See Chap. 7, paras. 7.4.15 *et seq.*

In the last five years there has been a quantum leap in the accounting **6.9.3** and external review requirements for Scottish charities. As the need for public accountability continues and increases as the voluntary sector takes on more responsibility for the direct provision of services previously carried out by statutory bodies,[27] it is likely that the requirements will continue to become more prescriptive.

[27]See Chap. 10.

APPENDIX 6:1

SUMMARY OF ACCOUNTING REQUIREMENTS IN SCOTLAND

Unincorporated Charities where annual receipts do not exceed £25,000

(Except where the founding deed or funder requires an audit or where the trustees elect to have an audit.)

1. Receipts and payments.
2. Statement of balances.
3. Notes to the accounts.
4. Annual report of the activities of the body.
5. Independent examination.
6. Accounts available to the public.

Unincorporated Charities with an annual income between £25,000–£100,000

(Except where the founding deed or funder requires an audit or where the trustees elect to have an audit.)

1. Income and expenditure account.
2. Balance sheet.
3. Notes to the accounts.
4. Annual report of the activities of the body.
5. Independent examination.
6. Accounts available to the public.

Unincorporated Charities where annual income exceeds £100,000

1. Income and expenditure account.
2. Balance sheet.
3. Notes to the accounts.
4. Annual report of the activities of the body.
5. Audit by registered auditor.
6. Accounts available to the public.

Incorporated Charities up to August 11, 1994

1. Full set of accounts in accordance with Companies Acts.
2. Audit by registered auditor (registration required by Companies Act 1989).

Incorporated Charities from August 11, 1994

(a) Income not exceeding £90,000
Exempt from audit

(b) Income between £90,000–£250,000
Independent accountant's report

(c) Income over £250,000
Full audit required.

Parent charitable companies and subsidiaries require an audit regardless of size.

Current size criteria defining small and medium sized companies and groups

Any two of the following:

Small Company

Turnover not more than £2.8 million, balance sheet total not more than £1.4 million and no more than 50 employees.

Medium Company

Turnover not more than £11.2 million, balance sheet total not more than £5.6 million and no more than 250 employees.

Small Group

Aggregate turnover not more than £2.8 million net or £3.36 gross, aggregate balance sheet total not more than £1.4 million net or £1.68 million gross, no more than 50 employees.

Medium Group

Aggregate turnover not more than £11.2 million net or £13.44 million gross, aggregate balance sheet total not more that £5.6 million net or £6.72 million gross, no more than 250 employees.

APPENDIX 6:2

The main references to Scottish charities in the SORP are paragraphs 223 to 236 which are outlined below:

para. 223
General guidance elsewhere in the SORP on treatment applicable to particular matters is to be followed unless there is a specific Scottish requirement.

para. 224
Scottish charities should provide in prominent form a SOFA by way of note to the accounts.

para. 225
Scottish charities should apply the same treatment to items to be included in their income and expenditure account as to be applied for their inclusion in the SOFA (*e.g.* income recognition; expenditure allocation) unless specifically noted.

para. 226
The income and expenditure account should be analysed in a manner appropriate to the charity, helpful to the reader, but not excessively detailed. There follows a list of information to be shown separately, which approximates to the requirements of the Charities Accounts (Scotland) Regulations 1992.

paras. 227-230
Expand the above with particular reference (in para. 229) to endowment funds which should not be dealt with in the income and expenditure account but should instead be dealt with in the SOFA as a note to the accounts, disclosing all movements on such funds.

para. 231
Relates to accounting for separate funds as follows: "Depending on the materiality of each fund the accounts should group **restricted funds** under one or more heads. **Unrestricted funds,** both **designated** and **undesignated,** should be grouped similarly. The columnar format of the income and expenditure account is designed to facilitate this, subject to any constraints imposed by the need to distinguish between continuing, discontinued and acquired operations in compliance with the financial reporting standard" (FRS3).

para. 232
Refers to grants payable, details of which should be given in the notes to the accounts in accordance with Charities Accounts (Scotland) Regulations 1992.

para. 233
A single note may be used to explain or to expand upon items which appear in both the income and expenditure account and the SOFA, providing the same level of disclosure to support items is disclosed.

paras. 234–235
Refer to small charities and the alternative format of accounts available for them, as detailed in the Charities Accounts (Scotland) Regulations.

para. 236
Refers to the size criteria which require a cash flow statement as required by FRS1. In deciding whether or not the charity falls within the size criteria a charity's turnover should be taken to equate to its gross income as defined in the regulations.

APPENDIX 6:3

STATEMENT OF FINANCIAL ACTIVITIES (SOFA)

Description	Un-restricted Funds	Restricted Income Funds	Endow-ment Funds	Total Funds
Incoming resources before transfers and revaluations - A	A	A	A	A
Direct charitable expenditure - B	B	B	B	B
Other expenditure - C	C	C	C	C
Total expenditure = B+C	D	D	D	D
Gross transfers between funds - E	E	E	E	(Total=NIL)
Net incoming resources before revaluations and investment asset disposals = A-D+E	F	F	F	F
Gains and losses on revaluation and on investment asset disposals - G	G	G	G	G
Net movement in funds = F+G	H	H	H	H
Total funds brought forward - I	I	I	I	I
Total funds carried forward = H+I	J	J	J	J

(J = Total funds in Balance Sheet)
H to J = Reconciliation of Funds required as link between SOFA and Balance Sheet.

All incoming resources becoming available to the charity during the year should be summarised in the first section, distinguishing between those belonging to the charity's endowment funds, its restricted income funds and its unrestricted funds.

A. The gross incoming resources should be summarised in the statement in a manner appropriate to the charity. The following items should be shown separately in the summary, where material:

   (i) donations, legacies and similar incoming resources;
   (ii) grants receivable from government and other public bodies;
   (iii) investment income;
   (iv) income from trading activities of the charity,
      distinguishing between: (a) trading activities permissible

within charity's objects; (b) trading activities which are outside the charity's objects;

(v) other incoming resources (*e.g.* net gains on disposals of fixed assets for use by the charity);

(vi) the total of the above resources arising in the year.

B. Direct charitable expenditure comprises all expenditure directly relating to the objects of the charity and should include, where the amount is material, the direct cost of supporting charitable activities and projects as well as depreciation, amortisation or losses on disposal of fixed assets used wholly or mainly for direct charitable activities, including where the assets are written off as project expenditure. Direct charitable expenditure should, where material, be analysed between the following two subheadings:

(i) grants payable;
(ii) other direct expenditure.

C. Other expenditure should be analysed under the following two subheadings:

(i) fundraising and publicity costs; and
(ii) expenditure on the management and administration of the charity.

G. Gains and losses arising on disposal or revaluation of fixed assets, whether held for functional or investment purposes, will form part of the particular fund in which the investment or asset concerned is or was held. Realised and unrealised gains and losses should be included in the SOFA, the former either as incoming resources (A) or additional depreciation (B) or (C), the latter as part of the revaluation section (G), but unrealised gains will be excluded from the summary income and expenditure account.

Detailed definitions of income and expenditure terms appear in Appendix 1 of the SORP.

APPENDIX 6:4

SUMMARY OF THE PRIMARY DOCUMENTS FOR SCOTTISH CHARITIES

Incorporated charity	Unincorporated charity	
United Kingdom (incl. N.I.)	England & Wales	Scotland
Primary Accounting Statements		
Statement of Financial Activities **(SOFA)** (*)	Statement of Financial Activities **(SOFA)** (*)	Income and Expenditure
Summary Income and Expenditure Account (*)	Summary Income and Expenditure Account (*)	
Balance Sheet	Balance Sheet	Balance Sheet
Cash Flow Statement (*per* FRS1 revised limits)	Cash Flow Statement (*per* FRS1 revised limits)	Cash Flow Statements (*per* old FRS limits)
Notes to Accounts		
SOFA could also be shown as a note		Prominent SOFA!

(*) if no capital fund could be the same.

APPENDIX 6:5

BRANCHES

Questions to be Answered to Assess Position of a "Branch" Relative to a Charity

The branch is a subsidiary undertaking of the charity if these questions are all answered **YES**:

1. Does a local charity require permission from the charity before establishing itself? ... and before calling itself a branch of the main charity?
2. Is the same trustee body responsible for administering both the charity and its branches?
3. Does the branch carry out its activities using the name and/or charity (Inland Revenue) number of the charity?
4. Does the charity prevent the branch from administering its own affairs totally independently?
5. Does the charity have legal control over important aspects of the branch administration, *e.g.* by prescribing the form of its constitution or by being constitutionally involved in the alteration of branch constitution or its dissolution?
6. Does the branch avail itself of the fiscal benefits of being part of the charity?
7. Is the branch financially dependent on the charity?
8. Does the charity have the right to control the use of branches' resources?
9. Do the branch members feel that their subscriptions support the main charity?
10. Are the branches themselves charities or parts of the main charity as opposed to being non-charitable clubs whose main purpose is to benefit their members?
11. Does the branch have to report annually to the charity on operational and financial matters?

The branch is a subsidiary undertaking of the charity if these questions are all answered **NO**:

1. Can the branch disburse funds as it pleases?
2. Does the branch "own" funds held at the local branch?
3. Are branch accounts separately prepared/audited and presented only to the branch members?
4. Would branch funds remain at branch/area level if the branch were to close?
5. Would legal action taken be against the branch?
6. Could the branch support another charity?

Implications if Branches are Autonomous

They will have to apply for separate registration with the Inland Revenue in Scotland or with the Charity Commissioners in England and Wales.

Chapter 7

TAXATION

Introduction

This chapter provides a summary of the reliefs and exemptions from   **7.1.1**
tax, stamp duty and rates which are available to bodies recognised as
charitable by the Inland Revenue. Space does not permit more than a
summary, and the reader is referred in Appendix 7:1 to specialist works
which examine the subject of charity tax in greater detail. The review
of reliefs and exemptions offered here is divided into three sections:
section 1 deals with the taxes administered by the Inland Revenue,
that is income tax, corporation tax, capital gains tax, inheritance tax,
and stamp duty; section 2 with value added tax (VAT); and section 3
with non-domestic rates. A preliminary section deals with the
interpretation of the word "charitable" in Scotland as it appears in
United Kingdom tax legislation.

"Charitable" for Tax Purposes

Application of the English Definition

Meaning of "Charitable" for Tax Purposes

The exemptions from the Inland Revenue administered taxes   **7.2.1**
described in section 1 and from non-domestic rates are made available
by reference, *inter alia,* to the fact that the body seeking relief is
established for "charitable" purposes only.[1] In the application of the
relevant legislation in each case to a Scottish company, association or
trust of the kind described in earlier chapters, the word "charitable"
is to be understood in its technical meaning in English law. The English
definition is based ultimately on the Charitable Uses Act 1601 which,
with the classification of charitable purposes which has grown out of
it, is discussed more fully in Chapters 1 and 8. It may be helplful to
recall at this point, however, that the English definition is usually

---

[1]Income and Corporation Taxes Act 1988, ss.505 and 506(1); Taxation of
Chargeable Gains Act 1992, s.256; Inheritance Tax Act 1984, s.272; Finance
Act 1982, s.129; Local Government (Financial Provisions) (Scotland) Act 1962,
s.4 as amended; and see sections 1 and 3 of this chapter.

summarised as incorporating four heads of charity: the relief of poverty, the advancement of education, the advancement of religion, and purposes beneficial to the community not falling under the first three heads.[2] There is also an overriding requirement of public benefit.

7.2.2   By contrast, the limited exemptions available to charities under the VAT legislation have only an oblique connection with the extended English concept of charity.[3]

Applicability in Scotland

7.2.3   The rule that the English meaning of charitable is to be applied in Scotland as in the rest of the United Kingdom in the interpretation of a taxation statute was established in *Income Tax Special Commissioners v. Pemsel*.[4] In that case the majority in the House of Lords declined to follow the decision of the Court of Session three years earlier in *Baird's Trustees v. Lord Advocate*[5] to the effect that the word "charitable" in a taxation statute should be interpreted in "nothing but its ordinary popular signification" and decided instead that, in the words of Lord Macnaghten, "the expression 'trust for charitable purposes' in [a taxation statute], and the other expressions [in a taxation statute] in which the word 'charitable' occurs, must be construed in their technical meaning according to English law".[6]

Role of Scottish Courts

7.2.4   The implications of the rule for the Scottish courts were developed by Lord Normand in *Inland Revenue v. City of Glasgow Police Athletic Association*[7]:

> "In *Pemsel's* case it was decided authoritatively that it was part of the jurisdiction of the Court of Session, as Court of Exchequer in Scotland, to administer this branch of English law in claims for exemptions by charities. ... The necessary effect of *Pemsel's* case ... is that the English law of charity has, for income tax purposes and for them alone,[8] to be regarded as part of the law of Scotland and not as a foreign law."

7.2.5   Lord Normand pointed out that the Scottish courts do, however, retain a measure of independence:

> "They are technically not bound by the decisions of the English Courts in the matter of charities, and it is not improper

---

[2]*Income Tax Special Commissioners v. Pemsel* [1891] A.C. 531, *per* Lord Macnaghten at 583.

[3]Value Added Tax Act 1983, s. 16(2) and Sched. 5, and s. 47(3).

[4][1891] A.C. 531.

[5](1888) 15 R. 682, *per* Lord President Inglis at 689.

[6]*Income Tax Special Commissioners v. Pemsel* [1891] A.C. 531, *per* Lord Macnaghten at 587.

[7]1953 S.C. (H.L.) 13, 21; 1953 S.L.T 105, 106.

[8]Now applicable for the purposes of the other taxes (excluding VAT), stamp duty and rates.

for them to discuss or criticise English decisions. The Court of Session is not reduced to the role of an obsequious follower of decisions either of a Judge of first instance or of the Court of Appeal, though it is only good sense to pay special regard and respect to the decisions and opinions pronounced by the English Courts on a branch of the law built up by English Judges, and familiar to them by long training and experience."

Interpretation of Scottish Deeds

While the Court of Session is bound to apply the technical English meanings of "charity" and "charitable" when interpreting a taxation statute, it does not cease to be a Scottish court and must interpret Scottish deeds according to the usual rules of construction of Scots law. Thus it was decided in *Jackson's Trustees v. Lord Advocate*[9] that a bequest for "charitable or benevolent" purposes in a Scottish will should receive the benefit of tax relief as a bequest for charitable purposes only. Lord President Clyde pointed out that there were two separate questions before the court: the first was the meaning of "charitable purposes" in the taxation statute, which *Pemsel's* case had established must be its English meaning, and the second was whether the trust purposes declared in the deed under consideration fell within the category of "charitable purposes" as defined by the law of England. The second question was to be answered by interpreting the deed according to the common law of Scotland, which, unlike the law of England, equates a trust for "charitable or benevolent" purposes with a trust for charitable purposes alone. In a Scottish deed, the words "or benevolent" are treated as merely exegetical of the word "charitable". It was further held that a trust which is charitable in Scots law is also charitable under English law. The result was that a wording which in an English deed would have rendered the bequest invalid (and so excluded it from relief) was brought within the scope of the English technical definition by application of the normal rules for the interpretation of deeds in Scotland.[10]

7.2.6

Benignant Approach

The overall approach adopted in England in considering the validity of a charitable gift is, however, a benignant one, and in *Guild v. Inland Revenue Commissioners*[11] Lord Keith of Kinkel qualified the rule that a Scottish deed constituting a charitable purpose must be interpreted according to Scots law as follows:

7.2.7

---

[9] 1926 S.C. 579, 587.

[10] In English law, the rule is that a general word such as "benevolent" cannot logically be treated as exegetical of a technical word such as "charitable" and that its effect is to add a further, ill-defined purpose which renders the whole bequest void from uncertainty. See *Chichester Diocesan Fund and Board of Finance (Incorp.) v. Simpson* [1944] A.C. 341.

[11] [1992] 2 A.C. 310, at 323; [1992] 2 All E.R. 10, at 18; also (as *Russell's Executor v. I.R.C.*) 1992 S.C. 71 (H.L.), at 102.

"But the importation into Scots law, for tax purposes, of the technical English law of charities involves that a Scottish judge should approach any question of construction arising out of the language used in the relevant instrument in the same manner as would an English judge who had to consider its validity as a charitable gift. The English judge would adopt the benignant approach in setting about that task, and so the Scottish judge dealing with the tax consequences should do likewise."

In other words, the Scottish court sets about interpreting any deed before it as a Scottish court interpreting a Scottish deed in the usual way but, influenced by the generally benign approach of the English courts in giving effect to charitable intentions, it will in marginal cases favour an interpretation which brings the tax benefits of charitable status into play.[12]

Influence of Charity Commissioners

7.2.8   The cases deal with the relationship between the English and Scottish courts in the application of charitable relief under the taxation statutes, but they say nothing of the practical influence of the Inland Revenue, and indirectly of the Charity Commissioners, on how eligibilty for relief is established at a day to day level in Scotland. In Scotland it is the Inland Revenue which determines eligibility for tax relief, subject to appeal to the Court of Session and the House of Lords, and the Charity Commissioners have, of course, no jurisdiction. It is only natural, however, that the Inland Revenue should be anxious to apply the same criteria in Scotland as are applied in England and Wales, where recognition of charitable status (by registration in the register of charities) is the responsibility of the Charity Commissioners, again subject to appeal in certain circumstances to the High Court.[13] In practice, the decisions of the Commissioners have built up into a body of persuasive authority which is available by analogy to the Inland Revenue when applying the reliefs in Scotland.[14]

---

[12]The benignant approach to be adopted in applying the tax legislation should presumably be distinguished from the rule of benignant construction applied under Scots common law in deciding the validity of bequests for public and "charitable" purposes. *Cf. Russell's Executor v. Balden*, 1989 S.L.T. 177, which considered the same will and bequest as *Guild*. Lord Jauncey, sitting in the Outer House, adopted a benignant approach to the construction of the deed in finding that a valid public trust had been constituted.

[13]The Inland Revenue may appeal against a decision to register, but a body seeking registration may only appeal if it would be subject to compulsory registration if its appeal were granted. A body seeking voluntary registration cannot appeal if its application is refused: Charities Act 1993, ss. 3 and 4.

[14]See also *Governors of Dollar Academy Trust v. Lord Advocate*, 1994 S.L.T. 596, in which in another context Lord President Hope referred with approval to the *Decisions of the Charity Commissioners*, April 1994, considering that circumstances taken into account by the Commissioners within their jurisdiction might apply equally in Scotland.

Applying for Recognition in Practice

Draft Constituting Document

Application for recognition of a body as charitable in Scotland is made   **7.2.9**
under section 505 of the Income and Corporation Taxes Act 1988 to
the Commissioners of Inland Revenue and is dealt with in practice
by the Financial Intermediaries and Claims Office (FICO).[15] The best
practice is to approach FICO before the body has been formally
constituted by submitting a draft of the proposed constituting
document for comment. FICO will give its view in writing on whether
the purposes disclosed in the draft will permit the body to be
recognised under the Act, and there is scope for adjustment where
FICO's initial view is that they will not. FICO will wish to satisfy
itself that all of the proposed purposes of the body are charitable in
terms of the English definition.[16] When provisional recognition has
been obtained, the body can be formally constituted in terms of the
approved draft and definitive recognition applied for. Submission of
the constituting document in draft is not mandatory, but it may save
embarrassment and expense in the event that the purposes of a body
which has already been constituted prove to be ineligible for
recognition and adjustment has not been allowed for in the document
or is procedurally cumbersome.

Formal Application

An application to FICO for formal recognition should be accompanied   **7.2.10**
by:

(1) in the case of a company, the memorandum and articles of
    association, a copy of the certificate of incorporation, and a note
    of the address of the registered office;
(2) in the case of a trust, the original of the stamped trust deed, or an
    extract after registration in the Books of Council and Session;
(3) in the case of an unincorporated association, a copy of the
    constitution certified as a true copy by two office bearers, the
    certificate to include a note of the date on which the constitution
    was adopted by the association and of the names and addresses of
    the certifying office bearers and the capacity in which they act.[17]

Charity Recognition Letter

Approval of the application is intimated in a formal charity recognition   **7.2.11**
letter, which contains both a reference number (the ED number) for
future correspondence with FICO itself and a Scottish charity number
(the SC number) which is the body's identifying number for the
purposes of the index of Scottish charities maintained by the Inland
Revenue for public inspection. Once a claim for repayment of tax has

---

[15]See Appendix 7:1 for telephone number.
[16]See, *e.g. Scottish Flying Club Co. Ltd. v. I.R.C.*, 1935 S.C. 817; *Trustees for the Roll of Voluntary Workers v. I.R.C.*, 1942 S.C. 47.
[17]Inland Revenue pamphlet CB(1) 1993.

been accepted, the ED number changes to a CR number. It is the SC number, however, which is the Scottish charity number and which should be cited on a body's notepaper and in dealings with the public.

Withdrawal of Recognition

7.2.12   The Inland Revenue may withdraw recognition where it appears that the purposes of the body are no longer exclusively charitable in terms of sections 505 and 506 of the 1988 Act. Some possible circumstances for withdrawal might be (1) where FICO has reason to believe that the real purposes and activities of the body do not correspond with those of its constituting document, (2) where there has been a change in the law as a result of a judicial decision as to what is or is not included in the term "charitable" for the purposes of the 1988 Act so that those of the body are no longer covered, and (3) where the body has altered its purposes in terms of its constituting document to purposes which are not exclusively charitable. Of these, the third is perhaps the most likely to arise, and a recognised body which is contemplating the alteration of its purposes would be wise to submit the proposed alterations in draft to FICO for an informal opinion on how they will affect the body's status under the 1988 Act.

Appeal

7.2.13   There is no right of appeal at the recognition stage against refusal by FICO to grant recognised body status. Reasons for refusal are given and can be discussed with FICO. An appeal is possible, however, at the point when FICO refuses a claim for repayment of tax. Such an appeal would be made to the Special Commissioners of Inland Revenue in the first instance, with further right of appeal to the Court of Session and the House of Lords.

THE RELIEFS AVAILABLE

7.3.1   For Inland Revenue and Customs and Excise taxes, it is of prime importance that a charity determines the source of its income, whether any goods or service transaction is expected in exchange for the income and how the income is spent. "For charitable purposes only" is the concept; although undefined, it is constantly referred to and is determined by voluminous case law concerning both Inland Revenue taxes and VAT.

SECTION 1: THE INLAND REVENUE TAX ENVIRONMENT

Direct Revenue Taxes on Income and Profits

7.4.1   The Income and Corporation Taxes Act 1988 (ICTA 1988) at section 505(1) grants:

"exemptions from taxes under Schedules A and D in respect of rents and profits of any lands, tenements, hereditaments or heritages ... vested in trustees for charitable purposes, so far as the same are applied to charitable purposes only" and

"exemption from tax under Schedule C in respect of any interest, annuities, dividends or shares of annuities from tax under Schedule D in respect of any yearly interest or other annual payment, and from tax under Schedule F in respect of any distribution."

By virtue of the Income and Corporation Taxes Act (ICTA) 1988, section 9(4), the above exemptions are equally applicable to the many charities which are liable to corporation tax whether they are companies or bodies such as societies and unincorporated associations. **7.4.2**

It might appear that there is a blanket exemption allowing charities to ignore the revenue taxes on income. This is not the case: charities are not absolved from all responsibilities as far as tax is concerned. ICTA 1988, section 505 imposes a requirement on charities to make a claim that they should be exempt from taxes. In theory, as income tax is an annual tax, such an application should be made annually. In practice an application for exemption will be required when the charity is making a claim for tax refunds. **7.4.3**

Reliefs from paying tax, therefore, are available to charities (*i.e.* bodies whose charitable status is "recognised" by FICO) on: **7.4.4**

(1) income from property (taxed under Schedule A);
(2) annual profits arising in respect of rents or receipts under leases of land in the U.K.;
(3) rent charges, ground annuals, feu duties or any other annual payment in respect of, charged on or issuing out of such land;
(4) other receipts arising from or by virtue of ownership of an estate or interest in or right over land or any incorporeal hereditament or incorporeal heritable subject in the U.K.

This includes normal rental income from lettings of properties, wayleaves and rights of way over land, and so on. There are allowable deductions in respect of insurance, routine repairs and maintenance and management. Expenditure on major structural repairs, such as a new roof or the subdivision of rooms, is not allowable as a deduction. **7.4.5**

Charities are normally exempt from taxes on net income from property, but charities which regularly undertake letting of property and provide a service, of, for instance, a caretaker to arrange meeting rooms, may be assessed as carrying on a trade which could be in breach of charitable status. (See "trading" below.) **7.4.6**

Schedule C charges to tax "all profits arising from public revenue dividends payable in the U.K." This includes income from U.K. and foreign government stocks paid through a U.K. paying-agent such as a bank. **7.4.7**

7.4.8   In practice most public dividends are paid under deduction of tax, the refund of which can be claimed by a charity which is exempt from paying tax, provided such income is being applied to charitable purposes.

7.4.9   Schedule D, Case III covers income received from any yearly interest, annuities and other annual payments. Such income will be received either subject to a tax deduction by the payer which can be reclaimed by the payee or gross if the paying institution (bank or building society) is satisfied regarding the payee's charitable status.

7.4.10   The ability to reclaim tax deducted or receive payment gross is the most important exemption for all charities because in conjunction with ICTA 1988, section 348 it provides the legislative background which enables a charity to reclaim substantial sums of tax in respect of deeds of covenant (considered below).

7.4.11   Other annual payments made under deduction of tax to a charity must show the following aspects:

(1)   a payment to which the charity is entitled, not an *ex gratia* payment;
(2)   a payment dealt with by reference such as "per annum";
(3)   one which is payable year by year;
(4)   "pure income profit" in the hands of charity, *i.e.* the charity does not undertake to do anything in return for the payment.

However, it is rare nowadays for charities to receive annual payments other than covenanted payments.

7.4.12   Schedule D, Cases I and II are dealt with below under "trading".

7.4.13   Schedule F, ICTA 1988, section 20 charges to tax "all dividends and other distributions" made in the year by a company resident in the U.K. By far the most common Schedule F receipt is in respect of dividends where the company pays the dividend net, paying over to the Inland Revenue, in the form of advance corporation tax, a sum which in the hands of the recipient is known as a tax credit. This tax credit can be reclaimed by a charity. It should be noted, however, that charities may well receive stock dividends and foreign income dividends, neither of which carry tax credit, so there is no entitlement to any repayment of tax in respect of such dividends.

7.4.14   Relevant key sections for charities in ICTA 1988 are:

235 Distribution to exempt funds.
339 Charges on income, donations to charity.
347a General rules on financial payments and interest.
505 Charity exemptions — general.
506 Qualifying and non-qualifying expenditure.
507 Extension of section 505 to certain other bodies.
508 Scientific research organisation.
510 Agricultural societies.

660 Covenanted payments.
671 Revocable settlements allowing release of obligation.
776 Transactions in land: taxation of capital gains.
832 Interpretation (definitions) section.
839 Connected persons.

Trading

Trading is one of the most difficult areas for a charity, particularly as more   **7.4.15**
and more charities are turning to trading as a fundraising source. Charities
are most at risk in having to pay tax on profits made, unless they understand
and plan for the tax position relating to trading. It is irrelevant that the
underlying objective of making a profit is to fund a charitable purpose.

It is essential to establish the Inland Revenue concept of trade which   **7.4.16**
is widened by ICTA 1988, section 832, to include "every trade,
manufacture, adventure or concern in the nature of trade". The
wording "adventure or concern in the nature of a trade" has been
exhaustively considered by the courts, but the main guidelines to arise
from the cases are:

(1) profit motive (where the objective is to raise funds for a charity a
profit motive may be implied)
(2) an adventure can be a "one-off" occurrence and need not be an
established trade (running a charity shop for the Christmas period
is classed as an adventure)
(3) factors such as the type of goods, what is done to them and how
the transaction was financed all influence the decision.

There are two broad categories of trading by charities, each of which   **7.4.17**
has a different tax treatment:

Primary trade — profits exempt from tax
Where the trade is either carried out in the course of the primary
purpose of the charity or is carried on by the beneficiaries of the charity
then profits earned are exempt from tax.

Example (1): charges levied by an educational charity for courses
it runs would be exempt as this would come within the main
purpose of the charity, but the sale of Christmas cards by such a
charity would not be exempt unless the cards were produced by
the charity's beneficiaries.

Example (2): a church having charitable status sells books to raise
funds. Religious books sold would qualify as a primary purpose
but secular books would not.

Example (3): charity shops which only sell donated goods are
regarded as converting goods donated into cash donated, but if
goods are bought in for resale then a trade could be construed as
taking place.

Evidence that the "profit" or surplus is generated through the primary
purpose and is applied to the purposes of the charity (not just any

charitable purposes but within the specific objects of the charity in question) is an essential pre-requisite to exemption.

Secondary trade — profits subject to tax
Where such trade, in itself is not part of the primary purpose of the charity but is designed to raise funds to be applied for charitable purposes, then profits earned are subject to tax. Such trade should be channelled through a trading subsidiary with the surplus, which is subject to corporation tax, covenanted to the charity (see below).

Reliefs by Concession

7.4.18   Because the unsatisfactory definition of section 832 of ICTA 1988 would catch activities which are traditional fundraising routes for charities, the Inland Revenue issued Statutory Concession C4:

> "Bazaars, jumble sales, gymkhanas, carnivals, firework displays and similar activities arranged by voluntary organisations or charities for the purposes of raising funds for charity may fall within the definition of "trade" in Section 832, ICTA 1988, with the result that any profits will be liable to corporation tax. Tax is not, however, charged on such profits provided the following conditions are satisfied:
>
> a. the organisation or charity is not regularly carrying on these trading activities;
> b. the trading is not in competition with other traders;
> c. the activities are supported substantially because the public are aware that any profits will be devoted to charity; and
> d. the profits are transferred to charities or otherwise applied for charitable purposes."

7.4.19   Contentious areas arise in the following phrases:

"Similar activities"
These are basically "small beer" events, but one charity's large event (and therefore taxable) may be another charity's "small beer". The Revenue is likely to look carefully at large events such as pop concerts.

"Regularly carrying on"
Once a year is regular, but the Revenue is more likely to regard frequency as regular, for example, an event which takes place more than three times a year.

"Not in competition"
A major gala at a prime venue with celebrities would be in competition with other theatres and therefore not within the concession.[18]

---

[18]See Inland Revenue booklets CS2 *Trading by Charities* and *Fund-Raising for Charity* for further guidance.

Tax-Effective Income

(i) Trading Profits

The problem described above of trading profits for a charity can, like   **7.4.20**
certain other sources of income, be treated in a tax advantageous
manner. A charity, having carefully reviewed its activities in the light
of tax, is quite at liberty to carry out any trading activities within a
separate legal entity, usually a subsidiary trading company, and
transfer any profit generated to the charity under a deed of covenant
as a single gift.

Covenanted payments by a company to its parent charity must be   **7.4.21**
paid net of tax, although the parent charity, if properly exempted,
will be able to recover the tax paid.

(ii) Other Donations

Companies and individuals (including individuals carrying on a trade)   **7.4.22**
can obtain tax relief for payment to a charity made under a legally
binding deed of covenant for a period of more than three years.

Companies can obtain tax relief for a single payment made to charity   **7.4.23**
under the Gift Aid scheme. For a close company (a company under
the control of five or fewer people) the gift has to be for at least £250
net, being treated as grossed up at the current basic rate of tax.[19] For
companies which are not close companies there is no limit for a single
payment. Such "gift" payments should be kept separate from
payments for "sponsorship" for which a return is expected. Although
the net effect of these payments for the company is the same, the
Revenue views them separately and applies different rules in
reviewing them. The company must, however, deduct income tax at
the basic rate and account for that tax under Schedule 16 to ICTA
1988. Failure to do so will result in loss of tax relief in respect of the
company's mainstream corporation tax liability.

Charity officials often do not realise that the tax mechanism for   **7.4.24**
company Gift Aid and covenant payments is different from that for
individuals in that companies always have to account for the tax on
these payments.

Individuals (including individuals carrying on a trade) can obtain   **7.4.25**
tax relief for a single payment made to charity under the Gift Aid
scheme. The gift again has to be at least £250 net (and is treated as
grossed up at the current basic rate of tax).[20] Smaller amounts have to
be covenanted over a four-year period.

Trading and investment companies and individuals carrying on a   **7.4.26**
trade can obtain tax relief by seconding staff to work temporarily for

---

[19]See Inland Revenue leaflets IR 64 and IR 113.
[20]See Inland Revenue leaflet IR 113.

a charity. Trading companies and individuals carrying on a trade can also get tax relief for payments made wholly and exclusively for business purposes but not of a capital nature, for example:

(1) small annual subscriptions to charities related to the payer's trade, profession or vocation
(2) small donations to local charities which benefit the payer's employees
(3) a sponsoring payment for a charitable activity if the sole purpose is to raise public awareness of the payer's product and such publicity is commensurate with the payment.

Payment under Deed of Covenant

7.4.27 A deed of covenant is a legally binding agreement and if the covenanted sum is not paid the charity is entitled to take action for recovery. However, in exceptional circumstances, such as unemployment, a charity could release a covenanter from his or her obligations for further payment. Covenants are terminated by the death of the covenanter.

7.4.28 The covenanter cannot receive anything in return for his or her payment, except for:
ordinary small membership subscriptions, where the benefits available are ignored if they are worth less than 25 per cent of the subscription; or, where a charity's main purpose is the preservation of the national heritage or wildlife, the benefit of the member's right of entry to view is ignored. In either case any literature distributed to the members is also ignored.

7.4.29 To obtain tax relief:

(1) the obligation to make annual payments must cover a period longer than three years (three years and one day is possible, for example April 5, 1991, 1992, 1993 and April 6, 1994, but usually covenants are written for four years);
(2) the payment made is for the net amount, *i.e.* what the payer wished to pay less the basic tax rate in force at the time of payment.

7.4.30 If the payer wished to contribute a specific gross amount, therefore, (s)he would actually pay the gross amount less the current basic rate of tax to a charity and the charity would then reclaim that tax from the Inland Revenue. Charities must be able demonstrate that covenanted payments have actually been received before the tax refund is met, and current annual accounts for the charity must be available for the Inland Revenue to peruse.

7.4.31 It is generally assumed that the payer must be a taxpayer, but this, in fact, has no bearing on whether the charity is entitled to repayment. If the payer has not paid income tax at the basic rate on at least an amount equal to the aggregate of the gross amounts of all covenant and Gift Aid payments for the year concerned, the consequence will be a tax bill for the payer. This will be either the whole amount of the tax or, if the payer paid tax at the lower rate only, the difference between the lower and basic rates.

Both companies and individuals can give a charity the benefit of an immediate lump sum, incorporating the tax advantages of covenants, by means of a "deposited covenant". Effectively, there are two transactions:

1.   an interest-free loan repayable in four equal instalments; and
2.   a deed of covenant for four annual payments, the net amount of each covenanted payment equalling one-quarter of the loan.

7.4.32

The loan must not be made before the deed of covenant is executed by the payer.

The annual repayments cover the net amount due under the covenant, and the charity benefits because it has immediate use of the total net cash covenanted, reclaiming tax each year on the "covenanted" payment.

7.4.33

Employees

By joining a payroll giving scheme (Give As You Earn), if one is operated by the employer, employees can agree to a regular deduction from their pay to give to a charity or charities up to a maximum (£100 per month from April 6, 1996) per tax year by payroll deduction. The deduction is handed over to an agency charity which will in turn pass it on to the charity or charities of the employee's choice. The deduction is made from the gross pay to the employee before tax is deducted leaving a lower amount of pay subject to tax, hence there is tax relief to the donor.[21]

7.4.34

Investment Income

Charities holding deposits in banks and building societies are entitled to receive such income gross before tax. This is not so, however, as regards interest and dividends paid by companies. When companies pay interest they must deduct tax at the basic rate and when they pay dividends the dividend declared carries a tax credit. Charities have to claim repayment of tax deducted (or payment of tax credit) and must fulfil the application test in section 505, under which the income must be applied "for charitable purposes only".

7.4.35

The mechanics are as follows: the interest on stocks and the dividends from shares will be paid to the charity in common with other stockholders and shareholders net after tax. However, the charity can reclaim the tax from the Inland Revenue using form R68. Since April 6, 1993 all dividends have a tax credit at 20 per cent as compared with the basic rate of tax, effectively reducing the tax reclaimable. In order that charities would not suffer a sudden drop in income, transitional tapering arrangements were established whereby between 1993 and 1997 charities can reclaim the 20 per cent plus a small fraction of the

7.4.36

---

[21]Inland Revenue leaflet IR 65.

net in order partially to compensate for the loss in income. The fractions are:

> 1993–94 1/15th
> 1994–95 1/20th
> 1995–96 1/30th
> 1996–97 1/60th.[22]

The time limit within which such tax can be reclaimed is the normal tax limit of six years except for the above transitional relief, where the time limit is two years.

7.4.37 Where charities are residuary beneficiaries of estates of deceased persons, they will either during or on completion of the administration of the estate be deemed under the rules in ICTA 1988 Part XVI (as amended by the Finance Act 1995) to have received income from the estate. No part of this deemed income will qualify for transitional relief because the dividends concerned were received by the executors, not the charity.

Capital Gains Tax

7.4.38 The Taxation of Capital Gains Act 1992, section 257(2) provides that a gift by an individual or a corporation to a charity or to trustees to be held for charitable purposes is exempt from capital gains tax as a disposal giving rise to neither a gain nor a loss. By section 257(3) of the 1992 Act a transfer of property from a trust to a charity is also exempt. Accordingly, where the source of a gift to a charity is to be property which carries an inherent taxable gain, it is better to transfer the property with the benefit of the exemption than to realise it and transfer only the net proceeds after tax to the charity. This is as true for executors as for individuals and trustees of a continuing trust, because executors will be taxed on gains arising during the period of the administration.

7.4.39 By section 256(1) of the 1992 Act, gains accruing to a charity and applicable and applied in furtherance of its purposes are exempt from capital gains tax. Transfers between charities are also exempt.[23]

Inheritance Tax

7.4.40 The Inheritance Tax Act 1984, section 23(1) provides that transfers of value are exempt from inheritance tax to the extent that the values transferred by them are attributable to property which is given to charities. By section 23(6) property is "given" to charities if it becomes the property of charities or is held on trust for charitable purposes

---

[22]See the Finance Act 1993, s.80.
[23]See Inland Revenue leaflet IR 75.

only. Under section 272, "charity" and "charities" have the same meaning as in section 506(1) of ICTA 1988. There is no longer a limit on the amount which may pass under the exemption.[24]

In principle, therefore, gifts to charity by individuals (by lifetime transfer or by will) and by companies pass free from inheritance tax. Transfers between charities are also exempt. Property held in trust for charitable purposes will not suffer the periodic charges imposed on property held in discretionary trusts for other purposes, nor any exit charge when assets are distributed, provided the assets are applied for charitable purposes only.[25] **7.4.41**

Various anti-avoidance provisions exist to prevent artificial advantage being taken of the exemption.[26] **7.4.42**

Stamp Duty

No stamp duty is payable on documents transferring assets or interests in heritable property to charities (Finance Act 1982, section 129). Documents should, however, be adjudicated. **7.4.43**

Abuse of Charity Tax Reliefs (ICTA 1988, sections 505, 506 and Schedule 20)

Tax relief may be restricted if a charity uses its funds for non-charitable purposes, or makes payments to overseas bodies without taking reasonable steps to ensure that their use is for charitable purposes, or makes certain loans or investments for tax avoidance rather than for the benefit of the charity. **7.4.44**

Schedule E — Taxes on Earnings and Benefits

Clearly persons "concerned in the management or control" of a charity should not themselves receive gratuities from the charity. They must not profit improperly from their position. Nevertheless, such persons may carry out administrative or specialist work for a charity for which financial reward is justified and is authorised by the charity's founding document. For instance, professionals such as lawyers and accountants can be appointed to a position of management or control and an appropriate charging clause be written into the charity's constitution or trust deed. As far as others who "work" for a charity are concerned, particular care should be taken in three areas: **7.4.45**

---

[24]The upper limit for gifts exempted from inheritance tax was removed in March 1983.

[25]Inheritance Tax Act 1984, s.58(1)(*a*).

[26]Inheritance Tax Act 1984, ss.23(2)–(5) and 56.

(1) employees on formal contracts of employment,
(2) sessional workers to whom a fee is paid,
(3) volunteers.

Employees on Formal Contracts of Employment

7.4.46 As with any other employer, charities with staff having contracts of employment are required to apply the normal Pay As You Earn (PAYE) and national insurance (NI) rules by making deductions on behalf of the Inland Revenue and Contributions Agency. Failure to do so could give rise to a formal determination by the Inland Revenue under section 49 of the Income Tax (Employments) Regulations 1993[27] against the employer or, if it is with the employee's collusion that tax has not been deducted, against the employee as well. Emoluments include wages, salaries, commissions, bonuses, tips and certain benefits in kind, as well as profit-related pay in excess of £4,000 per annum.

7.4.47 Normally all directors and employees earning in excess of £8,500 including any benefits in kind require to have such benefits declared annually to the Inland Revenue. However, directors of charities or non-profitmaking concerns are excluded from this requirement under certain conditions.[28] Commonly such benefits are meal vouchers in excess of 15p per day(!), use of cars provided by the charity, reimbursement above the accepted scale rate of mileage to an employee owning his/her own car, mobile phones and beneficial loans.

7.4.48 Dispensations for normal reimbursement of expenses incurred by staff "wholly, exclusively and necessarily" in connection with the charity's work can and should be sought from the Inland Revenue and will be accepted by the Contributions Agency.

7.4.49 "Pay" for national insurance purposes is broadly the same as that for income tax Schedule E assessment under PAYE.

Penalties relating to PAYE and National Insurance

7.4.50 There are stricter timetables coming into force for the submission of monthly tax and national insurance payments to the Inland Revenue, quarterly returns (P46 "Car") regarding changes in the provision of cars and fuel, and also the year end returns. P14, the employee's end of year summary (part of which is the P60), and P35, the employer's annual return, require to be in by May 19, and P11D, showing details of expenses payments and benefits provided,[29] by June 6, in 1996 and

---

[27]S.I. 1993 No. 744.
[28]Income and Corporation Taxes Act 1988, Pt. V, Chap. II, s.167(5).
[29]This applies to current and former employees earning £8,500 or more per annum and all directors irrespective of earnings, excluding directors of charitable companies. See n. 28.

July 6, from 1997. Failure to adhere to the timetable will trigger automatic penalties which, currently available, will be increasingly enforced by the Inland Revenue.

From tax year 1996–97 employers will be required to provide employees with their form P60 by May 31, following the tax year-end and similarly details of expenses payments and benefits by July 6, in order to enable the employee to complete the new self-assessment forms.   **7.4.51**

Sessional Workers to whom a Fee is Paid

It is important to establish whether or not the sessional worker is employed or self-employed. Ideally the sessional worker should produce a letter from the Inland Revenue indicating that (s)he is paying tax under Schedule D, Case I, whereafter (s)he should render an invoice to the charity for the sessional work carried out. There is a joint booklet (IR56/NI39) issued by the Revenue and the Contributions Agency which outlines the main points of definition as far as they are concerned. Common factors pointing to employment or self-employment relate to who controls the time and content of employment and who reaps profit or bears losses from the operation.   **7.4.52**

Many employers are justifiably wary of paying fees in full since they could be held liable for PAYE and NI they should have deducted if someone is later held to be employed rather than self-employed.   **7.4.53**

Volunteers

Volunteers are just that and should receive no emolument at all for work done. They can however receive reimbursement of legitimate expenses (supported by detailed vouchers) "wholly, exclusively and necessarily" incurred on behalf of the charity. If a volunteer receives payments which are in excess of what are deemed "reasonable" subsistence and expenses then the Inland Revenue will normally regard such payments as earnings.   **7.4.54**

"Volunteers" who do receive an emolument are technically employees or sessional workers as the case may be and should be treated as such.[30] This also applies to those in receipt of welfare benefits, even if the payments fall within the amount they can receive without affecting their benefit payments. (Those on unemployment benefit may receive a payment of up to £2 per day without affecting their benefit for that day or under £58 per week without affecting their benefit for the week,   **7.4.55**

---

[30]For an illuminating survey on payments to volunteers see Blacksell, S. and Phillips, D.R., *Paid to Volunteer* (1994), Volunteer Centre U.K.
[31]See Benefits Agency Leaflet IS 20, *A Guide to Income Support*, pp. 105–107.

and those in receipt of income support may receive a maximum of £5 or £15 per week, depending on their circumstances,[31] and must work for less than 16 hours per week if their income support payment is to remain unaffected.)

7.4.56 Volunteer drivers using their own cars are allowed to claim a tax-free mileage allowance up to a maximum rate per mile (depending on the car's engine size). A reduced rate applies for mileage over 4,000 miles in the tax year. Tax is only payable if the allowance received is more than the expenses incurred, in other words, if a profit is made. Further details are given in the Inland Revenue leaflet IR 122 *Volunteer drivers.* The mileage allowances described in the leaflet do not affect the special system which operates for volunteer drivers for the hospital car service.

7.4.57 Details of payments (emoluments) to "volunteers" must be maintained and if in excess of an annual amount (currently £100) within the tax year, must be reported on the annual return form P38.

SECTION 2 — THE VALUE ADDED TAX ENVIRONMENT

7.5.1 Value added tax (VAT) is in principle a simple tax whereby any business registered for VAT making a supply of goods and services adds value to the transaction. This value is taxed as follows:

sale £100 plus VAT at 17.5% = £17.50 = Total £117.50

cost £80 plus VAT at 17.5% = £14.00 = Total £ 94.00

surplus £20 plus VAT at 17.5% = £ 3.50 = Total £ 23.50

7.5.2 The £20 surplus remains in the business as profit and the net £3.50 is remitted to Customs and Excise. The total £117.50 is collected from the customer and the £94.00 is paid to the supplier. The amount of £17.50 is known as tax on "outputs" of £100 or "output tax" and the amount of £14.00 is known as tax on "inputs" or "input tax". The ultimate customer is unlikely to be registered for VAT and so bears all the VAT, that is, all the input tax charged (known to VAT officers as the "sticking tax"). The other businesses in the chain have only paid over their portion of tax on the value they have added. This is not as easy as it might appear.

7.5.3 Unlike Inland Revenue taxes, there is no exemption for charities from VAT. If the value of what are known as "taxable supplies" exceeds the threshold (£47,000 from November 28, 1995) the charity must register for VAT. Late registration can incur penalties. A charity can choose to register voluntarily in advance of the anticipated income from taxable supplies exceeding the threshold.

A diagram at this point will assist the reader to understand the complexities:

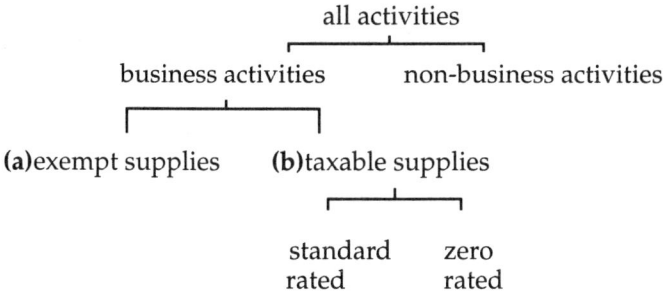

7.5.4

```
                        all activities
            ┌─────────────┴─────────────┐
    business activities          non-business activities
    ┌────────────┴────────────┐
(a)exempt supplies    (b)taxable supplies
                      ┌────────┴────────┐
                  standard         zero
                   rated           rated
```

Business and Non-Business Activities

First, the charity has to review all its activities and establish what are business and non-business activities. For VAT purposes business has a very wide meaning. It includes any continuing activity which is mainly concerned with making supplies to other persons for any form of payment or "consideration", whether monetary or otherwise. The activity must have a degree of frequency and scale and be continued over a period of time. Paragraph 12 of VAT Notice 700, "The VAT Guide", expands on the meaning of business.

7.5.5

An important case expanding the meaning of business was the *Morrison Academy* case.[32] In his judgment, Lord Cameron usefully summarised the meaning of business activity by saying that the school:

7.5.6

> "has every mark of a business activity; it is regular, conducted on sound and recognised business principles, with a structure which can be recognised as providing a familiar constitutional mechanism for carrying on a commercial undertaking, and it has as its declared purpose the provision of goods and services which are of a type provided and exchanged in the course of everyday life and commerce. Not only so, but to some extent the association is necessarily competing in the market with other persons and concerns offering precisely similar services to the same clients and customers."

It may be necessary to compare and contrast the Inland Revenue interpretation of trading with that of Customs and Excise.

Charities — Business or Non-Business Activities?

Examples of business activities are:

7.5.7

(1) Provision of services to a member for payment. (A subscription

---

[32]*Customs and Excise Commissioners v. Morrison's Academy* [1978] S.T.C. 1.

may be considered as non-business for VAT if the member receives no more than the annual report and accounts and the right to attend and vote at the AGM. In practice, it is also possible to provide the member with a regular newsletter.)

(2) Sales of goods including publications and services to clients, even for fundraising.
(3) Certain property transactions such as renting out.
(4) Admission to any premises or to any event for a consideration.
(5) Provision of consultancy or advice.

7.5.8   Examples of non-business activities for charities are:

(1) Voluntary services given free of charge in accordance with the charity's objects.
(2) Supplies made below cost for the relief of distress (at a subsidy of at least 15 per cent).
(3) Flags or other emblems given in recognition for a donation — flag days.
(4) Religious activities for which the clergyman receives an offering.
(5) Grants, legacies and donations given without any expectation of return to the donor (apart from a reasonable acknowledgment and a right to vote at the AGM).

7.5.9   If a charity's income is purely from non-business activities then it cannot register for VAT and there are no further VAT problems (except for paying VAT as a sticking tax on purchases or "inputs", and minimising the impact of VAT by taking advantage of particular "zero-rated supplies" relevant to its operations).

Business Activities: (a) Exempt Supplies and (b) Taxable Supplies

7.5.10   However, if there is any business activity the next point that has to be considered is whether, under VAT law, the activity and therefore the supply is what the VAT law describes as an:

Exempt supply
on which no VAT is charged; or a

Taxable supply
when it is taxable at zero per cent or at a positive rate.

7.5.11   If the activities of the charity are exempt, VAT is neither charged nor recovered on related purchases. If the organisation mainly undertakes exempt activities, or a combination of exempt and non-business activities, it is unable to register for VAT.

7.5.12   If, on the other hand, as stated earlier, the activities of the charity are taxable and the level of income generated exceeds the registration level, then the charity must register for VAT.

7.5.13   There is a third scenario which is very common for many charities, namely, where the level of taxable activities requires registration and there is also a substantial level of exempt supplies. This leads to a state of "partial exemption" (see below).

(a) Exempt Activities and Supplies

An exempt supply is determined by the business activity which itself is considered to be an exempt business activity as defined in VAT law. The charity has no choice in the matter (except for certain transactions concerning the renting of property).

7.5.14

Examples of exempt supplies generally include:

7.5.15

(1) many transactions related to land;
(2) rental income from residential buildings;
(3) insurance;
(4) postal services;
(5) education by schools, universities or certain other non-profit making bodies;
(6) financial services — bank interest;
(7) health services — provision of medical care by recognised professionals;
(8) lotteries and bingo, including raffles;
(9) provision by a youth club of facilities available to its members;
(10) burial and cremation.

Examples of exempt supplies specifically made by charities include:

7.5.16

Provision of welfare service otherwise than for profit
i.e. services directly connected with:

(1) provision of care, treatment or instruction designed to promote the physical or mental welfare of elderly, sick, distressed or disabled persons;
(2) the protection of children and young persons; or
(3) the provision of spiritual welfare by a religious institution as part of a course of instruction or a retreat.

"Otherwise than for profit" means that any surplus made is applied solely to the furtherance of the activity which generated the surplus. Cross subsidies to other charitable activities could jeopardise the exempt status.

Supply of goods and services by a charity in connection with a one-off fundraising event organised for charitable purposes by a charity

(1) Certain "one-off" fundraising events held by charities (or other similar qualifying bodies as defined) are eligible for exempt business activity. The exemption applies to all admission charges, sale of commemorative brochures, including the advertising space therein and other items sold at the event and sponsorship payments directly connected with the event.
(2) The type of event envisaged covers banquets, gala balls, film premières, theatre first nights and single-day concerts. A number of the same type of events can be held each year but they must all be stand-alone. Annual events of the same type also qualify.

Remember that the VAT guidance in connection with fundraising events should be read in conjunction with the Inland Revenue guidance.

(b) Taxable Activities and Supplies

7.5.17 Taxable activities and, therefore, taxable supplies basically cover all goods and services provided to U.K. and overseas customers, apart from those specifically exempted above. The rate of tax to be charged can be a zero rate or a standard rate (which currently stands at either 8.5 per cent or 17.5 per cent).

Zero-rated supplies

7.5.18 (1) Supply of most food (not hot foods and certain luxuries).
(2) Books, newsletters and certain other printed matter.
(3) Children's clothing.

7.5.19 Of particular interest to charities is a group of zero-rated supplies specific to them which include:

(1) Export of any goods by a charity.
(2) Advertising supplied to a charity when it is for fundraising or educational purposes.
(3) Sale of donated goods — charity shops selling donated goods.
(4) Video and refrigeration equipment for use in medical treatment, diagnosis and research.
(5) Welfare vehicles supplied to an eligible body caring for the blind, the deaf or the mentally handicapped for use in transporting those persons.

Standard-rated supplies

7.5.20 All those items neither exempt nor zero-rated.

Registration — Practical Steps to Determine whether or not to Register

Step 1

7.5.21 From a list of total gross income review the sources of income and categorise them for VAT purposes.[33]

(1) Non-business activity (or outside the scope of VAT).
(2) Business activity of an exempt nature.
(3) Business activity of a taxable nature, but at zero per cent.
(4) Business activity of a taxable nature at standard rate.
(5) Not sure (need to check) category.

Step 2

7.5.22 Total up all the business activities of a taxable nature, determining particularly standard and zero-rated activities.

---

[33]Income must be considered gross because it represents the total output of the charity; and zero per cent is considered to be a rate of tax, *i.e.* taxable at zero per cent.

Step 3
Has the total at step 2 exceeded the registration limit? **7.5.23**

If so, from November 30, 1994, the charity is liable to be registered for **7.5.24**
VAT at the end of the month where the taxable income of all business
activities in the year ended on the last day of the month has exceeded
the registration limit (unless the charity can satisfy Customs and Excise
that the taxable income in the next 12 months will not exceed a limit
just below the registration limit (currently £45,000). Notification of
intention to register must be made to Customs and Excise within 30
days of the end of the month in which the yearly limit was exceeded.
Registration will start from the beginning of the next month or such
earlier date as is mutually agreed.

The charity's own financial year is irrelevant; the totals required at **7.5.25**
steps 2 and 3 above are those for the current and preceding 11 months.
It is therefore important to maintain a moving annual total to monitor
the levels, particularly if the income over the previous 12 months or
less is approaching the registration level or if there is one month with
excessive income.

The "not sure" category must be analysed to fit the items into the **7.5.26**
other categories. It may be necessary to take advice either from
Customs and Excise (in writing) or from professional VAT advisers.
Early advice is essential to avoid penalties for underdeclarations found
later.

Above is only a summary of the legislation. A charity must review its **7.5.27**
own position individually with reference to the Customs and Excise
booklets. Those asterisked are essential for any charity registered for VAT.

700*	The VAT guide
700/1/94	"Should I be registered?"
701/1/95*	Charities
701/5/90	Clubs and associations
701/7/94	VAT reliefs for people with disabilities
701/10/85	Printed and similar matter
701/28/84	Lotteries
701/41/95	Sponsorship
706*	Partial exemption
731	Cash Accounting
742	Property

The booklets are regularly updated and available from a local VAT
inquiry office. Currently, Notice 701/6/86 *Donated medical and scientific
equipment* has been withdrawn for revisions.

Treatment of VAT Charged to Charities on Inputs

Having established which outputs are within or without the scope of **7.5.28**
VAT, it is now important to consider the status of the inputs to a charity
and how much of the input tax can be recovered by the charity.

7.5.29 A review of the diagram at paragraph 7.5.4 will help because input tax is claimable based only on taxable outputs.

7.5.30 As highlighted earlier, given the complexity of a charity's activities and consequently its income, it is highly likely that there will be a mixture of business and non-business activities, taxable and exempt (non-taxable) supplies, standard and zero-rated taxable supplies! This mixture leads to many charities being in the VAT position referred to at paragraph 7.5.12 and known as "partial exemption".

7.5.31 As it is not possible to reclaim VAT on supplies relating to non-business or exempt business activities and only possible to reclaim VAT on supplies relating to taxable activities, it will be important to maintain records in such a way as to identify VAT on purchases as they directly relate to income in the different categories outlined above.

7.5.32 It is possible that such identification will be required over four headings:

(1) VAT on purchases relating to non-business supplies — not recoverable;

(2) VAT on purchases directly attributable to exempt supplies **(a)** in the diagram will only be recoverable if *de minimis* rules apply. If VAT on purchases exceeds the current *de minimis* level, then none is recoverable;

(3) VAT on purchases directly attributable to taxable supplies **(b)** in the diagram will be recoverable in full whether it relates to standard-rated or zero-rated business activities;

(4) Non-attributable VAT, being the remaining "pot" of VAT which cannot be identified as attributable to the three activity categories above, will have to be apportioned and the portion which can be related to the taxable activity will be recovered. It can be a complex calculation to arrive at the percentage basis, but usually a basis will be agreed with Customs and Excise. The basis will be affected by the partial exemption *de minimis* rules: currently where VAT on purchases relating to exempt supplies is less than £625 per month on average and less than 50 per cent of total input VAT then such VAT, being below the current *de minimis* level, may be reclaimed in full. There is also an annual adjustment possible.

Specific Reliefs for Charities

7.5.33 As referred to earlier, charities are eligible for special concessions which enable them to buy goods at zero rate even although they are normally standard-rated. It is necessary to provide a certificate to allow the supplier to waive the VAT charge to zero if it applies to:

(1) Aids for handicapped persons.

(2) Vehicles and ambulances.

(3) Disabled access.
(4) Advertising.[34]

A Practical Guide to VAT for Charities[35] suggests steps to: minimise VAT paid on expenditure; minimise the VAT compliance burden; minimise VAT due on income; and maximise recovery on expenditure.

A further step is to avoid any penalties which can be incurred. **7.5.34**

Penalties

Through Late Registration

The net VAT which should have been paid from point of registration **7.5.35** plus 5 per cent of net VAT is incurred up to nine months late, 10 per cent up to 18 months late and 15 per cent thereafter. Reasonable excuse is possible, such as awaiting a reply to a written inquiry regarding registration from Customs and Excise, or death!

Through Late Returns (due within a month of the due date)

On an "accumulator" basis — after two late returns within 12 months **7.5.36** (a warning follows the first late return) a default surcharge of 2 per cent of the net VAT due is incurred, then 5 per cent, 10 per cent and a maximum 15 per cent for subsequent late returns, subject to *de minimis* rules. Non payment of VAT due can lead to assessment and ultimately seizure of assets by Customs and Excise.

Through Errors or Serious Misdeclaration or Underdeclaration

If the aggregate error is less than £2,000, correction can be made on **7.5.37** the next return; over £2,000 it must be voluntarily disclosed, paid, and interest will be due from the date when the error occurred. If it is not disclosed voluntarily, then a serious misdeclaration penalty plus the VAT and interest may be due when discovered by a Customs and Excise officer in the course of a VAT visit.

It pays to be accurate with VAT. **7.5.38**

SECTION 3 — NON-DOMESTIC RATES

Business Rates and Council Tax

Business premises occupied by a recognised charity and used wholly **7.6.1** and mainly for charitable purposes can apply to the local authority

---

[34]See relevant VAT leaflets for details and *pro forma* certificates.
[35]Sayer, K., *A Practical Guide to VAT for Charities* (1992), Directory of Social Change.

for relief from the unified business rate. The local authority will give mandatory relief of 80 per cent with up to a further 20 per cent discretionary relief available.[36] It is possible, therefore, for a charity to attain 100 per cent relief from rates. The additional 20 per cent relief may be awarded to non-profitmaking organisations such as schools, societies concerned with arts and literature and recreational clubs and societies. The relief does not extend to water and sewerage charges.

7.6.2 An important case — *Oxfam v. Birmingham City District Council*[37] — led to a change in the legislation over the interpretation of "wholly and mainly". The case held that Oxfam's charity shops were not wholly or mainly used for charitable purposes, but the effect of this case was overturned by the Rating (Charity Shops) Act 1976 which allows a property to be treated as wholly or mainly used for charitable purposes if it is wholly or mainly used for the sale of goods donated to a charity and the proceeds of sale are applied for the purpose of a charity.

7.6.3 Under section 22 of the Valuation and Rating (Scotland) Act 1956, as amended by section 21 of the Local Government (Scotland) Act 1966, churches, church halls and similar buildings belonging to a religious body are exempted from rates provided that the building's use is "wholly or mainly for purposes connected with that body and no profit is derived by that body from its use for any other purpose" (section 22(1)). The exemption is mandatory and the local authority has no discretionary powers. The exemption again does not extend to water and sewerage charges.

7.6.4 Council tax carries no specific reliefs for charities. The occupier, failing whom the owner, of property must rely on the general rules to take advantage of any exemption.

CONCLUSION

7.7.1 There are many benefits for charities in the tax legislation, but there are also many pitfalls and frequent changes in the legislation and differing treatments under the Inland Revenue and Customs and Excise régimes. Updates are essential and clear recording of income and expenditure vital to ensure maximum benefit to the charity. This chapter does not attempt to answer all the issues which may arise and detailed advice should be sought. We believe the facts to be correct at November 30, 1995 but they are, of course, subject to change in future budgets.

---

[36] Local Government (Financial Provisions etc.) (Scotland) Act 1962, s.4, as amended by the Local Government (Scotland) Act 1966 and the Rating (Charity Shops) Act 1976.

[37] [1976] A.C. 126.

APPENDIX 7:1

OTHER SOURCES OF INFORMATION AND SPECIALIST TEXTS

Assistance from the Inland Revenue, the Contributions Agency and Customs and Excise

From October 2, 1995 the above three organisations have joined forces to provide a "phone one for three" inquiry service for all business and employers (including charities) on tel. 0345-143 143.

Specialist Texts

Update Manuals and Books

Tolley's Charities Manual (looseleaf service) written and updated by Neville Russell.
Tolley's Tax Guide 1995/96, ISBN 1 86012 014 8.
Sayer, K., *A Practical Guide to VAT for Charities*, ISBN 0 907164 99 4.
Dymond's Capital Taxes (looseleaf service), Longman Group UK Ltd ISBN 0 85120 851 7.
Stair Memorial Encyclopaedia of the Laws of Scotland, Vol. 3, ISBN 0 406 237 034.

Guidance Notes produced by Accounting Firms

Binder Hamlyn Charity Unit
Moores Rowland Charities Unit
Sayer Vincent

Guidance Notes and Booklets produced by

Inland Revenue (FICO) Edinburgh   (tel. 0131-551 8127).
Customs and Excise   (tel. 0131-469 2000).
or the "phone one for three" helpline mentioned above.

CHAPTER 8

CROSS-BORDER ISSUES

8.1.1 The fact that there are different regulatory frameworks for charities under English and Scots law may cause problems for some charities and their advisers. Some of these difficulties have already been considered in earlier chapters. It is important, however, to deal with these issues in more depth and to present readers with other problems which may arise from the different treatment of charities in the two jurisdictions. The position is complicated because of the need to take into account both the long established tradition of charity law in England and Wales and the recent development of this branch of the law in Scotland. This chapter identifies some of these problems and attempts to suggest possible answers.

ENGLISH CHARITY LAW

Application of English Definition of Charity Law in Scotland

8.2.1 Legal practitioners in Scotland have had to live with some aspects of English charity law for a long time. This is because revenue law is the same in both jurisdictions. In order to claim tax exemption, therefore, Scottish charities need to demonstrate to the satisfaction of the Inland Revenue that they are recognised bodies engaged in charitable activities as defined by centuries of English cases.[1] The starting point for the development of English charity law was the Preamble to the Charitable Uses Act of 1601,[2] which defined "charitable" in terms of several categories. The courts later extended and updated those categories and applied them to charities judged to be "within the equity" (*i.e.* the general spirit or intention of the Act).[3]

---

[1]See Lord Wilberforce in *Scottish Burial Reform and Cremation Society v. Glasgow Corporation* [1968] A.C. 138 at 153-154.
[2]Repealed by the Charities Act 1960, s.48 and Sched. 7.
[3]See *Incorporated Council of Law Reporting for England and Wales v. Att.-Gen.* [1972] Ch. 73 at 87–88.

The Four Heads of Charity

There is no modern statutory definition of charitable purposes,[4] although in 1952 the Nathan Committee[5] recommended one based on the classification by Lord Macnaghten (namely the relief of poverty, the advancement of education and religion and other purposes beneficial to the community).[6] The tax privileges of charities are not the only benefits of charitable status in English law as charitable trusts are exempt from some of the technical rules governing the creation and nature of non-charitable trusts. The four categories or "heads" of charity, which are used in establishing eligibility for tax relief throughout the U.K., will now be considered separately.

8.2.2

The Relief of Poverty

Poverty, as defined through the cases, does not have to be absolute but covers those who have to "go short" as Sir Raymond Evershed M.R. explained in *Re Coulthurst*.[7] Thus, gifts to "indigent" or "needy" persons will come under this head as will donations to victims of a particular disaster such as the Lockerbie air crash or an earthquake. The recipients may be limited by other criteria such as locality or religion. The major restriction is that those who are not poor cannot benefit from the gift.

8.2.3

The Advancement of Education

The scope of this head has widened substantially since 1601 and today it covers most teaching and learning activity in schools and universities not operated for profit, as well as research likely to produce a public benefit. Vocational courses which are prerequisites for entry to professions are not covered. However, the teaching, studying and research activity does not have to take place within a school, university or other recognised educational institution. Thus, a trust for the promotion of the music of Delius[8] and one for the publication of law reports[9] have been recognised as charitable. Political propaganda is not charitable, however, and in *Baldry v. Feintuck*[10] the use of student union funds to campaign for free school milk to be restored was held not to be charitable.

8.2.4

---

[4]The definition of "charity" in s.96(1) of the Charities Act 1993 refers to "charitable purposes" but does not define these.

[5]*The Committee on the Law and Practice relating to Charitable Trusts* (1952), Cmnd. 8710, HMSO, para. 140.

[6]*Commissioners for Special Purposes of Income Tax v. Pemsel* [1891] A.C. 531 at 583.

[7][1951] Ch. 661 at 665-666.

[8]*Re Delius* [1957] Ch. 299.

[9]*Incorporated Society of Law Reporting for England and Wales v. Att.Gen.* [1972] Ch. 73.

[10][1972] 1 W.L.R. 552.

The Advancement of Religion

8.2.5 The requirement of "advancement" under this head has thwarted a number of apparently strong contenders for charitable status as it is not enough simply to set up a foundation with religious overtones; it is necessary for there to be an involvement in spiritual teaching and the maintenance of religious doctrines.[11] The interpretation of religion in the context of this head has become progressively broader over the centuries beginning with the recognition of other Christian sects apart from the established Church of England and moving on to embrace non-Christian religions.[12] Today it has been suggested that all that is necessary to qualify as a religion is some form of monotheistic deism,[13] but even the need for monotheism is now questioned[14] and the position of Buddhism was left undecided in *Re South Bank Ethical Society*.[15] This breadth of approach contrasts sharply with the narrower approach adopted in Scotland which is discussed later in this chapter. It has the merit of not discriminating against the religions followed by significant numbers of immigrants, but gives rise to uncertainty in the case of new or minority cults. Purposes related to the advancement of religion, such as the maintenance of religious buildings and the clergy, may also be charitable.[16]

Other Purposes Beneficial to the Community

8.2.6 This fourth head of charity is essentially a residual category and in practice it is used to give charitable status to gifts, purposes, trusts and other bodies which do not fit into even the most extended definitions of the other three heads. It must be shown that the purposes are beneficial to the community within the spirit and intention of the Preamble to the 1601 Act, or by analogy from the principles established by the cases. Since the criteria for this head are even less precise than for the other three heads, the courts are faced with difficult decisions in balancing the perceived benefits to the community of particular purposes against probable disadvantages, as in *National Anti-Vivisection Society v. Inland Revenue Commissioners*,[17] where the total suppression of vivisection was held not to be a charitable object because of its likely adverse effect on medical research. The consequence is that the variety of charitable purposes under this head

---

[11] See *Keren Kayemeth Le Jisroel v. I.R.C.* [1932] A.C. 650.
[12] See *Straus v. Goldsmid* (1837) 8 Sim. 614, Charities (Religious Premises) Regulations (S.I. 1962 No. 1421) and Charities (Exception from Registration and Accounts) Regulations (S.I. 1963 No. 2074).
[13] See *Bowman v. Secular Society* [1917] A.C. 406.
[14] See Warburton, J., *Tudor on Charities* (8th ed., 1995), Sweet and Maxwell, pp. 63-64.
[15] [1980] 1 W.L.R. 1565.
[16] See *Att.-Gen. v. Day* [1900] 1 Ch. 31 and *Re Forster* [1939] Ch. 22.
[17] [1948] A.C. 31.

is extremely wide, ranging from a non-profitmaking cremation society[18] to the provision of housing for the aged.[19]

The Public Benefit Requirement

This must not be confused with the fourth head as it is an initial **8.2.7** hurdle which must be cleared in all cases where a body seeks charitable status under U.K. law for tax purposes. However, this general requirement is differentially applied, depending on which of the four heads is in issue. This requirement is of comparatively recent development[20] and the hurdle is set at its highest in respect of education as the scope for manipulation for private benefit is greatest under this head,[21] while it is set at its lowest in respect of relief of the poor as a class.

Increasing Regulation in England and Wales

Charitable trusts are public trusts and enforced by the Attorney- **8.2.8** General in the name of the Crown, while the general regulation of charities, including the initial decision whether or not to register a body as a charity, is a matter for the Charity Commissioners, who were set up under the Charitable Trusts Act 1853 and had their powers extended by the Charities Act 1960. In addition, the Trustee Investments Act 1961 controls the investment powers of charity trustees. They may invest up to half of a trust fund in shares of certain companies quoted on a recognised stock exchange. Tax exemption and other benefits of charitable status have led to public scrutiny and calls for greater regulation to control abuse of that privileged status. Parliament has responded to public concern by increasing regulatory powers over charities operating in England and Wales. The 1992 Act extended further the regulatory powers of the Commissioners, particularly in relation to disqualifying certain persons from acting as charity trustees,[22] requiring charities to keep accounting records, imposing controls on professional fundraisers engaged by charities, and issuing directions for charities to change their names. The Charities Act 1993 is essentially a tidying-up or consolidation measure, which has superseded the 1960 Act.

---

[18]See *Scottish Burial Reform and Cremation Society v. Glasgow Corporation* [1968] A.C. 138.

[19]See *Re Glyn's Will Trusts* [1950] 2 All E.R. 1005.

[20]See Newark, F.H., "Public Benefit and Religious Trusts" (1946) 62 L.Q.R. 234.

[21]See *Oppenheim v. Tobacco Securities Ltd.* [1951] A.C. 297.

[22]See Chap. 1 for definition.

Powers of the Charity Commissioners

8.3.1 In considering the relationship between the two regulatory frameworks it is necessary to examine the English legislation, principally the Charities Acts 1992 and 1993, as well as the new regulatory provisions contained in Part I of the Law Reform (Miscellaneous Provisions) (Scotland) Act 1990 governing charitable bodies active in Scotland.

8.3.2 The starting point for these new provisions was the need to ensure that there was some form of cross-border co-operation between the appropriate regulatory bodies to maintain a check on persons or organisations attempting to exploit the different legal requirements of the two systems. However, the legal, terminological and historical differences between the two legal systems have led to problems in achieving this goal.

8.3.3 Some of the problems become evident from an examination of section 80 of the Charities Act 1993, which covers supervision by the Charity Commissioners of "certain Scottish charities". Subsection (1) lists the sections of the Act caught by this cross-border provision which will apply in respect of any "recognised body" which is managed or controlled wholly or mainly in or from England and Wales. The relevant sections are: section 8, which gives the Charity Commissioners a general power to institute inquiries with regard to charities or a particular charity or class of charities; section 9, which gives the Commissioners powers to call for documents and search records; section 18 (except (2)(ii)), which provides that if the Commissioners discover any misconduct or mismanagement in the administration of an investigated charity they may take certain steps, including the suspension or removal of any of its trustees, officers, agents or employees, if they are satisfied it is necessary or desirable to do so in order to protect or secure the proper application of its property; and section 19, which contains supplementary provisions relating to receivers and managers.

8.3.4 The problems start to emerge in subsection (2), which refers to a recognised body "managed or controlled" wholly or mainly in or from Scotland and to any person in England and Wales holding any property on behalf of that body or of any person concerned in its management or control. This subsection empowers Commissioners, in the circumstances set out in subsection (3), to make an order requiring the person holding the property not to part with it without their approval. This will arise where there has been any misconduct or mismanagement in the administration of the body, and where it is necessary or desirable to make an order under this subsection for the purpose of protecting the property of the body or securing a proper application of such property for the purposes of the body. Subsection (2) requires that the Commissioners are satisfied as to these matters and subsection (3) specifies that they must be so satisfied on the basis of such information as may be supplied to them by the Lord Advocate.

As well as the powers listed above, subsections (4) and (5) of section 80 give the Charity Commissioners powers, in certain circumstances, to vest or transfer property in or to a recognised body or registered charity. Subsection (4) provides that where "any person in" England and Wales holds "any property" on behalf of a "recognised body" (defined by subsection (6) as having the same meaning as in Part I of the Law Reform (Miscellaneous Provisions) (Scotland) Act 1990) or of "any person concerned in the management or control" of such a body, provided the Commissioners are satisfied, whether on the basis of information supplied by the Lord Advocate "or otherwise", both that there has been "any misconduct or mismanagement" in the administration of the body and that it is "necessary or desirable" to do so, they may make an order to protect or secure a proper application of the property for the purposes of the body. This order may vest the property in such recognised body or registered charity as is specified in the order, subject to the provisions of subsection (5), or require any persons in whom the property is vested to transfer it to any such body or charity, or appoint any person to transfer the property to any such body or charity.

8.3.5

The provisions of subsection (5) referred to above permit the Commissioners to specify in an order made under subsection (4) a recognised body or registered charity as "they consider appropriate", provided it is a body or charity whose purposes are, in the opinion of the Commissioners, as similar in character to those of the body referred to in subsection (4)(*a*) so far as is reasonably practicable. However, the Commissioners may not specify any body or charity unless they have received written confirmation from the persons concerned in the management or control of the body or from the charity trustees of the charity that they are willing to accept the property.

8.3.6

These provisions create potential problems of interpretation. For example, a key phrase in subsections (2) and (4) is where "any person in England and Wales holds any property". The first question to be addressed is the strange use of the preposition "in" as opposed to more widely used terms such as "resident", "ordinarily resident" or even "domiciled". How long do these persons have to be "in" England and Wales for the provisions of section 80 to apply? If they live in North Berwick but visit Berwick-upon-Tweed for a day will they be "in" England? Lawyers could make a good living from resolving these matters. Charities, however, could find themselves spending money given for charitable purposes on legal advice about the interpretation of this provision.

8.3.7

Of course, these legal perils do not affect most persons ordinarily resident in Scotland but only those holding "any property on behalf of the body or of any person concerned in its management or control" (subsections (2) and (4)). Presumably the courts and the Commissioners will take a sensible approach in such cases, but it would have been

8.3.8

more helpful if terms such as "resident", "ordinarily resident" or "principally resident" had been used. However, this raises other questions such as what types of property are to be included. For example, in strict law the account books or software records of a charity based in Dumfries would be its "property", so catching an accountant who takes them home to Carlisle, particularly if (s)he has taken the petty cash home too, but how strictly is the law to be applied? One hopes that the *de minimis* principle will apply. The issue of just who is in management or control raises further problems which are discussed in Chapter 4.

The Powers of the Lord Advocate

8.3.9   Cross-border problems are not confined, however, to issues about the interpretation of section 80, as it is also necessary to consider the relevant provisions of the Law Reform (Miscellaneous Provisions) (Scotland) Act 1990, notably sections 6 and 7.

8.3.10   Section 6 gives powers to the Lord Advocate to investigate charities and to suspend trustees, comparable to those found in sections 6 and 7 of the Charities Act 1960 (which are now contained in sections 8 and 9 of the Charities Act 1993). Under section 6(1)(*b*) the power to make inquiries extends to non-Scottish charities since it includes a registered or non-registered charity operating in Scotland. Section 6(13) defines "registered charity" as meaning a body which is registered as a charity in England and Wales under section 4 of the Charities Act 1960 (now section 3 of the Charities Act 1993) and "non-registered charity" as meaning a charity which, by virtue of section 4(4), is not required to register under section 4. In addition, section 6(1)(*c*)(iii) extends the Lord Advocate's powers of investigation to include non-registered bodies having any moveable or immoveable property situated in Scotland.

8.3.11   Section 7(6) applies to a registered or non-registered charity which is managed or controlled wholly or mainly outside Scotland but on behalf of which a bank or person in Scotland holds moveable property. The Court of Session may, on the application of the Lord Advocate acting on information received from the Charity Commissioners for England and Wales, make an order requiring the bank or person not to part with that property without the court's approval and such an order shall be subject to such conditions as the court thinks fit. This order will be subject to the provisions of subsections (7) to (9).

8.3.12   Section 7(7) provides that where the court has made an order under subsection (6) and is satisfied that there has been any misconduct or mismanagement in the administration of such a charity and it is necessary or desirable to act for the purpose of protecting its property or securing a proper application of such property for its purposes then, on the further application of the Lord Advocate, it may make an order confirming that order, subject to such conditions as it thinks fit. Thus, the court can act quickly under subsection (6) to "freeze" the situation and prevent moveable property belonging to the charity being dissipated. The court can then consider the matter more fully before deciding the conditions to be attached to any order it may decide to make under subsection (7).

Section 7(8) provides that where the court has made an order under subsection (6) and is satisfied as to the matters specified in subsection (7) if, in its opinion, the moveable property would not be applied for the purposes of the charity it may, on the application of the Lord Advocate, transfer that property to such body as the Lord Advocate specifies in the application. Subsection (8) requires this body to be either a recognised body or a registered or non-registered charity, the purposes of which closely resemble the purposes of the charity subject to the order. The charity to which it is proposed to transfer the assets must have intimated that it will receive that property.

8.3.13

Enforcement of the Legislation

The Lord Advocate and the Court of Session have a key role to play in enforcing the cross-border provisions of both the English and Scottish Acts. Thus, section 80(3) of the 1993 Act refers to the Charity Commissioners being satisfied "on the basis of such information supplied to them by the Lord Advocate", although subsection (4) adds the words "or otherwise" to the same format, suggesting that the Charity Commissioners may act on information supplied by others, for example, another recognised body or a registered charity. Similarly, those provisions of the 1990 Act affecting this area and discussed above require an application by the Lord Advocate to the Court of Session to give them effect, although section 7(6) appears to limit that power of application by requiring the Lord Advocate to be "acting on information received from the Charity Commissioners for England and Wales". The interaction of the Charity Commissioners and the Lord Advocate — in practice the Scottish Charities Office, a division of the Crown Office[23] — is of considerable importance in the implementation of the cross-border provisions and will be examined below.

8.3.14

The first situation to be considered is where a recognised body, as defined by section 1(7) of the 1990 Act,[24] is managed or controlled wholly or mainly in or from England or Wales. Section 80(1) of the 1993 Act permits the Charity Commissioners to exercise their supervisory powers under sections 8, 9, and 18 (except subsection (2)(ii)) and 19) just as if it were an English charity, although they will not be empowered to make schemes. These sections give the Commissioners wide powers, including a general power to institute inquiries, a power to call for documents and search records and to remove trustees, officers, agents or employees where there has been any misconduct in the administration of a charity. Subsections (4) and

8.3.15

---

[23]See Chap. 1, para. 1.7.8 and Chap. 5, paras. 5.2.1 *et seq.*
[24]*ibid.*

(5) give the Commissioners a jurisdiction corresponding to section 7(5) of the 1990 Act in respect of the protection of property belonging to a recognised body held in England and Wales, but it will be necessary for them to refer the matter to the Lord Advocate to take action under section 7 of the 1990 Act in respect of property held by the recognised body in Scotland. This provision will not apply to land situated in Scotland.

8.3.16 The second situation is where a recognised body is managed or controlled wholly or mainly in or from Scotland, but where any person in England or Wales holds any property on behalf of the body (or on behalf of any person concerned in its management or control). Here the key provisions are to be found in subsections (2) and (3) of section 80 of the 1993 Act as set out in paragraph 8.2.12. Where such a situation exists the Commissioners may make an order requiring a person not to part with such property without their approval, but they may do so only if satisfied on the basis of information supplied by the Lord Advocate both that there has been mismanagement in the administration of that body and that it is necessary or desirable so to do in order to protect its property or secure its proper application for the purposes of that body. Land in Scotland cannot be the subject of an order under these provisions.

8.3.17 The position of property requires further consideration. Where any person in England and Wales holds any property on behalf of a recognised body or of any person concerned in its management and control and where the Commissioners are satisfied that there has been mismanagement in the administration of that body and that it is necessary or desirable so to do in order to protect its property or secure its proper application for the purposes of that body then they may by order vest property in or transfer property to bodies with similar purposes whether or not they are recognised bodies or registered charities. The Commissioners may act on the basis of information provided by the Lord Advocate or otherwise for the purposes of subsections (4) and (5). These subsections do not apply to land situated in Scotland.

8.3.18 It is difficult to predict with any certainty how aspects of these provisions will be applied by the regulatory authorities or interpreted by the courts. These issues may be complicated by the differences in legal terminology between the two jurisdictions, particularly with regard to property, as well as the different regulatory structures. Conflict of law issues may arise in certain situations as where, for example, a trust has been established under English law but, before registering it with the Charity Commissioners, the trustees put it in the hands of the trusters' agents in Scotland who decide to seek recognised-body status under the 1990 Act and thus bring this trust constituted under English law within the regulatory provisions of the 1990 Act, including the appointment and removal of trustees. This would mean that a trust constituted in England would be subject to Scots law, contrary to the rules of private international law, while a Scottish trust caught by the provisions of section 80 of the 1993 Act would come under the supervision of the Charity Commissioners.

OTHER CROSS-BORDER ISSUES

Fundraising

Fundraising is often a cross-border activity and charities operating throughout the U.K. should conduct their fundraising on a consistent basis. An imbalance has arisen, however, with the introduction of fundraising regulations[25] in England and Wales with no comparable legislation for Scotland. This situation has given rise to fears, apparently confirmed by newspaper reports,[26] that "professional" fundraisers will move into Scotland to take advantage of this discrepancy, particularly as they do not seem to be caught by the cross-border enforcement provisions considered earlier in this chapter.[27] Where Scottish charities undertake fundraising in England and Wales they will need to comply with English charity legislation. As already indicated, section 80 of the Charities Act 1993 empowers the Charity Commissioners to act in the case of Scottish charities which are managed and controlled wholly or mainly in England and Wales, or which have property or other assets there.

8.4.1

Fundraising appeals in the U.K. media can cause particular difficulties because they are seen, heard or read in areas where the charity does not carry out its charitable purposes. This problem is particularly acute for Scottish charities as they frequently have English-registered equivalents competing for funds. Scottish donors may not realise that the charitable purposes of these charities do not extend to Scotland. This problem is exacerbated by the lack of regulation in Scotland in respect of misleading names, and this is considered in more detail in the next paragraph.

8.4.2

Names

Section 6 of the Charities Act 1993 empowers the Charity Commissioners to give a direction requiring a charity, other than an exempt charity, to change its name in certain circumstances. These circumstances include cases where the charity's registered name is the same as or, in the opinion of the Commissioners, too like the name of any other charity and where the name of the charity is, in the opinion of the Commissioners, likely to mislead the public as to the true nature of the purposes or activities of the charity. Details of what words in the charity's name the Commissioners are likely to find misleading are contained in the Charities (Misleading Names) Regulations 1992.[28] No similar protection for charities exists in

8.4.3

---

[25] S.I. 1994 No. 3024.
[26] See, for example, *The Scotsman*, May 19, 1995.
[27] This and other issues relating to fundraising are examined in detail in Chap. 9.
[28] S.I. 1992 No. 1901.

Scotland. Thus, the Royal Scottish Society for the Prevention of Cruelty to Children (RSSPCC) may have lost funding from individual Scottish donors as the result of a television fundraising advertising campaign extending to Scotland by the National Society for the Prevention of Cruelty to Children (NSPCC), which does not provide services in Scotland. The RSSPCC is now campaigning under the new name of "Children First", retaining its original name for formal purposes, but if it were to advertise in the English media there could be some confusion with the NSPCC or other children's charities registered in England and Wales. The Charity Commissioners have ruled that they can register every name under which a charity operates, whether it is a formal title or a working name,[29] but this ruling does not extend to Scotland and there is no comparable provision in the Scottish legislation.

Powers of Investment

8.4.4   This important area is one where the position of charity trustees is substantially the same in both jurisdictions. Section 100(5) of the Charities Act 1993 (formerly section 79(5) of the Charities Act 1992) provides that sections 70 and 71 of the 1993 Act (formerly sections 38 and 39 of the 1992 Act) apply to Scotland as well as to England and Wales. Section 70 permits the relaxation of wider-range investments as defined by the Trustee Investments Act 1961, and section 71 permits the extension of powers of investment, although in both cases an order has to be be made by the appropriate Secretary of State with the consent of the Treasury. The Charities (Trustee Investments Act 1961) Order 1995[30], which came into force on April 25, 1995 and which applies to charities in Scotland as well as in England and Wales, allows charities to invest up to 75 per cent of their assets in "wider range" investments such as equities and only 25 per cent in "narrower range" investments such as gilts.[31]

Accounting Provisions

8.4.5   The Charities Accounts (Scotland) Regulations 1992,[32] which came into force on September 30, 1992, were introduced before the revised Statement of Recommended Practice or SORP[33] was adopted as representing "best recommended practice" for accountants and auditors throughout the U.K. The English and Welsh regulations, which were issued in October 1995 for implemention on March 1,

---

[29]*Decision of the Charity Commissioners on Registered Charity Names* (1995), *Decisions of the Charity Commissioners*, Vol. 4, September 1995, HMSO, 22.

[30]S.I. 1995 No. 1092.

[31]Chap. 3 considers this in greater detail.

[32]S.I. 1992 No. 2165.

[33]Charity Commissioners for England and Wales, *Accounting by Charities: Statement of Recommended Practice* (1995), Charity Commission.

1996, were drawn up in parallel with the SORP and also differ in other respects from the Scottish Regulations. The Scottish Office is reviewing the Scottish accounting regulations in the light of these developments.

The question of branches, which may, of course, be in the "other" jurisdiction, has not been considered in the 1990 Act and ensuing regulations. Issues relating to branches and details of the requirements of the SORP are considered in the treatment of financial accounting requirements in Chapter 6. **8.4.6**

Designated Bodies

Certain classes of recognised bodies (namely Scottish charitable statutory corporations, local authority trusts and registered housing associations) have been exempted from the need to comply with certain of the accounting requirements of Part I of the Law Reform (Miscellaneous Provisions) (Scotland) Act 1990 by the Charities (Exemption from Accounting Regulations) (Scotland) Regulations 1993,[34] as have those religious bodies listed in the Charities (Designated Religious Bodies) (Scotland) Order 1993.[35] Details of these exemptions are contained in Chapter 6. The remainder of this chapter will compare the legal position of religious organisations in Scotland and in England and Wales. **8.4.7**

Religious Organisations

The Position under Scots Law

Section 3(1) of the Law Reform (Miscellaneous Provisions) (Scotland) Act 1990 gives the Secretary of State for Scotland the power to designate by order such recognised bodies as appear to have as their principal purpose the promotion of a religious objective and have as their principal activity the regular holding of acts of public worship. These bodies must satisfy each of the conditions set out in section 3(2). The first condition is that the body has been established in Scotland for not less than 10 years, although the Secretary of State can waive this condition in certain cases. The second condition is that the body can demonstrate that it has a membership of not less than 3,000 persons aged at least 16 resident in Scotland. The third condition relates to the internal organisation of the body with particular reference to accounting and auditing requirements (corresponding to those required by sections 4 and 5 of the 1990 Act). These must be imposed by one or more authorities in Scotland exercising supervisory and disciplinary functions over the component elements of a religious organisation. **8.4.8**

---

[34] S.I. 1993 No. 1624.
[35] S.I. 1993 No. 2774.

8.4.9   Such designation exempts these bodies from the following provisions of Part I of the Act: section 1(6) (the court's power to interdict the body and any person engaged in its management or control when there has been a failure to provide an explanatory document); section 4 (the duty to keep accounting records); section 5 (detailed provisions governing the preparation of accounts and reports) other than subsections (6)–(8) (the duty to provide on request a statement of accounts to the Lord Advocate or any person requesting it and the Lord Advocate's power to require that a failure to prepare a statement of accounts be noted for the purposes of section 1(3)); section 6(2) and (6) (suspension of persons in management or control); section 7 (powers of Court of Session to deal with management of charities); and section 8 (disqualification of persons concerned in the management or control of recognised bodies).[36]

8.4.10   An order made under section 3, the Charities (Designated Religious Bodies) (Scotland) Order 1993 (S.I. 1993 No. 2774), listing the designated religious bodies in Scotland, came into force on December 7, 1993. The Order covers most of the main Christian denominations in Scotland, although not the Methodist Church or the Baptist Church. The latter is excluded because its decentralised organisation does not meet the organisational requirements specified in section 3(2)(*c*) of the Act. Other denominations are excluded because of their failure to satisfy the membership threshold of not less than 3,000 persons resident in Scotland who are 16 years of age or more, which is contained in section 3(2)(*b*).

The Position under English law

8.4.11   This also requires to be considered since various churches active in Scotland, such as the Methodists, are registered in England and Wales, or are exempt from registration. Section 3(5)(*c*) of the Charities Act 1993, which replaces section 4(4) of the Charities Act 1960 as amended by section 2 of the Charities Act 1992, exempts charities from the need to register with the Charity Commissioners in respect of any registered place of worship. Certain religious charities are included in the list of "exempt charities" listed in the Charities Act 1993, Schedule 2 (replacing Schedule 2 to the 1960 Act) exempting them from sections 41 to 45 of the 1993 Act. Section 41 places charity trustees under a duty to keep accounting records, section 42 requires them to prepare an annual statement of accounts, section 43 requires an annual audit or examination of charity accounts, section 44 contains supplementary provisions relating to audits and section 45 imposes a duty on the charity trustees to prepare an annual report for each financial year of the charity.

---

[36]See Chap. 4, paras. 4.8.1–4.9.2 for further details.

CONCLUSION

The key issues raised by cross-border regulation have been discussed **8.5.1**
in this chapter. Inevitably, there may be difficulty in operating
interacting provisions between two jurisdictions with very different
traditions in this area. It might be argued that it would have been
simpler to have brought Scotland totally under the control of the
Charity Commissioners in view of the fuller development of English
law in relation to the control of charities, but as indicated earlier in
this chapter there are still unclear and controversial areas in the English
law of charities in spite of centuries of case law and statutes. Perhaps
the best solution might be to develop a new approach, adopting a
European perspective in the light of modern social concerns, rather
than a repealed statute of 1601!

CHAPTER 9

FUNDRAISING

9.1.1   Charities derive their funding from a wide variety of sources. Some obtain grants from statutory bodies, charitable trusts or commercial organisations. Some rely on membership subscriptions, donations, legacies, Give As You Earn schemes and deeds of covenant from members of the public.[1] Others engage in trading activities of various kinds, selling goods and/or services.[2] Most charities engage in fundraising activities of one kind or another. In the Nuffield study[3] only two of the interview sample of 50 said that fundraising played no part in their activities (because staff did not have the time to get involved in fundraising activities). The powers of a charity to solicit funds depend to some extent on its constituting document and this needs to be borne in mind when defining the objects clause.[4]

9.1.2   This chapter looks at the law relating to some of the most common forms of fundraising undertaken by charities: public collections, lotteries, disaster appeals, commercial fundraising and sponsorship.

CHARITABLE COLLECTIONS

9.2.1   Collecting from members of the public, whether in the street ("tin-rattling") or by house to house collections, is one of the most widespread forms of fundraising and is regulated in Scotland by district or islands councils[5] under section 119 of the Civic Government (Scotland) Act 1982 and the Public Charitable Collections (Scotland) Regulations 1984 as amended (S.I. 1984 No. 565). Section 119(1) makes it an offence for anyone to organise a public charitable collection without the permission of the relevant district or islands council. Local authorities have no powers to regulate collections taking place inside supermarkets, football grounds and other such establishments, although a collection in a shop doorway or outside a football club requires a local authority licence.

---

[1] See Chap. 7.
[2] See Chaps. 2, 7 and 10.
[3] See Chap. 1, paras. 1.1.4–1.1.5 and Chap. 11, paras. 11.3.4 *et seq.*
[4] See Chaps. 2 and 3.
[5] From April 1, 1996 the regulatory function will be taken over by the new unitary councils created by the Local Government etc. (Scotland) Act 1994.

The 1984 Regulations

The Public Charitable Collections (Scotland) Regulations 1984, made **9.2.2**
under section 119 of the 1982 Act, apply both to street collections
and house to house collections. They replace section 5(3) of the Police,
Factories etc. (Miscellaneous Provisions) Act 1916 and the House to
House Collections Act 1939, which were repealed by section 119(15)
of 1982 Act. Part III of the (English) Charities Act 1992 introduces
similar provisions for street and house to house collections in
England and Wales and will similarly replace the separate existing
legislation on street and house to house collections. No date has yet
been set for the implementation of the new regulations in England
and Wales.

Definitions

Section 119 defines "public charitable collection" as "a collection **9.2.3**
from the public of money ... for charitable purposes taken either in
a public place or by means of visits from place to place". "Charitable
purposes" is defined as "any charitable, benevolent or philanthropic purposes whether or not they are charitable within the
meaning of any rule of law" (subsection (16)). It does not, therefore,
apply solely to appeals by recognised bodies in Scots law or
registered and non-registered charities under English law, nor is it
confined to appeals which are charitable in Scots common law.[6]
The extension of the definition to include "benevolent" and
"philanthropic" purposes means that to fall within the regulations
an appeal need not necessarily meet the requirement of "public
benefit" but can also extend to other "good causes" such as money
raised to benefit a particular individual, for example, a sick child
requiring specialised medical treatment.

Application Procedure

Written applications under section 119 must be made by the organiser **9.2.4**
not later than one month before the date of the collection or within
such other period as the council may fix (section 119(3)). It is worth
noting that in practice many councils insist on much more than one
month's notice as they receive far more applications than there are
dates available and are loath to allow more than one collection on the
same date. Some councils place all applications on hold and make an
allocation in January each year. House to house collections are
generally requested immediately prior to a flag day or other street
collection.

---

[6]See definitions in Chap. 1.

9.2.5   Having received an application, the council must then consult the chief constable for the area and may make other inquiries as it thinks appropriate (section 119(4)). A council may also impose such conditions as it sees fit with regard to the date, time and frequency of the collection, the area in which it takes place, the regulation of its conduct and the type of collection box to be used (section 119(5)).

Refusal or Withdrawal of Consent

9.2.6   Reasons for refusal of an application are public inconvenience, a clash with another collection, if it appears that the amount to be applied for charitable purposes is inadequate given the likely proceeds, or if the organiser has been convicted of certain offences (section 119(6)). Normally the reason given will be the lack of an available date, although on occasion it is because a local authority finds that individuals rather than the charity are likely to benefit.

9.2.7   A council may withdraw permission or vary a condition if it has reason to believe that there has been a change in circumstances or a condition has been breached (section 119(7)). The council must provide a written statement giving reasons for refusal or withdrawal of permission (section 119(8)), and an organiser has the right of appeal to the sheriff not only against refusal or withdrawal of permission but also against any of the conditions (section 119(9)). Appeals by way of summary application must be lodged within 14 days of the decision or, where applicable, within 14 days of receipt of the reasons for refusal.

Exempted Persons

9.2.8   Under section 119(11) the Secretary of State, if satisfied that a person "pursues charitable purposes throughout the whole or a substantial part of Scotland", for example, large charities such as Barnardo's or Age Concern, may exempt that person from the offence of organising a public charitable collection without permission of the district or islands council. Section 119(12), however, states that persons so exempted shall (unless otherwise directed by the Secretary of State) give three months' notice of intent to hold a public charitable collection. The council does not have discretion to insist on more than three months' notice. Any discretion regarding the period of notice given lies with the Secretary of State. In practice exempted charities generally hold their flag day or other collection on the same day each year.

Exclusions

9.2.9   Section 119(1) does not apply to a collection which takes place in the course of a public meeting or to a collection by means of "an unattended receptacle kept in a fixed position in a public place" (section 119(2)). Peter Luxton, writing about similar provisions contained in Part III of the Charities Act 1992 which are due to be implemented in England and Wales, describes the latter omission as "regrettable", pointing to evidence of abuse in the use of such boxes.[7] He suggests that there should be a requirement that such boxes should be sealed or secured and also regularly checked and emptied to prevent the unauthorised removal of money.[8]

Duties of Organisers

The 1984 Regulations impose certain duties on the organiser of the collection. An "exempted promoter", defined as a person exempted under the terms of section 119(11) by the Secretary of State, must appoint a qualified accountant to act as auditor, and an organiser not so exempted must appoint an independently responsible person or a qualified accountant to act as auditor (regulation 2). The organiser may appoint an agent to carry out certain of his/her functions under the regulations (regulation 3). — **9.2.10**

Organisers or their agents are required to issue each collector with a certificate of authority bearing the name and address of the organiser and the collector, the name of the funds or organisation to benefit from the collection, the area and period of time within which (s)he can collect, as well as the signature of the collector and organiser or his/her agent (regulation 4(1)). — **9.2.11**

The organiser (or agent) must give each collector a supply of sealable envelopes or a numbered collecting box (regulation 4(2)) and must ensure that collectors are 14 years or over in the case of street collections and 16 or over in the case of house to house collections (regulation 5). Collectors must also be "fit and proper persons to act as collectors" and be aware of their obligations under the regulations (regulation 5). — **9.2.12**

Collection Requirements

It is an offence to collect without a certificate of authority and badge bearing the name of the organisation which is to benefit from the collection (regulation 6), although not all local authorities insist on a badge. It is also an offence to collect contributions except in a sealed envelope or collecting box (regulation 7). A "collecting box" is defined — **9.2.13**

---

[7]Luxton, P., "Public Charitable Collections: The New Régime" (1992-93) Vol.1, 1 *Charity Law & Practice Review* 37. Dr Luxton cites *Jones v. Att.-Gen., The Times,* November 10, 1976; *Report of the Charity Commissioners for England and Wales for the Year 1976* (1977), HMSO, paras. 26-9; and *Malpractice in Fundraising for Charity* (1986), NCVO, para. 5.35.
[8]*ibid.*

in regulation 1 as "a box or other similar receptacle which is securely closed and sealed so as to prevent it from being opened without the seal being broken". It must also prominently display the name of the funds or organisation which are to benefit from the collection. The envelope too must bear the name of the cause which will benefit and must be sealable with a gummed flap.

9.2.14   Collecting boxes or envelopes must be returned unopened to the organiser or agent who must either open them him/herself in the presence of another responsible person, or take them to a bank where they will be opened by a bank official (regulation 10(2)). Accounts in the form stipulated must then be submitted to the council by organisers (other than exempted promoters) (regulation 11) and to the Secretary of State by exempted promoters (regulation 12). Organisers must also publish a summary of the accounts in one or more newspapers circulating in the area, or, in the case of exempted promoters, a summary of the accounts must be published in one or more newspapers circulating throughout Scotland (regulation 13). Where a collection has taken place within the area of a single district or islands council, however, the requirement may be waived by the council, subject to a summary of the accounts being made available for inspection by members of the public.

Policing Public Collections

9.2.15   There are difficulties in policing public collections because of their frequency and because of lack of available police resources. In practice local authorities will warn each other about any dubious collectors (who are easily refused a licence given the excess of demand). Otherwise they and the police rely largely upon complaints from members of the public. Complaints are most frequently made about persons collecting without permission.

9.2.16   The requirement to publish a summary of accounts in newspapers is difficult to verify, and for this reason councils frequently prefer the option of having a summary of accounts available for inspection in their offices. They are also aware of the cost implications for charities of placing notices in newspapers.

LOTTERIES

9.3.1   Lottery activity in Scotland is governed by the same primary legislation as in England and Wales, namely, the Lotteries and Amusements Act 1976, as amended. This, together with subsequent regulations and orders, some of which apply only in Scotland, contains the necessary guidance for charities wishing to run a lottery. The introduction of the National Lottery etc. Act 1993 brought significant changes.

Definitions

There is no statutory definition of a lottery, but the criteria established by the House of Lords in *Reader's Digest Association Ltd. v. Williams*[9] are as follows:

> "A lottery is the distribution of prizes by chance, where the persons taking part in the operation, or a substantial number of them, make a payment or consideration in return for obtaining their chance of a prize."

9.3.2

Examples are manifold and include scratchcard games, local raffles and, of course, the National Lottery. Everyone should have an equal chance of winning the prize, and there should be no skill involved such that it removes the element of chance.[10]

The relevant lottery for charities will normally be either a small lottery or a society lottery. A third form of lottery referred to in the 1976 Act is a private lottery which permits the sale of tickets only to members of a society or people who either work or reside on the same premises, for example, an office raffle where no tickets are on sale to members of the public (section 4). Small and private lotteries do not need to be registered with any statutory body, although local authorities do sometime receive applications in respect of lotteries which qualify as "small". Even when it is pointed out that they do not need to register some prefer to do so to ensure that they are on the right side of the law.

9.3.3

Small Lotteries

Although small lotteries do not need to be registered they must be incidental to "exempt entertainments", which are defined as a bazaar, sale of work, fête, dinner, dance, sporting or athletic event or other entertainments of a similar character (section 3). Certain conditions have to be met which include the provision that the sale and issue of tickets and the announcement of the results must be carried out during the entertainment and on the premises where it is held. There is also a limit (currently £250) to the amount which can be spent on buying prizes and no money prizes can be awarded.

9.3.4

Society Lotteries

A society lottery is defined as including any club, institution, organisation or association of persons, and any separate branch or

9.3.5

---

[9][1976] 3 All E.R. 737 at 739; [1976] 1 W.L.R 1109 at 1113. See also *Imperial Tobacco Ltd. v. Att.-Gen.* [1980] 1 All E.R. 866 and *Taylor v. Smetten* (1883) 11 Q.B.D. 207.

[10]See *Moore v. Elphick* [1945] 2 All E.R. 155, which found that a football pool was not a lottery.

section of such a club, institution, organisation or association. Section 5(1) of the 1976 Act defines a society lottery as one which is conducted wholly or mainly for charitable purposes; for sports, games or cultural activities; or for other purposes which are not for private gain or a commercial undertaking.

9.3.6   In the case of all three types of lottery the whole of the proceeds of the lottery, after the deduction of expenses and cost of prizes, must be applied to the purposes of the society.

Registration Procedure for Society Lotteries — The Gaming Board

9.3.7   A "society" will need to register with the Gaming Board in cases where

(a)   the total value of tickets or chances to be on sale in any lottery is to exceed £20,000, or

(b)   the total value of tickets or chances to be put on sale, added to the value of those already sold or put on sale in all earlier lotteries in the same calendar year, is to exceed £250,000.[11]

9.3.8   It is the value of tickets put on sale rather than the final income which is the determining factor for registration. Once an organisation has registered with the board the 1976 Act requires it to conduct all further lotteries, of whatever size, under board registration until three calendar years have elapsed during which no lottery which would otherwise have required board registration has taken place. (A local authority wishing to promote a lottery must register with the board a scheme approved by the local authority.) The relevant application form and further information about the application procedure can be obtained from the board's lotteries section.[12]

Local Authority Registration

9.3.9   More frequently, recognised bodies in Scotland wishing to conduct a society lottery (where tickets are sold to the general public) will need to register with the licensing department of the local authority within whose area the office or head office is situated. The application process varies with each district or islands council. A registration fee at a level set by the Secretary of State (currently £35) is payable and thereafter an annual renewal fee, currently £17.50.

---

[11]s.3 of the 1976 Act as amended by s.48(3) of the National Lottery etc. Act 1993.

[12]Lotteries Section, The Gaming Board for Great Britain, Berkshire House, 168-173 High Holborn, London WC1V 7AA. The board has produced a helpful booklet entitled *Lotteries and the Law* which is available free of charge.

The maximum permitted price of a lottery ticket is £1 and the price of each ticket must be the same.[13] This means that inducements such as five tickets for the price of four are not permitted. A person can only participate in the lottery once the full ticket price has been paid, and this sum is not refundable. Prizes must not exceed £25,000 or 10 per cent of the total value of tickets sold, whichever is the greater, and no more than 50 per cent of the lottery proceeds may be used to provide prizes. This also applies in cases where prizes are donated, and the Gaming Board takes the view that the value of any prize should be based on the recommended retail price plus any relevant taxes but less any generally available discount.[14]

9.3.10

Every ticket and advertisement must state the price of the ticket, the name of the society promoting the lottery, and the date of the lottery (section 11). Regulations made under under section 12 of the 1976 Act further specify what must appear on tickets, including the name of the local authority which has registered the society. They also state that tickets may not be sold to any person under the age of 16 or be sold in the street.[15] A return certified by two other members of the society must be sent to the local authority no later than the end of the third month after the date of the lottery. This should show the proceeds of the lottery, expenses and prizes deducted, and the purpose(s) to which the proceeds were applied.[16]

9.3.11

IMPACT OF THE NATIONAL LOTTERY

The National Lottery etc. Act 1993 provided for the establishment of a national lottery in the U.K. Its launch as a weekly game in November 1994 was acclaimed as an outstanding success, with an estimated 58 per cent of the adult population taking part. "Good causes" receive 28 per cent of the takings, and of this charities receive 5.6 per cent. Partly as a result of misleading comments in various sections of the media, many members of the public mistakenly believe that "good causes" and "charities" are synonymous, and this has increased fears that donations from individuals directly to charities will fall dramatically and that the deficit will not be made up by the allocation of lottery funds.

9.4.1

Although it is too soon as yet to assess accurately whether or not these fears are justified, figures from a National Opinion Poll (NOP) survey have shown a fall in charitable giving since the launch of the

9.4.2

---

[13]s.11 of the 1976 Act as amended.
[14]*op. cit.*, n. 11.
[15]Lotteries Regulations 1993 (S.I. 1993 No. 3223).
[16]1976 Act, Sched. 1, Pt. II.

National Lottery. Figures released in October 1995 revealed that the proportion of the Scottish population giving to charities had fallen from 86 per cent in November 1994 to 74 per cent in September 1995, suggesting a net loss of £10 million to Scottish charities if the trend continues.[17] While Scots surveyed in September 1995 still believed that 19.1p in the pound of money raised by the National Lottery went specifically to charity, this figure did represent a fall from the March figure of 25.9p, and while 66 per cent of those interviewed in March thought the National Lottery was a good way of helping charity, this had fallen to 37 per cent in September 1995 (compared with a national average of 54 per cent). In October 1995 the Home Office announced that it too is to monitor the effect of the National Lottery on charities by looking at all their main sources of income before and after its introduction, and charities are hoping that any negative impact will be compensated for by an allocation of funds from the 12p in the £1 which the Government receives from the sale of National Lottery tickets.

9.4.3   Although not all charities will benefit from Lottery funding, and some, like the Church of Scotland, have objections of principle to applying for funding from this source, it would seem that not all eligible charities are applying to the National Lottery Charities Board. It was reported in July 1995 that less than 10 per cent of Scottish charities had requested application forms for the first round of awards.[18] Those which did apply did relatively well in the first round of grants, announced in October 1995. A total of 223 Scottish organisations received £17.6 million of the £40 million allocated by the Charities Board, with the largest single award of £666,177 going to the Strathclyde Poverty Alliance in Glasgow. However, in the same month as the first grants were announced, some leading charities reported substantial losses in revenue. The Royal National Institute for the Blind, for example, reported a loss of £500,000 since the introduction of the National Lottery, and a £90,000 deficit announced at the annual general meeting of the learning disabilities charity Enable was attributed at least in part to the effect of the National Lottery.[19] There has also been some criticism that groups benefiting from Lottery funds are not those which stand to lose from competition with the Lottery.[20]

---

[17]Figures from SCVO. The survey is part of a research programme by SCVO, NCVO and the Welsh Council for Voluntary Action, aimed at providing as accurate an estimate as possible of the impact of the National Lottery on charities.

[18]*Scotland on Sunday*, July 23, 1995.

[19]*Scotland on Sunday*, October 29, 1995.

[20]See, for example, comments made by David Mellor, M.P., as reported in *The Scotsman*, October 24, 1995.

DISASTER APPEALS

Another form of fundraising which may be charitable is that of an appeal made following a sudden mass disaster. In 1981 the Attorney-General issued guidelines on disaster appeals following problems which arose in connection with the Penlee Lifeboat Disaster Fund and, before that, with the Aberfan Disaster Fund.[21] There seems no reason why the taxation implications of the guidelines should not apply in Scotland. It is important to decide at the outset of the appeal whether or not it is to be charitable. Although charitable funds qualify for tax reliefs and donations to them may do so, they are essentially public in nature and cannot be used to give individuals benefits over and above those appropriate to their needs.[22] The public's generosity in the wake of a disaster frequently means that if all the donations were to be given to the bereaved and injured they would receive more than would be considered appropriate to their needs, particularly where the numbers of people affected by the tragedy are relatively small.

9.5.1

A non-charitable fund attracts no special tax treatment but does not limit the amount which can be paid to individual beneficiaries or impose other restrictions on how the money can be spent.

9.5.2

One solution is to set up two funds, one charitable, the other non-charitable, which would give donors a choice and also benefit not only individuals directly affected by the disaster but also appropriate charities. However, as Andrew Phillips points out,[23] it is important to make it clear which of the two appeals will benefit from a contribution if the giver fails to specify. Phillips also points out that the tax disadvantages of a non-charitable appeal may not be all that great since few of the donations will attract tax either by the donor or the fund, and tax on the interest earned on the fund can be negligible given swift administration (as in the Bradford Fire Disaster).[24]

9.5.3

COMMERCIAL FUNDRAISERS

There has been concern in recent years about dubious methods of fundraising and about the percentage taken by some commercial

9.6.1

---

[21]For an account of the difficulties which arose and for a description of a successfully managed appeal see Suddards, R.W., *Bradford Disaster Appeal* (1986), Sweet & Maxwell.

[22]For a further discussion of taxation issues, see Chap. 7.

[23]Phillips, A., *Charitable Status. A Practical Handbook* (1994), Directory of Social Change, p. 28.

[24]Phillips, *op. cit.*, p. 30.

fundraisers. For example, in the 1994 case brought against the Leukaemia and Cancer Children's Fund (LCCF) in the Court of Session, the Lord Advocate, Lord Rodger, described as "excessive" the 58 per cent retained by the fundraiser engaged by the charity, Ross Macfarlane Associates.[25] The fundraising agent was receiving at least 58 per cent of all money raised and in one month the charity received just 26.2 per cent. The Lord Advocate critised an arrangement whereby the fundraiser had complete access to a joint account with the charity which had been continually in debit. This, he suggested, amounted to mismanagement.[26]

9.6.2 The Charity Commission reported that 51 (or 17 per cent) of the 523 inquiry cases completed in 1994 were concerned with fundraising abuse. While the Commissioners were able to recover over £300,000 which would otherwise have been lost to charities, they point out that in many cases it is not possible to recover funds:

> "Often the most we can hope to achieve is to stop a bogus fundraiser from operating and, where there is sufficient evidence to show that a criminal offence has been committed, to refer the matter to the police. Preventing unlawful fundraising activities is, nevertheless, immensely worthwhile. Public confidence can be badly damaged by such activities and it is important that potential charitable donations do not fall into the wrong hands. We estimate that in 1994 our intervention saved the public from being defrauded of some £1.5 million."[27]

Fundraising Regulations

9.6.3 On March 1, 1995 new legal requirements came into force in England and Wales regarding the control of fundraising practice. Part II of the Charities Act 1992 introduces controls on fundraising activities by professional fundraisers and commercial participators, and the Charitable Institutions (Fund-Raising) Regulations 1994 (S.I. 1994 No. 3023) made under sections 59 and 64 of the 1992 Act, prescribe the form and content of agreements made between charitable institutions and fundraisers. The controls introduced involve (1) mandatory agreements in a prescribed form between charities and professional fundraisers or commercial participators; (2) mandatory disclosure of information to potential donors with regard to the proportion which will go to the charity; (3) refunds to donors in certain situations; and (4) the granting of injunctions to prevent objectionable methods of fundraising.

---

[25]Reported in *The Scotsman*, September 10, 1994.
[26]*ibid*.
[27]Charity Commissioners for England and Wales, *Report of the Charity Commissioners for England and Wales for the Year 1994* (1995), HMSO, p. 12.

The controls also prohibit professional fundraisers from soliciting for a charity except where there is an agreement with the charity to do so. The Charity Commissioners for England and Wales reported that in 1994 all but four of the cases where complaints about fundraising were justified involved either self-styled fundraisers who were collecting money for non-existent charities or for registered charities without the trustees' knowledge.[28] Under the new regulations trustees can now prevent the raising of funds in the name of their charity without their agreement. They can also put a stop to dubious methods of fundraising and to fundraising by someone who is not considered to be a "fit and proper person".

9.6.4

Any agreement reached between a fundraiser and a charity must indicate the proportion by which the charity will benefit and the fundraiser's remuneration. "Commercial participators", that is, those selling goods such as Christmas cards with the representation that a proportion of the purchase price will go to charity, and those providing services, such as charity credit cards, must also state the proportion which will go to the charity. There is also a right to a "cooling-off" period in respect of payments of at least £50 made in response to certain appeals on television or radio or by telephone.

9.6.5

The Situation in Scotland

The 1990 Act did not make provision for the introduction of fundraising controls in Scotland and the above measures are not part of the legislative framework governing recognised bodies unless they undertake fundraising in England and Wales. The fact that regulations were introduced in one part of the U.K. and not another[29] has led to fears that those wishing to exploit charities might move to Scotland. Concern has been expressed, *inter alia*, by the Institute of Charity Fundraising Managers (ICFM), established in 1983 to provide an individual membership body committed to the highest standards in the management of fundraising for "not for profit" organisations and charities. The Institute's director has said that he knows of seven or eight organisations which have moved north of the border specifically in order to escape the new controls in England and Wales and feared that more would follow.[30]

9.6.6

In an attempt to provide Scottish charities with some form of protection, ICFM, together with SCVO, has produced a voluntary code of practice which was published in May 1995. The Scottish Code of Fundraising Practice provides a framework of standards for fundraising in Scotland equivalent, in most respects, to those provided

9.6.7

---

[28]*op. cit.*, p. 13.
[29]Regulations on fundraising comparable to those introduced in England and Wales are to be introduced in Northern Ireland.
[30]*The Scotsman*, May 19, 1995.

by the English legislation and in certain areas imposing additional requirements. It contains no provisions corresponding to those outlined above concerning the prevention of unauthorised fundraising, but charities can, of course, report illegal or unacceptable activities to the police.

9.6.8 While the Scottish Code does not have the force of legislation, section 11 states that ICFM members who are professional fundraisers or commercial partners are personally bound by the Code and should do all in their power to ensure that charities which employ them adhere to the Code too.[31] Fundraisers, commercial partners and other advisers who are not ICFM members are also invited to support the Code. It is recommended that agreements should contain a provision for the non-charity party to the agreement to guarantee that all their fundraising activities or commercial partnership promotions are undertaken in compliance with the Code.

9.6.9 The term "charity" as used in the Code is not confined to charities registered in England and Wales and recognised bodies in Scotland; it also extends to "other bodies established for charitable, benevolent or philanthropic purposes". In including benevolent or philanthropic purposes the Code follows the definition in the (English) 1992 Act of "charitable institution" as "a charity or an institution (other than a charity) which is established for charitable, benevolent or philanthropic purposes"[32] and also the definition in section 119 of the Civic Government (Scotland) Act 1982.

Commercial Fundraisers and the Scottish Code

9.6.10 The Scottish Code of Fundraising Practice follows Part II of the (English) Charities Act 1992 in not seeking to regulate fundraising by charities on their own account or through connected companies under a charity's direct control. It does not, therefore, apply to in-house fundraisers employed by a charity or to a charity's trading companies. This is regretted by some, who fear that less reputable commercial fundraisers may try to escape the disclosure requirements by forming their own charities and employing themselves as in-house fundraisers at high salaries.[33] The Code does make it clear, however, that charities operating on their own account are expected to uphold the spirit of

---

[31]ICFM has over 1,600 members, working either within or for voluntary organisations in a fundraising capacity. Over 100 national, regional and local charities are affiliated to ICFM. All members agree, as a prerequisite to membership, to abide by its Code of Conduct and various codes of practice and guidance notes.

[32]s.58(1)(*b*) of the Charities Act 1992. The 1992 Act continues to govern fundraising in England and Wales because the relevant provisions were not carried forward into the consolidating Act, the Charities Act 1993.

[33]See Luxton, P., "Control of Fund-raising for Charitable Institutions: The New Law" (1992-93) Vol.1, 2 *Charity Law & Practice Review* 149.

the Code in all cases where its provisions would apply were a third party involved (section 5). It also refers to other ICFM Codes of Practice which apply throughout the U.K.[34]

Definitions

"Fundraising business" is defined as "a business carried on for gain and wholly or primarily engaged in soliciting money or property for charitable purposes".

9.6.11

A "professional fundraiser" is "a person (other than a charitable institution or a connected company) who carries on a fundraising business or who otherwise, for gain, solicits money or property for the benefit of a charity or to be applied to charitable purposes".[35]

9.6.12

As well as excluding a charity's own in-house fundraisers and connected companies and their employees, the definition also excludes those who receive only a small honorarium for their fundraising activities (anyone not paid more than £5 per day or more than £500 per annum). This provision therefore excludes volunteers who receive a small payment.

9.6.13

Potential donors must be advised of the means by which a fundraiser will be remunerated (normally a percentage of monies raised) and the way in which this is to be done must be agreed before donors are approached.

9.6.14

The Scottish Code also stipulates that verbal solicitations made by professional fundraisers, whether face-to-face, by telephone or via a broadcast appeal, should make it clear that the fundraiser is being paid by the charity concerned and also indicate in general terms the method by which the remuneration is calculated. In the case of promotions by commercial partners the method by which the contribution to the charity is to be calculated must likewise be stated, and where more than one charity is to benefit the proportion which each will receive.

9.6.15

The Scottish Code also follows the 1992 Act in providing for a "cooling off" period for credit card donations of more than £50 in cases where a broadcast appeal is made by a professional fundraiser.[36] It also provides for a right to a refund (less expenses) for donations solicited via the telephone by a professional fundraiser. All those making a

9.6.16

---

[34]These are: *Guidance Notes and Standard Form of Contract for dealing with Consultants; Code of Practice on Lotteries; Code of Practice on Reciprocal Mailing; Code of Practice on Schools; Code of Practice on Telephone Recruitment of Collectors; Guidance Notes on the Management of Static Collecting Boxes; Code of Practice on House to House Collections; Code of Practice on Outbound Telephone Support.*

[35]s.58(1) of the 1992 Act, as amended by s.25 of the Deregulation and Contracting Out Act 1994.

[36]Although para. 8.2 refers to "donations of £50 or more", the relevant Appendix (6) refers to payment of more than £50.

payment of more than £50 by whatever means must be given a written statement informing them of their right to a refund.

COMMERCIAL SPONSORSHIP

9.7.1   Another form of commercial involvement governed by the fundraising regulations made under the Charities Act 1992 is sponsorship, and the Scottish Code also seeks to address this issue.

Definition

9.7.2   A "commercial partner" (the equivalent of "commercial participator" in the 1992 Act) is defined as "any person or company carrying on a business which is not a fundraising business and who in the course of that business carries out an advertising, sales or other promotional campaign during which it is represented that contributions will be made to a charity or applied to charitable purposes".

9.7.3   The question of whether or not a charity's trading company was a commercial participator as defined in section 58(1) of the Charities Act 1992 was resolved by section 25(2) of the Deregulation and Contracting Out Act 1994 which amended the original definition to exclude a company connected with the institution. By stating that "commercial partner" in the Code is the equivalent to "commercial participator" in the 1992 Act the Code is presumably following the amended definition and intends it to apply to a commercial organisation otherwise unconnected to the charity which in the course of its business states that part of the proceeds of its sales or services will be donated to a charity.

Agreements between Charities and Commercial Organisations

9.7.4   Section 6 of the Code deals with the requirement for agreements between charities and fundraisers and/or commercial partners. The minimum requirements are described in section 4 of the Appendix and generally follow those set out in sections 2 and 3 of the 1994 Regulations in England and Wales, with certain additions. Importantly, the Scottish Code also extends the requirement for a written agreement to external advisers as well as fundraisers and commercial partners, pointing out that as a matter of good governance charities should have written agreements with all outside consultants and advisers, whether paid or unpaid, on fundraising and marketing issues, whether or not the outside parties will be directly soliciting money or goods on the charity's behalf.[37] Section 6 also imposes a duty on trustees

---

[37]para. 6.1.

and/or directors to ensure that clear lines of authority exist establishing who may sign contracts on behalf of the charity.

As well as requiring that an agreement shall specify the amount of remuneration and expenses which a fundraiser or adviser will be entitled to receive and the way in which the amount is to be determined, the Code also requires a specification of the terms under which money and property raised by a fundraiser or commercial partner are to be transferred to the charity or charities which are party to the agreement. The Code imposes a general duty on charities to ensure that agreements contain a clear statement of costs and likely returns so that potential risks and liabilities are understood by the charity. There have been several instances of fundraising events losing rather than making money and the Code is clearly seeking to minimise the risk of such an eventuality.

9.7.5

Payment of Sums Due

The Code states that all monies received on behalf of a charity should be paid forthwith into a bank or building society account directly controlled by the charity or be paid directly over to an appropriate officer of the charity. Where money or other property goes first to the fundraiser or commercial partner it should be passed over to the charity within 28 days or sooner, unless specifically otherwise provided for by agreement. In the case of fundraising businesses and professional fundraisers monies should be paid over gross without prior deduction of expenses.[38]

9.7.6

Fundraising for general charitable purposes[39] is discouraged by the Scottish Code, except where an appeal is made by recognised press and broadcasting media or by formally constituted non-profit organisations. In such cases an appeal should be accompanied by an explanatory statement clarifying how it will be determined which charitable purposes will benefit, whether any expenses will be deducted (and if so, how they will be calculated) and when the monies will be paid over. Charities are advised to discourage any other parties from soliciting funds in this way.

9.7.7

Potential Problems

Both the 1992 Act and the Scottish Code use the phrase "in general terms" in connection with the method by which a fundraiser's remuneration or a commercial partner's charitable contribution is to be calculated. However, section 7 of the Code strongly recommends

9.7.8

---

[38] s.9.

[39] That is, where money is solicited not for the benefit of a specific charity but for some general purpose, such as helping the homeless.

that the statement indicates "as accurately as possible the exact amount or proportion of the contribution to be made to the benefiting charity or charities" and states that the wording of the statement should be part of the agreement between the parties. Home Office guidelines likewise recommend that an exact percentage or amount should be included in the statement and where this is impossible that a minimum contribution should be stipulated.[40]

9.7.9   The words "in general terms" were not in the original Bill, but it was recognised that it would be impossible in many cases to include details of the exact proportion of each sale which would go to charity. A principal reason for this is because agreements between charities and commercial partners and fundraisers are frequently made via a trading subsidiary, which has to meet its own overheads before covenanting its profits to the charity. For example, a manufacturer may agree to donate a percentage of the sale price of certain goods but will be unable to predict with any accuracy how many will be sold.

9.7.10   If the agreement is not made via a trading subsidiary then the charity is in danger of carrying out non-charitable trading activity. Such activity is not covered by the exemptions from income tax as contained in section 505 of the Corporation Taxes Act 1989.[41] Noting that payments to charities for promoting commercial products are usually taxable, the Charity Commissioners' leaflet *Charities and Fundraising* (the principles of which are also followed by the Inland Revenue in Scotland) states that direct tax will be avoided only if the relationship between the charity and the commercial product is a purely passive one, that is, if the charity provides nothing material in return.[42]

CONCLUSION

9.8.1   There is a variety of legislation governing the various methods of fundraising for charities as outlined in this chapter and in Chapter 7, but as far as both public collections and society lotteries are concerned, it will generally be to the local authority that application should be made and each authority has an established procedure and set of regulations for the guidance of charities. Once an initial application has been made future applications will normally be a matter of routine.

9.8.2   While legislation in England and Wales will soon introduce provisions similar to those in Scotland for public collections in that jurisdiction,

---

[40]*Charitable Fundraising: Professional and Commercial Involvement* (1995), HMSO.

[41]See Chap. 7, paras. 7.4.15 *et seq.*

[42]Charities are advised to seek advice from the Inland Revenue before entering into an arrangement of that kind.

and the law governing lotteries, like tax law, is already the same throughout the U.K., the disparity in the law governing commercial fundraisers and sponsors is a cause for some concern. It is difficult to see how the Scottish Code of Fundraising Practice can be as effective as the regulations in England and Wales which have the force of law, and while ICFM members must comply as a condition of membership, it remains to be seen whether non-members will adhere to the Code. It is unfortunate that the 1990 Act did not make provision for fundraising regulations to be made so that Scottish charitable givers could enjoy the same protection from fraud and mismanagement as their English, Welsh and Northern Irish neighbours.

CHAPTER 10

CHARITIES AND THE CONTRACT CULTURE

10.1   The aim of this chapter is to provide an overview of the legal consequences for charities of their increasing involvement with formal contracts. It briefly explains the background to this development and outlines the implications which the particular legal situation of charities has for the formation and management of contracts. It then discusses some of the main practical problems which have arisen for charities and looks in detail at some of the particular provisions of service contracts. The use of contracts has grown far faster than the ability of many charities (and indeed funders) to understand and deal with their many legal consequences. This chapter is intended to assist charities and those who represent charities to ensure that contracts are negotiated, drafted and monitored in a reasonable and competent manner.

WHAT IS THE CONTRACT CULTURE?

10.2.1   The phrase "the Contract Culture" has gained wide currency within the voluntary and public sectors.[1] It has been used to describe a number of different, but related, developments. These include:

(1)   the move by bodies such as local authorities and Scottish Homes away from acting as "providers" to becoming "enablers": from directly providing services such as housing and community care to contracting with private and voluntary bodies for these services;

(2)   a desire for greater clarity in the roles and responsibilities of the various people and agencies involved in delivering public services (both from funders concerned with value for money and charity trustees concerned with their own potential liability);

(3)   an increased emphasis on tendering by charities to provide a service whose remit is predefined by funders rather than by the charity itself.

---

[1]For the origins of this phrase, see Davies and Edwards, *Twelve Charity Contracts*(1990) .

Historical Background

The rise of the contract culture reflects the major shifts in the welfare **10.2.2** state which occurred in the 1980s, both in the United Kingdom and internationally.[2] Before then, it was generally assumed that charities would play a limited and marginal role in the provision of welfare services, which would principally be provided by central and local government.[3] The roles of charities were defined as advocating for clients, pioneering new and innovative ways of responding to need which would ultimately be adopted by other providers, and providing "extras" above what the state could reasonably afford.

This ideological model was replaced by one which saw charities as **10.2.3** potential large-scale providers of public services. This, it was argued, would benefit service users by challenging the perceived inefficiency and remoteness of the public sector and promoting diversity and choice. While these developments offer new opportunities for charities, they have been viewed with some concern by the voluntary sector. There are fears that the sector's distinctive values could be eroded.[4]

The Government's White Paper on Community Care[5] stated as one **10.2.4** of its key objectives: "to promote the development of a flourishing independent sector". Social work departments are moving to become enabling agencies, focussing on assessing individual and overall need, planning and commissioning services to meet that need, and monitoring the quality of those services. (In some ways, this mirrors the purchasing role of health boards in the NHS reforms.)[6]

In residential and nursing care independent agencies are entitled to a **10.2.5** greater degree of DSS subsidy than either local authority or NHS-run homes. This has led in some cases to the creation of more or less "arm's length" charitable bodies to manage care homes formerly run by social work departments or health boards.

In housing, the Scottish Special Housing Association, which owned **10.2.6** and managed public housing, was replaced by Scottish Homes which

---

[2]See Kühnle, S. and Selle, P., *Government and Voluntary Organisations* (1992), Avebury.

[3]Wolfenden, J., *The Future of Voluntary Organisations: Report of the Wolfenden Committee* (1977), Croom Helm.

[4]*The Contract Culture — The Challenge for Voluntary Organisations* (1989), NCVO.

[5]*Caring for People — Community Care in the next decade and beyond* (1989), Cm. 849, HMSO, para. 1.11.

[6]NHS and Community Care Act 1990, Pt. II and *Working for Patients* (1989), Cm. 555, HMSO.

funds a network of independent housing associations. Housing associations are governed by the provisions of the Friendly Societies Acts 1974 and 1992. Although they could be characterised as non-profitmaking, they are generally not recognised bodies within the terms of the Law Reform (Miscellaneous Provisions) (Scotland) Act 1990. The role of independent housing bodies in the rental sector has also increased with the reduced significance of local authority housing through the sale of council houses to tenants.

10.2.7   In training and employment, the Department of Employment and local enterprise companies increasingly look to charities to provide programmes, particularly for people with special needs. Charities have also entered into contracts to provide training through European Community initiatives such as the European Social Fund.

10.2.8   Even social security has seen some moves away from State and towards charitable provision, such as the creation of the Independent Living Fund, a State-funded charitable trust to support disabled people.[7]

10.2.9   Charities have an advantage over statutory bodies in that their activities are less circumscribed by statute. A charity may provide a combination of different services in a way which a single-purpose department cannot. Increasingly, this will involve the charity in contracts with several different agencies.

10.2.10 Thus a mental health charity, for example, may contract with a housing association to obtain housing which it then provides to residents referred under contracts with health boards and social work departments. The residents may undertake employment and training under contracts with the local enterprise company, the Department of Employment, and possibly the local further education college.

10.2.11 The creation of new unitary authorities, often much smaller than the previous regional councils, may also mean that social work and education departments will turn increasingly to charities for specialised services, and those charities will have to negotiate with more local authorities.

---

[7]The history of this fund exemplifies many of the dilemmas for charities in these developments. Initially, there was considerable hostility to the fund as a derogation from the principle of universal entitlements. However, some disability organisations become involved in administering the fund and it became a successful means of providing flexible packages to support independent living. Nevertheless, this success (and therefore the cost of continuing the fund) contributed to the government replacing it by two new schemes with much more restricted discretion, the Independent Living (Extension) Fund and the Independent Living (1993) Fund.

CONTRACTS AND CHARITY LAW

Powers of Charities

A charity can only engage in contracts to the extent to which it is **10.3.1**
explicitly or implicitly authorised so to do by its constituting document
(whether a constitution, memorandum and articles of association or
trust deed) or by statute.[8]

Any contract must fulfil or be reasonably incidental to the stated **10.3.2**
purposes of the charity. Where the charity has as one of its main
purposes the provision of a service to a particular group and the
contract pertains to this it should not be difficult to satisfy this
requirement.

It has been suggested[9] that the requirement for a charity's activities to **10.3.3**
be directed to public rather than private benefit could call into question
the legitimacy of some contracts. The case law in this area is complex
and it is difficult to give clear guidance. The basic principle is that a
charity must benefit the community or an appreciably important class
of the community and not private individuals, or even a fluctuating
body of private individuals.[10] However, it is submitted that where a
contract relates to a small group or even one person (*e.g.* a contract to
provide a residential place or training opportunity for an individual)
this should be considered in the context of the overall service provided,
and other contracts entered into by the charity.

Most modern constituting documents will contain clear powers to **10.3.4**
enter into contracts with a range of bodies in order to fulfil the stated
purpose of the charity. (Where a charity is part of a group or network
this might be limited geographically, for instance to local authorities
within the particular charity's area.) Even if such a power is not
explicitly stated it can probably be implied where the activity to be
undertaken under the contract would fulfil the charity's purpose.
Nevertheless, a potentially lucrative contract which took up a
substantial part of the charity's time and effort and which did not
directly relate to the charitable aims of the organisation would not be
acceptable, however the profits were used. The charity would have
ceased to be established or be operating for charitable purposes only.[11]

---

[8]See Chaps. 2 and 3.

[9]Warburton, J. and Morris, D., "Charities and the Contract Culture" (1991)
55 *The Conveyancer* 419. See also Chaps. 1 and 8 for discussion of the public
benefit requirement.

[10]See *Blair v. Duncan* (1901) 4.F (H.L.) 1; *McCaig v. University of Glasgow*,
1907 S.C. 231; *Aitken's Trs. v. Aitken*, 1927 S.C. 374; and *Salvesen's Trs. v. Wye*,
1954 S.C. 440.

[11]*Inland Revenue v. Falkirk Temperance Cafe Trust*, 1927 S.C. 261; *Tennent Plays
Ltd. v. IRC* [1948] All E.R. 506, esp. Cohen L.J. at 510.

10.3.5 As well as the power to enter the contract itself, the charity must have express or implied powers to carry out the activities required to fulfil the contract, such as employing staff. In particular, if a security over a property is to be granted, this should be explicitly allowed by the constituting document of the charity.

10.3.6 A well-drafted constitution will clearly specify who has authority to bind the charity in contracts, and how their identity can be verified. For charities which are limited companies the provisions of the Companies Act 1985 apply.[12]

10.3.7 Smaller charities may provide that all contracts should be signed by office bearers, but larger organisations will often delegate signing responsibility to managers. All charities must meet the stipulations for documents relating to interests in land, wills, and trust dispositions laid down in the Requirements of Writing (Scotland) Act 1995.

Contracts and Trading

10.3.8 A charity which contracts to provide a service is trading. Therefore all the restrictions outlined in Chapters 2 and 7 apply. The trade must be carried out in the course of fulfilling the primary purposes of the charity. For example, a charity whose task is to assist disabled people could contract to provide training to disabled people. It could also contract to provide training to non-disabled people if disabled people received a service as part of the training programme. However, it could not simply run a training programme for able-bodied people, even if the profits were to be used to benefit disabled people. To do this, a separate trading company, or perhaps a charity with different objects, would be needed. Provided the trade is in furtherance of the primary purposes, it is legitimate for the charity to make a profit or surplus which is then applied for these same purposes.

Revenue Law

10.3.9 In order to avoid an assessment for income tax any profits from trading must be applied solely for the purposes of the charity and it is necessary that:

(i)   the trade is exercised in the course of carrying out a primary purpose of the charity, or
(ii) the work in connection with the trade is mainly carried out by beneficiaries of the charity.[13]

If the trading activity of a charity consistently fails to meet these requirements that charity may not only be liable to pay tax but may

---

[12]See Chap. 2.
[13]s.505, Income and Corporation Taxes Act 1988.

also be deemed to be acting in a way which is incompatible with charitable status. Again, the classic solution to these dilemmas is to form a separate trading company.

KEY CONCERNS IN CONTRACTING

When is a Contract Appropriate?

The Government has strongly promoted contracting as a mechanism to ensure greater accountability and clarity in the provision of services. However, it has also recognised that contracts may not always be beneficial and that some activities undertaken by charities are more appropriately supported by traditional mechanisms such as grant aid. This particularly applies to advocacy and campaigning.[14] This view is shared by the Scottish Council for Voluntary Organisations whose *Voluntary Sector Code of Practice for Community Care Contracting* (1991) states: **10.4.1**

> "The move to greater reliance on contracting as a source of funding rather than traditional grant aid may squeeze out vital voluntary sector activities such as advocacy, co-operation, development, education, innovation and representation. SCVO believes that grant aid should continue to be available for the voluntary sector's full range of activities, other than contracted services."

The Contracting Process

Although one of the reasons for the increased use of contracts has been the introduction of market philosophies to health and welfare services, most charities do not openly compete to provide services to public bodies. This is not simply because they find such activities distasteful. The funding body will wish to be assured that the service provider is able to provide a high quality service. Charities often work in areas where few other organisations would wish to be involved or have appropriate skills. Sometimes the impetus to develop a service will have come from the charity, rather than the funder. The contracting process may therefore take a variety of forms, for example: **10.4.2**

Open tendering
This procedure might be adopted where the service is one which can clearly be specified in advance and there are many possible providers. This may create problems for charities if they are unfamiliar with   **10.4.3**

---

[14]Social Work Services Group Circular SW19/1991 *Commissioning And Purchasing*, para. 18.

tendering processes or incur considerable expenditure in unsuccessful bids.

Select list tendering
This is a procedure where organisations which have previously been approved by the funder are invited to tender for the service.

Negotiated commissioning
Approved organisations will be provided with an outline of the service the funder is seeking to provide and invited to submit detailed proposals which will be assessed according to a range of criteria (not simply cost).

Partnership
The funder will work with a single provider to develop the service.

Defining the Service

10.4.3   For charities contracting raises both ideological dilemmas and practical concerns. The key dynamic in the contracting process is essentially about who "owns" or controls the service which is to be delivered. From the point of view of charities, they may wish to enter into a contract because they believe they can offer a particular service in a way which is more attuned to the needs of service users than a similar service offered by a statutory agency with broader purposes. A charity may accept that the funding body has a legitimate monitoring role in ensuring that money is spent for the agreed purpose, but may feel that the definition of what kind of service is to be provided should be largely left to the charity. The charity will often prefer to offer a high quality service to a limited number of users.[15] For funding bodies the service must fit in with their overall strategy.[16] There should be broad consistency between different services funded by the same body (for example on the level of charges). Because funders have a responsibility to all those in need in their area of responsibility, there may be a tendency to offer a limited service to all, rather than an excellent service to some.

10.4.4   Charities whose new services are successful may find themselves under pressure to compromise their initial aims, or to grow more quickly than is desirable. Charities may often be dependent on funding from a single agency, which both puts them in a weak negotiating position and makes the terms of the funding contract of even greater significance. Even where charities have a broader market, they tend

---

[15]See Leat, D. *et al*, *A Price Worth Paying?*(1986), Policy Studies Institute No. 651.

[16]See *Efficiency Scrutiny of Government Funding of the Voluntary Sector* (1990), HMSO; *Working Together: The Scottish Office, Volunteers and Voluntary Organisations* (1994), Scottish Office.

not to operate as commercial enterprises would by borrowing funds and taking a business risk in order to obtain contracts. Charitable trusts are bound to exercise particular caution in investing the funds of the charity. Most charities in Scotland do not have large surpluses to absorb unsuccessful ventures.[17]

In short, there tends to be a clear imbalance of power in negotiating   **10.4.5**
contracts which means that charities and their advisers must be vigilant in protecting their vital interests.

The Knowledge Gap

There is considerable concern amongst small and medium-sized   **10.4.6**
charities about contracting because staff may have limited experience in negotiating contracts, and little knowledge of the legal consequences of entering into a contract. The trustees, committee members, or directors, who ultimately bear responsibility (as persons concerned in management or control under the 1990 Act) for the implementation of the contract, may be even more inexperienced. In Scotland there are only a few charities which employ in-house lawyers and smaller charities may have limited expertise in financial matters.

It has been suggested that the contract culture will inevitably favour   **10.4.7**
large, "efficient" charities at the expense of smaller groups with links in local communities.[18] The danger is that this may result in replacing one set of bureaucratic institutions (local authorities and other public agencies) with another, arguably less publicly accountable, group of charities. If this is to be avoided charities need to be able to obtain adequate advice from the legal and financial professions (which will often require to be paid for out of the funds which are under negotiation).

It would be wrong to assume that the knowledge gap only pertains   **10.4.8**
to charities. It is still often the case that those representing the funding agency in negotiations have little legal knowledge. They may be using a standard form contract prepared elsewhere which they may not be allowed or prepared to modify to meet an individual case.

In the writer's experience, it is not uncommon for contracts to be   **10.4.9**
signed even though neither party has any intention of implementing some of the stated provisions. Indeed, even lengthy contracts involving considerable sums of public money may be executed in ways which are not probative in Scots law.

---

[17]See Chap. 3 for the restrictions on the investment powers of trustees.
[18]Taylor, M., *New Times, New Challenges: Voluntary Organisations Facing 1990* (1990); Kramer, R. and Grossman, B., "Contracting for Social Services: Process Management and Resource Dependencies" (1987) 61 *Social Service Review* 32.

Negotiating Contracts

10.4.9 Most funding bodies are entering into contracts with a considerable number of charities. For reasons of efficiency and equity, they will tend to develop standard forms of contract and may be reluctant to negotiate variations to suit an individual charity. Nevertheless, public bodies are bound by general principles of administrative law. In exercising a discretion they must not rigidly bind themselves by policy decisions. Therefore they should be prepared to negotiate amended contracts in appropriate cases.[19] Umbrella bodies, such as the Scottish Council for Voluntary Organisations and the Scottish Federation of Housing Associations, have also sought to protect service providers by promoting codes of practice which should influence both funders and charities. Sometimes funders have entered into negotiations with a range of service providers to agree a contract which is then used as a standard model. (This was done by Strathclyde Regional Council when drawing up a contract for providers of residential care for people being transferred from NHS services.)

Funding Shortfalls

10.4.10 Charities typically enter into contracts where they are assisting a public body to fulfil a statutory function. Most charities do not regard it as appropriate that their own donated income should be used to subsidise public bodies by making up shortfalls in funding (except perhaps by providing start up finance). Nevertheless, many charities, notably the Church of Scotland with its old people's homes, have found themselves running services at a loss. Ideally, from the charity's point of view, any contract should make provision for payments which will cover costs. At the very least, the budget should make clear the extent to which the charity's own resources may be called upon.

Pre-Contract Expenditure

10.4.11 Reaching the stage at which a service can be sold may be extremely expensive. Premises may need to be obtained, and sometimes improved, particularly for registration purposes. Business plans need to be prepared. Staff may have to be recruited, and negotiating the contract may be a lengthy process. In cases where the charity is tendering to provide a service against competition all of this expenditure may result in no return. Even in a non-competitive

---

[19]*Holt v. Watson*, 1983 S.L.T. 588.

The Government has also made it clear that, since it sees the voluntary sector as providing greater choice, local authorities should not seek to impose uniform standards. See, *e.g.* para. 7 of the Social Work (Scotland) Act 1968 (Choice of Accommodation) Directions 1993.

situation the charity is at risk until a binding commitment is given. In a local authority this will often require approval by the relevant committee.

From the point of view of the charity it is obviously helpful if this initial expenditure can be recouped. This may happen in three ways. One is for the contract budget to include an agreed element of compensation for pre-contractual expenditure. A variant is to have a pre-contractual agreement, typically an exchange of letters, which should provide sufficient assurances to allow the charity to incur development costs. The alternative to reimbursement of specific bid costs is for public bodies (not necessarily those buying a service from the charity) to provide core funding to the charity, which will allow it to prepare contract proposals.   **10.4.12**

Unfortunately, there has been considerable reluctance from funding bodies to adopt such measures. Their expectation seems to be that this expenditure should come from the charity's own resources obtained through voluntary fundraising, which seems likely to aggravate the bias towards larger and wealthier charities. It may also be doubted whether the public will be eager to donate money towards what would be seen as administration, rather than more visible services.   **10.4.13**

THE CONTRACT — SPECIFIC CONSIDERATIONS

The Service Specification

Alongside the budget this is the most crucial part of the contract since it sets out exactly what service will be provided, and to what standards. For innovative or specialised services charities may have considerable latitude in defining the type of service they offer. In practice, the written specification is often based on an initial project proposal, and care needs to be taken that the final specification is consistent with the larger contract and contains all the necessary elements. These might include: **10.5.1**

(1) client group (perhaps specifying precisely who is regarded as an appropriate user of the service and who is not, and how selection criteria will be applied);
(2) number of clients;
(3) the aims of the service;
(4) type and extent of service (and the degree to which it may vary);
(5) the rights of service users;
(6) value base of the service (meaning the moral or ideological aims and values which influence how the service is organised and how service users are treated. This might include concepts such as user choice, empowerment, and non-discrimination);
(7) how the service will be monitored and quality assured;

(8) how the service will be managed;
(9) staffing issues, including qualifications, training, the use of volunteers.

10.5.2   For more mainstream services (*e.g.* residential care of the elderly) the funding body may take a more active role in drafting the service specification. Whoever prepares it, one of the most difficult tasks is to be sufficiently specific to ensure a high quality service without creating such rigid requirements that the service is institutional and inflexible. In some fields (for example training) this can be done by focusing on expected outcomes, but even this may be difficult if the clients' skills and needs vary. In care services, evidence of, for example, the ways in which the involvement of service users will be secured may be more helpful than an exhaustive list of what services will be offered and how often.

Start Date

10.5.3   At the moment, many contracts are not formally completed until just before, or even some time after, the service is to be delivered. This obviously places both parties at considerable risk. Where the service is a continuing one which is annually renewed the charity may be forced to issue redundancy notices to staff while awaiting confirmation of the next year's contract. Clearly the solution to this problem does not lie with charities, but they should seek to be familiar with the planning and committee cycle of the relevant funding bodies so that they can pursue negotiations at the appropriate time.

Duration

10.5.4   Most charities will prefer a contract of a reasonable duration, as offering some degree of continuing security (subject to the issue of uprating — see below). In the case of community care the SCVO Code of Practice recommends three to five year contracts.[20] However, funders may only be prepared to offer an annual contract. One reason is a wish to preserve flexibility. Another, at least for local authorities, is the principle of "annuality" — that local authorities should not fetter their future discretion by committing resources which they do not yet control.[21]

10.5.5   One possible compromise is a contract which lasts for one year but which is automatically renewed unless either body has withdrawn following a stated period of notice (and perhaps consultation or formal review). This protects the charity and its clients from precipitate

---

[20]*Community Care Contracting — A Voluntary Sector Code of Practice* (1991), SCVO.
[21]*Re Westminster City Council* [1986] A.C. 668.

withdrawals of funding, while allowing the funders to change priorities in future. It also avoids both parties having to issue, revise and execute lengthy and repetitive contracts every year.

The Budget

When negotiating the funding or charges charities must of course be careful to consider all the costs of providing the service and complying with their contractual obligations. In particular, costings should include a realistic amount for management and administration (and professional advice). If the charity has not been funded separately for development costs it may wish to include an element to pay for the cost of developing further services.   **10.5.6**

Payment Arrangements

Because charities rarely have large reserves, cash flow is of major importance. From the charity's viewpoint it is important to ensure that: **10.5.7**

(1) the due date for payment is acceptable, bearing in mind when significant expenditure will be incurred by the charity (particularly salaries);
(2) the information required by the funder in order to process payment can easily and timeously be provided by the charity;
(3) there are penalties or interest clauses for late payment unless the charity can confidently expect payment in good time.

Uprating

If the contract is to last beyond one year it should contain provisions for payments to be uprated to take account of inflation. A standard measure, such as the Retail Price Index, may be used, sometimes combined with formulae reflecting actual increases in costs in specific areas (*e.g.* rent or salaries). However, a contract drafted by a funding body will often state that this formula is a maximum, rather than guaranteed, uprating. If the charity cannot obtain a firm guarantee then the issue of terminating or withdrawing from the contract becomes crucial.   **10.5.8**

Salaries

Charities often provide services which are comparable to those provided by public bodies, such as local authorities and health boards. Most charities aspire to give their staff the same salaries as comparable public sector staff and to recognise national salary awards. This would need to be reflected in the original budget for any contract and in provisions for uprating.   **10.5.9**

"Spot" or "Block" Contracts

10.5.10   When the contract is being negotiated it may be impossible to be sure that enough suitable clients will wish to use the service throughout the contract period. The contract must establish upon whom this risk should fall. From the charity's point of view the best option may be a "block" contract, where the charity is funded to provide an appropriate level of service, whether or not it is used. This may be particularly justifiable if, for example:

(1)   there is only one purchaser of the service;
(2)   the service is innovative or experimental;
(3)   the funding agency is responsible for selecting appropriate clients;
(4)   the unit cost is so high that the charity cannot sustain a shortfall in places; or
(5)   the number of clients is large or inherently unpredictable (for example, an advice service).

10.5.11   The other extreme is the "spot" contract. This is where the purchaser contracts to buy individual places at an agreed rate when required. There is no guarantee to the charity that any places will be used. This type of contract may be found where the charity deals with many funders (for instance, a residential school offering places to children from throughout the U.K.).

10.5.12   A variant of the spot contract is the "call off" contract. This is where the charity agrees general terms and conditions in advance with a funder, and the funder then buys places when required at an agreed unit price. This might be used, for example, for a charity providing domiciliary care services. In some cases it may be possible to negotiate an undertaking by the funder of a minimum number of referrals which will provide some basis for planning.

10.5.13   Slightly more stability is offered by "cost and volume" contracts. There is still no guarantee that all the places in a service will be taken up by the funder. However, the unit price will be set on the basis of agreed overall budgets and estimated take up levels. These were recommended in a recent Scottish Office research study.[22]

10.5.14   The level of use or occupancy specified in the contract should make allowances for the time it may take to fill places if clients leave. The contract may also allow for extra funding for clients with special needs. It should stipulate a mechanism for review if expectations regarding use of the service are not met.

Unanticipated Expenditure

10.5.15   Because services run by charities are often innovative, and because

---

[22]Scottish Office Central Research Unit, *The Cost and Quality of Care for People with Disabilities* (1995), HMSO.

the needs of clients are often unpredictable, a charity may well find that it cannot meet all of a client's needs within the original budget. Obviously no funder will give an open ended commitment to meeting all unanticipated expenditure. The options are:

(1) specific agreement on additional expenditure in the event of particular defined situations arising;
(2) a procedure for formal review of the funding of the service or of a particular client at the charity's initiative; or
(3) raising the possibility of increased costs during negotiations and obtaining whatever assurances are available.

In the care field it is worth remembering that local authorities have a duty formally to assess the needs of people for community care and to review this when appropriate. The charity would be perfectly entitled to request a council formally to review a client's care needs.[23]   **10.5.16**

Underspend/Extra Income

In some cases the funder may seek to recover any of the payment to the charity which turns out not to have been required to provide the agreed level of service, which is a significant difference from ordinary commercial contracts. This is reasonable in the case of block funding, and to some extent with a cost and volume contract, but may be resisted where the charity receives no guarantees from the funder as to the level of use which will be made of the service or in relation to future uprating.   **10.5.17**

Funders may also seek to offset higher than expected income from other sources against the contract price. One example is income from increases in social security benefits which may reduce the social work department's contribution to a residential care place. More contentious would be an attempt to take account of donations or legacies to the charity itself, or money raised to provide extra benefits to the clients of the charity.   **10.5.18**

Monitoring

It is obviously legitimate that funders should have powers to ensure that funds are being spent appropriately and a high quality service is being delivered. Indeed some charities express frustration, not at intrusive monitoring, but at the difficulty of getting funders to take an interest in the project once it is under way. However, there are some caveats: **10.5.19**

---

[23]NHS and Community Care Act 1990, s.55. Similar procedures are being introduced for disabled children (Children (Scotland) Act 1995, s.22) and already exist in education for children with special educational needs (Education (Scotland) Act 1980, s.60).

(1) visits to the service and information provided should respect the right of clients to privacy;
(2) the standards by which the service is evaluated should be those set down in the original contract;
(3) access to computer data by funders may have implications for the charity's registration under the Data Protection Act 1984;
(4) funders should not expect information in a form which is unnecessarily detailed or inconvenient to the charity (for example requiring separately audited accounts for a particular service which may be financially integrated into the charity's general accounts);
(5) procedures for contract monitoring should be consistent with the exercise of statutory monitoring functions (such as registration and inspection of care homes and nursing homes).

Reviews/Changes of Conditions

10.5.20 Incorporating provisions for review of a contract is often helpful, particularly if both parties have the right to initiate a review. However, charities must guard against contracts which allow the funder to change the service specification or funding level following a review without the agreement of the charity. At the very least, a charity should insist on a right to terminate the contract if such a change means it feels unable to sustain the service.

10.5.21 Even more unreasonable is a clause, often found in training and supported employment contracts, to the effect that the contract is subject to the funding agency standing conditions which may be unilaterally amended at any time.

Disputes

10.5.22 Few parties would wish disputes to result in litigation, and some form of arbitration clause may be appropriate. At all costs, charities should resist the standard clause proposed by one health board to the effect that disputes between the board and the service provider should be referred for arbitration to an employee of the health board! Unfortunately, formal arbitration can now be almost as expensive and time-consuming as litigation. Therefore it may be helpful if the contract provides a process for mediation, perhaps between stated officials in the agencies in dispute facilitated by an independent mediator.[24] It should also ensure that aspects of the contract unaffected by the dispute should continue, and particularly that both parties should have regard to the need to ensure that clients do not suffer during the dispute.

---

[24]See Quint, F., *Alternative Dispute Resolution in the Charitable Sector* (1995), The Henderson Top 2000 Charities.

Complaints Procedures

Funders may specify that the charity provide a complaints procedure for clients. In the field of social work local authorities are obliged to ensure that bodies providing a service on behalf of the local authority have a procedure which meets the minimum requirements imposed by statute on social work authorities themselves.[25]   **10.5.23**

Staff Qualifications and Training

Many contracts will specify that the staff should have the appropriate skills and training to deliver a high quality service and may require particular staff to have appropriate qualifications. Charities will wish to ensure that budgets allow for appropriate professional development. It should also be borne in mind that to require qualifications which are not objectively necessary for the job in question may be indirectly discriminatory, and thus breach equal opportunities policies or even legislation.   **10.5.24**

Section 7 of the Sex Discrimination Act 1975
Allows for appointment of a specified gender where this is a genuine occupational qualification, including situations involving physical contact, the knowledge of intimate details of a person's life, the provision of care within an establishment, and the provision of personal services.

Section 5 of the Race Relations Act 1976
Also allows a person's ethnic origin to be considered where this is a genuine occupational qualification, including where the employee provides persons of a particular racial group with personal services which can most effectively be provided by a person of that racial group.

Section 10 of the Disability Discrimination Act 1995
Grants exemption from Part II of that Act (which makes discrimination against disabled people in employment unlawful) to:

(a)   any charitable instrument which provides for conferring benefits on one or more categories of persons determined by reference to any physical or mental capacity; and
(b)   any act done by a charity or recognised body in pursuance of any of its charitable purposes, so far as those purposes are connected with persons determined by reference to any physical or mental capacity.

---

[25]Social Work (Scotland) Act 1968, s.5B and Direction 10, Social Work (Representations) Procedure (Scotland) Directions 1990 (contained in Annex to Social Work Services Group Circular SW5/91). The Scottish Office recently issued a consultation paper on revisals and guidance to the directions.

It also allows anyone who provides supported employment to treat members of a particular group of disabled persons more favourably than other persons in providing such employment.

Equal Opportunities

10.5.25 Funders often wish to see a commitment to equal opportunities from service providers. However, local authorities and some other public bodies[26] are restricted in the extent to which they may take this into account by the provisions of the Local Government Act 1988. Section 17 of the Act prohibits public authorities from having regard to any "non-commercial matter" in exercising functions in relation to contracts for the supply of services. Non-commercial matters include the composition of the workforce. Therefore a public authority covered by the Act cannot ask questions about staffing matters such as the proportion of women or ethnic minorities employed by the charity, or make a contract conditional upon adopting the funder's equal opportunities policy.

10.5.26 There is an exception to this general prohibition against consideration of non-commercial matters. Local authorities are entitled to seek certain information to ensure that their own functions are carried out in compliance with their statutory duty to promote the elimination of racial discrimination.[27] The local authority is also entitled to require that no one should be denied access to the service or receive a poorer service on the grounds of his or her gender, race, disability, and so on.

10.5.27 Of course, some charities specifically offer services to a particular client group, either because of the nature of the service itself or the aims of the charity. They may be entitled to disregard the normal legal restrictions preventing discrimination on the grounds of gender, ethnic origin and disability.

10.5.28 If their work involves dealing with vulnerable people, charities may also be exempted from the requirements of the Rehabilitation of Offenders Act 1974 to treat some convictions as "spent".[28] Charities

---

[26]Sched. 2 of the Local Government Act 1988, as amended by Sched. 13A of the Local Government (Scotland) Act 1994, brings development corporations, passenger transport executives, water development boards, Scottish Homes and any local authority joint board or joint committee within the scope of these restrictions. For Government guidance, see SDD Circular 7/88 and SO Environment Department Circular 6/91.

[27]Local Government Act 1988, s.18 and Race Relations Act 1976, s.71.

[28]The Rehabilitation of Offenders Act 1974 (Exceptions) Order 1975 (S.I. 1975 No. 1023) entitles prospective employers to seek information regarding otherwise "spent" convictions where, *inter alia*, the employment is in connection with the provision of "similar services" to local authority social services, and the holder of the post would have access to ill or disabled people, persons aged over 65, or persons addicted to alcohol and drugs; the

have no right to ask for police checks themselves, unlike central government, local authorities and health boards.[29] It is therefore a matter for the contractor, if it is a public body, to seek such information.

Selecting Clients

Some charitable services are available to everyone in an area or using a particular facility (*e.g.* an information service). Other services are only available to a specific and limited number of clients with particular needs. Whether the funder or the charity selects the client can be a point of contention. Funders may fear that charities will tend to select those clients whose needs are comparatively easy to satisfy. (This is a particular concern in areas where the funder may in effect be a provider of last resort for those whom the independent sector will not accommodate.) Conversely, charities may fear being forced to provide a service for clients whom they regard as unsuitable, or incompatible with other clients. **10.5.29**

Relevant considerations in negotiating this issue would include: **10.5.30**

(1) whether the level of service to clients is uniform or variable. Where everyone receives the same service, for example a window-replacement scheme, the funder would be likely to specify who should benefit;
(2) whether the funder or the charity has the necessary expertise to assess client needs;
(3) whether existing clients have any say in who should receive a service (for example, in a home where the residents may have influence over the selection of new residents);
(4) whether the charity is the sole provider of a particular service or one of a number from whom the funder can choose. In the latter case the charity may have a greater expectation of being able to select clients.

Often there will be an element of joint selection. This could be by a committee or a mechanism through which referrals from the funder are vetted and approved by the charity. The discretion may also be **10.5.31**

---

employment is in connection with the provision of health services and the holder will have access to persons in receipt of such services; the employment is concerned with the provision of accommodation, care, leisure and recreational facilities, schooling, social services, supervision or training of persons under 18 and the holder would have access to such persons or would work on the premises where such provision takes place.

[29]See *Protection of Children: Disclosure of Criminal Convictions of those with access to Children,* Scottish Office Circular SW9/89 referring to local authorities and NHS Circular 1989 (GEN) 22 with reference to health boards. Extension of this circular to voluntary organisations providing care to children is under consideration. The position regarding police checks for those working with vulnerable adults, rather than children, is less clear and tends to be based on local arrangements between statutory agencies and police forces.

exercised within the agreed eligibility criteria set out in the service specification.

10.5.32 The same issues arise when it may become necessary to stop providing a service to a client, either because the type of service is no longer appropriate, or because the client is creating problems for the charity or other clients. The contract should specify clearly how such a decision would be taken and who, ultimately, has the final say. Ideally, it should also set out what responsibility the funder and/or the charity accept for assisting the client to move to another appropriate service.

Contracts and Clients

10.5.33 While a charity may be under a contractual obligation to a funder, the intended beneficiaries are typically third parties, namely the clients or users of the service. Both charities and funders are increasingly concerned that clients should be "empowered", that is, actively involved in a service rather than passive objects of charity. This can be difficult to achieve when the client is not the purchaser or contracting party, but various attempts have been made to accommodate this.

10.5.34 Sometimes a tripartite contract is entered into, involving the client, the charity and the funder. However, contracts may be lengthy and complex, and clients may have little opportunity to negotiate. Asking the client to sign such a contract may contribute little.

10.5.35 A more realistic option may be for clients to sign a separate agreement, setting out both what is expected of them and what their rights are in relation to the funder and the charity. Ideally, such an agreement should:

(1) be clear about the extent to which it is legally binding or simply a statement of expectations;
(2) refer to and be consistent with the statutory rights of clients (for example, employment and tenancy rights).

It is to be hoped that increased legal involvement in contracting will assist these aspirations.

10.5.36 Many charities provide services for children or adults with some degree of mental disorder or learning disability. Contracts should reflect the fact that some clients may lack the capacity to sign binding agreements or comply with contractual obligations.

Indemnity of Funder

10.5.37 Contracts drafted by public bodies typically state that the charity is acting as a principal and not an agent of the funder, and that the charity indemnifies the funder in respect of any claims arising out of the operation of the service. Charities will wish to ensure that such clauses do not require them to indemnify the funder for claims arising out of the negligence of the funder or the funder's employees, and that they are adequately insured for any potential liability.

Confidentiality

Contracts often specify that service providers treat information relating   **10.5.38**
to clients and to the contract itself as confidential. Whilst it is important
to respect the right of clients to privacy, some confidentiality clauses
are so widely drawn that they are likely to be observed only in the
breach. There are a number of situations where disclosure of
information would be appropriate, including where:

(1) it has been authorised by the client;
(2) it is reasonably necessary to fulfil the obligations of the contract;
     or
(3) it is legally required or justifiable as a matter of policy (for instance,
     to prevent serious harm to an individual).

So far as information relating to the contract or the funder is concerned   **10.5.39**
there should not be an obligation of confidentiality where the information:

(1) is already in the public domain;
(2) has been disclosed to the charity by a third party without an
     obligation of confidence; or
(3) is trivial.

Some contracts go further and specify that the charity should not say or   **10.5.40**
do anything which may bring the funder into disrepute. Charities which,
as well as providing services, undertake an advocacy or campaigning
role will wish to consider carefully whether such clauses might prevent
them from commenting on matters of legitimate public interest.[30]

Responsibilities of Funder

It is helpful if contracts specify not only the obligations of the service   **10.5.41**
provider but those of the funder. The most obvious of these is to make
prompt payment of sums due. Other responsibilities might include:

(1) provision of complementary services to clients (or fallback
     services if the charity's service proves to be inappropriate);
(2) support in managing or overseeing the service; or
(3) financial assessments where clients are being charged for the
     services (for example, residential care).

Termination

Contracts will almost always provide for the possibility of termination   **10.5.42**
of the contract prior to the end date, particularly if one party is in

---

[30]See Chap. 1, esp. paras. 1.5.1–1.5.7 for consideration of the campaigning
role of charities.

breach. Charities will wish to ensure that rights and obligations are reciprocal: they should have the same right as the funder to end the contract if the other side is in breach. Normally it would be appropriate to provide that the party in breach be given a reasonable opportunity to remedy the breach before the contract is terminated.

10.5.43 Sometimes a contract may allow one side to terminate on giving notice, without any prior breach of contract by the other side. Again, the charity should seek the same rights to terminate as the funder. It will also be important to negotiate an adequate period of notice both for the charity (which may have to issue redundancy notices or sell property) and the clients.

10.5.44 Whether the contract should allow for termination by either side on giving notice is a difficult question of balance. The charity will normally wish as much certainty as possible with regard to future finance. However, if there is any reason to suppose that the charity may not be able to maintain the service throughout the full contract period (for example because there is no guarantee of increased funding for inflation) then the option of early termination will be an important safeguard.

CONCLUSION

10.6.1 Both charities and the Welfare State have undergone major changes in the last decade and there is every reason to suppose that this will continue. However matters develop, charities are likely to find themselves becoming involved in more, and larger, contracts. Many public bodies are only now developing the internal systems necessary to operate contracts effectively. The challenge for charities is to develop the expertise and obtain the resources to ensure that contracting operates to provide better services for their clients.

Chapter 11

CONCLUSIONS

Introduction

This book has sought to describe and analyse the law on charities in **11.1.1**
Scotland and to offer a comprehensive picture of the current legal
situation. Contributors have focused on presenting the current
situation and have for the most part avoided speculative comment.
However, the impact of changes introduced by the 1990 Act and trends
in the development of the charitable sector generally require
consideration so that the key issues which may lie ahead for charities
and their professional advisers can be identified. This concluding
chapter attempts to outline recent trends in the regulation of charities,
considers the debate about the appropriate legal form for charities
and assesses the ability of the new regulatory structure in Scotland to
meet the aim of a better managed and more accountable charitable
sector.

Trends in the Regulation of Charities

The chapters in this book and empirical studies of charities identify a **11.2.1**
number of key themes in the management and regulation of charitable
bodies. Some of these themes stem from wider debates about the
nature of regulation in a market economy, others, such as the tension
between voluntary effort and professionalisation, are specific to
charities. In identifying these themes we are aiming to set the
presentations of the law given in preceding chapters within a wider
social and economic context.

Professionalism v. Voluntarism

Voluntary effort lies at the core of most charities. Unpaid labour far **11.2.2**
outweighs employed personnel, ranging from the delivery of basic
services, such as meals-on-wheels, to the demanding and complex
skills required of many honorary office bearers in major Scottish
charities. At the same time, an examination of the annual reports and
accounts of leading Scottish charities shows that they are responsible
for significant financial, personnel and capital resources and that they
offer an enormous variety of services, including work which is highly

specialised and innovative. Most of these services are required to meet exacting standards laid down by the contracting funding body. It is increasingly the case that the public expects the same quality of service from charities which are mainly staffed by volunteers as they do from organisations entirely staffed by paid employees. Even where the charity is a provider of funds rather than services there are nevertheless demands on such charities to streamline decision-making and specify the criteria which are applied in making grants.

11.2.3	Charities have also traditionally been vehicles for local community effort on a small scale. This "grassroots" movement away from centralised bureaucracies has been encouraged by the provision of grant aid to such groups (for instance through Urban Aid grants) and also by a focus, at national and European level, towards subsidiarity, in which decisions are taken locally. Government here has invoked the notion of "community" as a powerful symbol of social and economic regeneration and charities are regarded as playing a key role in communities. Numerous groups have sprung up which depend solely on voluntary effort and operate with very limited funds. Volunteers in such groups may become involved because of their commitment and may lack the administrative and financial skills which are necessary to run a charity. Funds may not be available to provide administrative support and management training for such groups.

11.2.4	The 1990 Act does not directly address this issue but it may create difficulties for those charities which depend mainly on voluntary effort. Are such charities able to produce the information which the law now requires them to make available to the Lord Advocate and to the public on request? Can such charities meet the accounting requirements set down in the regulations, which are more onerous than those imposed on small businesses? Will charities become increasingly more professionalised and no longer reflect the communities which they serve?

11.2.5	The tension between voluntarism and professionalism has become particularly acute where charities tender for contracts.[1] On the one hand, the service they offer must be of a high standard. On the other, the acceptance of the constraints which the market imposes may undermine the voluntary ethos. Establishing an appropriate balance between the encouragement of voluntary community-based endeavour and the delivery of high-quality services is a challenge for charities. Regulation should also be seeking to balance these sometimes competing interests.

11.2.6	The role of professional advisers in maintaining this balance is also significant. If regulation requires charities to employ lawyers, accountants and business managers this will have implications for expenditure. Indeed, this is happening already, as the Nuffield research

---

[1] See Chap. 10.

shows. While the growth of regulation offers new markets for advisers and is therefore to be welcomed by such professions it also may discourage the "active citizen" from involvement in charitable work. Volunteers may feel that they do not want to work within an ethos where the emphasis seems to have shifted away from altruism towards professional goals.

Accountability v. Autonomy

The 1990 Act has highlighted the importance of accountability and it is designed to put in place forms of regulation which make the activities of recognised bodies, particularly their financial affairs, open to scrutiny by the public and by the State, through the office of the Lord Advocate. It is clearly important that the public goodwill towards charities and the public's willingness to donate to charitable causes should not be undermined by a fear of fraudulent or incompetent dealings by charities. The recent cases brought under section 7 of the Act demonstrate that some charities do engage in activities which are an abuse of their charitable status.   11.2.7

However, there is also no doubt that charities have benefited from their independence, both from the demands which the imperative to generate profit impose on businesses and the freedom from direct control by government. From the nineteenth century onwards, charities have been at the forefront of change, in the identification of needs hitherto unmet, in the provision of innovative services, in funding new initiatives and in campaigning on a wide range of social, economic and environmental issues. If accountability inevitably means the imposition of such tight controls that inventiveness is stifled then it will produce undesirable consequences. How can a satisfactory balance be struck between accountability and autonomy? Are the regulatory structures presently in place designed to do so?   11.2.8

The regulatory structures are not the only potential threat to the autonomy of charities. Their increasing dependence on securing contracts, as has been seen in Chapter 10, may make it difficult for these bodies to retain a critical edge and to strive for those standards which are compatible with their purposes. The requirements of monitoring and accountability included in contracts are often far more onerous than those which the legislation expects of recognised bodies. The funders of contracts frequently require a charity's accounts to be audited, regardless of the charity's level of income, and may also require an audit to be carried out quarterly. It is important that the resource implications of any such requirements are clearly understood by both parties to the contract.   11.2.9

Regulation v. Freedom

Paradoxically, the first attempts in Scotland to regulate charities, whatever their legal form, have coincided with increasing emphasis   11.2.10

by government and business on deregulation, cutting out "red tape" and other bureaucratic constraints inhibiting development. The trend towards deregulation is particularly noticeable so far as small businesses are concerned, as recent papers by the Department of Trade and Industry demonstrate. It would appear, therefore, that the trend for more regulation of charities is at odds with the current climate in the commercial sector. This is also evident from a comparison between the accounting requirements for limited companies and the regulations which govern unincorporated recognised bodies. Whereas incorporated charities are now exempt from external review provided their income does not exceed £90,000, there is as yet no such exemption for unincorporated charities in Scotland.[2] They must submit their accounts for an independent examination where annual receipts do not exceed £100,000, and above that limit require an audit by a registered auditor.

11.2.11   Charities were not included in the original Deregulation Initiative, set up in 1992 by the Department of Trade and Industry, and were only added to the seven Deregulation Task Forces after lobbying by charities themselves. These task forces were given the remit to consider whether regulation was over-burdensome and reduced effective working and to recommend improvements in the quality and consistency of regulation across a range of areas. The Deregulation Task Force on Charities, which included Scottish representation, published its report in July 1994. As far as Scotland is concerned, the report recommends that the Scottish Office should clarify the role of the Scottish Charities Office, establish a register of Scottish charities, provide a central resource of consistent information and support, make fundraising controls consistent with England and Wales, and address cross-border issues affecting charities operating in both jurisdictions. It further recommends that the Scottish Office should publish guidance on the role and responsibilities of the independent examiner to whom unincorporated charities with an income under £100,000 must submit their accounts.[3]

11.2.12   There are important similarities between service-providing charities and businesses, but there are also significant differences. Efficiency and effectiveness are key to success in both, necessitating sound financial and administrative controls. However, while recognised bodies may also be limited companies they do enjoy a favoured status for tax purposes.[4] They are also permitted to appeal to the public's sense of altruism under the banner of "charity", whereas non-recognised bodies cannot. In this jurisdiction, therefore, tighter

---

[2] The Charities Accounts (Scotland) Regulations 1992 are, at the time of writing, under review by the Scottish Office.

[3] Charities and Voluntary Organisations Task Force, *Proposals for Reform* (1994), Deregulation Task Forces, pp. 31–32. The section of the report in which these recommendations are contained is headed "Task Force Proposals under Review by Departments".

[4] See Chap. 7.

regulation of charities may be justified. However, the degree to which this may adversely affect the ability of charities to meet their objects is an open question.

THE LEGAL FORM OF CHARITIES

A further important issue is the most appropriate legal form in which charities should be constituted. Earlier chapters have considered the current situation, under which recognised bodies can assume a variety of legal forms, including the company, the trust or the unincorporated association.[5] The term "recognised body" is entirely concerned with function rather than structure and does not require the adoption of any specific legal form. Guidance is given both in the legal texts[6] and in guidelines from umbrella organisations[7] about the form best suited to the particular needs of a new body with charitable objects. Larger charities are encouraged to be incorporated and funders may insist on incorporation in order to secure the advantages of limited liability for those concerned in the management or control of the charity. Grant-making bodies have traditionally been established as trusts, often under the provisions of the truster's will. The majority of recognised bodies are unincorporated associations, whose powers depend entirely on the terms of their constitution. This variety of legal forms has the great advantage of offering choice and flexibility to charities, which may change their legal structures as their activities develop in scale and sophistication.

11.3.1

Other jurisdictions have adopted a very different approach. In many European countries, including France, Germany and Italy, non-profit organisations must adopt a particular legal form unique to them so that they are granted legal personality as and only as non-profit organisations. This may be explained by the lack of a secular voluntary tradition in those jurisdictions and, in some instances, concerns about the impact of such organisations on pre-existing relations between the State and the citizen. Thus the French Law of 1901, under which charities were first given legal recognition, contains detailed requirements on matters of internal structure, dissolution and the roles of members. It appears to give such organisations a coherence and clarity which is lacking in Scotland.

11.3.2

Research is being undertaken at the University of Liverpool which is considering whether a separate legal form for charities is desirable.

11.3.3

---

[5] See Chaps. 2 and 3.
[6] See, for instance, Cairns, E., *Charities: Law and Practice* (1993), Sweet and Maxwell.
[7] See, for instance, Phillips, A., *Charitable Status — A Practical Handbook* (1993), Directory of Social Change.

This research has looked at the legal structures adopted by non-profit organisations in several other countries, including Australia and New Zealand. This would have the advantage of streamlining structures within charities. It might prove difficult, however, to apply the same form to the huge variety of recognised bodies in Scotland, covering small community-based groups staffed entirely by volunteers, large grant-making trusts, national service-providing charities and special interest groups.

11.3.4   The current definition of charity has already been considered in Chapters 1, 3, 4, 5 and 8. It is clear that non-recognised bodies, which do not have charitable purposes conforming to those required for tax exemption, are not the subject of any regulation except in so far as they represent themselves as charities. There is still scope, therefore, for non-profit voluntary endeavours to continue without regulation provided no claim is made that they are "charitable". The Nuffield research uncovered several instances of bodies which had been recognised by the Inland Revenue deciding to have their names removed from the Index and foregoing charitable status. This might be because they did not wish to have to meet the financial accounting standards or because they did not wish to provide information to the general public. Concerns have been raised by legal advisers about the administrative burden which compliance with the 1990 Act may entail for small grant-making trusts, and also about public access to information about the trust's purposes which the trustees may not wish to divulge and which may be of little relevance to most of the general public.

11.3.5   A further concern is raised by "self-help" groups, which may fail to meet the public benefit requirement. The membership of such groups may be limited to people in the same circumstances (for instance, sufferers of a particular illness or disability), the groups may not have an educative function and may be staffed entirely by people having the illness or disability. They may, therefore, not meet the requirement of "public benefit", and if they are neither educational nor confined solely to the relief of poverty their objects may not be defined as "charitable", under the test of the four heads of charity set down in *Pemsel*.[8]

REGULATORY MECHANISMS

Successful Regulation

11.4.1   Writers on regulation have identified the key issues in successful regulation as clarity and feasibility of purpose, use of the most

---

[8] *Income Tax Special Commissioners v. Pemsel* [1891] A.C. 531.

appropriate form of regulation, and securing compliance without undue cost.[9] Applying these criteria to the current system for regulating charities suggests that both the changes which were designed to affect charities directly (introduced by the 1990 Act and subsequent regulations) and those more general developments which also have an impact on charities (such as the Contract Culture) have had both beneficial and adverse effects.

It is clear from the background papers to the changes and from the legislation itself that it was intended on the one hand to improve the management and accountability of charities and to allay public concern about "bogus" or poorly administered charities and on the other to introduce a regulatory system which would be inexpensive and not unduly intrusive. The Scottish Office did consult widely, but there appears to have been a lack of consensus among charities themselves as to what was needed. The consultation process was not informed by any research specifically commissioned to investigate the existing management and accountability structures for Scottish charities and to make comparison with other jurisdictions. Demands of parliamentary time meant that there were limited opportunities for debate on the Bill, which incorporated a wide range of other, equally important, issues.

11.4.2

Knowledge and Understanding of the Provisions

Inevitably, it is taking time for charities to adjust to the new régime. The findings of the Nuffield research study reveal that the purpose of the new provisions and indeed the provisions themselves are not known or not understood by many of the bodies which must adhere to them. Although in 1992 the staff of the Inland Revenue's Claims Branch sent out information detailing the changes to 19,500 charities with whom they had been in contact since January 1, 1970, many smaller charities which had not reclaimed tax since that date, if ever, and which had not been in contact with the Inland Revenue for any other reason were totally unaware of the legislation. Also, the Inland Revenue in some cases had out-of-date correspondence addresses because charities had not kept them up to date with relevant changes.

11.4.3

Professional advisers must also take some of the responsibility for this failure of communication since in many cases the contact address on the Index was that of the charity's professional adviser, a lawyer or accountant, and many of these had not passed on the relevant information to the charity in question. In some instances this was because solicitors had assisted with a charity's founding document and then had no further contact with them, and in others because solicitors assumed that the Inland Revenue or Scottish Charities Office

11.4.4

---

[9]See, for instance, Cranston, R., *Legal Foundations of the Welfare State* (1985), Weidenfeld and Nicolson.

would also be writing to the charity's registered office and/or, in the case of companies, to its business address.[10] This raises the question of whether or not it is the responsibility of professional advisers to advise their clients of legislative changes affecting them. The prudent course of action would be to do so.

11.4.5 The gaps in the Inland Revenue's Index certainly need to be rectified and the Index is constantly being updated. The Scottish Council of Voluntary Organisations (SCVO) is also compiling a register of charities, as recommended by the Deregulation Task Force, and this will help to maintain an up-to-date record of Scottish charities. Further efforts might also be made to inform such bodies and to clarify the legal requirements more specifically.

Impact of Regulation on Scottish Charities

11.4.6 Undoubtedly recognised bodies have had to alter their financial management systems and to make available to members of the public information which was previously available to members or trustees only. This should be welcomed by professional advisers, funders and the public. However, the extent to which all charities comply with the requirements is very difficult to assess, particularly as there is no requirement routinely to file accounts, although incorporated charities continue to file their annual accounts at Companies House.

11.4.7 It is also not clear how many bodies which are not recognised by the Inland Revenue may be representing themselves as charities. It is the public who alert the Scottish Charities Office to alleged irregularities. The resources currently available to the Lord Advocate do not permit the Scottish Charities Office to operate in a more proactive way. Its director explained to us the role of the Scottish Charities Office as follows :

> "the role of the office is quite clear and it is to act in the public interest in the investigation of concerns about misconduct and mismanagement in the administration of charities and in appropriate cases to seek remedies through civil proceedings before the Court of Session.... In this jurisdiction the regulatory framework is such that trustees of charities seeking general advice must consult their own professional advisers."[11]

11.4.8 There is a concern among charities that "whistle-blowers" may not always be well-intentioned (and this is one of the reasons given by the Scottish Charities Office for maintaining strict confidentiality).

---

[10]In most cases where the Inland Revenue wrote to professional advisers theirs was the only address available for the charity concerned and the Inland Revenue had no other means of contacting the charity.
[11]Letter of January 6, 1995 from Mr Brian Logan, Director of the SCO.

Significant damage might be done to the reputation of bona fide charities were it to be known that they were under investigation even if there was no foundation for the allegations being made against them. Even where the "whistle-blowers" are disinterested their coverage of the voluntary sector can only be patchy so that fraud and incompetence in certain charities may be overlooked. Umbrella organisations, which provide advice and support to particular groupings of charities, might fulfil this role but not all recognised bodies have access to or choose to belong to such organisations. In any case, umbrella organisations may feel that their supportive role might be undermined were they to be seen as "policing" the voluntary sector.

11.4.7 It appears from the information provided by the Scottish Charities Office that the majority of recognised bodies reported to them require nothing more than advice and help and that court proceedings are not usually necessary to secure compliance. Much work has clearly been done to assist such charities. It is unfortunate, therefore, that the guidelines which the Scottish Charities Office are undoubtedly applying in the case of these charities are not disseminated more widely. The availability of such guidance, issued perhaps on the same basis as the decisions and recommendations of the Charity Commissioners, might be an excellent preventive measure which would in many cases pre-empt the necessity for intervention by the Lord Advocate.

11.4.8 Some charities are finding it difficult to meet the new statutory requirements because of the resource implications. The Nuffield research shows that there may be an increased administrative burden on charities, regardless of their existing infrastructure or size, although it is undoubtedly the smaller charities which are finding the greatest difficulties in complying with the legislation. In some instances they are incurring "one-off" costs such as that of rewriting a constitution in order to replace the word "audit" by "independent examination" or the cost of becoming a limited company in order to give some measure of liability protection to those in management or control. However, some charities in our research sample reported increases in accountancy fees ranging from 50 per cent to 300 per cent, and others had been obliged to employ a paid treasurer. Although the change to the format of the accounts was a one-off cost, interviewees said that most increased costs would be ongoing because of all the additional information they were now required to supply in the accounts and in writing a report on the charity's activities. This has implications both for the charities' administrators and for their auditors and many charities complained that the time spent on "administration" was time taken from their charitable work.[12]

---

[12]The paid director of one incorporated charity in our sample said he would be asking his board whether they wished him temporarily to cease his charitable work in order to devote the requisite time to completing the accounts within the period prescribed under company law or whether to continue with his charitable work and risk a fine for late lodging of accounts.

11.4.9   Neither private funders nor the public look favourably on appeals by charities to cover their administrative costs. Thought should be given to ensuring that charities do have recourse to advice and assistance in meeting their new obligations. Funding from central government specifically for the administration of charities and preparation of accounts would greatly assist the situation, as would the provision of model styles of accounts for smaller charities which are unable to afford to pay an accountant.[13] The burdens on the smallest charities might be made lighter by the introduction of a "small charities" régime on the English model, freeing charities whose income does not exceed £10,000 from the requirement to submit their accounts to an external review and excepting charities with an income of £1,000 or less from some of the requirements of the 1990 Act.

CONCLUSION

11.5.1   Many charities are in need of help with legal issues and a consultation with a professional adviser may be beyond the means of many charities. Access to authoritative, free advice on general legal matters was something the majority of the Nuffield interviewees felt was much needed, especially when they became aware of their own ignorance of the full implications of the legislation. They regarded it as unfair that charities in England and Wales should have the benefit of free advice whereas those in Scotland did not. The Scottish Charities Office is not geared towards a general advisory role in its present form, and it may, in any event, be preferable to keep such a role separate from the regulatory. An authoritative source of legal advice is, however, highly desirable. Ideally this would be located in an independently constituted body similar to the Charity Commission in England and Wales.

11.5.2   The Inland Revenue is continuing to expand its information services with a wide range of user-friendly booklets and a telephone helpline, and members of the public can telephone or write to FICO to find out whether an organisation is on the Index of charities. It might also be useful if the role of the Inland Revenue or some other body could be developed to include a system whereby all unincorporated charities were required to file annual accounts, adopting a similar system to that employed by Companies House. The introduction of a system of random checks would also help to increase the accountability of charities, since at present there is little check on whether they are, in fact, complying with the legislation. If the Inland Revenue became actively involved in this way with all Scottish charities, more charities

---

[13]SCVO has produced some styles of receipts and payments and income and expenditure accounts.

might be encouraged to make use of its helpline and other sources of assistance. As the Inland Revenue follows the same criteria as the Charity Commission in matters relating to tax law, it might also be helpful to make available to charities any Charity Commission booklets which would not be incompatible with Scots law.

In England and Wales, where registered charities must file accounts   **11.5.3**
and annual reports with the Charity Commissioners, copies of accounts can be obtained from them upon payment of a nominal charge.[14] The 1990 Act refers to a "reasonable charge in respect of copying and postage".[15] There is no reference to the inclusion of any professional fee, although we were advised by solicitors that they normally charge £25–£30 for supplying the relevant documents in respect of charities which they manage, based on the usual feeing structure of the firm. While this is to some extent understandable, it may well deter members of the public from pursuing those charities, and this raises the question of whether the public accountability of charities can be achieved in this way. We understand that the Scottish Charities Office is considering establishing a maximum level of what constitutes a "reasonable charge" and this would certainly be desirable.[16]

Charities, already major employers, service providers and campaig-   **11.5.4**
ners, continue to grow in numbers, with new recognised bodies being added to the Index on a regular basis. Charities also represent a growth area for advisers, as they are increasingly requiring specialist advice, particularly in selecting the appropriate legal form and in ensuring that the legal document does not impose unnecessary obligations on charities, over and above the requirements of legislation. In recent years England and Wales has seen the development of growing numbers of specialist charity units within legal and accountancy firms, and this is now happening in Scotland too. The increasing complexities of the legal environment for Scottish charities, particularly where their activities also extend into England and Wales with its different regulatory framework, make it likely that this trend will continue. This book has drawn together the various elements of the legal framework for charities in Scotland and it is hoped that the presentation of the material for the first time in a single book will both help to establish charity law in Scotland as a field of expertise in its own right and provide users with practical guidance within the component areas which are of particular interest to them.

---

[14] The Charity Commission currently charges £1.80 for six pages or less (inclusive of postage) and 30p per page thereafter.

[15] ss.1(4) and 5(7).

[16] The latest figure to be mentioned was £10 plus VAT (to a researcher compiling a guide to Scottish trusts for the Directory of Social Change in June 1995).

CONTENTS

CIVIC GOVERNMENT (SCOTLAND) ACT 1982

(1982 c.45)

PART IX

MISCELLANEOUS AND GENERAL

Regulation of charitable collections

Regulation of charitable collections

[1]**119.**—(1) Subject to the provisions of this section, any person who organises a public charitable collection in respect of which the local authority for the area in which it is to be held have not given their permission under this section shall be guilty of an offence and liable, on summary conviction, to a fine not exceeding £200.

(2) Subsection (1) above does not apply to a collection which takes place in the course of a public meeting or to a collection which takes place by means of an unattended receptacle kept in a fixed position in a public place.

(3) An application for permission under this section shall be made in writing to the local authority by the organiser of the collection not later than 1 month before the date of the collection, or within such other period as the local authority may fix.

(4) On receipt of an application for permission under this section the local authority shall consult the chief constable for the area which comprises or includes their area and may make such other inquiries as they think fit.

(5) In granting permission under this section a local authority may, subject to the provisions of any regulations made under subsection (13) below, impose such conditions as they think fit, having regard to the local circumstances in which the collection is to be held, including conditions—
  (a) specifying the date, time or frequency of the collection;
  (b) specifying the area within which it is to take place;
  (c) regulating its conduct;
  (d) specifying the form of collection boxes, other containers and any other articles used for the purposes of the collection; and

---

[1] As amended by the Local Government etc. (Scotland) Act 1994, Sched.13, para.129(16).

(e) as to any other matter relating to the local circumstances of the collection.

(6) A local authority may refuse to grant permission under this section on any of the following grounds—

(a) that the date, time, frequency or area of the collection would cause undue public inconvenience;

(b) that another collection in respect of which permission under this section has been granted or which is exempt under subsection (11) below is due to take place on the same or a proximate day;

(c) that it appears to them that the amount likely to be applied for charitable purposes in consequence of the collection is inadequate having regard to the likely amount of the proceeds of the collection;

[2](d) that the organiser of the collection has been convicted of an offence under section 5 of the Police, Factories, etc. (Miscellaneous Provisions) Act 1916 or the House to House Collections Act 1939, or under this section or regulations made under subsection (13) of this section or under Part III of the Charities Act 1992 or regulations made under section 73 of that Act or of any other offence which involved dishonesty or the commission of which would be likely to be facilitated by the grant of permission under this section.

(7) A local authority may—

(a) if they have reason to believe that there has been a change in the circumstances which prevailed at the time when they granted a permission under this section and they are of the opinion that, in consequence, grounds of refusal under subsection (6) above apply, withdraw the permission or vary any condition imposed by them under subsection (5) above in relation to that permission;

(b) if they have reason to believe that there has been, is or is likely to be a breach of any condition imposed by them under subsection (5) above, withdraw a permission under this section.

(8) Where permission for a collection is refused under subsection (6) above or withdrawn under subsection (7) above, the local authority shall give written notice of that fact to the organiser of the collection and such notice shall include a statement of the reasons for such refusal or withdrawal.

(9) The organiser of a collection may appeal to the sheriff against the decision of a local authority—

(a) under subsection (6) above, refusing permission for a collection;

(b) under subsection (7) above, withdrawing any condition;

---

[2] As amended by the Charities Act 1992, Sched. 6, para.10.

(c) under subsection (5) above, imposing any condition;

(d) under the said subsection (7), varying any condition,

and an appeal under this subsection shall be made by way of summary application and shall be lodged with the sheriff clerk within 14 days of the date of the decision appealed against, or in a case where reasons for a decision have been given, within 14 days from the date of receipt of those reasons.

(10) In upholding an appeal under subsection (9) above, the sheriff may—

(a) remit the case with the reasons for his decision to the local authority for reconsideration of their decision; or

(b) reverse or alter the decision of the local authority.

(11) If he is satisfied that a person pursues charitable purposes throughout the whole or a substantial part of Scotland, the Secretary of State may direct that that person shall, subject to such conditions as may be specified in the direction, be exempt from subsection (1) above.

A direction made under this subsection may be revoked or amended by a further direction so made.

(12) Notwithstanding the provisions of subsection (11) above, any person who has been exempted from subsection (1) above by a direction of the Secretary of State under subsection (11) above shall, unless the Secretary of State otherwise directs, give to the local authority in whose area he intends to organise a public charitable collection 3 months notice of that intention.

A direction under this subsection may be revoked or amended by a further direction so made.

(13) Subject to the provision of this section, the Secretary of State may make regulations for the purposes of regulating public charitable collections and, without prejudice to that generality, regulations may include provision about the keeping and publication of accounts; provision for prevention of annoyance to the public and provision making it an offence to fail to comply with any obligation imposed by the regulations which is specified in the regulations as an obligation breach of which is an offence and making any person guilty of such an offence liable on summary conviction to a fine not exceeding £50 or such lesser sum as may be specified in the regulations.

(14) Regulations under this section shall be made by statutory instrument subject to annulment in pursuance of a resolution of either House of Parliament.

(15) [Repeated by the Statute Law (Repeals) Act 1993, Sched. 1, Pt. X.]

(16) In this section "public charitable collection" means a collection from the public of money (whether given by them for consideration

or not) for charitable purposes taken either in a public place or by means of visits from place to place and "charitable purposes" means any charitable, benevolent or philanthropic purposes whether or not they are charitable within the meaning of any rule of law.

LAW REFORM (MISCELLANEOUS PROVISIONS) (SCOTLAND) ACT 1990

(1990 c.40)

PART I

CHARITIES

Recognition of charities

Information as to recognised charities

1.—(1) No obligation as to secrecy or other restriction upon the disclosure of information imposed by statute or otherwise shall prevent the Commissioners of Inland Revenue (in this section referred to as "the Commissioners") from disclosing—

(a) to the Lord Advocate, information as regards any recognised body such as is mentioned in subsection (2) below,

(b) to any person who requests it, the name of any recognised body and the address last used by the Commissioners for any communication with the body and the year when such communication occurred.

(2) A recognised body referred to in subsection (1)(a) above is a body—

(a) which appears to the Commissioners to be or to have been carrying on activities which are not charitable or to be or to have been applying any of its funds for purposes which are not charitable;

(b) which is certified by the Lord Advocate as being a body in respect of which information has been provided to the Scottish charities nominee by a relevant institution in pursuance of section 12 of this Act.

(3) Where any information is made available to any person as mentioned in subsection (1)(b) above, the Commissioners shall include in such information any matter noted by them in respect of the body in pursuance of a requirement made by the Lord Advocate under this Part of this Act.

(4) A recognised body shall provide to any person who requests it, on payment of such reasonable charge in respect of copying and postage as the body may stipulate, a copy of its explanatory document.

(5) Where any recognised body, within one month of its being requested to do so by any person, fails to provide to that person a copy of its explanatory document as mentioned in subsection (4) above, the Lord Advocate, on a complaint being made to him by such person, may direct that the fact of such failure shall be noted for the purposes of subsection (3) above.

(6) Where there has been a failure such as is mentioned in subsection (5) above, the court may, on an application being made by the Lord Advocate, interdict the body and any person concerned in its management or control from engaging in any activity specified in the application until the Lord Advocate intimates to the court that he is satisfied that the explanatory document has been provided.

(7) In this Part of this Act "recognised body" means any body to which the Commissioners have given intimation, which has not subsequently been withdrawn, that relief will be due under section 505 of the Income and Corporation Taxes Act 1988 in respect of income of the body which is applicable and applied to charitable purposes only, being a body—

(a) which is established under the law of Scotland; or
(b) which is managed or controlled wholly or mainly in or from Scotland,

and a recognised body shall be entitled to describe itself as "a Scottish charity".

(8) For the purposes of any proceedings under or by virtue of this Part of this Act, a certificate purporting to be signed by a person authorised to do so by the Commissioners and certifying that a body is a recognised body shall be sufficient evidence of that fact and of the authority of that person.

(9) In this section "explanatory document" means—

(a) the trust deed of a body or other document constituting the body; or
(b) such other document as the Lord Advocate may approve,

being a document which describes the nature of the body and of its charitable purposes.

Non-recognised bodies

2.—(1) A non-recognised body shall not be entitled to represent itself or hold itself out as a charity.

(2) For the purposes of this Part of this Act, any body which is not—

(a) a recognised body; or
(b) body which is—

(i) registered as a charity in England and Wales under section 4 of the Charities Act 1960; or
(ii) a charity which is not required to register by virtue of subsection (4) of that section,

is a non-recognised body.

(3) Where a non-recognised body represents itself or holds itself out as a charity, the court may, on an application made by the Lord Advocate, interdict the body from so representing itself or holding itself out until it becomes a body such as is mentioned in paragraph (a) or (b) of subsection (2) above.

Designated religious bodies

3.—(1) The Secretary of State may from time to time, by order, designate for the purposes of this section such recognised bodies as appear to him—

    (a) to have as their principal purpose the promotion of a religious objective;

    (b) to have as their principal activity the regular holding of acts of public worship; and

    (c) to be bodies which satisfy each of the conditions mentioned in subsection (2) below.

(2) The conditions referred to in subsection (1)(c) above are—

    (a) subject to subsection (4) below, that the body has been established in Scotland for not less than 10 years.

    (b) that the body can demonstrate to the satisfaction of the Secretary of State that it has a membership of not less than 3,000 persons resident in Scotland who are 16 years of age or more; and

    (c) that the internal organisation of the body is such that one or more authorities in Scotland exercise supervisory and disciplinary functions in respect of the component elements of the body and, in particular, that there are imposed on such component elements requirements as to the keeping of accounting records and the auditing of accounts which appear to the Secretary of State to correspond to those required by sections 4 and 5 of this Act.

(3) Where a body is, for the time being, designated under subsection (1) above the following provisions of this Part of this Act shall not apply to the body nor to any component or structural element of the body which is, itself, a recognised body—

    section 1(6);

    section 4;

    section 5, other than subsections (6) to (8) and subsection (12);

    section 6(2) and (6);

    section 7; and

    section 8.

(4) The Secretary of State may determine that the condition mentioned in subsection (2)(a) above shall not be required in the case of a body—

    (a) which has been created by the amalgamation of two or more bodies each of which, immediately before the amalgamation, either was designated under this section or appears to the Secretary of State to have been eligible for such designation; or

(b) which has been constituted by persons who have removed themselves from membership of a body which immediately before such removal, was so designated or appears to the Secretary of State to have been eligible for such designation.

Charities accounts

Duty to keep accounting records

4.—(1) The persons concerned in the management or control of every recognised body shall ensure that there are kept in respect of the body, accounting records which are sufficient to show and explain the body's transactions and which are such as to—
  (a) disclose with reasonable accuracy, at any time, the financial position of the body at that time; and
  (b) enable them to ensure that any statement of accounts prepared under section 5 of this Act complies with the requirements of that section.

(2) The accounting records shall in particular contain—
  (a) entries showing from day to day all sums of money received and expended by the body, and the matters in respect of which the receipt and expenditure takes place; and
  (b) a record of the assets and liabilities of the body.

(3) The accounting records which are required by this section to be kept in respect of a recognised body shall be preserved, without prejudice to any requirement of any other enactment or rule of law, for six years from the date on which they are made.

(4) The Secretary of State may, by regulations—
  (a) prescribe requirements as to the places where and the persons by whom the accounting records of recognised bodies, including bodies which have been wound up or have ceased to be active, are to be kept; and
  (b) provide that such class or classes of recognised body as may be prescribed shall be exempt from such requirements of this section and section 5 of this Act as may be prescribed.

Annual accounts and report

5.—(1) The persons concerned in the management or control of every recognised body shall ensure that, in respect of each financial year of the body, there is prepared a statement of accounts.

(2) Subject to subsection (3) below, the statement of accounts of every recognised body shall comprise—
  (a) a balance sheet as at the last day of the year;
  (b) an income and expenditure account; and
  (c) a report as to the activities of the body, having regard to its charitable purposes.

(3) As regards such class or classes of recognised body as the Secretary of State may, by regulations, prescribe a recognised body may elect that in respect of any financial year its statement of accounts shall, instead of the requirements in subsection (2) above, comprise—
  (a) a statement of balances as at the last day of the year;
  (b) a receipts and payments account; and
  (c) a report as to the activities of the body, having regard to its charitable purposes.

(4) The balance sheets shall give a true and fair view of the state of affairs of the body as at the end of the financial year; and the income and expenditure account shall give a true and fair view of the surplus or deficit of the body for the financial year.

(5) The Secretary of State may, by regulations, prescribe—
  (a) the form and content of the statement of accounts;
  (b) any additional information to be provided by way of notes to the accounts; and
  (c) such requirements as to auditing of the balance sheet, statement of balances, income and expenditure account and receipts and payments account and any notes thereon and as to the consideration of the report as he considers appropriate,
and different provision may be prescribed for different bodies or classes of bodies.

(6) The Lord Advocate may require any recognised body to furnish him, without payment therefor, with a copy of its statement of accounts.

(7) Every such body shall—
  (a) make available to any person who requests it, on payment of such reasonable charge in respect of copying and postage as the body may stipulate, a copy of its most recent statement of accounts;
  (b) inform any person who requests it of its accounting reference date.

(8) Where any recognised body fails, within 10 months, or such longer period as the Lord Advocate may allow, after the end of the financial year, to have prepared a statement of accounts, the Lord Advocate may require that such fact shall be noted for the purposes of section 1(3) of this Act.

(9) Where a body has failed to have prepared a statement of accounts as mentioned in subsection (8) above, the Lord Advocate may require the persons concerned in the management of control of the body to have prepared a statement of accounts, by such date as he may require.

(10) In any case where the statement of accounts has not been prepared by the date specified under subsection (9) above, the Lord Advocate may appoint a suitably qualified person to prepare a balance sheet and income and expenditure account or, in the case of a body

which belongs to a class to which subsection (3) above applies if it appears to such person more appropriate to do so, a statement of balances and receipts and payments account; and a person so appointed shall be entitled, for that purpose—

    (a) on giving prior notice in writing, to enter, at all reasonable times, the premises of the body;

    (b) to take possession of any document appearing to him to relate to the financial affairs of the body;

    (c) to require any person concerned in the management or control of the body to give him such information as he may reasonably require relating to the activities of the body,

and the persons concerned in the management or control of the body shall be personally liable jointly and severally for the expenses incurred in the performance of his functions under this section by any person so appointed.

(11) A person appointed under subsection (10) above shall make a report to the Lord Advocate as to the affairs and accounting records of the body and shall send a copy of the report to any person appearing to him to be concerned in the management and control of the body.

(12) Where any such body, within one month of its being requested to do so by any person—

    (a) fails to provide to that person a copy of its most recent statement of accounts as mentioned in subsection (7) above; or

    (b) fails to inform that person of its accounting reference date,

the Lord Advocate, on a complaint being made to him by such person, may direct that the fact of such failure shall be noted for the purposes of section 1(3) of this Act.

(13) Where in the case of any recognised body, there has been a failure such as is mentioned in subsection (9) or (12) above the court may, on an application being made by the Lord Advocate, interdict the body and any person concerned in its management or control from engaging in any activity specified in the application until the Lord Advocate intimates to the court that he is satisfied that the failure has been rectified.

(14) Section 4 of this Act and subsections (1), (2), (3), (4), (5), (8), (9), (10) and (11) and, so far as it relates to a failure such as is mentioned in the said subsection (9), subsection (13) of this section shall not apply to any recognised body which is—

    (a) a company within the meaning of section 735 of the Companies Act 1985; or

    (b) an unregistered company to which Part VII of that Act (accounts and audit) applies by virtue of section 718 of that Act,

and, in the application of the remainder of this section to such a body, references to its income and expenditure account and its report shall be construed as references to its profit and loss account and its directors' report.

Supervision of charities

Powers of Lord Advocate to investigate charities and to suspend trustees

6.—(1) The Lord Advocate may at any time make inquiries, either generally or for particular purposes, with regard to—

(a) a recognised body;

(b) a registered, or non-registered, charity operating as such in Scotland; or

(c) a non-recognised body with appears to him to represent itself or hold itself out as a charity and—

(i) is established under the law of Scotland;

(ii) is managed or controlled wholly or mainly in or from Scotland; or

(iii) has any moveable or immoveable property situated in Scotland,

or with regard to any class of any such bodies.

(2) Where it appears to the Lord Advocate—

(a) in the case of a body referred to in paragraph (a) or (b) of subsection (1) above—

(i) that there is or has been any misconduct or mismanagement in its administration; or

(ii) that it is necessary or desirable to act for the purpose of protecting its property or securing a proper application of such property for its purposes; or

(b) in any other case, that a body is a non-recognised body which appears to him to represent itself or hold itself out as a charity,

he may, if the body is managed or controlled wholly or mainly in or from Scotland, suspend any person concerned in its management or control from the exercise of his functions (but not for a period longer than 28 days), and may make provision as respects the period of the suspension for matters arising out of it.

(3) The Lord Advocate may from time to time nominate officers for the purpose of making inquiries such as are mentioned in subsection (1) above.

(4) A nominated officer may by notice in writing require any person who he has reason to believe has relevant information to answer questions or otherwise furnish information with respect to any matter relevant to inquiries being made under this section at a specified place and either at a specified time or forthwith.

(5) A nominated officer may, for the purpose of making inquiries under this section—

(a) require any person having in his possession or control any records relating to a body which is the subject of inquiries under this section to furnish him with copies of or extracts from any such records; or

    (b) unless it forms part of the records of a court or of a public body or local authority, require such a person to transmit the record itself to him for inspection,
either by a specified time or forthwith.

(6) If any person fails or refuses to comply with a requirement made under subsection (4) or (5) above, the nominated officer may apply by summary application to the sheriff for an order requiring that person to—

    (a) attend and to answer such questions or to furnish such information at a time and place specified in the order;

    (b) furnish the nominated officer with copies or extracts of such records as are specified in the order and by such time as is specified in the order;

    (c) transmit to the nominated officer such records as are specified in the order by such time as is specified in the order,
and the sheriff shall, if he considers it expedient to do so, make such an order.

(7) A person shall not be excused from answering such questions as he may be required to answer by virtue of subsection (6) above on the ground that the answer may incriminate or tend to incriminate him, but a statement made by him in answer to any such question shall not be admissible in evidence in any subsequent criminal proceedings against him, except in a prosecution for an offence under section 2 of the False Oaths (Scotland) Act 1933.

(8) A person who fails to comply with an order under subsection (6) above shall be guilty of an offence and liable on summary conviction to a fine not exceeding level 5 on the standard scale.

(9) Any person who wilfully alters, suppresses, conceals or destroys any record which he may be required to furnish or transmit under this section shall be guilty of an offence and liable on summary conviction to a fine not exceeding level 5 on the standard scale or to imprisonment for a term not exceeding 6 months or to both.

(10) Subject to subsections (11) and (12) below, there shall be paid to any person who complies with a requirement under subsection (4) or (5) above such expenses as he has reasonably incurred in so complying.

(11) A nominated officer shall, for the purpose of making inquiries under this section, be entitled without payment to inspect and take copies of or extracts from records in respect of which no requirement can be made under paragraph (b) of subsection (5) above.

(12) A nominated officer shall, for the purpose of making inquiries under this section, be entitled without payment to keep any copy or extract furnished to him under this section; and where a record transmitted to him for his inspection relates only to one or more recognised body and is not held by any person entitled as trustee or otherwise of such a body to the custody of it, the nominated officer

may keep it or may deliver it to the trustees of such a body or to any person who may be so entitled.

(13) In this section, "record" means a record held in any medium and includes books, documents, deeds or papers; and, in this Part of this Act—
> "registered charity" means a body which is registered as a charity in England and Wales under section 4 of the Charities Act 1960; and
> "non-registered charity" means a charity which, by virtue of subsection (4) of section 4 of that Act, is not required to register under that section.

Powers of Court of Session to deal with management of charities

7.—(1) Where it appears to the court, in the case of a recognised body or a registered, or non-registered, charity which is managed or controlled wholly or mainly in or from Scotland, that—
> (a) there is or has been any misconduct or mismanagement in its administration; or
> (b) it is necessary or desirable to act for the purpose of protecting its property or securing a proper application of such property for its purposes,

it may, on the application of the Lord Advocate, exercise any of the powers specified in paragraphs (a) to (f) of subsection (4) below.

(2) Where the court is satisfied, in the case of such a body as is mentioned in subsection (1) above, that—
> (a) there is or has been any misconduct or mismanagement in its administration; and
> (b) it is necessary or desirable to act for the purpose of protecting its property or securing a proper application of such property for its purposes,

it may, on the application of the Lord Advocate, exercise any of the powers specified in paragraphs (f) to (j) of subsection (4) below.

(3) Where the court is satisfied that a non-recognised body—
> (a) represents itself or holds itself out as a charity; and
> (b) is established under the law of Scotland or is managed or controlled wholly or mainly in or from Scotland or has moveable or immoveable property situated in Scotland,

it may, on the application of the Lord Advocate, exercise any of the powers specified in subsection (4) below.

(4) The powers which may be exercised under this subsection by the court are—
> (a) to interdict *ad interim* the body from representing itself or holding itself out as a charity or from such other action as the court, on the application of the Lord Advocate, thinks fit;
> (b) to suspend any person concerned in the management or control of the body;

    (c) to appoint *ad interim* a judicial factor to manage the affairs of the body;

    (d) to make an order requiring any bank or other person holding money or securities on behalf of the body or of any person concerned in its control and management not to part with the money or securities without the court's approval;

    (e) to make an order, notwithstanding anything in the trust deed or other document constituting the body, restricting the transactions which may be entered into, or the nature or amount of the payments which may be made, in the administration of the body without the approval of the court;

    (f) to appoint a trustee, and section 22 of the Trusts (Scotland) Act 1921 shall apply to such a trustee as if he had been appointed under that section;

    (g) to interdict the body from representing itself or holding itself out as a charity or from such other action as the court, on the application of the Lord Advocate, thinks fit;

    (h) to remove any person concerned in the management or control of the body;

    (j) to appoint a judicial factor to manage the affairs of the body.

(5) Where the court is satisfied, in the case of such a body as is mentioned in subsection (1) above, that—

    (a) there has been in its administration any misconduct or mismanagement;

    (b) it is necessary or desirable to act for the purpose of protecting its property or securing a proper application of such property for its purposes;

    (c) it is not practicable nor in the best interests of the body to retain its existing administrative structure and, if appropriate, trustee body; and

    (d) in its opinion, the body's purpose would be achieved better by transferring its assets to another such body,

or where the court is satisfied as mentioned in subsection (3) above in the case of a non-recognised body, it may approve a scheme, presented to it by the Lord Advocate and prepared by him in accordance with regulations made by the Secretary of State, for the transfer of any assets of the body to such body as the Lord Advocate specifies in the scheme, being a recognised body or a registered, or non-registered, charity which is managed or controlled wholly or mainly in or from Scotland.

(6) In the case of a registered, or non-registered, charity which is managed or controlled wholly or mainly outside Scotland but on behalf of which a bank or other person in Scotland holds moveable property, the court may, on the application of the Lord Advocate acting on information received from the Charity Commissioners for England and Wales, make an order requiring the bank or person not to part with the property without the court's approval and such an order shall be subject to such conditions as the court thinks fit.

(7) Where the court has made an order under subsection (6) above and is satisfied, in the case of such a charity, that—

(a) there has been in its administration any misconduct or mismanagement; and

(b) it is necessary or desirable to act for the purpose of protecting its property or securing a proper application of such property for its purposes,

it may, on the further application of the Lord Advocate, make an order confirming the order made under subsection (6) above and such an order shall be subject to such conditions as the court thinks fit.

(8) Where the court has made an order under subsection (6) above and is satisfied as to the matters specified in subsection (7) above in respect of such a charity, if in its opinion the moveable property would not be applied for the purposes of the charity, it may, on the further application of the Lord Advocate, transfer that property to such body as the Lord Advocate specifies in the application, being a body—

(a) which is a recognised body or registered, or non-registered, charity the purposes of which closely resemble the purpose of the charity whose moveable property is transferred; and

(b) which has intimated that it will receive that property.

(9) The court shall have power—

(a) to vary or recall an order made under paragraph (d) or (e) of subsection (4) above or under subsection (6) or (7) above;

(b) to recall the suspension of a person under paragraph (b) of subsection (4) above;

(c) to approve a scheme under subsection (5) above subject to such modifications as it thinks fit;

(d) subject to subsection (10) below, to award expenses as it thinks fit in any proceedings before it under this section.

(10) In a case where, but for the provisions of this subsection, the court would have awarded expenses against the body which is the subject of the proceedings, the court—

(a) shall have regard to the desirability of applying the property of the body for the charitable purposes of that body, or the charitable purposes which are purported to be the purposes of that body, and

(b) may award expenses against a person concerned in the control or management of the body, or against any such persons jointly and severally.

(11) Where the court exercises in respect of a recognised body any power specified in subsection (4) or (5) above, the Lord Advocate may require that exercise to be noted for the purposes of section 1(3) of this Act.

(12) In this section "the court" means the Court of Session.

Disqualification of persons concerned in the management or control of recognised bodies

8.—(1) A person who—

(a) has been convicted of an offence involving dishonesty;

(b) is an undischarged bankrupt;

(c) has been removed, under section 7 of this Act, from being concerned in the management or control of any body; or

(d) is subject to a disqualification order under the Company Directors Disqualification Act 1986,

shall, subject to the provisions of this section, be disqualified from being concerned with the management or control of a recognised body.

(2) A person shall not be disqualified under subsection (1) above if—

(a) the conviction mentioned in that subsection is spent by virtue of the Rehabilitation of Offenders Act 1974; or

(b) the Lord Advocate has thought fit to grant in writing a waiver of that disqualification in respect of that person,

but the Lord Advocate shall not grant a waiver where to do so would prejudice the operation of the Company Directors Disqualification Act 1986.

(3) A person who is concerned with the management or control of a recognised body whilst disqualified by virtue of this section shall be guilty of an offence and liable—

(a) on summary conviction, to imprisonment for a term not exceeding 6 months or a fine not exceeding the statutory maximum or to both; and

(b) on conviction on indictment, to imprisonment for a term not exceeding 2 years or to a fine or to both.

(4) The acts, in relation to the management or control of such a body, of such a person as is mentioned in subsection (1) above shall not be invalid only by reason of his disqualification under that subsection.

(5) Proceedings for an offence under subsection (3) above shall not be commenced after the end of the period of 3 years beginning with the day on which the offence was committed but, subject to that, may be commenced at any time within 6 months from the date on which evidence sufficient in the opinion of the procurator fiscal to warrant proceedings came to his knowledge; and a certificate of the procurator fiscal as to the date on which such evidence came to his knowledge shall be conclusive evidence of that fact.

(6) In this section, "undischarged bankrupt" means a person who has had his estate sequestrated, been adjudged bankrupt or has granted a trust deed for or entered into an arrangement with his creditors and has not been discharged under or by virtue of—

(a) section 54 or section 75(4) of the Bankruptcy (Scotland) Act 1985;

(b) an order under paragraph 11 of Schedule 4 to that Act of 1985;

(c) section 279 or section 280 of the Insolvency Act 1986; or

(d) any other enactment or rule of law subsisting at the time of his discharge.

Reorganisation of public trusts by the court

9.—(1) Where, in the case of any public trust, the court is satisfied—

(a) that the purposes of the trust, whether in whole or in part—

(i) have been fulfilled as far as it is possible to do so; or

(ii) can no longer be given effect to, whether in accordance with the directions or spirit of the trust deed or other document constituting the trust or otherwise;

(b) that the purposes of the trust provide a use for only part of the property available under the trust;

(c) that the purposes of the trust were expressed by reference to—

(i) an area which has, since the trust was constituted, ceased to have effect for the purpose described expressly or by implication in the trust deed or other document constituting the trust; or

(ii) a class of persons or area which has ceased to be suitable or appropriate, having regard to the spirit of the trust deed or other document constituting the trust, or as regards which it has ceased to be practical to administer the property available under the trust; or

(d) that the purpose of the trust, whether in whole or in part, have, since the trust was constituted—

(i) been adequately provided for by other means; or

(ii) ceased to be such as would enable the trust to become a recognised body; or

(iii) ceased in any other way to provide a suitable and effective method of using the property available under the trust, having regard to the spirit of the trust deed or other document constituting the trust,

the court, on the application of the trustees, may, subject to subsection (2) below, approve a scheme for the variation or reorganisation of the trust purposes.

(2) The court shall not approve a scheme as mentioned in subsection (1) above unless it is satisfied that the trust purposes proposed in the scheme will enable the resources of the trust to be applied to better effect consistently with the spirit of the trust deed or other document constituting the trust, having regard to changes in social and economic conditions since the time when the trust was constituted.

(3) Where any of paragraphs (a) to (d) of subsection (1) above applies to a public trust, an application may be made under this section for the approval of a scheme—

(a) for the transfer of the assets of the trust to another public trust, whether involving a change to the trust purposes of such other trust or not; or

(b) for the amalgamation of the trust with one or more public trusts,

and the court, if it is satisfied that the conditions specified in subsection

(2) above are met, may approve such a scheme.

(4) Subject to subsection (5) below, an application for approval of a scheme under this section shall be made to the Court of Session.

(5) From such day as the Lord Advocate may, by order, appoint, an application for approval of a scheme under this section may be made by a public trust having an annual income not exceeding such amount as the Secretary of State may, by order, prescribe—

    (a) to the sheriff for the place with which the trust has its closest and most real connection;

    (b) where there is no such place as is mentioned in paragraph (a) above, to the sheriff for the place where any of the trustees resides;

    (c) where neither paragraph (a) nor (b) above applies, to the sheriff of Lothian and Borders at Edinburgh.

(6) Every application under this section shall be intimated to the Lord Advocate who shall be entitled to enter appearances as a party in any proceedings on such application, and he may lead such proof and enter such pleas as he thinks fit; and no expenses shall be claimed by or against the Lord Advocate in any proceedings in which he has entered appearance under this subsection.

(7) This section shall be without prejudice to the power of the Court of Session to approve a cy-près scheme in relation to any public trust.

Small trusts

10.—(1) Where a majority of the trustees of any public trust having an annual income not exceeding £5,000 are of the opinion—

    (a) that the purposes of the trust, whether in whole or in part—

        (i) have been fulfilled as far as it is possible to do so; or

        (ii) can no longer be given effect to, whether in accordance with the directions or spirit of the trust deed or other documentation constituting the trust or otherwise;

    (b) that the purposes of the trust provide a use for only part of the property available under the trust;

    (c) that the purposes of the trust were expressed by reference to—

        (i) an area which has, since the trust was constituted, ceased to have effect for the purpose described expressly or by implication in the trust deed or other document constituting the trust; or

        (ii) a class of persons or area which has ceased to be suitable or appropriate, having regard to the spirit of the trust deed or other document constituting the trust, or as regards which it has ceased to be practicable to administer the property available under the trust; or

    (d) that the purposes of the trust, whether in whole or in part, have, since the trust was constituted—

        (i) been adequately provided for by other means; or

(ii) ceased to be such as would enable the trust to become a recognised body; or

(iii) ceased in any other way to provide a suitable and effective method of using the property available under the trust, having regard to the spirit of the trust deed or other document constituting the trust,

subsection (2) below shall apply in respect of the trust.

(2) Where this subsection applies in respect of a trust, the trustees may determine that, to enable the resources of the trust to be applied to better effect consistently with the spirit of the trust deed or other document constituting the trust—

(a) a modification of the trust's purposes should be made;

(b) the whole assets of the trust should be transferred to another public trust; or

(c) that the trust should be amalgamated with one or more public trusts.

(3) Where the trustees of a trust determine as mentioned in subsection (2)(a) above, they may, subject to subsections (4) to (6) below, pass a resolution that the trust deed be modified by replacing the trust purposes by other purposes specified in the resolution.

(4) The trustees shall ensure that, so far as is practicable in the circumstances, the purposes so specified are not so far dissimilar in character to those of the purposes set out in the original trust deed or other document constituting the trust that such modification of the trust deed would constitute an unreasonable departure from the spirit of such trust deed or other document.

(5) Before passing a resolution under subsection (3) above the trustees shall have regard—

(a) where the trust purposes relate to a particular locality, to the circumstances of the locality; and

(b) to the extent to which it may be desirable to achieve economy by amalgamating two or more trusts.

(6) As regards a trust which is a recognised body, the trustees shall ensure that the purposes specified as mentioned in subsection (3) above are such as will enable the trust to continue to be granted an exemption from tax by the Commissioners of Inland Revenue under section 505(1) of the Income and Corporation Taxes Act 1988 (exemption from tax for charities).

(7) Subject to subsection (14) below, a modification of trust purposes under this section shall not have effect before the expiry of a period of two months commencing with the date on which any advertisement in pursuance of regulations made under subsection (13) below is first published.

(8) Where the trustees determine as mentioned in subsection (2)(b) above they may pass a resolution that the trust be wound up and that

the assets of the trust be transferred to another trust or trusts the purposes of which are not so dissimilar in character to those of the trust to be wound up as to constitute an unreasonable departure from the spirit of the trust deed or other document constituting the trust to be wound up.

(9) Before passing a resolution under subsection (8) above, the trustees shall—
    (a) where the trust purposes relate to a particular locality, have regard to the circumstances of the locality;
    (b) where the trust is a recognised body, ensure that the purposes of the trust to which it is proposed that the assets be transferred are such as will enable the trust to be granted an exemption from tax by the Commissioners of Inland Revenue under section 505(1) of the Income and Corporation Taxes Act 1988 (exemption from tax for charities); and
    (c) ascertain that the trustees of the trust to which it is proposed to transfer the assets will consent to the transfer of the assets.

(10) Where the trustees determine as mentioned in subsection (2)(c) above, they may pass a resolution that the trust be amalgamated with one or more other trusts so that the purpose of the trust constituted by such amalgamation will not be so dissimilar in character to those of the trust to which the resolution relates as to constitute an unreasonable departure from the spirit of the trust deed or other document constituting the last mentioned trust.

(11) Before passing a resolution under subsection (10) above, the trustees shall—
    (a) where the trust purposes relate to a particular locality, have regard to the circumstances of the locality;
    (b) where any of the trusts to be amalgamated is a recognised body, ensure that the trust purposes of the trust to be constituted by such amalgamation will be such as to enable it to be granted an exemption from tax by the Commissioners of Inland Revenue under section 505(1) of the Income and Corporation Taxes Act 1988 (exemption from tax for charities); and
    (c) ascertain that the trustees of any other trust with which it is proposed that the trust will be amalgamated will agree to such amalgamation.

(12) Subject to subsection (14) below, a transfer of trust assets or an amalgamation of two or more trusts under this section shall not be effected before the expiry of a period of two months commencing with the date on which any advertisement in pursuance of regulations made under subsection (13) below is first published.

(13) The Secretary of State may, by regulations, prescribe the procedure to be followed by trustees following upon a resolution passed under subsection (3), (8) or (10) above, and such regulations may, without prejudice to the generality, include provision as to

advertisement of the proposed modification or winding up, the making of objections by persons with an interest in the purposes of the trust, notification to the Lord Advocate of the terms of the resolution and the time within which anything requires to be done.

(14) If it appears to the Lord Advocate, whether in consideration of any objections made in pursuance of regulations made under subsection (13) above or otherwise—

(a) that the trust deed should not be modified as mentioned in subsection (3) above;

(b) that the trust should not be wound up as mentioned in subsection (8) above; or

(c) that the trust should not be amalgamated as mentioned in subsection (10) above,

he may direct the trust not to proceed with the modification or, as the case may be winding up and transfer of funds or amalgamation.

(15)The Secretary of State may, by order, amend subsection (1) above by substituting a different figure for the figure, for the time being, mentioned in that subsection.

(16) This section shall apply to any trust to which section 223 of the Local Government (Scotland) Act 1973 (property held on trust by local authorities) applies.

Expenditure of capital

11.—(1) This section applies to any public trust which has an annual income not exceeding £1,000 where the trust deed or other document constituting the trust prohibits the expenditure of any of the trust capital.

(2) In the case of any trust to which this section applies where the trustees—

(a) have resolved unanimously that, having regard to the purposes of the trust, the income of the trust is too small to enable the purposes of the trust to be achieved; and

(b) are satisfied that either there is no reasonable prospect of effecting a transfer of the trust's assets under section 10 of this Act or that the expenditure of capital is more likely to achieve the purposes of the trust,

they may, subject to subsection (3) below, proceed with the expenditure of capital.

(3) Not less than two months before proceeding to expend capital, the trustees shall advertise their intention to do so in accordance with regulations made by the Secretary of State and shall notify the Lord Advocate of such intention.

(4) If it appears to the Lord Advocate that there are insufficient grounds for the expenditure of capital he may apply to the court for an order prohibiting such expenditure, and if the court is satisfied that there are insufficient grounds it may grant the order.

(5) The Secretary of State may, by order, amend subsection (1) above by substituting a different figure for the figure, for the time being, mentioned in that subsection.

Dormant charities

Dormant accounts of charities in banks, etc.

12.—(1) The Secretary of State may appoint a person to be the Scottish charities nominee (in this section referred to as "the nominee") who shall have the functions conferred by this section.

(2) Where the nominee receives from a relevant institution the following information—
   (a) that every account held by the institution in the name of or on behalf of a named body is dormant; and
   (b) the amount of the balance standing to the credit of the body in each such account,
and he is satisfied that the body is a recognised body, subsection (3) or, as the case may be, subsection (5) below shall apply as regards the body and such accounts.

(3) Where the aggregate amount standing to the credit of the body in such accounts as are mentioned in subsection (2) above does not exceed £5,000, unless it appears to the nominee—
   (a) that a person is concerned in the management or control of the body; or
   (b) that there are circumstances relating to the body which would make it inappropriate to do so,
he shall transfer the balance standing to the credit of the body in such accounts to such other recognised body as he may determine, having regard to the purposes of the body in whose name or on whose behalf the accounts are held and those of the body to which it is proposed to transfer the funds; and the body to which the funds are transferred under this subsection or subsection (4) below shall be entitled to apply such funds for its purposes as it thinks fit.

(4) Where, in the case of a body to which subsection (3) above applies, the nominee is unable to ascertain the purposes of the body in whose name or on whose behalf such accounts are held, he shall transfer the balance standing in the name of the body concerned to such other recognised body as appears to him expedient.

(5) Where the aggregate amount standing to the credit of the body in such accounts as are mentioned in subsection (2) above exceeds £5,000 or in any case to which paragraphs (a) or (b) of subsection (3) above applies, the nominee shall advise the Lord Advocate of the information received by him in respect of the body and of any other matter which appears to him to be relevant in the circumstances.

(6) Where the Lord Advocate receives information in pursuance of subsection (5) above he shall inform the nominee—

    (a) in the case of a body which is a trust, whether he intends to exercise his power under section 13(2) of this Act to appoint new trustees to the body; or

    (b) in any case, if he intends to apply to the Court of Sessions for the appointment of an interim judicial factor under section 7(4)(c) of this Act,

but if the Lord Advocate informs the nominee that he does not intend to proceed under either paragraph (a) or (b) above, subsection (3) above shall apply as regards the body and such accounts as are mentioned in subsection (2) above as if the aggregate amount of the balance referred to in subsection (3) did not exceed £5,000 and neither paragraph (a) nor (b) of that subsection applied.

(7) Notwithstanding anything in any enactment or rule of law to the contrary, the nominee shall, by virtue of this subsection, have the right to effect any transaction (including a transaction closing the account) in relation to any account to which subsection (3) above applies; and the receipt of the nominee in respect of any funds withdrawn or transferred from an account by virtue of this subsection shall, as regards the interest of the nominee in respect of such funds, be a full and valid discharge to the relevant institution holding the account.

(8) No liability (other than liability for a criminal offence) shall attach to the nominee in consequence of any act or omission of his in the performance of his functions under this section.

(9) The power of the nominee to effect transactions in relation to the accounts of a body shall cease to have effect—

    (a) when the Lord Advocate notifies him of his intention to proceed under subsection (6) above;

    (b) if the relevant institution by which the accounts are held notifies the nominee that the accounts held by or on behalf of the body are no longer dormant; or

    (c) where the nominee becomes aware of the identity of a person concerned in the management or control of the body, when he informs the institution of that fact,

and in any case to which paragraph (c) above applies, the nominee shall also inform the Lord Advocate of that fact.

(10) The Secretary of State may, by regulations made under this section—

    (a) make provision as to the procedure to be followed by the nominee in exercising his powers under this section;

    (b) require the nominee to make to the Secretary of State an annual report as regards the exercise of his functions and such regulations may specify the form and content of such report; and the Secretary of State shall lay a copy of such report before each House of Parliament;

    (c) prescribe the circumstances in which and the extent to which the nominee may apply any interest accruing to any account as regards which subsection (3) above applies during any period for which he is entitled to effect transactions in respect of the account for the purpose of defraying his expenses in connection with the exercise of his functions under this section;

(d) require the nominee to keep accounts as regards his outlays and expenses in connection with the exercise of his functions under this section; and

(e) amend subsections (3) and (5) above by substituting a different figure for the figure for the time being mentioned in those subsections.

(11) Where every account held by or on behalf of a body which appears to a relevant institution to be a recognised body is a dormant account, no obligation of confidentiality or requirement of secrecy (whether imposed by any enactment or rule of law or otherwise) shall prevent the institution from supplying to the nominee information such as is mentioned in subsection (12) below.

(12) Information referred to in subsection (11) above is information relating to any account such as is mentioned in that subsection which consists of any of the following—

(a) the amount of the balance of the account as at the date the information is supplied;

(b) the last date on which a transaction (other than a transaction consisting only of the accrual of interest to the account) was effected in relation to the account;

(c) so far as is known to the institution, the terms of the trust deed or other document constituting the body or any information as to the nature of the purpose of the body.

(13) For the purpose of this section—

(a) a "relevant institution" is—

(i) an institution which is authorised by the Bank of England to operate a deposit-taking business under Part I of the Banking Act 1987;

(ii) a building society which is authorised by the Building Societies Commission under section 9 of the Building Societies Act 1986 to raise money from its members;

(iii) such other institution mentioned in Schedule 2 to the Banking Act 1987 as the Secretary of State may, by regulations made under this section, prescribe;

(b) an account is dormant if—

(i) in the period of ten years preceding the date on which the institution reviews the account, no transaction (other than a transaction consisting only of the accrual of interest to the account) has taken place in respect of the account; and

(ii) the institution has no knowledge of the identify of any person concerned in the management or control of the body in whose name or on whose behalf the account is held.

Miscellaneous

Appointment of trustees

13.—(1) Where a recognised body is a trust, notwithstanding anything to the contrary in the trust deed or other document constituting the trust, the trustees shall have power to appoint such number of additional trustees as will secure that, at any time, the number of trustees shall be not less than three.

(2) Where in the case of any trust which is a recognised body—
   (a) the number of trustees is less than three; and
   (b) it appears to the Lord Advocate that the trustees will not, or are unable to, exercise their power under subsection (1) above,
if it appears to the Lord Advocate expedient to do so, he may exercise the power in place of the trustees.

Alteration of purposes and winding-up of charitable companies

14.—(1) This section applies to a recognised body which may be wound up by the Court of Session under or by virtue of Parts IV or V of the Insolvency Act 1986.

(2) Where a body to which this section applies has power to alter the instruments establishing or regulating it, it shall not alter any charitable purposes in those instruments except in such a way as will enable the body to continue to be granted an exemption from tax by the Commissioners of Inland Revenue under section 505(1) of the Income and Corporation Taxes Act 1988 (exemption from tax of charities).

(3) Notwithstanding section 124 of the Insolvency Act 1986, a petition for the winding-up under section 122 of that Act of a body to which this section applies may be presented by the Lord Advocate to any court in Scotland having jurisdiction.

Interpretation

Interpretation of Part I, regulations and orders

15.—(1) In this Part of this Act—
   "annual income" in relation to a recognised body means the income of the body for the financial year to which its most recent statement of accounts relates;
   "accounting reference period", "accounting reference date" and "financial year" shall be construed in accordance with subsections (2) to (7) below;
   "body" includes the sole trustee of any trust and, as regards any reference in this Part of this Act to the institution of proceedings in any court or to any order of a court in relation to an unincorporated body, shall be construed—
      (a) in the case of a trust, as a reference to the trustees acting in their capacity as such;

(b) in any other case, as a reference to the persons concerned in the management or control of the body;

"court", for the purposes of establishing jurisdiction to hear or determine any matter other than under sections 7 and 9 of this Act, means the Court of Session or the sheriff court;

"non-recognised body" shall be construed in accordance with section 2 of this Act;

"non-registered charity" has the meaning given by section 6 of this Act;

"recognised body" has the meaning given by section 1 of this Act; and

"registered charity" has the meaning given by section 6 of this Act.

(2) For the purposes of this Part of this Act, a recognised body's first financial year begins with the first day of its first accounting reference period and ends with the last day of that period or such other date, not more than 7 days before or after the end of that period, as the persons concerned with the management or control of the body may determine.

(3) Subject to subsection (4) below, subsequent financial years begin with the day immediately following the end of the body's previous financial year and end with the last day of its next accounting reference period or such other date, not more than 7 days before or after the end of that period as the persons responsible for is management or control may determine.

(4) A recognised body's accounting reference periods are determined according to its accounting reference date.

(5) A recognised body's accounting reference date is the date upon which its accounting reference period ends in each calendar year and it shall be ascertained as follows—

(a) in the case of a body which is recognised at the commencement of this section and in respect of which accounts have been prepared up to a date not more than 12 months before such commencement, its accounting reference date shall be that date;

(b) in the case of a body which is recognised at the commencement of this section and in respect of which no such accounts have been prepared, its accounting reference date shall be 31 March or such other date as the Secretary of State may, by order, prescribe;

(c) in the case of a body which is not recognised at the commencement of this section and in respect of which accounts have been prepared up to a date not more than 1 months before its recognition, its accounting reference date shall be that date; and

(d) a body which is not recognised at the commencement of this section and in respect of which no accounts have been prepared up to a date not more than 12 months before such commencement, unless it determines that its accounting reference date shall be 31 March or such other date as the Secretary of State may, by order, prescribe, shall by notice given to the Lord Advocate specify its accounting reference date.

(6) A recognised body's first accounting reference period is—

    (a) in the case of a body which is recognised at the commencement of this section and in respect of which any accounts have been prepared for a period up to date not more than 12 months before such commencement, the period beginning with that date;

    (b) in the case of a body which is recognised at such commencement and in respect of which no such accounts have been prepared, the period beginning with such commencement;

    (c) in the case of any other body, the period of more than 6 months, but not more than 18 months, beginning with the date from which its recognition takes effect and ending with its accounting reference date.

(7) Its subsequent accounting reference periods are successive periods of 12 months beginning immediately after the end of the previous accounting reference period and ending with this accounting reference date.

(8) A recognised body may, on giving not less than one month's notice of its intentions to do so to the Lord Advocate, unless the Lord Advocate notifies the body that he objects to the proposal, specify a new accounting reference date having effect in relation to the body's current accounting reference period and subsequent periods.

(9) Nothing in this Part of this Act, except section 1, shall affect any educational endowment within the meaning of section 122(1) of the Education (Scotland) Act 1980.

(10) The War Charities Act 1940 shall cease to have effect as regards Scotland; but nothing in this subsection shall affect any prosecution for an offence under that Act which has been instituted before the commencement of this section.

(11) Any power in this Part of this Act of the Secretary of State to make regulations or orders shall be exercisable by statutory instrument subject to annulment in pursuance of a resolution of either House of Parliament.

CHARITIES ACT 1993

(1993 c.10)

Part II

Registration and Names of Charities

Registration of charities

Status of registered charity (other than small charity) to appear on official publications etc.

5.—(1) This section applies to a registered charity if its gross income in its last financial year exceeded £5,000.

[1](2) Where this section applies to a registered charity, the fact that it is a registered charity shall be stated in legible characters—
- (a) in all notices, advertisements and other documents issued by or on behalf of the charity and soliciting money or other property for the benefit of the charity;
- (b) in all bills of exchange, promissory notes, endorsements, cheques and orders for money or goods purporting to be signed on behalf of the charity; and
- (c) in all bills rendered by it and in all its invoices, receipts and letters of credit.

[2](2A) The statement required by subsection (2) above shall be in English, except that, in the case of a document which is otherwise wholly in Welsh, the statement may be in Welsh if it consists of or includes the words "elusen cofrestredig" (the Welsh equivalent of "registered charity").

(3) Subsection (2)(a) above has effect whether the solicitation is express or implied, and whether the money or other property is to be given for any consideration or not.

[2](4) If, in the case of a registered charity to which this section applies, any person issues or authorises the issue of any document falling within paragraph (a) or (c) of subsection (2) above which does not contain the statement required by that subsection, he shall be guilty of an offence and liable on summary conviction to a fine not exceeding level 3 on the standard scale.

[3](5) If, in the case of any such registered charity, any person signs any document falling within paragraph (b) of subsection (2) above which does not contain the statement required by that subsection, he shall be guilty of an offence and liable on summary conviction to a fine not exceeding level 3 on the standard scale.

(6) The Secretary of State may by order amend subsection (1) above by substituting a different sum for the sum for the time being specified there.

---

[1] As amended by the Welsh Language Act 1993, s.32 and Sched.2.
[2] Inserted by the Welsh Language Act 1993, s.32
[3] As amended by the Welsh Language Act 1993, s.32.

Part III

Commissioners' Information Powers

General power to institute inquiries

8.—(1) The Commissioners may from time to time institute inquiries with regard to charities or a particular charity or class of charities, either generally or for particular purposes, but no such inquiry shall extend to any exempt charity.

(2) The Commissioners may either conduct such an inquiry themselves or appoint a person to conduct it and make a report to them.

(3) For the purposes of any such inquiry the Commissioners, or a person appointed by them to conduct it, may direct any person (subject to the provisions of the scheme)—

  (a) to furnish accounts and statements in writing with respect to any matter in question at the inquiry, being a matter on which he has or can reasonably obtain information, or to return answers in writing to any questions or inquiries addressed to him on any such matter, and to verify any such accounts, statements or answers by statutory declaration;
  (b) to furnish copies of documents in his custody or under his control which relate to any matter in question at the inquiry, and to verify any such copies by statutory declaration;
  (c) to attend at a specified time and place and give evidence or produce any such documents.

(4) For the purposes of any such inquiry evidence may be taken on oath, and the person conducting the inquiry may for that purpose administer oaths, or may instead of administering an oath require the person examined to make and subscribe a declaration of the truth of the matters about which he is examined.

(5) The Commissioners may pay to any person the necessary expenses of his attendance to give evidence or produce documents for the purpose of an inquiry under this section, and a person shall not be required in obedience to a direction under paragraph (c) of subsection (3) above to go more than ten miles from his place of residence unless those expenses are paid or tendered to him.

(6) Where an inquiry has been held under this section, the Commissioners may either—

  (a) cause the report of the person conducting the inquiry, or such other statement of the results of the inquiry as they think fit, to be printed and published, or
  (b) publish any such report or statement in some other way which is calculated in their opinion to bring it to the attention of persons who may wish to make representations to them about the action to be taken.

(7) The council of a county or district, the Common Council of the City of London and the Council of a London borough may contribute to the expenses of the Commissioners in connection with inquiries under this section into local charities in the council's area.

Power to call for documents and search records

9.—(1) The Commissioners may by order—
- (a) require any person to furnish them with any information in his possession which relates to any charity and is relevant to the discharge of their functions or of the functions of the official custodian;
- (b) require any person who has in his custody or under his control any document which relates to any charity and is relevant to the discharge of their functions or of the functions of the official custodian—
  - (i) to furnish them with a copy of or extract from the document, or
  - (ii) (unless the document forms part of the records or other documents of a court or of a public or local authority) to transmit the document itself to them for their inspection.

(2) Any officer of the Commissioners, if so authorised by them, shall be entitled without payment to inspect and take copies of or extracts from the records or other documents of any court, or of any public registry or office of records, for any purpose connected with the discharge of the functions of the Commissioners or of the official custodian.

(3) The Commissioners shall be entitled without payment to keep any copy or extract furnished to them under subsection (1) above; and where a document transmitted to them under that subsection for their inspection relates only to one or more charities and is not held by any person entitled as trustee or otherwise to the custody of it, the Commissioners may keep it or may deliver it to the charity trustees or to any person who may be so entitled.

(4) No person properly having the custody of documents relating only to an exempt charity shall be required under subsection (1) above to transmit to the Commissioners any of those documents, or to furnish any copy of or extract from any of them.

(5) The rights conferred by subsection (2) above shall, in relation to information recorded otherwise than in legible form, include the right to require the information to be made available in legible form for inspection or for a copy or extract to be made of or from it.

PART IV

ASSISTANCE AND SUPERVISION OF CHARITIES BY COURT AND COMMISSIONERS

Powers of Commissioners to make schemes and act for protection of charities etc

Concurrent jurisdiction with High Court for certain purposes

16.—(1) Subject to the provisions of this Act, the Commissioners may by order exercise the same jurisdiction and powers as are exercisable by the High Court in charity proceedings for the following purposes—

    (a) establishing a scheme for the administration of a charity;

    (b) appointing, discharging or removing a charity trustee or trustee for a charity, or removing an officer or employee;

    (b) vesting or transferring property, or requiring or entitling any person to call for or make any transfer of property or any payment.

(2) Where the court directs a scheme for the administration of a charity to be established, the court may by order refer the matter to the Commissioners for them to prepare or settle a scheme in accordance with such directions (if any) as the court sees fit to give, and any such order may provide for the scheme to be put into effect by order of the Commissioners as if prepared under subsection (1) above and without any further order of the court.

(3) The Commissioners shall not have jurisdiction under this section to try or determine the title at law or in equity to any property as between a charity or trustee for a charity and a person holding or claiming the property or an interest in it adversely to the charity, or to try or determine any question as to the existence or extent of any charge or trust.

(4) Subject to the following subsections, the Commissioners shall not exercise their jurisdiction under this section as respects any charity, except—

    (a) on the application of the charity; or

    (b) on an order of the court under subsection (2) above; or

    (c) in the case of a charity other than an exempt charity, on the application of the Attorney General.

(5) In the case of a charity which is not an exempt charity and whose income from all sources does not in aggregate exceed £500 a year, the Commissioners may exercise their jurisdiction under this section on the application—

    (a) of any one or more of the charity trustees; or

    (b) of any person interested in the charity; or

    (c) of any two or more inhabitants of the area of the charity if it is a local charity.

(6) Where in the case of a charity, other than an exempt charity, the Commissioners are satisfied that the charity trustees ought in the interests of the charity to apply for a scheme, but have unreasonably refused or neglected to do so and the Commissioners have given the charity trustees an opportunity to make representations to them, the Commissioners may proceed as if an application for a scheme had been made by the charity but the Commissioners shall not have the power in a case where they act by virtue of this subsection to alter the purposes of a charity, unless forty years have elapsed from the date of its foundation.

(7) Where—
    (a) a charity cannot apply to the Commissioners for a scheme by reason of any vacancy among the charity trustees or the absence or incapacity of any of them, but
    (b) such an application is made by such number of the charity trustees as the Commissioners consider appropriate in the circumstances of the case,
the Commissioners may nevertheless proceed as if the application were an application made by the charity.

(8) The Commissioners may on the application of any charity trustee or trustee for a charity exercise their jurisdiction under this section of the purpose of discharging him from his trusteeship.

(9) Before exercising any jurisdiction under this section otherwise than on an order of the court, the Commissioners shall give notice of their intention to do so to each of the charity trustees, except any that cannot be found or has no known address in the United Kingdom or who is party or privy to an application for the exercise of the jurisdiction; and any such notice may be given by post, and, if given by post, may be addressed to the recipient's last known address in the United Kingdom.

(10) The Commissioners shall not exercise their jurisdiction under this section in any case (not referred to them by order of the court) which, by reason of its contentious character, or of any special question of law or of fact which it may involve, or for other reasons, the Commissioners may consider more fit to be adjudicated on by the court.

(11) An appeal against any order of the Commissioners under this section may be brought in the High Court by the Attorney General.

(12) An appeal against any order of the Commissioners under this section may also, at any time within the three months beginning with the day following that on which the order is published, be brought in the High Court by the charity or any of the charity trustees, or by any person removed from any office or employment by the order (unless he is removed with the concurrence of the charity trustees or with the approval of the special visitor, if any, of the charity).

(13) No appeal shall be brought under subsection (12) above except with a certificate of the Commissioners that it is a proper case for an appeal or with the leave of one of the High Court attached to the Chancery Division.

(14) Where an order of the Commissioners under this section establishes a scheme for the administration of a charity, any person interested in the charity shall have the like right of appeal under subsection (12) above as a charity trustee, and so also, in the case of a charity which is a local charity in any area, shall any two or more inhabitants of the area and the local council of any parish or (in Wales) any community comprising the area or any part of it.

(15) If the Secretary of State thinks it expedient to do so—
  (a) in consequence of changes in the value of money, or
  (b) with a view to increasing the number of charities in respect of which the Commissioners may exercise their jurisdiction under this section in accordance with subsection (5) above,
he may by order amend that subsection by substituting a different sum for the sum for the time being specified there.

Power to act for protection of charities

18.—(1) Where, at any time after they have instituted an inquiry under section 8 above with respect to any charity, the Commissioners are satisfied—
  (a) that there is or has been any misconduct or mismanagement in the administration of the charity; or
  (b) that it is necessary or desirable to act for the purpose of protecting the property of the charity or securing a proper application for the purposes of the charity of that property or of property coming to the charity,
the Commissioners may of their own motion do one or more of the following things—

(i) by order suspend any trustee, charity trustee, officer, agent or employee of the charity from the exercise of his office or employment pending consideration being given to his removal (whether under this section or otherwise);

(ii) by order appoint such number of additional charity trustees as they consider necessary for the proper administration of the charity;

(iii) by order vest any property held by or in trust for the charity in the official custodian, or require the persons in whom any such property is vested to transfer it to him, or appoint any person to transfer any such property to him;

(iv) order any person who holds any property on behalf of the charity, or of any trustee for it, not to part with the property without the approval of the Commissioners;

(v) order any debtor of the charity not to make any payment in or towards the discharge of his liability to the charity without the approval of the Commissioners;

(vi) by order restrict (notwithstanding anything in the trusts of the charity) the transactions which may be entered into, or the nature or amount of the payments which may be made, in the administration of the charity without the approval of the Commissioners;

(vii) by order appoint (in accordance with section 19 below) a receiver and manager in respect of the property and affairs of the charity.

(2) Where, at any time after they have instituted an inquiry under section 8 above with respect to any charity, the Commissioners are satisfied—

(a) that there is or has been any misconduct or mismanagement in the administration of the charity; and

(b) that it is necessary or desirable to act for the purpose of protecting the property of the charity or securing a proper application for the purposes of the charity of that property or of property coming to the charity,

the Commissioners may of their own motion do either or both of the following things—

(i) by order remove any trustee, charity trustee, officer, agent or employee of the charity who has been responsible for or privy to the misconduct or mismanagement or has by his conduct contributed to it or facilitated it;

(ii) by order establish a scheme for the administration of the charity.

(3) The references in subsection (1) or (2) above to misconduct or mismanagement shall (notwithstanding anything in the trusts of the charity) extend to the employment for the remuneration or reward of persons acting in the affairs of the charity, or for other administrative purposes, of sums which are excessive in relation to the property which is or is likely to be applied or applicable for the purposes of the charity.

(4) The Commissioners may also remove a charity trustee by order made of their own motion—

(a) where, within the last five years, the trustee—

(i) having previously been adjudged bankrupt or had his estate sequestrated, has been discharged, or

(ii) having previously made a composition or arrangement with, or granted a trust deed for, his creditors, has been discharged in respect of it;

(b) where the trustee is a corporation in liquidation;

(c) where the trustee is incapable of acting by reason of mental disorder within the meaning of the Mental Health Act 1983;

(d) where the trustee has not acted, and will not declare his willingness or unwillingness to act;

(e) where the trustee is outside England and Wales or cannot be found or does not act, and his absence or failure to act impedes the proper administration of the charity.

(5) The Commissioners may by order made of their own motion appoint a person to be a charity trustee—

    (a) in place of a charity trustee removed by them under this section or otherwise;

    (b) where there are no charity trustees, or where by reason of vacancies in their number or the absence or incapacity of any of their number the charity cannot apply for the appointment;

    (c) where there is a single charity trustee, not being a corporation aggregate, and the Commissioners are of opinion that it is necessary to increase the number for the proper administration of the charity;

    (d) where the Commissioners are of opinion that it is necessary for the proper administration of the charity to have an additional charity trustee because one of the existing charity trustees who ought nevertheless to remain a charity trustee either cannot be found or does not act or is outside England and Wales.

(6) The powers of the Commissioners under this section to remove or appoint charity trustees of their own motion shall include power to make any such order with respect to the vesting in or transfer to the charity trustees of any property as the Commissioners could make on the removal or appointment of a charity trustee by them under section 16 above.

(7) Any order under this section for the removal or appointment of a charity trustee or trustee for charity, or for the vesting or transfer of any property, shall be of the like effect as an order made under section 16 above.

(8) Subject to subsection (9) below, subsections (11) to (13) of section 16 above shall apply to orders under this section as they apply to orders under that section.

(9) The requirement to obtain any such certificate or leave as is mentioned in section 16(3) above shall not apply to—

    (a) an appeal by a charity or any of the charity trustees of a charity against an order under subsection (1)(vii) above appointing a receiver and manager in respect of the charity's property and affairs, or

    (b) an appeal by a person against an order under subsection (2)(i) or (4)(a) above removing him from his office or employment.

(10) Subsection (14) of section 16 above shall apply to an order under this section which establishes a scheme for the administration of a charity as it applies to such an order under that section.

(11) The power of the Commissioners to make an order under subsection (1)(i) above shall not be exercisable so as to suspend any person from the exercise of his office or employment for a period of more than twelve months; but (without prejudice to the generality of

section 89(1) below), any such order made in the case of any person may make provision as respects the period of his suspension for matters arising out of it, and in particular for enabling any person to execute any instrument in his name or otherwise act for him and, in the case of a charity trustee, for adjusting any rules governing the proceedings of the charity trustees to take account of the reduction in the number capable of acting.

(12) Before exercising any jurisdiction under this section otherwise than by virtue of subsection (1) above, the Commissioners shall give notice of their intention to do so to each of the charity trustees, except any that cannot be found or has no known address in the United Kingdom; and any such notice may be given by post and, if given by post, may be addressed to the recipient's last known address in the United Kingdom.

(13) The Commissioners shall, at such intervals as they think fit, review any order made by them under paragraph (i), or any of paragraphs (iii) to (vii), of subsection (1) above; and, if on any such review it appears to them that it would be appropriate to discharge the order in whole or in part, they shall so discharge it (whether subject to any savings or other transitional provisions or not).

(14) If any person contravenes an order under subsection (1)(iv), (v) or (vi) above, he shall be guilty of an offence and liable on summary conviction to a fine not exceeding level 5 on the standard scale.

(15) Subsection (14) above shall not be taken to preclude the bringing of proceedings for breach of trust against any charity trustee or trustee for a charity in respect of a contravention of an order under subsection (1)(iv) or (vi) above (whether proceedings in respect of the contravention are brought against him under subsection (14) above or not).

(16) This section shall not apply to an exempt charity.

Supplementary provisions relating to receiver and manager appointed for a charity

19.—(1) The Commissioners may under section 18(1)(vii) above appoint to be receiver and manager in respect of the property and affairs of a charity such person (other than an officer or employee of theirs) as they think fit.

(2) Without prejudice to the generality of section 89(1) below, any order made by the Commissioners under section 18(1)(vii) above may make provision with respect to the functions to be discharged by the receiver and manager appointed by the order; and those functions shall be discharged by him under the supervision of the Commissioners.

(3) In connection with the discharge of those functions any such order may provide—

(a) for the receiver and manager appointed by the order to have such powers and duties of the charity trustees of the charity concerned (whether arising under this Act or otherwise) as are specified in the order;

(b) for any powers or duties exercisable or falling to be performed by the receiver and manager by virtue of paragraph (a) above to be exercisable or performed by him to the exclusion of those trustees.

(4) Where a person has been appointed receiver and manager by any such order—

(a) section 29 below shall apply to him and to his functions as a person so appointed as it applies to a charity trustee of the charity concerned and to his duties as such; and

(b) the Commissioners may apply to the High Court for directions in relation to any particular matter arising in connection with the discharge of those functions.

(5) The High Court may on an application under subsection (4)(b) above—

(a) give such directions, or

(b) make such orders declaring the rights of any persons (whether before the court or not),

as it thinks just; and the costs of any such application shall be paid by the charity concerned.

(6) Regulations made by the Secretary of State may make provision with respect to—

(a) the appointment and removal of persons appointed in accordance with this section;

(b) the remuneration of such persons out of the income of the charities concerned;

(c) the making of reports to the Commissioners by such persons.

(7) Regulations under subsection (6) above may, in particular, authorise the Commissioners—

(a) to require security for the due discharge of his functions to be given by a person so appointed;

(b) to determine the amount of such a person's remuneration;

(c) to disallow any amount of remuneration in such circumstances as are prescribed by the regulations.

PART IX

MISCELLANEOUS

Powers of investment

Relaxation of restrictions on wider-range investments

70.—(1) The Secretary of State may by order made with the consent of the Treasury—

(a) direct that, in the case of a trust fund consisting of property held by or in trust for a charity, any division of the fund in pursuance of section 2(1) of the Trustee Investments Act 1961 (trust funds to be divided so that wider-range and narrower-range investments are equal in value) shall be made so that the value of the wider-range part at the time of the division bears to the then value of the narrower-range part such proportion as is specified in the order;

(b) provide that, in its application in relation to such a trust fund, that Act shall have effect subject to such modifications so specified as the Secretary of State considers appropriate in consequence of, or in connection with, any such direction.

(2) Where, before the coming into force of an order under this section, a trust fund consisting of property held by or in trust for a charity has already been divided in pursuance of section 2(1) of that Act, the fund may, notwithstanding anything in that provision, be again divided (once only) in pursuance of that provision during the continuance in force of the order.

(3) No order shall be made under this section unless a draft of the order has been laid before and approved by a resolution of each House of Parliament.

(4) Expressions used in this section which are also used in the Trustee Investments Act 1961 have the same meaning as that Act.

(5) In the application of this section to Scotland, "charity" means a recognised body within the meaning of section 1(7) of the Law Reform (Miscellaneous Provisions) (Scotland) Act 1990.

Extension of powers of investment

71.—(1) The Secretary of State may by regulations made with the consent of the Treasury make, with respect to property held by or in trust for a charity, provision authorising a trustee to invest such property in any manner specified in the regulations, being a manner of investment not for the time being included in any Part of Schedule 1 to the Trustee Investments Act 1961.

(2) Regulations under this section may make such provision—

(a) regulating the investment of property in any manner authorised by virtue of subsection (1) above, and

(b) with respect to the variation and retention of investments so made,

as the Secretary of State considers appropriate.

(3) Such regulations may, in particular, make provision—

(a) imposing restrictions with respect to the proportion of the property held by or in trust for a charity which may be invested in any manner authorised by virtue of subsection (1) above, being either restrictions applying to investment in any such manner generally or restrictions applying to investment in any particular such manner;

(b) imposing the like requirements with respect to the obtaining and consideration of advice as are imposed by any of the provisions of section 6 of the Trustee Investments Act 1961 (duty of trustees in choosing investments).

(4) Any power of investment conferred by any regulations under this section—

(a) shall be in addition to, and not in derogation from, any power conferred otherwise than by such regulations; and

(b) shall not be limited by the trusts of a charity (in so far as they are not contained in any Act or instrument made under an enactment) unless it is excluded by those trusts in express terms;

but any such power shall only be exercisable by a trustee in so far as contrary intention is not expressed in any Act or in any instrument made under an enactment and relating to the powers of the trustee.

(5) No regulations shall be made under this section unless a draft of the regulations has been laid before and approved by a resolution of each House of Parliament.

(6) In this section "property"—

(a) in England and Wales, means real or personal property of any description, including money and things in action, but does not include an interest in expectancy; and

(b) in Scotland, means property of any description (whether heritable or moveable, corporeal or incorporeal) which is presently enjoyable, but does not include a future interest, whether vested or contingent;

and any reference to property held by or in trust for a charity is a reference to property so held, whether it is for the time being in a state of investment or not.

(7) In the application of this section to Scotland, "charity" means a recognised body within the meaning of section 1(7) of the Law Reform (Miscellaneous Provisions) (Scotland) Act 1990.

Supervision by Commissioners of certain Scottish charities

80.—(1) The following provisions of this Act, namely—

(a) sections 8 and 9,

(b) section 18 (except subsection (2)(ii)), and

(c) section 19,

shall have effect in relation to any recognised body which is managed or controlled wholly or mainly in or from England or Wales as they have effect in relation to a charity.

(2) Where—

(a) a recognised body is managed or controlled wholly or mainly in or from Scotland, but

    (b) any person in England and Wales holds any property on behalf of the body or of any person concerned in its management or control,

then, if the Commissioners are satisfied as to the matters mentioned in subsection (3) below, they may make an order requiring the person holding the property not to part with it without their approval.

    (3) The matters referred to in subsection (2) above are—

    (a) that there has been any misconduct or mismanagement in the administration of the body; and

    (b) that it is necessary or desirable to make an order under that subsection for the purpose of protecting the property of the body or securing a proper application of such property for the purposes of the body;

and the reference in that subsection to the Commissioners being satisfied as to those matters is a reference to their being so satisfied on the basis of such information as may be supplied to them by the Lord Advocate.

    (4) Where—

    (a) any person in England and Wales holds any property on behalf of a recognised body or of any person concerned in the management or control of such a body, and

    (b) the Commissioners are satisfied (whether on the basis of such information as may be supplied to them by the Lord Advocate or otherwise)—

        (i) that there has been any misconduct or mismanagement in the administration of the body, and

        (ii) that it is necessary or desirable to make an order under this subsection for the purpose of protecting the property of the body or securing a proper application of such property for the purposes of the body,

the Commissioners may by order vest the property in such recognised body or charity as is specified in the order in accordance with subsection (5) below, or require any persons in whom the property is vested to transfer it to any such body or charity, or appoint any person to transfer the property to any such body or charity.

    (5) The Commissioners may specify in an order under subsection (4) above such other recognised body or such charity as they consider appropriate, being a body or charity whose purposes are, in the opinion of the Commissioners, as similar in character to those of the body referred to in paragraph (a) of that subsection as is reasonably practicable; but the Commissioners shall not so specify any body or charity unless they have received—

    (a) from the persons concerned in the management or control of the body, or

    (b) from the charity trustees of the charity,

as the case may be, written confirmation that they are willing to accept the property.

(6) In this section "recognised body" has the same meaning as in Part I of the Law and Reform (Miscellaneous Provisions) (Scotland) Act 1990 (Scottish charities).

PART X

SUPPLEMENTARY

Regulations and orders

86.—(1) Any regulations or orders of the Secretary of State under this Act—
  (a) shall be made by statuary instrument; and
  (b) (subject to subsection (2) below) shall be subject to annulment in pursuance of a resolution of either House of Parliament.

(2) Subsection (1)(b) above does not apply—
  (a) to an order under section 17(2), 70 or 99(2);
  (b) to any regulations under section 71; or
  (c) to any regulations to which section 85(3) applies.

(3) Any regulations of the Secretary of State or the Commissioners and any order of the Secretary of State under this Act may make—
  (a) different provision for different cases; and
  (b) such supplemental, incidental, consequential or transitional provision or savings as the Secretary of State or, as the case may be, the Commissioners consider appropriate.

(4) Before making any regulations under section 42, 44 or 45 above the Secretary of State shall consult such persons or bodies of persons as he considers appropriate.

THE PUBLIC CHARITABLE COLLECTIONS (SCOTLAND) REGULATIONS 1984

(S.I. 1984 No. 565)

(1st July 1984)

In exercise of the powers conferred on me by section 119 of the Civic Government (Scotland) Act 1982 and of all other powers enabling me in that behalf, I hereby make the following regulations—

Citation, commencement and interpretation

1.—(1) These regulations may be cited as the Public Charitable Collections (Scotland) Regulations 1984 and shall come into operation on 1st July 1984.

(2) In these regulations, unless the context otherwise requires—

"the Act" means the Civic Government (Scotland) Act 1982;

"agent" means a person appointed by the organiser in accordance with regulation 3 of these regulations;

"collection box" means a box or similar receptacle which is securely closed and sealed so as to prevent it from being opened without the seal being broken and bears prominently displayed thereon, so as to be readily legible by any person from whom money is solicited, the name of the funds or organisations which are to benefit from the collection;

"collection" means a public charitable collection;

"collector" means any person who solicits contributions in the course of a collection;

"council" means the district or islands council for an area in which a collection is to be organised;

"envelope" means an envelope which has a gummed flap by means of which it can be securely closed and which bears the name of the funds or organisations which are to benefit from the collection;

"envelope collection" means a house to house collection made by going from house to house presenting envelopes in which money may be placed for immediate collection or which may be called for separately;

"exempted promoter" means a person whom the Secretary of State by virtue of his powers under section 119(11) of the Act has directed should be exempt from section 119(1) of the Act;

"house" includes a place of business;

"house to house collection" means a collection made by going from house to house and soliciting contributions from the occupants thereof;

"organiser" means any person who either organises a collection in respect of which he has been given permission under section 119 of the Act or who is an exempted promoter;

"a qualified accountant" means a member of, or a firm all of the partners of which are members of, one of the following bodies—

(a) The Institute of Chartered Accountants of Scotland,

(b) The Institute of Chartered Accountants in England and Wales,

(c) The Institute of Chartered Accountants in Ireland, or

(d) The Association of Certified Accountants;

"street collection" means a collection made by soliciting contributions from passers by in a public place.

Duties of the organiser

2.—(1) On receiving permission to organise a collection the organiser if he is not an exempted promoter shall appoint an independent responsible person or a qualified accountant to act as auditor of the collection.

(2) An exempted promoter shall appoint a qualified accountant to act as auditor for all collections which he organises while an exempted promoter.

3.—(1) The organiser may appoint an agent to carry out certain of his functions under these regulations.

(2) The organiser shall exercise all due diligence to ensure that—
- (a) any agent that he appoints to carry out any functions is a fit and proper person to carry out such functions; and
- (b) any agent, collector or other person covered by these regulations complies with the obligations imposed by these regulations and with any conditions imposed under section 119 of the Act by the council, the sheriff or the Secretary of State.

4.—(1) The organiser of a collection or his agent shall issue to each collector participating in the collection a certificate of authority which shall bear—
- (a) the name and address of the organiser;
- (b) the name and address of the collector to whom the certificate is issued;
- (c) the name of the funds or organisations which are to benefit from the collection;
- (d) the area in which the collector is authorised to collect;
- (e) the period during which the collector is authorised to collect;
- (f) the signature of the collector;
- (g) the signature of the organiser or his agent; and
- (h) when the certificate has been signed by an agent the name and address of the agent.

(2) The organiser or his agent shall—
- (a) if the collection is an envelope collection, issue a supply of envelopes to each collector;
- (b) if the collection is not an envelope collection, issue a collecting box marked with a distinguishing number to each collector; and
- (c) record the name and address of each collector, and the number marked on the box given to him or the number of envelopes issued to him.

5. The organiser or his agent shall exercise all due diligence to ensure that the collectors to whom certificates of authority are issued are—
- (a) if the collection is a street collection, 14 years of age or over;
- (b) if the collection is a house to house collection, 16 years of age or over;
- (c) fit and proper persons to act as collectors; and
- (d) aware of their obligations under these regulations and under any conditions relating to the collection made under section 119 of the Act by the council, the sheriff or the Secretary of State.

Duties of collectors

6.—(1) No persons shall act as a collector unless he possesses a certificate of authority and displays a badge bearing the name of the funds or organisations which are to benefit from the collection.

(2) A collector shall produce his certificate of authority, on demand, to a police constable, to any person from whom he has solicited a contribution or to any other interested person.

7.—(1) A collector in an envelope collection shall not accept any contribution except in a sealed envelope.

(2) A collector in a collection which is not an envelope collection shall not accept any contribution except by permitting the donor to place it in a collecting box.

8. No collector shall importune any person to the annoyance of that person or remain in or at the door of any house if requested to leave by any occupants thereof.

9. A collector shall return his certificate of authority and his collecting box or envelopes, unopened, to the organiser or his agent on ceasing to act as a collector or at any other time on demand by the organiser or his agent.

Opening of collecting boxes and envelopes

10.—(1) Except as provided in paragraph (2) below, no person shall open a collecting box or sealed envelope.

(2) (a) A collecting box or sealed envelope shall be opened by the organiser or his agent in the presence of another responsible person or, if they are delivered unopened to a bank, they shall be opened by an official of the bank; and

(b) in the case of an envelope collection the person opening the envelopes shall note the number of envelopes returned by each collector and the total amount of money in them and convey this information to the organiser; or

(c) if the collection is not an envelope collection the person opening the collecting boxes shall note the number on each collecting box and the amount of money in it and convey this information to the organiser.

Accounts

11.—(1) The organiser, other than an exempted promoter, of a collection within the area of a council shall, within one month of the last date for which he possessed permission to organise a collection, submit to that council accounts relating to the collection unless the council are satisfied that there are special reasons for granting an extension in which case the one month period may be extended at their discretion.

(2) Where the organiser has received permission to collect for the same beneficiaries on the same dates in more than one area, the accounts may relate to the combined collection in all the relevant areas.

(3) The accounts shall disclose particulars of—
  (a) the amount collected in the collection;
  (b) any other amount attributable to the collection;
  (c) all expenses incurred in connection with the collection; and
  (d) the name of the funds or organisations which have benefited from the collection and the amount which each has been paid from the net proceeds of the collection.

(4) The accounts shall be accompanied by a statement by the organiser and a report by the auditor in the form set out in the Schedule to these regulations.

(5) If required by a condition imposed by a council under section 119(5) of the Act the accounts shall be accompanied—
  (a) in relation to an envelope collection, by a list showing the number of envelopes issued to and returned by each collector and the total amount in the envelopes; or
  (b) in relation to a collection which is not an envelope collection, by a list showing the distinguishing numbers of all collection boxes issued and the amount collected in each of them.

(6) The organiser shall retain all vouchers receipts and other papers relating to the collection for a period of 2 years from the date on which the accounts are submitted to the council. The organiser shall be obliged to exhibit such vouchers receipts or other papers which may be required by the council during that period shall supply any further information or explanation required by the council in relation to any of the particulars required by regulation 11(3) or in relation to any of the vouchers receipts or other papers retained in accordance with this regulation.

12.—(1) Subject to paragraph (2) below, an exempted promoter shall submit accounts at least once during every period of twelve months to the Secretary of State, and a person ceasing to be an exempted promoter shall submit accounts to the Secretary of State within 3 months of such cessation.

(2) The Secretary of State may accept accounts from an exempted promoter which include details of income and expenditure arising from collections organised by another exempted promoter; and in such circumstances the Secretary of State may waive the requirement for a submission of accounts by the other exempted promoter.

(3) The accounts shall, in respect of either the period since the previous accounts were submitted by the exempted promoter, or the period since the exempted promoter became an exempted promoter, disclose particulars of—
  (a) the amounts collected in collections organised by the exempted promoter;
  (b) any other amounts attributable to the collections;

(c) all expenses incurred in connection with the collections; and
(d) the name of the funds or organisations which have benefited from the collections and the amount which each has been paid from the net proceeds of the collections.

(4) The accounts shall be accompanied by a statement by the exempted promoter and a report by the auditor in the terms set out in the Schedule to these regulations.

(5) The exempted promoter shall give the Secretary of State any further information or explanation which the Secretary of State may require in relation to any of the particulars required by regulation 12(3).

13. The organiser shall within one month of submitting accounts publish a summary of them in one or more newspapers circulating in the area or areas for which permission had been granted to collect, or, if the organiser is an exempted promoter, in one or more newspapers circulating throughout Scotland. Where a collection has been undertaken within the area of a single district or islands council, that council may waive this requirement subject to their making a summary of the accounts available for inspection by members of the public for a reasonable period of time. The summary shall include the name of the organiser, the amount of the proceeds and expenses of the collection to which the summary relates, and the name of the funds or organisations which have benefited from the collection and the amount which each has been paid from the net proceeds of the collection.

Offences

14.—(1) Any person who acts in contravention of regulations 6, 7, 8 or 9 shall be guilty of an offence and shall be liable on summary conviction to a fine not exceeding £25 in respect of each offence.

(2) Any person who acts in contravention of regulations 2, 3, 4, 10, 11, 12 or 13 shall be guilty of an offence and shall be liable on summary conviction to a fine not exceeding £50 in respect of each offence.

SCHEDULE   Regulations 11(4) and 12(4)

STATEMENT BY THE ORGANISER

I certify, in relation to the collection(s) undertaken by me on behalf of [*insert the name of the funds or organisations which have benefited from the collections*] on [*insert date(s)*] that—

(i) I have complied with the requirements of regulations 4 and 10 of the Public Charitable Collections (Scotland) Regulations 1984 dealing with the issuing and opening of envelopes and collecting boxes and the recording of their contents;

(ii) the above accounts are a true account of the expenses and proceeds of the collection(s) and the payment of the net proceeds of the collection(s) to the named beneficiaries.

Date   (*Signed*)

REPORT TO DISTRICT OR ISLANDS COUNCIL OR THE SECRETARY OF STATE FOR SCOTLAND

I/We have examined the above accounts of the collection(s) undertaken on behalf of [*insert the name of the funds or organisations which have benefited from the collections*] on [*insert relevant date(s)*] and have obtained all the information and explanations which I/we considered necessary.

In my/our opinion—

(i) the organiser and his agents have complied with the requirements of regulations 4 and 10 of the Public Charitable Collections (Scotland) Regulations 1984 dealing with the issuing and opening of envelopes and collecting boxes and the recording of their contents;

(ii) the above accounts fairly present the recorded expenses and proceeds of the collection(s) and the payment of the net proceeds of the collection(s) to the named beneficiaries.

Date   (*Signed*)

Qualifications

THE CHARITIES (SCHEME FOR THE TRANSFER OF ASSETS) (SCOTLAND) REGULATIONS 1992

(S.I. 1992 No. 2082)

(30th September 1992)

The Secretary of State, in exercise of the powers conferred on him by section 7(5) of the Law Reform (Miscellaneous Provisions) (Scotland) Act 1990 and of all other powers enabling him in that behalf, hereby make the following Regulations:

Citation and commencement

1. These Regulations may be cited as the Charities (Scheme for the Transfer of Assets) (Scotland) Regulations 1992 and shall come into force on 30th September 1992.

Interpretation

2. In these Regulations—
"the Act" means the Law Reform (Miscellaneous Provisions) (Scotland) Act 1990;
"scheme" means a scheme for the transfer of any assets of the transferor body to the transferee body which is prepared by the Lord Advocate under section 7(5) of the Act;
"transferor body" means any body whose assets are or are proposed to be transferred to a transferee body in or under a scheme;
"transferee body" means any body to which the assets of the transferor body are or are proposed to be transferred in a scheme;
"trustees", in relation to any transferor or transferee body, means the persons concerned in the management or control of that body;
and any other expression used in these Regulations which is also used in Part I of the Act will have the same meaning in these Regulations as it has in that Part.

Procedures in preparing a scheme

3.—(1) Before specifying a transferee body in a scheme, the Lord Advocate—
  (a) shall have regard to the spirit of the trust deed or other document constituting, or the intentions as represented or held out by, the transferor body; and
  (b) shall obtain a written statement from the trustees of the transferee body that they are willing to accept the transfer of the assets of the transferor body and, if necessary, to meet any liabilities of the transferor body in accordance with the terms of the scheme.

(2) Before presenting a scheme to the Court of Session for approval, the Lord Advocate—
  (a) shall notify the trustees of the transferor body of his intention to do so by posting to such of them as are known to him at their last known address in the United Kingdom—
      (i) a draft of the scheme which he proposes to present to the Court of Session for their approval; and
      (ii) a notice of his intention to present the scheme for such approval,
  (b) shall invite them to make representations about the proposed scheme by sending them to him in writing within 4 weeks from the date on which he posted the draft scheme to them; and
  (c) shall consider any representations so made.

(3) Before presenting a scheme to the Court of Session for approval, the Lord Advocate shall publish, in at least one newspaper a notice—
  (a) which intimates his intention to present to the Court of Session for approval a scheme for the transfer of the assets of the transferor body to the transferee body; and

(b) which shall invite any person to make representations concerning the proposed scheme by sending them to him in writing within 4 weeks from the date of the publication of the notice in the newspaper,

and shall consider any representations so made.

Contents of scheme

4.—(1) A scheme shall state, so far as known to the Lord Advocate—
   (a) the name and address of the transferor body and of its trustees; and
   (b) the name and address of the transferee body and of its trustees.

(2) A scheme shall contain a list and valuation of all the assets and liabilities of the transferor body, so far as known to the Lord Advocate.

(3) A scheme shall provide for the transfer of the assets of the transferor body to the transferee body on a particular date.

(4) The scheme shall state what provision is being made to meet the liabilities of the transferor body.

(5) The scheme shall contain a statement—
   (a) of the reasons which led the Lord Advocate to prepare and present the scheme for the approval of the Court of Session;
   (b) that the Lord Advocate has complied with the procedures specified in regulation 3 above in the preparation of the scheme;
   (c) of any representations which may have been made in pursuance of regulation 3(2) or (3) above; and
   (d) of any observations by the Lord Advocate upon those representations.

(6) There shall be appended to the scheme a copy of the written statement referred to in regulation 3(1)(b) above.

THE CHARITIES ACCOUNTS (SCOTLAND) REGULATIONS 1992

(S.I. 1992 No. 2165)

(30th September 1992)

The Secretary of State, in exercise of the powers conferred on him by sections 4(4)(a) and 5(3) and (5) of the Law Reform (Miscellaneous Provisions) (Scotland) Act 1990 and of all other powers enabling him in that behalf, hereby makes the following regulations—

Citation and commencement

1. These Regulations may be cited as Charities Accounts (Scotland) Regulations 1992 and shall come into force on 30th September 1992.

Interpretation

2. In these Regulations:

"the Act" means the Law Reform (Miscellaneous Provisions) (Scotland) Act 1990;

"designated fund" means a fund which has been allocated or designated for specific purposes by a recognised body;

"founding deed" means the trust deed of a recognised body or other document constituting the body;

"gross income" in relation to a recognised body means the total of its income from all sources that is required in terms of the Schedules to these Regulations to be recorded in the income and expenditure account;

"gross expenditure" in relation to a recognised body means the total of its expenditure on all purposes that is required in terms of the Schedules to these Regulations to be recorded in the income and expenditure account;

"gross receipts" in relation to a recognised body means the total of the sums received from all sources after deducting the proceeds, if any, of the sale of investments and the sale of assets and receipts in respect of a permanent endowment fund;

"permanent endowment fund" means a fund which must be held permanently although its constituent assets may change from time to time;

"record" means a record kept either in documentary form, or where kept by means of a computer or in other non-documentary form, the information comprised in such computer or in such other non-documentary form produced in a form in which it is tangible and legible;

"trustees", in relation to any recognised body, means the persons in management or control of that body;

and any other expression used in these Regulations which is also used in Part I of the Act will have the same meaning in these Regulations as it has in that Part.

Alternative statement of accounts for each financial year

3. The class of recognised body to which section 5(3) of the Act applies (bodies which may elect in respect of any financial year to have a different statement of accounts from that required by section 5(2) of the Act) is any recognised body the gross receipts of which in the financial year in question do not exceed £25,000 per annum and the founding deed of which contains no requirement that its statement of accounts shall be audited.

Form and content of statement of accounts

4.—(1) A recognised body shall ensure that there shall be shown—

(a) in the statement of accounts—

(i) the duration of the financial year to which they relate and the immediately preceeding financial year; and

(ii) in respect of every item stated in them the corresponding amount for the financial year immediately preceeding that to which they relate;

(b) in respect of the balance sheet and income and expenditure account of such recognised body which has not elected in terms of section 5(3) of the Act the information referred to in Part 1 of Schedule 1 to these Regulations;

(c) in respect of the statement of balances and receipts and payments account of such recognised body which has elected in terms of section 5(3) of the Act the information referred to in Part 2 of Schedule 1 to these Regulations; and

(d) in respect of the report the information referred to in Part 3 of Schedule 1 to these Regulations.

(2) A recognised body shall ensure that the report shall be approved by the trustees and signed by one of their number on their behalf and as authorised by them; and every copy of the report which is circulated, published or issued shall state the name of the person who signed the report.

Additional information by way of notes to the accounts

5. A recognised body shall ensure that there shall be known—

(a) in the case of such recognised body that has not elected in terms of section 5(3) of the Act in respect of its balance sheet and income and expenditure account the additional information to be provided by way of notes to the accounts referred to in Part 1 of Schedule 2 to these Regulations; and

(b) in the case of such recognised body that has elected in terms of section 5(3) of the Act in respect of its statement of balances and receipts and payments account the additional information to be provided by way of notes to the accounts referred to in Part 2 of Schedule 2 to these Regulations.

Approval of accounts

6. The balance sheet and income and expenditure account and notes thereon or the statement of balances and receipts and payments account and notes thereon as appropriate of a recognised body shall be approved by the trustees and signed by one of their number on their behalf as authorised by them; the signature shall be on the balance sheet or statement of balances as appropriate; and every copy of the balance sheet or statement of balances as appropriate of the body which is circulated, published or issued shall state the date of approval and the name of the person who signed the balance sheet or statement of balances.

Audit

7.—(1) Where in any financial year or in either of the two immediately preceeding financial years a recognised body which satisfies either of the following conditions—

(a) the gross income exceeds £100,000 per annum; or

(b) the gross expenditure exceeds £100,000 per annum,

or such other recognised body with is either required in terms of its founding deed or elects to submit its accounts to audit, the accounts and notes thereon shall be audited by a person eligible for appointment as a company auditor under the provisions of section 25 of the Companies Act 1989.

(2) In respect of any recognised body to which regulation 7(1) above applies—

(a) an auditor shall be appointed in respect of each financial year who will hold office for that year and may not be removed in respect of that year unless he becomes no longer eligible or competent for such an appointment; and any auditor so removed may submit a statement to the trustees setting out his observations on the circumstances of such removal and such statement shall be included in the report for the year in question; and

(b) the appointment or removal of an auditor shall be made or effected by the trustees, except in the case where other provision is made in the recognised body's founding deed in which case the appointment or removal shall be made or effected in accordance with such other provision.

(3) An auditor of such a recognised body to which regulation 7(1) above applies who is appointed in terms of paragraph (2)(a) above may resign his office by depositing a notice in writing to that effect with the Trustees and—

(a) his term of office shall terminate on the date on which the notice is deposited or such later date as may be specified therein;

(b) the notice of resignation shall contain a statement as to any circumstances connected with his resignation which he considers should be stated in the report; and

(c) these circumstances or a statement that there are no such circumstances connected shall be stated in the report for the year in question.

(4) Any auditor of such a recognised body to which regulation 7(1) above applies shall have the right of access at all times to the records of that body and shall be entitled to require such information and explanations from the present or former trustees as he thinks necessary for the performance of his duties.

(5) The report of an auditor which shall be annexed to the balance sheet and income and expenditure account shall state—

(a) whether in his opinion in the balance sheet and income and expenditure account have been properly prepared;

(b) without prejudice to the foregoing, whether in his opinion, a true and fair view is given—

(i) in the balance sheet, of the state of affairs at the end of the financial year; and

(ii) in the income and expenditure account, of the surplus or deficit for the financial year.

(6) An auditor shall consider whether the information given in the report is consistent with the accounts; and if he is of the opinion that it is not he shall state that fact in his report.

(7) In addition to preparing his report an auditor—

(a) shall carry out such investigations as will enable him to form an opinion as to whether—

(i) proper accounting records have been kept by the body; and

(ii) the accounts of the body are in agreement with the accounting records;

(b) if he is of the opinion that proper accounting records have not been kept or if the accounts of the body are not in agreement with the accounting records, shall state that fact in his report;

(c) if he fails to obtain all the information and explanations, which, to the best of his knowledge and belief, is or are necessary for the purposes of his audit, shall so state in his report; and

(d) shall consider whether the accounts comply with the relevant statutory requirements or terms of the body's founding deed, or both, and make a statement to that effect in his report.

8.—(1) In the case of a recognised body to which regulation 7(1) above does not apply its balance sheet and income and expenditure account and notes thereon or its statement of balances and its receipts and payments account and notes thereon shall be subject to examination by an independent examiner; and an independent examiner shall be an independent person who is reasonably believed by the trustees to have the requisite ability and practical experience to carry out a competent examination of the accounts.

(2) In respect of any recognised body to which regulation 8(1) above applies—

(a) an independent examiner shall be appointed in respect of each financial year who will hold office for that year and may not be removed in respect of that year unless he becomes no longer competent for such an appointment; and any independent examiner so removed may submit a statement to the trustees setting out his observations on the circumstances of such removal and such statement shall be included in the report for the year in question; and

(b) the appointment or removal of an independent examiner shall be made or effected by the trustees except in the case where other provision is made in the recognised body's founding deed in which case the appointment or removal shall be made or effected in accordance with such other provision.

(3) An independent examiner appointed in terms of paragraph (2) above may resign his office by depositing a notice in writing to that effect with the Trustees and—
- (a) his term of office shall terminate on the date on which the notice is deposited or such later date as may be specified therein;
- (b) the notice of resignation shall contain a statement as to any circumstances connected with his resignation which he considers should be stated in the report; and
- (c) these circumstances or a statement that there are no such circumstances connected shall be stated in the report for the financial year in question.

(4) Any independent examiner of such a recognised body to which regulation 8(1) above applies shall have the right of access at all times to the records of the body and shall be entitled to require such information and explanations from the present or former trustees as he thinks necessary for the performance of his duties.

(5) The report of an independent examiner which shall be annexed to the balance sheet and income and expenditure account or statement of balances and receipts and payment account as appropriate shall state whether, according to the best of his knowledge and belief in accordance with the information and explanations given to him, the balance sheet and income and expenditure account and notes thereon, have been properly prepared from the records of such a recognised body as is described in paragraph (1) above, are in agreement therewith and comply with the terms of these Regulations and the body's founding deed, or both.

(6) An independent examiner shall consider whether the information given in the report is consistent with the accounts; and if he is of the opinion that it is not he shall state that fact in his report.

(7) In addition to preparing his report an independent examiner—
- (a) shall be required to carry out such investigations as will enable him to form an opinion as to whether—
  (i) proper accounting records adequate for the purposes of the body have been kept; and
  (ii) the accounts of the body are in agreement with the accounting records;
- (b) if he is of the opinion that proper accounting records have not been kept or if the accounts of the body are not in agreement with the accounting records, shall state that fact in his report; and
- (c) if he fails to obtain all the necessary information and explanations, which, to the best of his knowledge and belief, is or are necessary for the purpose of his examination, shall so state in his report.

Keeping of records

9.—(1) The accounting records of a recognised body shall be stored at the headquarters office of the body or such other place as the trustees may determine except that they may not be stored at a place outside Great Britain.

(2) The trustees may appoint a person to store the accounting records where no such person has been appointed by the founding deed of the body; and where such a recognised body has been wound up or ceased to be active without appointing such person, and where no person has been appointed in terms of founding deed of the body, the trustees at the winding up of the body or on the body's ceasing to be active shall store the accounting records at an address which shall immediately be notified to the Lord Advocate.

SCHEDULE 1 Regulation 4

ACCOUNTS, NOTES TO THE ACCOUNTS AND THE REPORT

PART 1

Information to be shown in the Balance sheet and Income and Expenditure Account

1. The balance sheet shall—

  (a) classify the assets into fixed assets, investments, including investment properties, and current assets; and classify the liabilities into current liabilities being amounts falling due within one year of the balance sheet date and long term liabilities being those falling due after more than one year after the balance sheet date, in such a way as will enable the user to gain a proper appreciation of their spread and character;
  (b) analyse the total amount of assets less liabilities between its major funds; and
  (c) indicate, wherever possible, which assets and liabilities form part of endowment and other restricted funds.

2. The income and expenditure account shall set out the aggregate income and expenditure and any appropriations therefrom for the financial year in sufficient detail as may reasonably enable the user to gain a proper appreciation of the transactions and the surplus or deficit for that year; and in particular the following, if any, shall be shown separately—

  (a) realised gains on investments;
  (b) realised gains on the disposal of fixed assets;
  (c) income from investments other than land and buildings;
  (d) rents from land and buildings;
  (e) gross income from fund raising activities
  (f) legacies but excluding any amounts provided to form part of a permanent endowment fund;
  (g) grants received and receivable but excluding any amounts provided to form part of a permanent endowment fund;
  (h) donations (excluding legacies) received and receivable but excluding any amounts provided to form part of a permanent endowment fund;

(i) gross income from trading activities;
(j) other material income;
(k) realised losses on investments;
(l) realised losses on the disposal of fixed assets;
(m) expenses of fund raising activities;
(n) publicity expenses;
(o) administrative costs detailing material items;
(p) the remuneration of the auditor or independent examiner in respect of—

> (i) audit services; and
> (ii) other services such as taxation advice, consultancy, financial advice and accountancy;

(q) grants and donations made relating directly to charitable activities;
(r) other expenditure relating directly to charitable activities;
(s) gross expenditure on trading activities; and
(t) other material expenditure.

PART 2

Information to be shown in the Statement of Balances and Receipts and Payments Account

1. The statement of balances shall—
   (a) reconcile the cash and bank balances at the beginning and end of the financial year with the surplus or deficit shown by the receipts and payments account;
   (b) summarise the changes in the holding of investments and other assets including gifted assets during the financial year;
   (c) distinguish between the major funds, the investments and other assets; and
   (d) state an estimate of the liabilities at the end of the financial year showing separately any contingent liabilities.

2. The receipts and payments account shall set out the aggregate receipts and payments for the financial year in sufficient detail as may reasonably enable the user to gain a proper appreciation of the transactions and the excess of receipts over payments or payments over receipts for that year; and in particular the following, if any, shall be shown separately—
   (a) proceeds of sale of investments;
   (b) proceeds of sale of assets;
   (c) income from investments other than land and buildings;
   (d) rents from land and buildings;
   (e) proceeds from fund raising activities;
   (f) legacies;
   (g) grants received;
   (h) donations (excluding legacies) received;
   (i) gross trading receipts;
   (j) other material receipts;
   (k) purchases of investments;
   (l) purchases of other assets;
   (m) expenses of fund raising activities;
   (n) publicity expenses;
   (o) administrative costs detailing material items;
   (p) gross trading payments;
   (q) the remuneration of the auditor or independent examiner in respect of—

(i) audit services; and

(ii) other services such as taxation advice, consultancy, financial advice and accountancy;

(r) grants and donations relating directly to charitable activities;

(s) other payments relating directly to charitable activities;

(t) other material payments.

PART 3

Information to be shown in the Report

The report shall contain, so far as it is applicable—

(a) details of the legal and administrative arrangements including the nature of the founding document, the names and designations of those who are or have been, at any time during the financial year, trustees, and the manner of their appointment, the principal address of the body and details of any restrictions in the way the body may operate;

(b) an explanation of the objectives and organisational structure of the body;

(c) a review of the financial position and an explanation of the salient features of the statement of accounts;

(d) a review of the development, activities and achievements during the year;

(e) any other information necessary, for a proper appreciation of the financial position taking into account future plans and commitments;

(f) particulars of any connected body including the address and nature of the relationship; and

(g) particulars of any material transactions between connected bodies.

SCHEDULE 2   Regulation 5

PART 1

Additional information to be provided by way of Notes to the Accounts

In respect of the balance sheet and income and expenditure account—

(a) a statement of the accounting policies adopted by the recognised body in determining the amounts to be included in the balance sheet and income and expenditure account including such policies with respect to but not restricted to such matters as fixed assets, the use of designated funds, legacies, grants payable and receivable, investments and income therefrom;

(b) the nature and purpose of each of the major funds;

(c) details of the movements on permanent endowment funds to be shown;

(d) except where provided in the statement of accounts and as required in paragraph (c) above a reconciliation of the total opening funds to the total closing funds, by major fund, summarising the income and expenditure of each fund and detailing any movements between them during the financial year;

(e) details of any grant or grants paid which exceeds or exceed in aggregate the greater of £1,000 or 2% of the gross income from all sources for the financial year; separate disclosure shall not be required where the grant or grants is or are made for the benefit of an individual; and grants made for the benefit of individuals should be aggregated and the total, number and range of grants shown;

(f)   particulars of all material commitments showing separately those in respect of specific charitable and other purposes;

(g) any guarantees given or other contingent liabilities and the conditions under which such liabilities might arise;

(h) any loans or other liabilities secured on the assets;

(i)   the aggregate amount, if any, of any remuneration or reimbursement of expenses paid to the trustees and the aggregate amount, if any of any consideration paid to or receivable by third parties for making available the services of the trustees unless disclosed in the statement of accounts;

(j)   the total emoluments paid to employees and the average number of employees during the financial year;

(k) such other information as may reasonably assist the user to understand the statement of accounts; and

(l)   in respect of those bodies who satisfy any two of the following conditions—

> (i) the gross income from all sources exceeds £2,000,000 per annum;
>
> (ii) the number of its employees exceeds 50; or
>
> (iii) the balance sheet total exceeds £975,000

a financial statement analysing cash flows under the headings of operating activities, returns on investments and servicing of finance, taxation, investing activities and financing.

PART 2

Additional information to be provided by way of Notes to the Accounts

In respect of the statement of balances and receipts and payments accounts—

(a) the nature and purpose of each of the major funds;

(b) except where provided in the statement of accounts, a reconciliation of the total opening funds to the total closing funds, by major fund, summarising the receipts and payments of each fund and detailing any movements between them during the financial year;

(c) details of any grant or grants paid which exceeds or exceed in aggregate 2% of the gross receipts from all sources for the financial year; separate disclosure shall not be required where the grant or grants is or are made for the benefit of an individual; and grants made for the benefit of individuals should be aggregated and the total, number and range of grants shown;

(d) the aggregate amount, if any, of any remuneration or reimbursement of expenses paid to the trustees and the aggregate amount, if any, of any consideration paid to or receiveable by third parties for making available the services of the trustees unless disclosed in the statement of accounts; and

(e) such other information as may reasonably assist the user to understand the statement of accounts.

THE CHARITIES (EXEMPTION FROM ACCOUNTING REQUIREMENTS) (SCOTLAND) REGULATIONS 1993

(S.I. 1993 No. 1624)

(28th July 1993)

The Secretary of State, in exercise of the powers conferred on him by section 4(4)(b) of the Law Reform (Miscellaneous Provisions) (Scotland) Act 1990 and of all other powers enabling him in that behalf, hereby make the following Regulations:

Citation and commencement

1. These Regulations may be cited as the Charities (Exemption from Accounting Requirements) (Scotland) Regulations 1993 and shall come into force on 28th July 1993.

Interpretation

2. In these Regulations—
"the 1990 Act" means the Law Reform (Miscellaneous Provisions) (Scotland) Act 1990;
[1]"Scottish charitable corporation" means any recognised body which is a body corporate established by statute or Royal Charter and whose accounts are required by statute or otherwise to be examined and certified by the Comptroller and Auditor General;
"local authority trust" means any recognised body which is a trust for any charity, foundation, mortification or other purpose where a local authority or some members or such an authority are its sole trustees as mentioned in section 106(1)(b) of the Local Government (Scotland) Act 1973;
"registered housing association" means any recognised body which is a housing association as defined in section 1 of the Housing Associations Act 1985 which is registered with Scottish Homes under section 5(d) of that Act,
and, unless the context otherwise requires, any other expression which is used in these Regulations and which is also used in Part I of the 1990 Act, shall have the same meaning in these Regulations as in that Part.

Exemption from accounting requirements

3. Any class of recognised body, which is prescribed in an entry in column 1 of the Schedule to these Regulations, shall be exempt from such of the requirements of sections 4 and 5 of the 1990 Act (relating to accounting matters) as are prescribed opposite to the entry in column 2 of that Schedule.

SCHEDULE   Regulation 3

Exemption from accounting requirements

Column 1 *Class of Recognised Body*	Column 2 *Exempt requirements of section 4 and 5 of the 1990 Act*
[1]Scottish charitable corporation	section 4 and subsections (1), (2), (3), (4), (5), (8), (9), (10), (11) and (13) of Section 5.
local authority trust	Section 4 and subsections (2), (3), (4), (5) and (13) of Section 5.
registered housing association	Section 4 and subsections (2), (3), (4), (5) and (13) of Section 5.

THE PUBLIC TRUSTS (REORGANISATION) (SCOTLAND) (NO. 2) REGULATIONS 1993

(S.I. 1993 No. 2254)

(22nd September 1993)

The Secretary of State, in exercise of the powers conferred on him by sections 10(13) and 11(3) of the Law Reform (Miscellaneous Provisions) (Scotland) Act 1990 and of all other powers enabling him in that behalf, hereby makes the following Regulations—

Citation and commencement

1. These Regulations may be cited as the Public Trusts (Reorganisation) (Scotland) (No. 2) Regulations 1993 and shall come into force on 22nd September 1993.

Interpretation

2. In these Regulations, unless the context otherwise requires—
"the Act" means the Law Reform (Miscellaneous Provisions) (Scotland) Act 1990;
"small trust" means a public trust in respect of which section 10(2) of the Act applies;
"trust deed", in relation to a public trust, means a trust deed of or other document constituting the trust;
"trustees" means the trustees of a small trust,

---

[1] Substituted by the Charities (Exemption from Accounting Requirements) (Scotland) Amendment Regulations 1995 (S.I. 1995 No. 645), reg. 3.

and any other expression used in these Regulations which is also used in Part I of the Act shall have the same meaning in these Regulations as it has in that Part.

Small trusts: advertisement

3.—(1) Subject to paragraphs (2) and (3) below, not later than 28 days after the date when the trustees of a small trust have passed a resolution under section 10(3), (8) or (10) of the Act or, if that date is before the date of coming into force of these Regulations, the date when these Regulations come into force, they shall publish, in a newspaper circulating throughout Scotland or, if the purposes of the trust relate to a particular locality, in a local newspaper circulating in that locality, a notice—

(a) in the case where the trustees have passed the resolution under section 10(3) of the Act, in the form set out in Schedule 1 to these Regulations;

(b) in the case where the trustees have passed the resolution under section 10(8) of the Act, in the form set out in Schedule 2 to these Regulations;

(c) in the case where the trustees have passed the resolution under section 10(10) of the Act, in the form set out in Schedule 3 to these Regulations;

or in a form substantially to the like effect.

(2) Where the trustees of more than one small trust have each passed a resolution under section 10(8) of the Act providing that the trusts be wound up and that the assets of the trusts be transferred to the same trust, the trustees may, instead of publishing a separate notice in respect of each trust in terms of paragraph (1)(b) above, publish a combined notice in the form set out in Schedule 4 to these Regulations or in a form substantially to the like effect, which combined notice shall be published—

(a) not later than 28 days after the earliest date when the trustees of any of the trusts have passed the resolution under that section or, if that date is before the date of coming into force of these Regulations, the date when these Regulations come into force; and

(b) in a newspaper circulating throughout Scotland or, if the purposes of all the trusts relate to a particular locality, in a local newspaper circulating in that locality.

(3) Where the trustees of more than one small trust have each passed a resolution under section 10(10) of the Act providing that the trusts be amalgamated with each other, the trustees may, instead of publishing a separate notice in respect of each trust as required by paragraph (1)(c) above, publish a combined notice in the form set out in Schedule 5 to these Regulations or in a form substantially to the like effect, which combined notice shall be published—

(a) not later than 28 days after the earliest date when the trustees of any of the trusts have passed the resolution under that section or, if that date is before the date of coming into force of these Regulations, the date when these Regulations come into force; and

(b) in a newspaper circulating throughout Scotland or, if the purposes of all the trusts relate to a particular locality, in a local newspaper circulating in that locality.

Small trusts: notification to Lord Advocate

4. The trustees shall send to the Lord Advocate the following documents to arrive not later than 7 days after the date of publication of the notice in a newspaper as required by regulation 3 above, namely—

(a) a copy of the trust deed;

(b) a copy of the newspaper containing the published notice;

(c) a copy of the most recent accounts of the trust; and

(d) in the case where the resolution is passed under section 10(3) of the Act—

(i) a copy of the resolution;

(ii) a statement of the date as to when the trustees propose, subject to section 10(14) of the Act, to give effect to the resolution; and

(iii) a statement of the reasons as to why the trustees consider that they have fulfilled their obligations under section 10(4) and (5) of the Act, together with, in the latter case, any supporting evidence from the Commissioners of Inland Revenue confirming the matters as to which the trustees are required to ensure by section 10(6) of the Act;

(e) in the case where the resolution is passed under section 10(8) of the Act—

(i) a copy of the resolution;

(ii) a statement of the reasons as to why the trustees consider that they have fulfilled their obligations under section 10(9)(a) of the Act and, where the trust is a recognised body, under section 10(9)(b) of the Act, together with, in the latter case, any supporting evidence from the Commissioners of Inland Revenue confirming the matters as to which the trustees are required to ensure by section 10(9)(b) of the Act;

(iv) a statement as to what is to happen about any liabilities of the trust and whether those liabilities are to be met by the trustees of the trust or trusts to which it is proposed to transfer the assets of the small trust; and

(v) a copy of a letter from the trustees of the trust or trusts to which it is proposed to transfer the assets of the small trust confirming that those trustees will consent to the transfer of those assets; and, if necessary, to meet any liabilities of the small trust; and

(f) in the case where the resolution is passed under section 10(10) of the Act—

(i) a copy of the resolution;

(ii) a statement of the date as to when the trustees propose, subject to section 10(14) of the Act, to give effect to the resolution;

(iii) a statement of the reasons as to why the trustees consider that they have fulfilled their obligations under section 10(11)(a) of the Act and, where the trust is a recognised body, under section 10(11)(b) of the Act, together with, in the latter case, any supporting evidence from the Commissioners of Inland Revenue confirming the matters as to which the trustees are required to ensure by section 10(11)(b) of the Act; and

(iv) a copy of a letter from the trustees of the other trust or trusts with which it is proposed that the small trust will be amalgamated confirming that those trustees will agree to such amalgamation.

Small trusts: objections

5.—(1) Where, following the publication of the notice in a newspaper as required by regulation 3 above, any person with an interest in the purposes of the small trust wishes to object to what is proposed in the resolution passed by the trustees, he shall send his objection in writing to the trustees at the address specified in the notice to arrive not later than 14 days after the date of publication of the notice in the newspaper and shall state, in his objection—

   (a) his name and address;

   (b) the nature of his interest in the purposes of the trust; and

   (c) the nature of his objection and the reasons for that objection.

(2) The trustees shall send to the Lord Advocate the following documents to arrive not later than 14 days after the end of the period of 14 days referred to in paragraph (1) above—

   (a) a copy of any objection which has been received by them; and

   (b) a letter containing any comments which they may have upon that objection,

and shall, at the same time, send a copy of that letter to the objector who made the objection and shall inform him of—

(i) his right under paragraph (3) below to send to the Lord Advocate comments upon the points raised in that letter;

(ii) the address of the Lord Advocate to which those comments should be sent; and

(iii) the date by which those comments must arrive at that address.

(3) Any objector, to whom the trustees have sent a copy of their letter to the Lord Advocate as mentioned in paragraph (2) above, may send to the Lord Advocate his written comments upon the points raised in that letter to arrive not later than 14 days after the date on which the trustees sent to him a copy of their letter to the Lord Advocate.

Small trusts: notification to Inland Revenue

6. Where the trustees of a small trust which is a recognised body have passed a resolution under section 10(3), (8) or (10) of the Act,

they shall, not later than 7 days after the date when that resolution takes effect, send to the Commissioners of Inland Revenue—
   (a) a copy of the resolution; and
   (b) a statement as to the date when the resolution took effect.

Public trusts under section 11: advertisement

7. For the purposes of subsection (3) of section 11 of the Act (requirement on trustees of certain public trusts to advertise their intention to expend trust capital), the trustees of any public trust to which that applies shall advertise their intention to expend the capital of the trust by publishing, in a newspaper circulating throughout Scotland or, where the purposes of the trust relate to a particular locality, in a local newspaper circulating in that locality, a notice in the form set out in Schedule 6 to these Regulations or in a form substantially to the like effect.

Sending documents to the Lord Advocate

8. Any document which is required by these Regulations to be sent to the Lord Advocate shall be sent to him at the Scottish Charities Office, Crown Office, Edinburgh.

Revocation

9. The Public Trusts (Reorganisation) (Scotland) Regulations 1993 (S.I. 1993 No. 2036) are hereby revoked.

SCHEDULE 1   Regulation 3(1)(a)

FORM OF NOTICE OF RESOLUTION UNDER SECTION 10(3) OF THE ACT

"[Name of small trust]
Notice of proposed modification of trust purposes

Notice is hereby given that the trustees of [specify name of small trust] have passed a resolution under section 10(3) of the Law Reform (Miscellaneous Provisions) (Scotland) Act 1990 that the trust deed be modified by replacing the trust purposes by other purposes specified in the resolution.

A copy of the trust deed and of the resolution may be inspected at [specify address] between [specify between what dates and hours].

Any person with an interest in the purposes of the trust may object to what is proposed by sending his objection, in writing, to the trustees at [specify address] to arrive not later than [specify date ie 14 days after the date of publication of this notice]. The objection should state the objector's name and address, his interest in the trust purposes, and his objection and reasons for the objection.

Any such objection will be sent to the Lord Advocate by the trustees with their comments and the objector will be given another opportunity to comment. The Lord Advocate has power to direct the trust not to proceed with the modification.".

SCHEDULE 2   Regulation 3(1)(b)

FORM OF NOTICE OF RESOLUTION UNDER SECTION 10(8) OF THE ACT

"[Name of small trust]
Notice of proposed winding-up and transfer of assets

Notice is hereby given that the trustees of [specify name of small trust] have passed a resolution under section 10(8) of the Law Reform (Miscellaneous Provisions) (Scotland) Act 1990 to wind up the trust and to transfer its assets amounting to [specify amount in sterling] to [specify name of receiving trust or trusts].

A copy of the trust deed of [specify names of small trust and receiving trust or trusts] and of the resolution may be inspected at [specify address] between [specify between what dates and hours].

Any person with an interest in the purposes of the [specify name of small trust] may object to what is proposed by sending his objection, in writing, to the trustees at [specify address] to arrive not later than [specify date ie 14 days after the date of publication of this notice]. The objection should state the objector's name and address, his interest in the trust purposes, and his objection and reasons for the objection.

Any such objection will be sent to the Lord Advocate by the trustees with their comments and the objector will be given another opportunity to comment. The Lord Advocate has power to direct the [specify name of small trust] not to proceed with the winding-up of funds.".

SCHEDULE 3   Regulation 3(1)(c)

FORM OF NOTICE OF RESOLUTION UNDER SECTION 10(10) OF THE ACT

"[Name of small trust]
Notice of proposed amalgamation

Notice is hereby given that the trustees of [specify name of small trust] have passed a resolution under section 10(10) of the Law Reform (Miscellaneous Provisions) (Scotland) Act 1990 that the trust be amalgamated with [specify name of the other trust or trusts]. The trust to be constituted by such amalgamation is proposed to be known as [specify name of proposed new trust].

A copy of the resolution, of the trust deeds of [specify names of small trust and of the trust or trusts with which it is proposed to be amalgamated] and of the draft of the trust deed of [specify name of proposed new trust] may be inspected at [specify address] between [specify between what dates and hours].

Any person with an interest in the purposes of the [specify name of small trust] may object to what is proposed by sending his objection, in writing, to the trustees at [specify address] to arrive not later than [specify date ie 14 days after the date of publication of this notice]. The objection should state the objector's name and address, his interest in the trust purposes, and his objection and reasons for the objection.

Any such objection will be sent to the Lord Advocate by the trustees with their comments and the objector will be given another opportunity to comment. The Lord Advocate has power to direct the [specify name of small trust] not to proceed with the amalgamation.".

SCHEDULE 4   Regulation 3(2)

FORM OF COMBINED NOTICE OF RESOLUTIONS UNDER SECTION 10(8) OF THE ACT

"Notice of proposed winding-up and transfer of assets of small trusts

Notice is hereby given that the trustees of each of the trusts listed in column 1 of the Annex to this notice have passed a resolution under section 10(8) of the Law Reform (Miscellaneous Provisions) (Scotland) Act 1990 that each of these trusts be wound up and that its assets amounting to the amount specified in column 2 of that Annex, be transferred to [specify name of receiving trust].

A copy of the resolutions passed by the trustees of each of those trusts, of the trust deeds of each of those trusts and of [specify name of receiving trust] may be inspected at the address or addresses specified in column 3 of the Annex to this notice between [specify between what dates and hours].

Any person with an interest in the purposes of any of those trusts may object to what is proposed by sending his objection, in writing, to the trustees of the trust concerned at the address specified in relation to that trust in column 3 of the Annex to this notice to arrive not later than [specify date ie 14 days after the date of publication of this notice]. The objection should state the objector's name and address, his interest in the trust purposes, and his objection and reasons for the objection.

Any such objection will be sent to the Lord Advocate by the trustees with their comments and the objector will be given another opportunity to comment. The Lord Advocate has power to direct the any or all of the small trusts not to proceed with the winding-up and transfer of funds.

ANNEX

Column 1 Name of small trusts	Column 2 Amount of assets	Column 3 Address of small trusts

SCHEDULE 5   Regulation 3(3)

FORM OF COMBINED NOTICE OF RESOLUTIONS UNDER SECTION 10(10) OF THE ACT

"Notice of proposed amalgamation of small trusts

Notice is hereby given that the trustees of each of the trusts listed in column

1 of the Annex to this notice have passed a resolution under section 10(10) of
the Law Reform (Miscellaneous Provisions) (Scotland) Act 1990 that these
trusts be amalgamated with each other. The trust to be constituted by such
amalgamation is proposed to be known as [specify name of proposed new
trust].

A copy of the resolution passed by the trustees of each of those trusts, of the
trust deeds of each of those trusts and of the draft of the trust deed of the
[specify name of proposed new trust] may be inspected at the address or
addresses specified in column 2 of the Annex to this notice between [specify
between what dates and hours].

Any person with an interest in the purposes of any of those trusts may object
to what is proposed by sending his objection, in writing, to the trustees of the
trust concerned at the address specified in relation to that trust in column 2 of
the Annex to this notice to arrive not later than [specify date ie 14 days after
the date of publication of this notice]. The objection should state the objector's
name and address, his interest in the trust purposes, and his objection and
reasons for the objection.

Any such objection will be sent to the Lord Advocate by the trustees with
their comments and the objector will be given another opportunity to
comment. The Lord Advocate has power to direct any or all of the small trusts
not to proceed with the amalgamation.

ANNEX

Column 1   Column 2
Name of small trusts   Address of small trusts

SCHEDULE 6   Regulation 7

FORM OF NOTICE OF PROPOSAL TO EXPEND THE CAPITAL OF A PUBLIC TRUST UNDER
SECTION 11(3) OF THE ACT

"[Name of small trust]

Proposed expenditure of capital

Notice is hereby given that, in accordance with section 11(2) of the Law Reform
(Miscellaneous Provisions) (Scotland) Act 1990, the trustees of [specify name
of public trust]—

    (a) have resolved unanimously that the income of the trust is too small
         to enable the trust purposes to be achieved; and

    (b) are satisfied [delete whichever of the following statements does
         not apply] [that there is no reasonable prospect of effecting a transfer
         of the trust's assets under section 10 of that Act] [that the expenditure
         of capital is more likely to achieve the purposes of the trust],

and, accordingly, intend to expend the capital of the trust which amounts, in
total, to [specify amount in sterling]. Such expenditure cannot take place before
[specify date which is not less than 2 months after the date of the
advertisement].

The Lord Advocate has been notified of this intention. If it appears to the
Lord Advocate that there are insufficient grounds for the expenditure of
capital, he may apply to the court for an order prohibiting such expenditure".

THE CHARITIES (TRUSTEE INVESTMENTS ACT 1961) ORDER 1995

(S.I. 1995 No. 1092)

(25th April 1995)

Whereas a draft of this Order has been approved by both Houses of Parliament:

Now, therefore, the Secretary of State, in exercise of his powers under section 70 of the Charities Act 1993 and with the consent of the Treasury, hereby makes the following Order:

1. This Order may be cited as the Charities (Trustee Investments Act 1961) Order 1995 and shall come into force on the fourteenth day after the day on which it is made.

2. It is hereby directed that, in the case of a trust fund consisting of property held by or in trust for a charity,[1] any division of the fund in pursuance of section 2(1) of the Trustee Investments Act 1961[2] shall be made so that the value of the wider-range part at the time of the division bears to the then value of the narrower-range part the proportion of three to one.

3.—(1) The Trustee Investments Act 1961 shall, in its application in relation to a trust fund consisting of property held by or in trust for a charity, have effect subject to the modifications specified in the following paragraphs of this article, being modifications which the Secretary of State considers appropriate in consequence of, or in connection with, the direction contained in article 2 of this Order.

(2) Paragraph (b) of section 2(3) and sub-paragraph (b) of paragraph 3 of the Second Schedule shall have effect as if for the words from "each" to the end there were substituted the words "the wider-range part of the fund is increased by an amount which bears the specified proportion to the amount by which the value of the narrower-range part of the fund is increased".

(3) Section 4(3) shall have effect as if for the words "so as either to be equal, or to bear to each other" there were substituted the words "so as to bear to each other either the specified proportion or".

---

[1] By virtue of sub. (5) of s. 70 of the Charities Act 1993 and s. 11 of the Interpretation Act 1978, the expression "charity", in the application of this Order to Scotland, means a recognised body within the meaning of s. 1(7) of the Law Reform (Miscellaneous Provisions) (Scotland) Act 1990.

[2] By virtue of sub. (4) of s. 70 of the Charities Act 1993, expressions used in that section which are also used in the Trustee Investments Act 1961 have the same meaning as in that Act.

(4) Section 17 shall have effect as if at the end there were added the following subsection—

"(6) In this Act, "the specified proportion" means the proportion specified in article 2 of the Charities (Trustee Investments Act 1961) Order 1995.".

SELECT BIBLIOGRAPHY

Annual Report of the Crown Office and Procurator Fiscal Service 1993/94, Edinburgh: Crown Office.
Annual Report of the Crown Office and Procurator Fiscal Service 1994/95, Edinburgh: Crown Office.

Burgess, R.A. (1991) *Annotations to Part I of the Law Reform (Miscellaneous Provisions) (Scotland) Act 1990* Edinburgh: W. Green & Son.

Cairns, E. (1993) *Charities: Law and Practice* London: Sweet & Maxwell.
Charity Commissioners for England and Wales (1994) *Charities: The New Law: A Trustees' Guide to the Charities Acts 1992 & 1993*, London: HMSO.
Charity Commissioners for England and Wales (1993) *Decisions of the Charity Commissioners* Vol 1, August 1993, London: HMSO.
Charity Commissioners for England and Wales (1994) *Decisions of the Charity Commissioners* Vol 2, April 1994, London: HMSO.
Charity Commissioners for England and Wales (1995) *Decisions of the Charity Commissioners* Vol 3, January 1995, London: HMSO.
Charity Commissioners for England and Wales (1995) *Decisions of the Charity Commissioners* Vol 4, September 1995, London: HMSO.
Charity Commissioners for England and Wales (1994) *Model Memorandum and articles of association for a charitable company* London: Charity Commission.
Charity Commissioners for England and Wales (1995) *Political Activities and Campaigning by Charities* London: HMSO.
Charity Commissioners for England and Wales (1995) *Report of the Charity Commissioners for England and Wales for the Year 1994* London: HMSO.
Cracknell, D.G., Framjee, P., Longley, A. and Quint, F. (1994) *Charities: The Law and Practice* London: Longman Law, Tax and Finance.
Cranston, R. (1985) *Legal Foundations of the Welfare State* London: Weidenfeld and Nicolson.

Homer, A. and Burrows, R. (1995–96) *Tolley's Tax Guide* Croydon: Tolley Publishing Company.

Knight, B. (1993) *Voluntary Action: Report for the Home Office* London: HMSO.
Kramer, R. (1981) *Voluntary Organisations in the Welfare State* London: London School of Economics.
Kramer, R. and Grossmann, B. "Contracting for Social Services: Process Management and Resource Dependencies" (1987) 61. *Social Service Review* 32.
Kühnle, S. and Selle, P. (1992) *Government and Voluntary Organisations* Aldershot: Avebury.

Leat, D. et al (1986) *A Price Worth Paying?* London: Policy Studies Institute No. 651.

Luxton, P. "Public Charitable Collections: The New Régime" (1992–3) Vol. 1, 1 *Charity Law & Practice Review*, 35.

Luxton, P. "Control of Fund-raising for Charitable Institutions: The New Law – Part I" (1992–3) Vol. 1, 2 *Charity Law & Practice Review*, 147, Part II (1992–93) Vol. 1, 3, *Charity Law and Practice Review*, 233.

McLaren, J. (1894) *Wills and Succession* (3rd edition) Edinburgh: W. Green & Son.

National Council for Voluntary Organisations (1989) *The Contract Culture – The Challenge for Voluntary Organisations* London: NCVO.

Norrie, K. and Scobbie, E. (1991) *Trusts* Edinburgh: W. Green & Son.

National Council for Voluntary Organisations and Charity Commission (1992) *On Trust: Increasing the Effectiveness of Charity Trustees and Management Committees* (Report of a Working Party chaired by Winifred Tumin) London: NCVO.

Phillips, A. (1994) *Charitable Status. A Practical Handbook* London: Directory of Social Change.

Randon, A. and 6, P., "Constraining Campaigning: the legal treatment of non-profit policy advocacy across 24 countries" in (1994) 5(1) *Voluntas* 27.

Sayer, K. (1992) *A Practical Guide to VAT for Charities* London: Directory of Social Change.

Scottish Charities Office (undated) *The Supervision of Charities in Scotland: A Brief Guide* Edinburgh: Scottish Charities Office.

Scottish Council for Voluntary Organisations (1994) *Faith and Hope in Charity* Edinburgh: SCVO.

Scottish Council for Voluntary Organisations (undated) *In Management & Control* Edinburgh: SCVO.

Scottish Council for Voluntary Organisations (1995) *SCVO's Guide to Constitutions and Charitable Status in Scotland* Edinburgh: SCVO.

Scottish Home and Health Department (1988) *Supervision of Charities in Scotland: A Consultative Memorandum* Edinburgh: Scottish Home and Health Department.

Scottish Home and Health Department (1989) *Charities in Scotland: A Framework for Supervision* Edinburgh: Scottish Office.

Scottish Office Central Research Unit (1995) *The Cost and Quality of Care of People with Disabilities* Edinburgh: HMSO.

(1994) *Stair Memorial Encyclopaedia of the Laws of Scotland*, Edinburgh: The Law Society of Scotland/Butterworths.

Suddards, R.W. (1986) *Bradford Disaster Appeal* London: Sweet & Maxwell.

Turner, R.T., Hurst, K.B. and Burgess, A.C. (1995) *Tolley's Charities Manual* Croydon: Tolley Publishing Company.

Walker, N.M.L. (1974) *Judicial Factors*, Edinburgh: W. Green & Son.

Warburton, J. (1995) *Tudor on Charities* (8th ed.) London: Sweet & Maxwell.

Warburton, J. and Morris, D. "Charities and the Contract Culture" in (1991) 55 *The Conveyancer* 419.

Ware, A. ed. (1989) *Charities and Government* Manchester: Manchester University Press.

Wilson, W.A. and Duncan, A.G.M. (1975) *Trusts, Trustees and Executors* Edinburgh: W. Green and Son.

Wolfenden, J. (1977) *The Future of Voluntary Organisations,* London: Croom Helm.

Woodfield, P. et al (1987) *Efficiency Scrutiny of the Supervision of Charities; Committee of Public Accounts.* London: HMSO.

USEFUL SOURCES OF INFORMATION

Inland Revenue
Financial Intermediaries
and Claims Office (FICO)
Trinity Park House
South Trinity Road
Edinburgh EH5 3SD
Tel. 0131-552-6255

Scottish Charities Office
25 Chambers Street
Edinburgh EH1 1LA
Tel. 0131-226-2626

Scottish Council for
Voluntary Organisations
18/19 Claremont Crescent
Edinburgh EH7 4QD
Tel. 0131-556-3882

Registrar of Companies
37 Castle Terrace
Edinburgh EH1 2EB
Tel. 0131-535-5859

Customs and Excise
44 York Place
Edinburgh EH1 3JW
Tel. 0131-469-2000

Legal Services Agency Ltd
11th Floor, Fleming House,
134 Renfrew Street
Glasgow G3 6ST
Tel. 0141-353-3354

The Law Society of Scotland
26 Drumsheugh Gardens
Edinburgh EH3 7YR
Tel. 0131-226-7411

Institute of Chartered Accountants
of Scotland
27 Queen Street
Edinburgh EH2 1LA
Tel. 0131-225-5673

The Society of Trust and Estate
Practitioners (Scottish Branch)
c/o Murray Beith & Murray WS
39 Castle Street

Edinburgh EH2 3BH
Tel. 0131-225-1200

The Scottish Charity Finance
Directors' Group
PO Box SCFDG
c/o The Wise Group
72 Charlotte Street
Glasgow G1 5DW
Tel. 0141-303-3131

Charity Commission
St Alban's House
57/60 Haymarket
London SW1Y 4QX
Tel. 0171-210-4477

National Council for
Voluntary Organisations
Regent's Wharf
8 All Saints Street
London N1 9RL
Tel. 0171-713-6161

Charities Aid Foundation
Kings Hill
West Malling
Kent ME19 4TA
Tel. 01732-520000

Directory of Social Change
24 Stephenson Way
London NW1 2DP
Tel. 0171-209-5151

Institute of Charity Fundraising
Managers
Market Towers
1 Nine Elms Lane
Vauxhall
London SW8 5NQ
Tel. 0171-627 3436

Charity Law Association
c/o Anne-Marie Piper
Paisner & Co
Bouverie House
154 Fleet Street
London EC4A 2DQ
Tel. 0171-353-0299

INDEX